MAN OF COURAGE

MAN OF COURAGE

The Life and Career of Tommy Farr

Bob Lonkhurst

The Book Guild Ltd
Sussex, England

The Book Guild Ltd.
25 High Street,
Lewes, Sussex

First published 1997
Reprinted 1997
© Bob Lonkhurst 1997

Set in 12/12pt Garamond
Typesetting by Acorn Bookwork, Salisbury

Printed in Great Britain by
Bookcraft (Bath) Ltd, Avon

A catalogue record for this book is
available from the British Library

ISBN 1 85776 167 7

To

my dear sons
Michael and Philip
who fill me with pride

and
not forgetting Kathleen
my mum

CONTENTS

FOREWORD

Tommy Farr became a legend in his own time, yet there was so much of his life – the fights, the fun, the dramas, even blow-by-blow – that was not accurately recorded. His autobiography was restricted because the Welsh hero did not recall every fight. The ring was just another day at the office.

This aptly titled biography, an intense piece of research, presents his career warts 'n all. The author has discovered more fights than previously listed. He is an Honorary Inspector of the British Boxing Board of Control, and his feel for the Fight Game is obvious. The account of Farr's most famous fight with Joe Louis is the most accurate I've read.

I first watched Farr as a schoolboy, kneeling near ringside at Harringay Arena when he defeated Ben Foord. He's quoted here saying 'He looks good to me' as he glanced at Foord's corner before the opening bell. On behalf of the late trainer of Foord I know he would have approved. My father, Dick, had also often seconded Farr. The Gutteridge Twins, as cornermen, were part of the scene as well.

I was reporting sixteen years later when in truth Farr was prostituting his talents to clear his debts.

I was a fellow traveller when he was writing for the *Sunday Pictorial* (now *Mirror)* and I always enjoyed his company. He was feisty, stubborn, often the natural traits of a successful prize fighter, but he possessed the intangible thing called class. His marriage to 'Monty', a showjumper and pilot, was admirably romantic until his dying days. The candlelit suppers and ball room dancing were the most unlikely pursuits for a man who had to punch and take a punch for a living.

In his last TV appearance he strolled along a Sussex Beach and said: "I owe everything to boxing, boxing owes me nothing."

We chroniclers and commentators owe him plenty for having passed our way. *Man of Courage* is the honest tribute.

Reg Gutteridge

ACKNOWLEDGEMENTS

I owe thanks to many people for making this book possible. Without their help and support the finished article would never have appeared. I make special mention of Frank Butler, Lord Brooks of Tremorfa, Harold Alderman, Derek Leney, John Ford, Trevor Phillips, Don Taylor, Aneurin Evans, Glanville Farr, Ann Farr and Gilbert Allnut.

Special thanks go to Reg Gutteridge for agreeing to provide a foreword for the book. Reg is known and respected throughout the world for his contribution to boxing journalism, and I am honoured that a man of his standing has agreed to assist a mere novice like me.

The staff of the National Newspaper Library at Colindale cheerfully provided an endless stream of items required during research. Valuable assistance was also given by the Editor and staff of the *Brighton and Hove Leader*, Brighton Central Reference Library, and East Sussex County Library.

Many people volunteered photographs, cuttings and illustrations, and I am particularly grateful to Larry Braysher, Derek O'Dell, George Zelaney, Bernard Hart and Bill Chevally of Lonsdale Sports, Glynn Moses, Tony Lee, the staff of Madam Tussauds, Claire Hamer of Big Pit, Blaenafon, and Karl Woodward of *Western Mail*.

My particular thanks go to Barry Hugman, a highly successful and established author and close friend, who was always on hand to advise me. When things went wrong he taught me never to give up, and I am eternally grateful for his patience. I mention also Fred Snelling, who, when editing magazine articles I had written, would politely batter me with constructive criticism about my punctuation. I am convinced that he has helped me in that area.

I am extremely appreciative of the enthusiasm and encouragement shown by the directors and staff at The Book Guild who gave me the opportunity to finally become a published author. In doing so I have been able to pay tribute to a real 'Man of Courage'.

ACKNOWLEDGEMENTS

Finally, my heart-felt thanks go to my special friend, Pennie Bracey. During my times of hardship and frustration she was always there for me, to advise, support, and in particular temper my moods. She made special efforts to provide me with important photographs. I know it was not easy for her but she played a big part in me finally completing what I set out to achieve. I will never forget that support.

INTRODUCTION

I knew Tommy Farr only briefly, having met him at various boxing functions in London during the 1960s and 70s. Yet I had been fascinated by him ever since 1950, when, as a mere 10-year-old lad, I vividly recall his first comeback fight. A great deal of publicity surrounded the occasion, and I remember having a strange, eerie feeling every time I saw pictures of this old, craggy-faced man who was about to fight again.

I was just beginning to take an interest in boxing, and I would read every fight report I could lay my hands on. Fighters became my heroes, and I cut pictures from newspapers and pasted them on to my bedroom wall.

Living in a small Kentish village, I was just a naive little country boy who would never have the courage to box. Yet I was being drawn towards the fight game like a pin towards a magnet. Fighters fascinated me and I admired their bravery; but with the exception of Randolph Turpin, Tommy Farr was the man who fascinated me the most. As I grew older, and my library of boxing books expanded, I searched for everything I could find about him. I was intrigued, not only by his ring career, but by his problems outside it as well. As the years passed by, I was amazed that no book was ever written about Tommy because I saw him as one of the most extraordinary men in boxing. I decided therefore, to give it a go myself, despite having no previous experience as a writer.

In 1990, the inevitable happened, and a book entitled *Thus Farr* appeared in the book shops. By this stage, my own efforts were well advanced, so I confess to being somewhat disappointed, believing they had been to no avail. On reading the book, however, I regained my composure because without wishing to be critical of anyone else's work, I was disappointed with the content. Although it was claimed to be in Tommy's own words, the book told only a small part of the Tommy Farr story. Perhaps he was too modest to tell his readers the full extent of his battles and hardships.

I decided therefore, to press on with my own research, knowing that with the limited time available to me, it would be some years before a finished article would appear. I'm glad I made that decision because researching Tommy's life and career has been an enthralling experience. It has also made me appreciate what I have, and the times in which I live. Life for Tommy Farr was a constant battle. Born into the poverty and squalor of the mining depression in the heart of the Rhondda Valley, he literally had to fight for everything, including his bread and butter. He was one of eight children and his mother died when he was just nine years old. The following year his father was crippled with paralysis and confined to a wheelchair. The eight children were forced to become bread winners overnight in order to survive.

Even as a young boy, the courage of Tommy Farr was very evident. By the age of 13, he was fighting in the small halls and fairground booths of the South Wales mining towns. At 14, he was working in the pits as a Collier Boy because every penny he earned was crucial to the family meal table.

The hard times he experienced as a child, however, turned Tommy into a natural fighter. As he got older and stronger, he progressed rapidly in the ring and eventually achieved his ambition by becoming British heavyweight champion in March 1937. Victories over world-rated fighters, Max Baer and Walter Neusel, set him up for a fight with Joe Louis for the world title. Although he was beaten on points, Tommy put up one of the most courageous challenges ever in a world heavyweight title contest. His bravery ensured that he would never be forgotten in boxing circles, and the less knowledgeable would remember him for that fight alone rather than for his many victories.

Tommy earned a great deal of money from boxing and commercial enterprise, yet by 1950 he was broke. His pub, restaurant, and book-making businesses all folded, and at one stage he was declared bankrupt. His battles in the ring were replaced by battles in the courts, but with typical courage, Tommy fought back. Although he had been out of the ring for more than 10 years, the old warrior embarked on a comeback at the age of 37. He had a further 16 fights before finally calling it a day. What he did was for the sake of his family, but in doing so he cleared his debts, provided a home and education for his children, and retained his dignity.

Research into the life and career of the man whom I consider to be the finest British heavyweight of all time, has been absorbing and thoroughly rewarding. I have gained tremendous satisfaction from tracing more than 60 of Tommy's early fights which have never previously been recorded. That factor alone reveals a new part of boxing history, and goes a long way to showing the extent of Tommy's plight as a youngster. My efforts have been a true labour of love spread over several years. Although very time consuming, and sometimes frustrating, it has been worth the effort. To be able to produce a story about a man's courage without having to rely on sleaze and misfortune is particularly satisfying. Although Tommy had more than his fair share of misfortunes, courage and positive thinking enabled him to over-come them.

A man of many words, Tommy often said, 'I claim that man is master of himself when he can stand life's blows and scars and leave this world a better place behind him.' They were the words of a man who withstood more than his share of blows and scars. He set an example for others to follow, and by fighting for everything he got and taking nothing for granted, he did indeed leave the world a better place.

Tommy Farr was a true 'Man of Courage', and deserves a place, not only in the history of boxing, but in the history of Wales as well. I sincerely hope that my efforts help portray a clear picture of the hardships he endured, and show him as a man of great dignity and a credit to the hard world of professional boxing. The finished article is intended as a tribute, not only to Tommy, but to all other fighting men. I believe his story highlights the hardships endured by many men, who, without boxing would probably have had nothing. Fighters are a very special breed, and I count myself lucky to be able to say that many are my friends.

Bob Lonkhurst
Potters Bar, 1996

1

EARLY HARDSHIP

Extreme poverty and high unemployment were sadly the features in many parts of Britain during the early 1930s, but the Rhondda Valley in South Wales was hit harder than most. Suffering from the effects of the coal strike and the mining depression, work was extremely hard to come by, and for the male population, it was basically mining or nothing.

To avoid starvation, many men turned to fighting as a means to earn a few extra pounds. Miners were tough, rugged men, and to many fighting came naturally. However, although there were numerous boxing shows in most of the little mining towns scattered across the Rhondda, the number of fighters far exceeded demand. For many men, contests became hard to come by, and some therefore decided to leave their homes and head for the big cities.

There has for long been a saying that 'the streets of London are paved with gold'. For more than a century, many people from depressed parts of Britain have flocked to the capital, intent on seeking fortune and fame. The vast majority have been disappointed.

During the early 1930s, the belief that there were easy pickings to be had in the capital encouraged one particular young Welshman to walk all the way from Tonypandy in the Rhondda Valley. He was convinced that he would soon find a job and earn regular money. Furthermore, he was a fighter and believed that he would be welcomed with open arms by the leading boxing promoters. He hadn't considered the possibility of total rejection.

Tommy Farr was a lonely, frail-looking youngster as he walked aimlessly along the Strand in the heart of London on a cold, wet

1

winter's evening. The threadbare clothes in which he stood were his sole possessions. There were holes in his pockets, and his boots had broken-down heels and worn-out soles. He was freezing cold, soaking wet and starving, and his feet were sore and aching having walked the 200 or so miles to reach London.

He was only 18 and it was several days since he had last eaten a square meal. An old leather belt strapped around his waist was done up as tightly as possible to help fight off his craving for food. He had no money, but despite his predicament, Tommy was a boy of great pride and determination. Resisting the temptation to beg or steal, he wandered through street after street in the hope that something would turn up.

Suddenly he found himself outside the Savoy, one of London's finest hotels. He watched in amazement as cabs dropped off wealthy-looking people clad in evening dress. Tommy had never seen anything like this before. Curiosity finally got the better of him, so he made his way to the rear of the hotel, where he climbed on to a window ledge. Peering inside, he saw dozens of people dining lavishly beneath chandeliers whilst a small band played at one end of the massive room. The young Welshman was extremely envious, but what he saw set him thinking. As he walked away, the more he thought about the expensive clothes and jewellery people were wearing and the vast quantities of food and drink on the tables, the more convinced he became that one day he too would have enough money to live like those people. He had, after all, already convinced himself he would become a great boxing champion.

The immediate problem facing Tommy, however, was how to escape from the desperate situation he was in. He was drifting from one place to another, sleeping rough and eating whatever he could find. Although he was trying to find work, nothing was coming his way, and the future looked extremely bleak. Fortunately, he had been born with tremendous courage and a character which would make him carry on against incredible odds. He was used to having to fight in order to earn extra shillings on which to survive. All he wanted now was a lucky break.

Tommy Farr was born on 12 March 1913 in a tiny miner's cottage at 3 Railway Terrace, Clydach Vale, a hillside mining community overlooking Tonypandy in the Rhondda Valley. The numerous rows of terraced cottages, mostly built of quarrystone, clustered about half a mile down the hill from the Cambrian Pit, one of a number of coal mines in this part of the valley. The area was one of terrible poverty and squalor, and there was very little work for the male population other than mining.

The house where Tommy was born still stands today, and a circular plaque donated by the Rhondda Civic Council identifying his birthplace hangs above the front door. Like many other records, it wrongly quotes his year of birth as 1914. Why this error appears so consistently is not known, but Tommy was once quoted as saying that he tore up his birth certificate long ago.

Christened Thomas George Paul Farr, he was one of a family of four boys and four girls. His father, George Farr, a big 17-stone man who had emigrated from Cork, worked underground at the Cambrian pit as a haulier. He had also been a bare-knuckle fighter, and many of his fights had taken place in the hills behind Tonypandy. The need for extra money was so great that, like many other men, he was forced to resort to this bloody and brutal sport to supplement the meagre wage he picked up at the pit.

As a child, Tommy was brought up amid grime and coal dust during the desperate conditions of the Welsh mining depression. To make matters worse the First World War broke out the year after he was born. It meant that he lived in troubled times almost from birth.

As their eight children continued to grow, George Farr and his wife Sarah Ann realised that the little cottage at Railway Terrace was simply not big enough any longer. With tremendous effort they managed to raise a modest sum, and in April 1920 purchased a bigger cottage at 59 Court Street. Their new home consisted of a living room and scullery downstairs, and three bedrooms upstairs. Court Street was on a steep hill just round the corner from Railway Terrace, and stretched up the hill from behind the Pandy Hotel almost to the Cambrian Pit. Their move meant that George could still get to work with ease, and the children could remain at the nearby Blaenclydach School. The three-bedroom cottage was still a tight squeeze for a family of ten, and it meant that the four boys, John, Douglas, Richard and Tommy, shared one bedroom, and the girls, Phyllis, Elizabeth Ellen, Sally and Doreen, slept in another, leaving the third for their mother and father.

The appalling conditions created firstly by war and then by the mining depression were bad enough, but the young Tommy Farr and his family soon had other terrible hardships to contend with. Tommy was just nine years old when his mother died at their home on 10 May 1922. For a period of 21 days, she had suffered from a bout of acute bronchitis. This, together with dilation of

3

heart syncope, was the cause of her death. She was just 39 years old.

Until that time George Farr had been extremely tough and hard, but with the passing of his beloved Sarah Ann, all the strength drained out of him and he became a broken man. He found himself having to do all the family chores that his wife had previously done, and bringing up eight young children single-handed was no easy feat. At night, after returning from the pit, he would secretly do the family washing, but it caused him tremendous embarrassment. So before starting, he would lock the door of the house because he was terrified that a neighbour would walk in and surprise him. The next morning, it was the children who would peg the clothes out on the line to dry. He did the best he could for his children, but he couldn't do the mending. Tommy, who liked to be neat and tidy, would often run across the road to his aunt and beg her, 'Auntie, please put a stitch in my trousers.'

Losing their mother had a devastating effect on the eight children, but despite the sadness and hardship, they stuck firmly together. They were just coming to terms with the situation when tragedy struck again. Less than a year after losing his wife, George Farr was suddenly crippled with paralysis. He became bedridden and could hardly speak.

Although friends, neighbours and relatives rallied round as best they could, the situation was desperate. So much more had to be done if the youngsters were to survive. With their mother dead and their father no longer able to contribute to the family budget, they were left as the sole breadwinners. It is difficult to imagine a family of children having to face a worse plight; it turned them into adults almost over night.

With Tommy's eldest sister Phyllis taking the leading role, they worked all hours, making anything they could think of that would sell and get them a few pennies for food. They walked the streets selling their wares no matter what the weather was like. Tommy built himself a handcart, and after school each day he pushed it around the streets of Clydach Vale and Tonypandy, trying to sell tape, cotton, vinegar and soap. Times were hard; if he made tuppence he was lucky, but it was better than nothing, and it went towards the family's next meal.

Tommy also did deliveries for local shopkeepers, and amongst those he worked for were Evan and Myrtle Evans, the grandparents of England football manager Terry Venables, who ran a grocery shop.

He loathed the peddling because he was terribly shy and hated talking to strangers. He was almost afraid to knock on street doors to offer his wares, yet he plodded on simply because he knew he had to.

Years later, neighbours recalled an occasion when Tommy and a bailiff both arrived at a customer's house at the same time. The youngster was there to sell whatever he could, but the unfortunate wife of an unemployed miner could not afford to buy anything from him that day; the bailiff was there to evict her. Realising the situation, young Tommy quickly took his day's takings from his pocket and silently pressed the money into the woman's hand. Even as a very young boy, there was a streak of kindness in Tommy Farr.

Although after a while George Farr was able to get around aided by a wheelchair, he was unable to work or do anything for himself. For a further nine long years of suffering, he needed constant attention. Despite still being very young, Tommy knew what his father was going through. Although George Farr rarely complained about his plight, the boy felt the hurt as he watched the once tough and rugged man lying helpless and virtually devoid of speech. More than once, Tommy wished it could all come to an end peacefully so that his father wouldn't have to suffer any more.

Tommy always remembered sitting at the bedside one day and his father telling him, 'Take all that is coming to you Tommy, and it will be plenty, and you will pull through. They'll knock you down, but you will get up and fight on, as I shall, to the last gasp.'

The family tragedies, combined with the poverty and squalor of the times, were causing great bitterness and resentment to build up inside the youngster at a very early age. As he wandered around the streets of Clydach Vale with his handcart he was rarely seen to smile. He was indeed entitled to ask the question, 'Why me?'

Despite everything, the eight Farr children pluckily stuck together. Driven on by desperation and a determination to survive, no task was too great for any one of them. It was no fun being a child in those depressing times, and being without parents made it harder still.

* * *

In the tough mining districts of the Rhondda Valley, fighting was one of the general forms of recreation for many men, youths and boys. Not only did it provide a means of supplementing their meagre incomes, it was also one of the few spare-time activities. Even for those who didn't take part, boxing invariably formed the topic of conversation in almost every pub, club and hotel in the area.

The densely populated communities of Tonypandy, Trealaw, Penygraig, Gilfach Goch and Clydach Vale were all within a very short distance of one another, and were havens for fighting. There were plenty of boxing clubs and gymnasiums, the majority of which were attached to pubs or hotels.

In Tonypandy alone during the late 1920s there was the Court Athletic Club attached to the Court Hotel, the Cross Keys, which was situated next to the Empire Theatre, the Dunraven Hotel, the Dewinton Athletic Club and the Hibernian Club, an Irish club in Kendry Street.

Down the road at Penygraig were the Gethin Hotel, Butchers Arms, Swan Hotel and the White Rock, whilst at Trealaw was the well-known Paddy's Goose Athletic Club. All of these establishments had busy boxing gymnasiums which were frequented by boys as young as eight as well as hardened professional fighters.

In Tonypandy, regular boxing shows were put on at all the hotels which had clubs. Other well-known venues included the Square Pavilion, the old Tonypandy Pavilion, which partially collapsed in November 1927, the Theatre Royal, the Picturedrome and the Empire. At nearby Gilfach Goch was the famous Hippodrome, whilst Trealaw had the Judges Hall.

The Hibernian Club was probably the most famous boxing establishment in the area, and back in the early 1920s it was one of the most flourishing boxing schools in the Rhondda. At one time or another some of the best-known boxers ever to come from the valleys appeared there. They included 'Peerless' Jim Driscoll, who was never so happy as when he could pay a visit to the Hibernian and meet old friends and chat about old times.

Another well-known boxing establishment was the Pandy Hotel, where weigh-ins for contests frequently took place. Important meetings were also held there, when fighters and their backers met to arrange contests, and the hotel was the scene of many a heated debate.

In addition to the many boxing hostelries and venues in the area, there were also the boxing booths attached to travelling fairs. They frequently visited the little mining communities, where there were always plenty of tough rugged men willing to challenge the booth fighters. The best-known of these were Jack Scarrott's Pavilion, the Joe Gess Pavilion and Taylor's Travelling Booth. Gess

6

in particular invariably put on a top-line contest on a Saturday evening, backed up by a couple of six-round contests between local lads, as well as encouraging challenges for his regular booth fighters. By using local boxers, Joe was always guaranteed a full house.

One of the top boxers in the Rhondda during this period was Frank Moody from Pontypridd. He often boxed for Gess, and as a boy Tommy Farr idolised him. Whenever Frank boxed in the vicinity of Tonypandy, young Tommy was there to watch him.

It was not surprising that Tommy became involved in fighting at a very tender age, because although he was very shy on the surface, he was a rough-and-ready youngster, full of adventure and more than able to hold his own. Many of his scraps were with other youngsters suffering from the frustrations and hardships of the times. The slightest little thing could spark off a row, and a fight invariably followed.

Tommy was very young when he first became fascinated by the travelling boxing booths. With a group of mates, he made frequent visits, often as far afield as Penygraig and Trealaw. He soon learned how to look after himself, and by the age of ten or eleven he was more than willing to take on other youngsters. It didn't take him long to realise that fighting was a way of picking up a few extra shillings. Plenty of other kids were fighting in the small halls and booths, so why couldn't he?

During 1926 when the coal strike was on, boxing shows were run in most of the little mining towns and villages across the Rhondda to help with the canteen funds. This meant that there was plenty of scope for youngsters like Tommy who would fight almost anybody for a couple of bob.

It was at the end of 1926 that the young Farr had his first recorded fight, in a charity show at the Tonypandy Square Pavilion, organised in aid of the Miners Strike Committee Canteen Fund. The record books vary as to who his opponent was, but the lad Tommy beat on points in their six-rounds fight was in fact Jack Jones, also from Clydach Vale.

Years later, many people in the little mining community actually remembered Tommy's first fight. 'Tommy beat Jack Jones right enough,' one old man assured a reporter from a national newspaper. 'Yes, it was a week before Christmas 1926,' added another. Jones himself was actually traced nearly 30 years later and remembered the fight only too well. 'I would rather have put my head into a beehive than fight Farr again,' he was once claimed to have said.

Long afterwards, when Tommy was reminded of the occasion, he brushed it aside. 'I don't even remember who he was or where it took place.' In fact, there were a number of matters about his early career which Tommy was unable to recall, prompting a reporter from a well-known national to remark, 'Tommy boy, you will be the despair of your biographer.' How right he was!

A week after beating Jones, Tommy fought another local lad known as 'Young Snowball'. Co-incidentally, this was the ring name of a man who some eight years later would become his manager. Young Snowball from South Wales had something of a reputation around Tonypandy, and he and Farr fought on Boxing Day afternoon under a fairground marquee pitched at Pandy Fields. Young Snowball was given a real battering, and it was claimed in some quarters that he never fought again.

After the gruelling fight was over, young Tommy's throbbing hand closed tightly over the two half-crown pieces handed to him by the booth owner. It was surely a sign of the times that a 13-year-old boy was fighting at a boxing match at Christmas when he should have been at home with his family. The money, however, was all-important to Tommy because it represented square meals for him and his family, and considerably reduced the aches and pains of battle.

Like many of Tommy's early fights, this one would never appear in the record books. Full details of the fights he had as a boy will never be known because many took place in the various booths at short notice. Some local papers had no real interest in boxing and therefore not all fights were reported. The *South Wales Echo* was one paper to give boxing good coverage, and the majority of organised promotions were reported. The paper was always prepared to mediate between camps, and published most of the boys' challenges. The *Echo* in fact did a great deal to promote the sport in the Rhondda, but even so it is thought that a lot of Farr's early contests were missed.

Following one of his early fights, the promoter refused to pay Tommy in cash. Instead he handed him a pair of plimsoles and boxing shorts, the tools of his trade.

When he began fighting, Tommy was one of a number of youngsters to train under 'Alby' May at the newly opened gym at the Dewinton Hotel, Tonypandy. He was billed as either 'Kid' Farr, Young Tommy Farr, Young 'Kid' Farr, or Battling 'Kid' Farr. Because they sang in chapel choirs on Sundays, some boys Tommy fought boxed under different names to avoid recognition and embarrassment to their families, but Tommy never did.

Tommy's first contest of 1927 was against 'Kid' Denham at the Square Pavilion. After six hard-fought rounds the result was a draw, but according to his opponent's brother, Farr was very impressive. Cyril Denham, who had been at ringside, was quoted years later as telling a national newspaper reporter, 'Even then Farr had the makings of a champion.'

If Tommy had indeed looked that good, his ability certainly wasn't reflected in the results of the fights which followed. Although he was a bit of a tearaway with a real appetite for fighting, he had very little success and looked anything but a promising young fighter. Over the next two and a half years, his record was very poor and from a total of 45 recorded flights between December 1926 and early May 1929, he was credited with just 11 victories, all on points.

* * *

Tommy was barely 14 when circumstances forced him to follow in his father's footsteps and seek work at the Cambrian Pit situated above Clydach Vale. Even at that young age, mining was the general fate of many boys in this depressed part of Wales.

Within a few weeks of starting work, Tommy became the victim of a horrible accident. Whilst working at the coal face one day, his lamp accidentally knocked into some loose coal in the tunnel wall, and suddenly everything crashed around him. There was an explosion and fragments of coal were sent flying into his body. Tommy sustained serious cuts to his face and body and carried the scars of his injuries for the rest of his days. It was more than three months before he recovered sufficiently to fight again.

Weighing no more than six and a half stones when he first went into the pit, Tommy was so small and puny that his safety lamp dragged along the floor. He was often kicked and cuffed around the head because he wasn't big enough or strong enough to carry out tasks more suited to grown men. Frequently he stood knee-deep in icy seep water as he helped load the coal trucks. Conditions were so filthy that as he toiled away stripped to the waist, sweat combined with coal dust ran down his face and body like black ink. Tiny fragments of coal became embedded in his pale skin, and for years to come he would carry blue spots and blotches about his body as a cruel reminder of those terrible times.

The days in the bowels of the earth were long, hard and extremely dark. Accidents were frequent and death always seemed

9

to be just around the corner. It wasn't long before Tommy realised that mining was probably the hardest job in the world. As a collier boy he earned just 15s 9d a week, (about 78p), working at the coal face. It was a pittance of a wage for grafting away for as long as 12 hours every day. Apart from having to contend with the dangers of accidents, explosions and landslides, Tommy suffered on more than one occasion from silicosis, the dreaded occupational disease of the pits caused by coal dust irritating the lungs. No child should have had to endure such conditions, but for him there was no other choice.

Miners and collier boys were a tough breed and took to fighting like ducks to water. Many would accept a fight as readily as others would agree to a quick hundred up at billiards or a frame of snooker. Bets were often laid, not only on who would win but on how long a particular contestant would last. Youngsters in the pits had to learn to fight because if a row broke out and a challenge was issued, refusal to take it up earned the contempt of the rest of the workers.

The hard life in the pit quickly built up Tommy's strength, and apart from organised fights, he also took part in an atrocity called pit fighting. Better known as 'in the holes', it was something which could only have been enjoyed by extremely rugged and savage men, although collier boys were often forced to fight by their mates who wanted to lay bets. Holes were dug in the ground a foot or so apart and to such a depth that contestants' waists were at ground level. The fighters climbed in and punched away at each other until one of them was knocked unconscious on his feet. Some pits had four pairs of holes so that eight contestants would be fighting at the same time, giving the gamblers a greater range of options.

It was brutal and atrocious, but the young Tommy Farr became quite an expert in the holes. Before long his workmates refused to fight him, and this was one of the factors which convinced him that he should take up fighting for a living rather than work in the pit, which he loathed. The Cambrian Pit was a mile and a quarter deep, the gas and heat were terrible, and there were many explosions. 'After the mines, what is fighting?' said Tommy. 'Fighting is child's play.'

Recalling in the holes years later, Tommy remarked, 'Those were fights, among the hardest I ever had. It taught you to parry, to duck, and above all to take it. It may not have been a proper school but it did establish your courage. If you were good in the holes, you were good anywhere.' Tommy was about ten years old

10

when he first saw men in the holes. 'They punched each other until they were virtually unconscious. I have never forgotten it,' he remembered.

For his family's sake, Tommy stuck at mining for almost two years. It was a long and grinding time and there was little happiness during his childhood. One of his childhood dreams was to be able to lie in bed and have an early morning cup of tea brought to him.

* * *

Although he had started work in the pit, Tommy continued to fight whenever he could. Quite often he would finish work at teatime and go straight off to fight at a fairground booth or smoky hall anywhere in the Rhondda.

It was during 1927 that he first met up with Joe Gess, an experienced booth owner who travelled all over Wales and the Midlands. During September that year at Pontypridd, Tommy had what is thought to be his first fight for Gess when he lost to Jackie Moody, one of a large well-known fighting family. Although he fought on other booths including Charles Taylor's Pavilion, Sullivan's Pavilion, and Scarrott's, this was the start of an association which would greatly enhance Tommy's fighting career.

Another significant event during 1927 occurred in November when Tommy agreed to stand in as a substitute against 'Kid' Evans in a no decision bout at the Dewinton Hotel. Evans, another local tearaway, was having a try-out, which was quite common before an important contest. He and Farr both trained at the Dewinton gym under Alby May, and they slugged out four tremendous rounds. Yet what took place between them in the ring that night became the start of a long-standing feud.

That same month, the huge hall of the Hibernian Club was let to some newcomers in the field of boxing promotion. They announced their intention to run high-quality weekly shows using local boys. Farr would appear in a supporting bout on their first promotion against old opponent Cliff Smith, who had forced him to retire in the fourth round of a fight at Tonyrefrail just two weeks earlier. They had already met five times that year, with Tommy winning two, Smith one, and two draws, but the contest was sufficiently attractive for the *South Wales Echo* correspondent to write:

The one between Kid Farr (Clydach Vale) and Cliff Smith (Williamstown) is sure to be productive of thrills for this pair will fight like demons. Both of them are well known in the district and they can be relied upon to put on a right royal battle.

Local fans were thrilled at the prospect of the fight, which was due to take place on 17 November. A full house seemed assured, but no sooner had it been announced than the show fell through. The shrewd promoter for the Tonyrefrail Pavilion wasted no time, and matched Farr and Smith for his show a couple of days later. They had fought a thriller two weeks earlier, so he wanted them on again. The fans were not disappointed. Farr and Smith engaged in what was described as a 'game and fine battle', and the result was a draw.

The following week Tommy was due to fight twice on the same bill at Central Hall, Treharris. Amongst the contests were two six-rounders:

Tommy 'Kid' Farr (Tonypandy)	v	Bob Evans (Merthyr Vale)
'Battling' Farr (Tonypandy)	v	Danny Andrews (Merthyr Vale)

The show was in fact cancelled at short notice so, desperate for money, Tommy walked to Pontypridd, where he got a fight at the Joe Gess Pavilion and drew over six rounds in a hard set-to against Dave 'Kid' Flowers of Penygraig. The decision meant he still hadn't managed a win in ten fights.

The overdue victory finally came in his next contest against old rival Cliff Smith. It was their third meeting in just five weeks, and again they were involved in a fierce battle. Although Smith had an advantage in weight, Farr boxed cleverly on the retreat, using a sharp left jab, and at the end received a well-earned decision. He was elated by the victory and the following day issued what was probably his first ever challenge through the pages of the *South Wales Echo:*

Young Farr (Clydach Vale) would like to meet any six stone ten pounds lad in Wales. He specifically mentions Evan Lane (Treor-chy), Jackie Moody (Pontypridd), Young Hazel (Pontypridd), Dixie Kid (Merthyr), and 'The Porthcawl Kid' amongst those he is anxious to oppose. Replies through the South Wales Echo.

Such challenges between youngsters from the mining towns of the Rhondda were contained in almost every edition of the *Echo*. Due to his cocky and belligerent attitude, Farr was often a central figure. He was not particularly liked as a youngster because, despite his poor record, he frequently boasted that he could beat most lads at his weight.

In January 1928 alone, three challenges were issued involving Tommy. Firstly, he was challenged by Danny Harris (Treharris) provided the Aberdare promoters offered a purse. Tommy then repeated his challenge to any boy in Wales over six or ten rounds for the best purse offered at any weight between six stone ten pounds and seven stone. A few days later a challenge was issued by the newly formed Paddy's Goose Club at Trealaw. Ted Evans (Trealaw), who trained at the Goose, was particularly keen to get to grips with Tommy.

Farr and Evans were quickly matched and boxed at the Dewinton Hotel on 16 January in what was billed as an exhibition bout. No-decision contests in those days invariably turned out to be far more competitive than many that were billed for a decision and purse. Local pride was often at stake and almost every bout developed into a fierce hitting affair. This one was no exception, with each boy firmly intent on sorting out the other. The contest was so bitterly contested that neither would concede superiority, so ten days later they went through it all again in another no-decision six-rounder.

Tommy had five bouts in the space of three weeks, and next met Evan Lane (Treorchy) at the Judges Hall, Trealaw, in a show staged to assist the Mid-Rhondda AFC. They had met twice before the previous summer, with Lane winning one and the other being a draw. In a contest which excited the fans, Lane confirmed his superiority as he outboxed and outfought Farr to take the decision.

The following week Tommy beat Young John Hazel at the Joe Gess Pavilion at Pontypridd in a really hard fight, and two days later boxed a no-decision contest with Young Howe at the Swan Athletic Club, Penygraig. One of a number of exhibition bouts that evening, it was yet another gruelling affair. The proprietor of the Swan was Tom Lewis, who had given a great deal of financial help to foster sport in the area over a number of years.

Within the space of five weeks during February and March, Tommy was challenged through the *Echo* by Jack Kilpatrick (Milford Haven), Young Pales, Young Howells (twice), and Danny Andrews, who reissued his earlier challenge. Farr responded

13

through the same pages: 'Kid Farr is prepared to meet any of his challengers over six or ten rounds for a purse.'

By this time Tommy was being trained by Harry Green, the coach of Bob Dowling, another Clydach Vale youngster who issued frequent challenges through the *Echo*. In one edition, any promoter requiring the services of Farr or Dowling was asked to write to Harry Green at 6 Charles Street, Tonypandy. In another edition, Green invited promoters to contact him regarding a fight between Farr and Kilpatrick, who had agreed terms, but nothing was forthcoming.

Tommy's next two contests were against Young Billie Grocutt (Porthcawl). He drew and lost in what were described as 'exhilarating set-to's', but after their second fight, which took place at the Queens Hotel, Porthcawl, for a cup, he was very annoyed at not getting the decision. The following day he issued a challenge to Grocutt stating that he could easily find backing of up to £10 a side for a rematch at seven stones. Farr added that he was even willing to fight on a winner-take-all basis for whatever purse might be offered. But as far as is known, Farr and Grocutt never fought again.

Although dozens of challenges were issued, many were not taken up. Disputes often arose over the weight at which particular contests should be made, or over the number of rounds. The lads and their backers always argued for terms which suited them best, and if agreement couldn't be reached, the fights never took place. There were also occasions when they refused to fight because the purses offered were too small.

Tommy had a further ten fights during 1928 but won only three. Two of those were in the Joe Gess Pavilion at Ogmore Vale against Herbie Williams, a coloured lad from Merthyr who boxed under the name of 'Dixie Kid'. His other victory was against Young Parry in the main event at the New Inn Athletic Club, Clydach Vale. It was a tremendous local affair and the huge crowd cheered themselves hoarse as the two youngsters pounded away at one another. It was Farr's first ten-rounder, and although he was frequently warned for low punching and use of the head, he had the better strength and ringcraft. In the last two rounds there were some tremendous exchanges, but at the end it was Tommy who got the hard-earned decision.

Although Tommy was convinced he would become a champion, he hadn't made much progress in that direction. Nevertheless, nothing seemed to deter him, and by the time he was 15 he had fought at halls and fairgrounds at Bridgend, Cardiff, Porthcawl,

Pontypridd, Ogmore Vale and Blaengwynfi, as well as local ones at Clydach Vale, Tonypandy, Penygraig, Gilfach Goch, Tonyrefrail, Trealaw and Cwmparc.

In those early days he had to contend with no end of criticism and teasing. He had a very disheartening time because only his close friends and relatives had a good word to say about his ability to fight. Promoters laughed at the idea of him ever becoming a champion, and he was turned down so often when he tried to get a fight that only a desperate lad with courage, determination and a great heart would have persisted as he did.

Many of his fights by this stage were either as a late substitute or for a promoter who felt sorry for him. Things were made more difficult by the fact that his father was crippled with paralysis, and for much of the time he had to go it alone. When recalling those bleak times many years later, Tommy remarked, 'Jimmy Wilde got five bob for his first fight, but I sometimes fought a week for that much.'

* * *

At the beginning of July, Evan Lane beat Tommy yet again when he forced him to retire after five rounds at Blaengwynfi. It was at about this time that he had the good fortune to meet up with Job Churchill, a one-legged man who had a small saddler's shop at Penygraig. He had once worked in the pits but had been forced to quit following a horrific accident in which one of his legs was torn from his body.

Job had a reputation in the valleys for his knowledge of the fight game, and it wasn't long before Tommy explained how he intended becoming a champion. Being a local man, Job had seen Tommy fight on a number of occasions without being particularly impressed. 'Why have you come to me son?' he asked.

'Well,' said Tommy as he nervously shuffled his feet in the dirt, 'everyone keeps telling me what you did for Tom Farmer, and I want you to do the same for me.' Farmer, also from Penygraig, boxed professionally under the name of Tom Thomas, and won the British middleweight title in 1906, defending it six times before losing it in 1910.

Churchill was not a man to discourage anyone from doing what he wanted, least of all a lad who was only 15. 'We'll see,' he said casually. 'There's plenty of time.'

Once he knew the extent of Tommy's desperate family situation, Job became very caring towards him. The youngster

15

gradually came to look upon him as a father figure. They built up a strong and trusting relationship, and Tommy spent a lot of time in the old saddler's company. Job was a knowledgeable man and passed on his wisdom about many subjects apart from boxing.

Job recognised that Tommy was badly in need of a change of environment away from the filth and poverty of the Rhondda, so during the summer holidays sent him off to work in an hotel at Ilfracombe. It was the first time the boy had ventured outside the valley, and he travelled on the ferry from Barry across to North Devon. Tommy's duties at the hotel consisted of washing up dishes and waiting at tables. It was very different from the pits because not only was it cleaner and quieter, but the people were much more friendly. He loved every minute of it and when recalling those days, once chuckled, 'Training I was for when the time came for me to dine with Dukes and Duchesses, so I'd know which knife and fork to use.'

While working at the hotel, Tommy got regular meals and generous portions which helped build up his frail body. He was thrilled when appreciative diners gave him tips, and realized it was a much healthier life than he had been used to back home.

All good things come to an end, and at the end of the summer the hotel closed down. For Tommy it meant the return to life in the pits and the boxing booths. However, Job arranged for him to return the following year.

2

SLOW PROGRESS

After returning from his holiday in Devon, Tommy struggled to get fights, so he reissued his challenge, to any boy in Wales at seven stones two pounds. When he did return to action, he sustained a badly cut eye against Albert Davies at Gilfach Goch, forcing him to retire after four rounds. Although the injury put him out of action for two months, worse was to follow.

Earlier in the year Farr had been challenged on a number of occasions by Danny Andrews of Treharris but for a variety of reasons they had not fought. When they eventually met over ten rounds at the Cinema, Llanelli, Tommy took a real hiding and suffered the most shattering defeat of his career so far. He was floored for counts of eight and nine in the fourth before being knocked out in the sixth. It was Andrews' second fight of the day, having boxed a four-rounds no-decision bout at Bargoed in the afternoon.

Although he was devastated, Tommy challenged Andrews to a rematch through the *Echo* the following week, but no agreement could ever be reached. Farr then turned his attention to Idris Pugh, another Tonypandy lad, whom he particularly disliked. They were due to meet at Pontypridd Town Hall on 22 December but the show was cancelled. Feelings ran high, and they were eventually matched at the Dunraven Hotel Assembly Rooms in February, with Pugh winning clearly on points.

A few days later, Tommy challenged Pugh to a return, and stated that he was also prepared to box any lad in Wales at seven stones four pounds. When there were no takers he renewed the challenge through the *Echo* a couple of weeks later. Pugh responded, saying that a fight would be made provided Farr attended the Swan Hotel at noon on Friday 1 March with stake money of up to £10. Times were hard, and this was one of many occasions when Tommy couldn't raise the money, so the fight wasn't made.

Tommy issued yet another challenge through the *Echo*:

to anyone in Wales at seven stone four pounds, especially Herbie Hill (Blaengwynfi), Billy Howells (Clydach Vale), and Idris Pugh.

He stressed that if no promoter was prepared to stage a fight between him and Pugh, he would fight him on a mountainside.

It was with Job Churchill's help that Tommy began to get regular fights in 1929, most of which were on Saturday nights. Purse money, however, was low so travel to the various venues was by the cheapest means possible. There was one occasion when he even hitched a lift to a fight on a horse and cart.

Boxing was incredibly popular in the Rhondda, and there were often several shows on the same night within just a few minutes of each other. Most venues were small, smoky arenas, crammed to capacity with fans sitting or standing shoulder to shoulder. Often when two popular local boys met, the police made the organisers close the doors in the interest of safety.

When Tommy beat Eddie Thomas of Tonypandy at the Labour Assembly Hall, Ystrad, in February, it was his first win for more than seven months. The six-rounder was completely devoid of science but Thomas missed more than Farr.

The Imperial Athletic Club, Porth, was the venue for his next two fights. He got a draw in a poor contest with local boy Len Jones in March, and the following month disappointingly dropped a close decision to George 'Kid' Spurdle, who was having only his third fight in a conventional ring.

During May, Farr took three fights within the space of 14 days. He drew over ten rounds with Idris Pugh, outpointed Herbie Hill (Blaengwynfi) and Trevor Herbert (Tylorstown) over six and eight rounds respectively. Against Herbert, Tommy surprised even his most ardent followers by his performance in a close but thrilling contest. Herbert was extremely angry not to get the decision and immediately challenged Tommy to a return. It was staged at the Ferndale Servicemens Club two weeks later in front of a full house. The fight was over the shorter distance of six rounds and this time Tommy was hard pressed to get a draw. However, the Ferndale promoter was impressed with Tommy's performance and put him on again two weeks later against old rival Idris Pugh. After their draw at Mardy a month earlier, both had a score to settle, and after a thrilling contest it was Pugh who emerged victorious after ten rounds.

Three days before meeting Pugh, Tommy took on Johnny 'Dooner' Davies, another lad who he had frequently challenged through the *Echo*. They met at Nant-y-Moel, with Tommy winning easily over ten rounds.

Despite having failed to beat Pugh in three fights, Tommy still wouldn't accept being second best, and so they were matched again at Llanelli in August. Pugh once again got the decision after ten rounds.

With the fighting blood that was in him, Tommy frequently had rows with other collier boys at the Cambrian Pit. His arch rival was Dick Evans, who boxed as 'Kid' Evans of Clydach Vale. There was considerable bad feeling between them, which stemmed from the night they met in a no-decision contest at Tonypandy in 1927. They had engaged in a real set-to, and each was convinced he had the beating of the other.

Both now trained at the Court Hotel, where Tommy had gone after teaming up with Job Churchill, and there were often rows in the gym. Suddenly one day at the pit, a few hasty words led to an almighty row. Challenges to a real fight became commonplace, but nothing definite could be agreed upon.

Early in July 1929, a meeting was arranged at the Court Hotel between the boys and their backers, but Farr and his people failed to turn up. Evans and his backers angrily claimed that Tommy was scared, and promptly issued a challenge for a fight over 15 two-minute rounds at catchweights for any amount up to £50 a side or a promoter's purse. Evans' backers contacted the *South Wales Echo*, insisting that full details be published.

Surprisingly, nothing was heard from Farr so a few days later Evans' father, who ran the Court Hotel, issued another statement through the *Echo* claiming that Tommy had withdrawn. Farr's behaviour was somewhat strange. Completely ignoring the latest challenge, he issued his own through the *Echo* stating that he was willing to meet either Johnny 'Dooner' Davies or Herbie Hill for a promoter's purse, and asked for replies to be sent to him care of the Court Hotel.

In July 1929, Bill Phillips, Evans' trainer, told the Rhondda correspondent of the *Echo*, 'There appears to be a lot of controversy amongst the various paperweights in Wales as to their capabilities.' He believed that the air would be cleared nicely if someone accepted Evans' challenge. 'Evans will fight any seven stone, six pounds lad in Wales for £25 a side,' added Mr Phillips,

19

'with or without the title at stake.' He said that Evans was prepared to forward his £25 to the Welsh Boxing Association as soon as his challenge was met, but stressed that Kid Farr would be given preference at coming in at catchweights for a money match. Phillips went on to say that Evans had called in response to Farr's challenge to lay odds of 6–4 on the result of a fight between them, but found there was nothing doing when money was mentioned.

In the summer of 1929 Tommy was packed off to Devon by Job Churchill. In early September, however, things at last got moving between Farr and Evans, and they were finally matched in the big boxing tournament to celebrate the reopening of the once-famous Court Athletic Club on 14 September. The huge hall had been completely refurbished, with a splendid, fully equipped ring and seating for several hundred spectators.

Both boys had previously belonged to the Court Hotel boxing club, and trained there daily in the gymnasium. Over a period of time, however, more than 20 cross-challenges had been issued between the pair, due to their constant bad feeling. The question of weight was usually the fly in the ointment, but that difficulty had finally been overcome.

Their differences of opinion finally led to a split in the camp, and Tommy moved away. On the advice of Job Churchill, he and trainer Harry Green went about three-quarters of a mile down the road to the Swan Club at Penygraig to train for the Evans fight.

Once the match had been made, it became almost the sole topic of conversation amongst Rhondda boxing fans because they all knew of the needle that existed between the two boys. The fight had been anxiously awaited for months, and now it was on, there was tremendous excitement, especially after Tommy told the *Echo* that if he failed to beat Evans, he would realise that it would be better if he gave up boxing. Evans openly made numerous bets that he would make sure Farr gave up.

It was an incredible build-up to the fight between the two 16-year-olds. Many fans who fancied Tommy's chances went out and pawned their house-hold treasures to back him.

A couple of days before the fight, there were ridiculous rumours that neither boy had done any serious training. In fact, neither left anything to chance. At the Swan, Penygraig, Farr had been sparring with old foe Idris Pugh and a number of others, whilst Evans went through his own strenuous preparations at the Court Hotel.

The fight itself was for £5 a side, and as anticipated, was a thriller. Tommy finally won on points, but a great deal of credit had to be given to Evans because he was giving away a lot of weight. Nevertheless, he stuck valiantly to his task and proved to be a formidable opponent. The battle was typical of many that took place between collier boys, although despite the bad feeling between them, it was a particularly clean and sporting one.

Tommy took the first three rounds in great style, but on more than one occasion was guilty of pushing his opponent across the ring. Evans was very fast and Tommy had difficulty in landing his punches, which frustrated him. In the fourth, Evans came out of his shell and attacked strongly. He caught Farr with good lefts but they had little effect because Tommy was too powerful. Although Evans tried hard during the next few rounds, Farr did a lot of damage. By the seventh, Evans' left eye was very swollen, and from this point Tommy's greater strength and physical advantages were the telling factors. The last round was a thriller as they engaged in an almighty punch-up, trying to land the decisive knockout.

The victory seemed to be the turning point in Tommy's career. It was a tremendous boost for his confidence, and instead of losing consistently as he had in the past, he gradually started to progress. He would lose just once in his next 13 contests. Around Tonypandy he had the air of the kid in charge, and immediately challenged any flyweight in Wales over ten two-minute rounds for a £5 side stake or promoter's purse. He reminded everyone that he was the only lad to hold a decision over Trevor Herbert in 20 contests.

Tommy's boasting brought immediate response from Young Howley (Clydach Vale), who stated that he could find backing in any sum up to £20 for a fight over 10 or 15 rounds of either two or three minutes' duration at eight stones four pounds. The same day another Clydach Vale youngster, 'Kid' Morgan, from the same camp as Howley, challenged Farr to a fight over any distance for a £5 side stake. Although only seven stones ten pounds, he was confident he could give away the weight, and offered Tommy a fight at catchweights. Farr was told that if he really meant business he should post his stake money to the Boxing Editor of the *Echo* and it would immediately be covered by Howley or Morgan. Tommy was desperate to fight either boy but couldn't raise the money. He offered to fight on a winner-take-all basis, but this didn't suit Howley or Morgan.

The latest series of challenges brought about a strong protest from 'Kid' Hughes of Maestag, who wanted to know why all the 'paperweights' were avoiding him. He was willing to fight anyone at seven stone nine for the Welsh title over 15 three-minute rounds with a side stake of anything from £10 to £25. He particularly wanted to meet Farr or 'Dooner' Davies; the first one to make a deposit with the *Echo* would get the fight.

Ignoring this challenge, Tommy took four fights in eight days. He stopped local lad Eddie Worton at Porth, outpointed Billy Hazel at Pontypridd, and boxed a no-decision contest at Treherbert with Rees Owen. The following day he again drew with Trevor Herbert over six rounds at Porth. It was another thrilling battle, with Tommy proving to be a real bogeyman for the young prospect from Tylorstown.

After boxing a six rounds no-decision contest with George Williams (Treherbert), Tommy met the promising 'Young' Jim Driscoll (Ferndale) over ten rounds in the main event at the British Legion Club, Ynyshir. Driscoll won the decision but most spectators were of the opinion that Tommy was extremely unlucky. He made a determined attack from the opening bell, forcing Driscoll all over the ring. Although Jim used his left to check the two-fisted attacks, he lacked power and Tommy was never troubled. Farr's left, however, was so strong that he frequently punched his man into the ropes, but his attempts at following up were very crude, allowing Driscoll to escape from some tight corners. In the seventh, Driscoll was floored for a count of seven, but again Farr's attempts to finish the fight were too wild and Jim survived. In the closing rounds Jim rallied well but the decision in his favour was met with a torrent of boos and stamping of feet.

Over the months there were claims by lads beaten by Tommy that he had only won because of his weight advantage. Certainly several fights were made at catchweights because the lighter boys fancied their chances and desperately wanted to beat him. Farr was furious when one newspaper report referred to him as a featherweight, and he immediately asked the *South Wales Echo* to refute the statement. He claimed that the story had resulted in three agreed contests being cancelled. In order to prove his weight he threw out a challenge to anyone in Wales at eight stone four, and should there be no takers he said he was willing to fight any second-class Welsh bantamweight.

Tommy's next fight was a much-awaited affair against Young Billy Howley at the Court Hotel. They were keen rivals who had been after one another for some while. The contest was originally made for £5 a side but again Tommy failed to deposit the money so it went ahead for the promoter's purse only. Tommy had advantages in weight, height and reach, and used them to good effect to take the 10 rounds decision.

The once famous Labour Club at Penygraig reopened at the end of 1929. There was a large hall, which was ideal for training, and seating could be arranged for up to 700 spectators for shows, with standing room for a further 200 or more. A number of prominent local boxers, including Ashton Jones of Trealaw, Albert Davies (Gilfach Goch), Ivor Drew (Trealaw), Owen Evans and Roy Thomas (Clydach Vale), and Idris Pugh (Tonypandy), moved there to train.

The venue was officially reopened by Councillor Mark Harcombe on 7 December 1929, and it was planned that Farr would meet old rival Albert Davies in the main event. When Tommy pulled out at the last minute, Davies was very angry and claimed Tommy was scared of him because he had won their previous encounters. The fact was, Tommy had been offered more money to fight 'Young' Teddy Baldock (Treherbert) at the Nanthir Boxing Club, Blaengarw, the same night, where he won an easy ten-rounds decision.

The victory over Baldock was followed by a points win over Phil Gardner (Dowlais) at Blaengawr a week later in what was thought by Tommy's followers to be his best performance to date. He then beat Billy Jones (Tonypandy) at the Court Hotel and Cliff Llewellyn at Newport on Boxing Day.

The fight with Jones was for £5 a side but both lads were so confident of victory that they agreed to fight for purse money on a winner-take-all basis. Jones was known to be a heavy puncher and Tommy was warned not to treat him lightly. Again, weight proved to be the deciding factor. Farr was heavier and the clever Pandy southpaw was forced to box mainly on the retreat as Tommy made powerful rushes, and from the fourth round his left jab was the fight winner although he was warned on a number of occasions for holding and boring his opponent. After the fight Jones challenged Tommy to a return strictly at eight stone four whilst Bob Dowling (Clydach Vale) wanted to fight the winner.

Tommy had improved tremendously during 1929, losing just 5 of his 23 recorded contests, all on points. Evan Lane, who held four victories over him, was anxious to fight him again now that he had progressed. Both he and Dowling issued challenges backed by large side stakes. Lane claimed he could easily get backing in any amount up to £25 whilst Dowling could go to £10. As usual Tommy was asked to respond through the *Echo*, but the amounts were too great for him to cover. The Penygraig Labour Club did offer a purse for Farr to meet Dowling, but the boys failed to reach agreement over side stakes.

After a break of about three weeks, Tommy met Billy Pritchard (Treherbert) over ten rounds at Blaengarw. At the end of the fight, the referee failed to separate them but many onlookers felt that the drawn decision flattered him. Tom Partridge, who looked after Pritchard, was so convinced that his boy should have got the decision, that after the fight he made a remarkable challenge to Farr: 'I have a lad in my camp who I do not consider the equal of Pritchard, who shall box Farr, and if he doesn't win, he shall fight for nothing.' The boy in question was Rees Owen of Treherbert. Tommy readily accepted the challenge, and the promoter immediately agreed to stage it at the same venue the following week on a Saturday night.

Tommy had also been booked to fight on the Friday night, against Lew Haydn (Clydach Vale). Lew, a well-known flyweight and brother of the popular Johnny Haydn, was making a comeback after two years and had been training for some months for a showdown with Farr. They were matched over ten rounds in the main event at the New Inn Athletic Club at Clydach Vale, and had agreed to fight for £25 a side. There was no doubt that this was going to be a 'needle' match, and with both men having big local followings, the bout caused tremendous interest and excitement in the little mining community.

Although he appeared extremely tired at the end of the contest, Haydn boxed superbly throughout and sprang something of a surprise by winning on points. His touches and moves were those of a real artist, and he frequently tricked the younger Farr into false situations. He also cleverly got himself out of trouble on a number of occasions when it looked as though Tommy might take him.

Haydn won the first round with ease, and Tommy was completely outclassed. As in many of his previous fights, he was cautioned for holding and trying to bore into his man. Lew's left hand was a revelation, and he showed that even at close quarters he had lost none of his old skill.

Occasionally Tommy did well with a long left lead, but he did not make use of his considerable advantages in height and reach. He also showed his inexperience by trying to knock Haydn out instead of standing up and boxing correctly behind his talented left hand. Nevertheless, it was a tremendous learning fight for Tommy.

24

In the fifth round, the huge crowd yelled themselves hoarse when Farr took a tremendous right to the jaw. He withstood the shot well, and actually fought back viciously, landing several good right hooks to the head. In the next round, it was Tommy's supporters who became excited, when Haydn was rocked by a big right to the head. Tommy's inexperience again told, and his attempts at following up were very crude.

The bout swung one way and then the other, and throughout the final session Haydn was very tired and hanging on, but in the end he finished up a good points winner.

Tommy came out of the bout unscathed, and went ahead with his fight against Rees Owen the following night at Blaengarw. It was a rather one-sided affair, with Farr using all of his physical advantage to the full. His left hand was a dangerous weapon, and in the sixth round, following some long-range exchanges, he opened a cut over Owen's left eye with a vicious right hook. He played on the injury for the rest of the round, and the referee finally called a halt.

Tommy's next contest was the eagerly awaited return with Billy Pritchard, and it was the main contest on a bill at the Labour Club, Penygraig. It was another real needle match, because despite the drawn decision when they met a month earlier, both boys were convinced they had won. This time Pritchard won easily, due mainly to his clever boxing at long range. As the bout progressed, Farr became very wild and many of his punches were well wide of the target. Although he was taller and heavier, he failed to make use of those advantages.

Old foe Albert Davies was still angling for another fight with Tommy and issued a challenge with a £25 side stake. At the beginning of April, however, Tommy stated that he was unable to find the money, but added that he was more than willing to meet Davies over any distance at eight stone eight, for a purse. He also issued another challenge to Billy Pritchard, but neither Davies nor Pritchard showed any interest in meeting Tommy again.

Despite being shunned, Tommy was not short of work, and in April took part in four contests in the space of just 16 days, but with widely contrasting results. He won the first two, against Billy Thomas (Trealaw) and Emlyn Jones (Tumble), but lost to Billy Saunders (Tonypandy), and to Jones in a return.

In the fight against Thomas at the Labour Club, Penygraig, Farr was too strong, putting his opponent down for seven in the fourth round, before the towel was thrown in. The next three contests all took place at Charles Taylor's booth, which was pitched at Tonypandy and known as the Taylor Pavilion. Against Jones, Tommy was very impressive, hitting with great power, although he did receive several stern warnings from referee Fred Starn for holding during the early rounds. It was not until the seventh, when he realised that he had no chance of a points victory, that Jones really attacked. He was very wild though, and rarely came close to catching Farr with a telling punch, leaving Tommy as a good points winner.

The following Saturday, Charles Taylor put on one of the finest boxing shows seen on a Saturday night in Tonypandy for some years. Emlyn Jones topped the bill against Young Beckett (Pentre), while Farr met Billy Saunders (Clydach Vale). Saunders caused a surprise by beating Tommy on points. He was aggressive throughout, and often had Farr trapped in a neutral corner. Tommy's usually reliable left jab was completely ineffective, and throughout the contest it appeared more of a push than a punch.

Three days later Emlyn Jones caused a sensation at the Taylor Pavilion when he knocked Tommy out in the fourth round. A tremendous right to the jaw was the punch that finished the fight and handed Tommy only his second knock-out defeat. Determined to reverse the decision Tommy gained over him nine days earlier, Jones did it in grand style.

For the first three rounds Farr had the better of the exchanges by prodding good left leads into the face. Jones, however, bided his time, waiting to land his famous right. Their previous fight had been a thriller and this one was becoming the same. In the third Tommy took a heavy right to the body but fought back well during some big hitting exchanges at close quarters. Then in the fourth, following further heavy exchanges in Farr's corner, Jones cracked home a vicious right to the jaw and Tommy crashed to the floor. It was several minutes before he came round. The punch had been perfectly delivered and was so hard that Tommy's gumshield was badly damaged.

This setback put Farr out of action for a while. When he did return he suffered another surprise stoppage defeat, this time at the hands of local man Josh Sullivan at the Llanelli Working Men's Club. It was a fierce-hitting affair and Tommy retired at the end of the seventh round after being reduced to a very weak state by some heavy body punching.

* * *

Although there were no indications that Tommy was a rising star in the ring, he had always fancied himself as a fighter. Even as a boy he ducked nobody, and many he fought between 1927 and 1930 themselves went on to become highly successful professionals. Even Lane challenged for the Welsh lightweight title, only to lose on points; George Williams and Herbie Hill both won Welsh flyweight titles, while Jackie Moody became Welsh welterweight champion. Tommy had met Williams and Hill in their own backyards and neither had got the better of him.

In his early teens Tommy was a bit of a tearaway and not particularly liked because he had a tendency to shoot his mouth off. With a group of mates, he was a regular at the Victoria Billiard Hall in Tonypandy, and at one stage had a job there as a billiard marker. One night when he was about 16, he was playing with Jack Bessant, who had an artificial leg, when a dispute arose during the game. 'You one-legged bastard,' Tommy yelled at Jack. Lashing out viciously with his cue, Bessant chased Tommy around the table, and Tommy was lucky not to receive a serious injury.

Job Churchill recognised that Farr badly needed a complete break from fighting. He had been involved in some real rough-and-tumbles in the gyms as well as in the ring, and there had been plenty of others in the street and at the pit. The strenuous work at the pit also took a great deal out of him. Sometimes he got five bob for a fight, but more often it was only half a crown, and some of that went to his trainer.

After joining up with Churchill, Tommy trained at the Court Hotel, Hibernian Club, the Cross Keys, and also the Butchers Arms at Penygraig. He had worked out and sparred with good men, including Idris Pugh and Ivor Drew, and it was rumoured that he was once knocked cold by Pugh whilst sparring at the Court Hotel.

On Job's advice, Tommy didn't box for more than five months. The *South Wales Echo* reported that he had in fact been on a tour of the Midlands, but there were no reports of him taking any fights away from the Rhondda. If the *Echo* was correct, then it is possible he went with a travelling booth.

When he returned he eased back with a no-decision bout against Windsor Williams at Penygraig and a narrow points win over Herbie Nurse, a coloured lad from Cardiff, at the same venue on Boxing Day. Churchill still advised him to take things easy, and it was five weeks before Tommy fought again. Then at Job's suggestion he travelled across the valleys to Ebbw Vale, Blackwood and Bargoed for his next four contests. The old saddler

27

believed that if the youngster was to progress he needed to fight away from the Tonypandy area. His judgement again proved sound; Tommy won two and drew two of his next four fights, beating Jack Powell (Markham) twice and drawing with Bryn Powell (Abertridwr) and Chris Shea (Tredegar).

The bout against Bryn Powell took place on the Joe Gess Pavillion on a Saturday night at Blackwood. Although he gave away quite a lot of weight, Powell gave a fine display of double-handed hitting and caused Farr plenty of problems. Despite taking solid lefts to the face, he continually waded in with attacks to the body. The last three rounds were particularly hard-fought, and at the end the drawn decision was a popular one.

The Coliseum, Bargoed, was the scene of Tommy's fights against Shea and Jack Powell, and both were gruelling affairs. Against Shea, he came in as a late substitute, and the opening exchanges were so fierce that an early finish seemed likely. Although Shea sustained a badly cut left eye in the second round, he continually tried to end matters with big punches. Tommy was in good shape and too elusive to be caught cleanly, although in the last two rounds they stood toe to toe with neither prepared to give an inch. Again, the drawn decision was well received.

Tommy had beaten Jack Powell on a third-round disqualification at Ebbw Vale, but in the return there were plenty of thrills. Although he was in control for most of the fight, there was something of a sensation in the last round when, during a hectic free-swinging rally, he was sent hurtling through the ropes. He only just made it back into the ring before the count reached ten, but fought back viciously to take the decision.

At the time there was something of a lull at boxing venues in Tonypandy. Many well-known sportsmen were disappointed at the decreasing numbers of good shows in the area despite the fact that Welsh champions Jerry Daley and Freddie Morgan lived locally. In May 1931, however, the operators of the skating rink at Dunraven Street suddenly announced that they intended staging boxing shows. There was a hall with the capacity for 800 spectators, and the stated intention was to 'separate the wheat from the chaff' in the Rhondda. At the time Farr was one of at least a dozen youngsters living within a ten-mile radius who had the makings of becoming first-class fighters.

The ice rink's first show was staged on 23 May and the main event was a ten-round contest between Farr and Steve Donoghue, a young Tonypandy lightweight. Donoghue had been a good flyweight, then moved to London. He had returned to the

Rhondda about three months earlier and was extremely popular with the Tonypandy fans. Throughout the fight, shouts of 'Come on, Steve' rang out around the arena.

The difference between the two lads was that although Tommy's punches were not powerful, they were connecting. Donoghue, on the other hand, countered and connected, but his blows were poorly timed. Although he used the ring cleverly, sparred in a fancy way and showed excellent movement of the head to avoid blows, he rarely carried the fight to Farr. In the later rounds Tommy was conscious that many of the local element were against him, so he attacked furiously to take a clear decision.

It was fitting that he won because this was to be his last official contest for quite some time. He had already taken part in almost 80 recorded contests, yet he was still barely 18. They had been hard, gruelling fights with very few precautions, fought in the smoky, dimly lit halls of the Rhondda mining towns and the intimidating atmosphere of the fairground booths where the punters were baying for blood. There had been plenty of unofficial scraps as well, and many would never appear on any record. Tommy knew he could handle himself in the ring and was convinced he had what was required to go all the way. He also knew that now he had to move away from the small halls of the Rhondda and into a harder school. Even so, he would only do so with Job Churchill's blessing.

3

THE BOXING BOOTHS

At a very young age, Tommy Farr was convinced that fighting for a living would be a far less hazardous occupation than working underground in the pits. He absolutely hated the filth and dangers associated with mining. There was also a certain glamour attached to the prize ring, and this was very attractive to him. He liked to be recognised as a fighter because it made him feel that he was somebody.

Tommy had got to know his way around the booths – a common feature in Wales and the West Country in the twenties and thirties. Working in the pits had built up his strength and stamina tremendously, and it was not long before he realised that the booths – which paid a regular wage to boxers attached to them – might provide him with an alternative to mining.

The boxing booths were invariably attached to travelling fairgrounds, and there were a number which made frequent visits to the mining towns around Tonypandy. Tommy had already boxed for Joe Gess and Charles Taylor, but he knew all the others as well. Probably the best-known was Jack Scarrott, who travelled the length and breadth of Wales for many years. He provided the schooling for dozens of fine fighters who went on to become first-class professionals. Men such as Jim Driscoll, Jimmy Wilde, Freddie Welsh, Johnny Basham, and Frank Moody boxed for Jack at some stage of their careers.

The boxing booths were the breeding grounds for many of the great fighters of that era, and of those who fought in them during their early days, Jimmy Wilde, Freddie Welsh, Benny Lynch, Freddie Mills and Randolph Turpin all went on to become world champions. Their trade was well and truly learned as they took on as many as seven or eight opponents in a day, and Jim Driscoll once took on 15 or 16 opponents in a day.

The booth itself consisted of a large tent which had a glamorously painted false front bearing life-sized pictures of former great champions such as Jack Johnson and Jack Dempsey. The ring was erected inside the tent, and was usually very small so that as big an audience as possible could be crammed in. The show would commence with the owner or a master of ceremonies introducing the fighters and trying to get challenges from the audience.

The rules were simple. A challenger had to stay on his feet for the duration of three rounds to earn his money, which in Tommy Farr's day was about a pound. That was good money, but the booth fighter would try to stop his challenger to avoid his boss having to pay up. The challenger was allowed to pick the fighter he wanted to take on, but was told very firmly that he put the gloves on entirely at his own risk. The booth would accept no responsibility for any injuries sustained.

Life in the booths was extremely hard, but with a proper spirit of camaraderie prevailing, everyone was usually cheerful and generally healthy. The best part of working with a travelling booth was the incalculable advantages derived from the experience of taking on all comers. There were hardly ever two opponents precisely alike, and even with similar weight, they often differed in build, temperament, style of boxing and overall ability. Some challengers had a degree of skill and boxing knowledge, whilst others were just strong, crude sluggers.

Size and weight, however, were often ignored in the booths, and consequently serious injuries were sometimes sustained. There was no medical supervision, and broken noses, chipped and broken teeth, and the familiar cauliflower ears were all part of the scene. The competitors, though, were tough, and accepted the hazards of the game. For many men, fighting was their only skill and the only means by which they could survive. The top-class fighters went on to become successful professionals, whilst others, even punch-drunk boxers, just drifted along with the booths until they were either too old or not good enough to continue.

Suddenly things were made easy for Tommy. One day he became involved in a heated row with his foreman, who accused him of being lazy. Even at 16 Tommy had his principles and a strong will; he had slaved in the filthy pit for almost two years, suffered serious injury and illness, and the accusation was the last straw. Seething with anger, he told the foreman exactly what he could do with his job, and stormed out of the pit to join the ever-increasing numbers of unemployed.

With lots of time on his hands, Tommy spent countless hours at Job Churchill's workshop, and if anyone could come up with a solution, it was Job.

By this time, Tommy had been fighting in one form or another for over four years. One day, Job suddenly said, 'My attitude to life is, if you are going to get killed, then do so in broad daylight.' They had both worked in the pits and knew the dangers and horrors that lay deep beneath the ground. Tommy understood exactly what Job was telling him.

Being unemployed worried Tommy because the last thing he wanted was to become a burden on his family. He knew he had to go off somewhere on his own. Although only a youngster, Tommy was full of ambition. 'I know what I'll do,' he said. 'I'll join the booths. I'll be a champion like Jem [Driscoll], Jimmy and Freddie,' [Wilde and Welsh].

Driscoll was Tommy's hero, and although he'd never seen him fight, he knew everything about the former 'Jewel of Cardiff'. Everybody in the booths talked about Driscoll, and Tommy pestered them for stories about the ex-champion, who had died back in 1925. Older men demonstrated some of Driscoll's moves, and Tommy practised them in front of a little cracked mirror which hung on his bedroom wall, trying to perfect the left jab.

Tommy discovered that in his early days Driscoll had boxed for Joe Gess, another well-known booth owner who travelled the villages and coalfields of Wales. Having made up his mind to join a booth, there could be none better than that run by Joe Gess, which at the time, was pitched at Tylorstown, a small village not far from Tonypandy, and the birthplace of Jimmy Wilde. Tommy walked there and found the booth owner, but to his horror Gess said, 'Sorry, son, but you are too small.'

Tommy may have lacked many things but determination was not one of them. 'Please, Joe, if you will take me on, I guarantee that you will not be sorry. I don't seem to have anyone willing to coach me, but I know you understand the fight game from A to Z.'

Gess was still not convinced. Tommy refused to give up, and proceeded to explain about the desperate situation at home, that he was an orphan, and how he had started fighting at the age of 12. 'I intend becoming a great champion,' he said proudly. 'All I require is advice and guidance.'

Although Gess was a hard man, he possessed a kindly streak, and when Tommy looked up pitifully at him and said, 'Please Mr

32

Gess, I've just got to get some work somewhere,' the booth owner relented.

'OK, son, you can help pull down that tent for a start.'

Tommy ran over and got stuck into the task. He weighed no more than nine stone, but Gess was sufficiently impressed by his willingness to recognise that he would be useful to have around, although not as a fighter. He offered Tommy a job as a handyman, and Tommy was absolutely thrilled, because not only would it enable him to earn some money, but also put him in immediate contact with fighting people. Thrilled at the prospect, he ran all the way home to gather some clothes, and joined the booth that very same day.

Gess told Tommy he would be on a pound a week plus his keep, but he would have to earn it. And he did, taking down the tent every time the booth moved on, and then helping to erect it again on the new site; besides carrying buckets of water and numerous other laborious tasks. Bed was a bunk under a tarpaulin. But everything was a far sight cleaner than those horrendous pits, and a lot less dangerous.

Tommy was extremely happy and settled into the booth a lot quicker than most lads of his age. He got on well with all the fighters, and loved meeting the different characters who frequented the booths. He grew up quickly and learned to look after himself. It was just as well because one of his jobs was to prevent gatecrashers from getting in. If any succeeded, he had to throw them out, and there were plenty of rough characters ready to have a go. One remark Tommy learned very early in the booth was 'if they get you on the floor, don't let them jump on you'.

One night when Tommy was guarding the canvas wall, he turned and looked across at the action, but as he did so heard a loud ripping sound by his right ear. As he spun round, he saw to his horror, the blade of a large double-edged hunting knife protruding through the canvas at the end of a two-foot tear, narrowly missing Tommy. As the intruder stuck his head through the slit, Farr pounced on him like a terrier, grabbing him by the hair and ears, and with a massive jerk hauled him into the booth.

The teenaged Farr soon found that his prisoner was a fully grown man, a good two stones heavier than him, and as strong as an ox. Within seconds they were involved in a real set-to, rolling about on the ground, punching wildly at each other. Many onlookers forgot the action taking place in the ring, and formed a human ring around Tommy and his opponent, cheering wildly.

Joe Gess heard the commotion and rushed over. As he

attempted to pull them apart, he realised that the youngster could really fight and was handling matters very well on his own. He stood back and watched as Tommy gradually got the better of his man and then finished him off with some well-placed shots.

'I didn't realise you could handle yourself as well as that,' Gess remarked. Tommy's grin turned into the broadest smile when Joe told him that he was being promoted to booth fighter. Thrilled to bits, Tommy leapt into the air, grabbed Joe and hugged him.

Gess made sure that Tommy didn't get carried away, and warned him of what lay ahead. 'When a boxer joins a booth,' he said, 'he can expect plenty of bumps and very little money. But let me assure you, these are the things that have made fighters.'

The next night Joe fixed Tommy up with a swagger cap and brightly coloured sweater, and he proudly lined up on the platform in front of the booth with the other fighters. 'Kid' Farr was introduced to the crowd along with the others, and Joe Gess invited challengers for them. Tommy didn't have to wait long before he was called into action; weighing just over nine stones and looking quite frail, he was seen as an easy touch by some of the rough bully-boys who frequented the booths. Most were miners who had gone into the pits as boys but were now unemployed. With families to feed, the chance to win some extra money was a temptation some could not resist.

Even as a youngster, Tommy was well aware of the hardships of the men who stepped up to face him, but the booth ring was no place for sentiment. Even though he knew they were fighting for the extra pound that would provide a few square meals for themselves and their starving families, his job was to knock them out. He showed no mercy because his future was at stake and he had waited too long for his chance. If Tommy was beaten, Joe Gess would have to pay up, and if that happened the likelihood was that he would be thrown out of the booth and back to join the masses of unemployed.

Farr had one aim and one dream, and that was to become a champion. If that were to become a reality, he had to hammer every challenger who climbed through the ropes to face him. He set about his task with grim determination, and those who saw him as an easy touch got the shock of their lives once they were in the ring. Kid Farr was a real tearaway and really knew how to fight. He was like a bull terrier as he tore into his clumsy opponents and hammered away at them until they either fell or quit, bloodied and exhausted.

By the time Tommy was promoted to booth fighter, Joe Gess's

troupe was in the west of Wales. They went on a long tour, visiting practically every town in Carmarthenshire and Pembrokeshire. Joe told Tommy he would have to beat everybody he met, otherwise he would get no money. He warned him that the opponents would be husky, rough types who knew no rules, but the youngster was unconcerned.

During his first week as a fighter, Tommy was challenged by a huge navvy from the Swansea Docks. Gess didn't like the look of the situation, and even the apparently fearless Farr looked pale and apprehensive as the man climbed into the ring. As soon as the action started, though, it was a different story because although the navvy was a fearsome sight, he was slow and easy to hit. Tommy landed a good shot to the body, followed by a swift right to the jaw, and it was all over in a few seconds. Joe Gess was immensely relieved, and amazed at Tommy's ability and knowledge of boxing. He recognised that he had another possible champion on his hands.

Tommy had tremendous belief in his ability and his future, and he talked of very little else. He hardly left Gess alone. 'Come on, Joe,' he would say, 'tell me what's wrong with my left hand', or 'Do I use my feet properly?' There were times when Joe got thoroughly fed up with all the pestering, but Tommy lived for fighting, and it was his attitude which won the admiration of the booth owner.

There were times after a hard day's graft, that Tommy would sit in Joe's caravan and tell him about his life as a child, and of how he and his brothers and sisters had struggled after their mother died. Joe felt extremely sorry for the boy, but when Tommy became moody and discontented, Joe spoke harshly to him because he believed that it was for the boy's own good.

There was a time when Farr and Gess were very close to parting company. One day at Pontardulais, a row broke out over the carrying of a bucket of water. Everyone was on edge because at the time they were covering as much as 30 miles in a day and running several shows. It was, however, a row about nothing and arose purely because of the conditions and pressure under which they were working.

Worse was to follow, because the next day when they were on the way to Pontardawe, the engine of the lorry cut out. Gess told Tommy to restart it using the starting handle, but try as he did, nothing happened. There was still tension between them, and Gess suddenly jumped down from the cab of the lorry and swore at Tommy. 'You're finished,' he fumed. 'Get your cards and clear off home.'

Joe then had a go at starting the lorry, but with no more success. Eventually he discovered that something was wrong with the starting switch, which he soon fixed, but he was still in a foul temper and refused to give in to Tommy.

The party reached their new site and opened on time. Tommy was still hanging about, and three or four times Gess told him to clear off, but he refused. Throughout the evening, the atmosphere between them was very tense. The other resident boxers on the tour were Eddie Davies, Johnny Griffiths and Dixie Kid, who all got on well with Tommy. When the show was over, they had a talk with Joe and calmed him down, and he and Tommy eventually shook hands. They agreed to forget everything and carry on as though nothing had happened.

Taking on challenger after challenger in the booths day after day was extremely tiring, and apart from the fighting, there were many other strength-sapping chores. Every time the booth moved on to a new location, the tent had to be dismantled. The poles which held it up were heavy and the canvas cumbersome, yet everything had to be loaded onto the lorry in double quick time. If it had been raining, things were made much more difficult because the canvas was heavier and the ground more treacherous. The booth owner's livelihood depended on moving frequently to new locations to attract new punters, which meant that everyone was on the go all the time. There were no days off, and the only time for rest was between about midnight and 6 a.m. Then it was up early and back to the grindstone of the daily chores. But Tommy's strength was increasing day by day.

Once he became a booth fighter, Tommy slept in a caravan with several others, although there were times when Joe Gess got his fighters into lodgings. Tommy's back and arms ached almost permanently. The hardest job of all was taking down the booth after the final evening show before moving on. Limbs were weary from fighting, but there was no time for rest because everything had to be dismantled ready for an early start the next morning.

The regular breakfast in the booth was 'gypsy gruel', a porridge-like concoction generously dosed with bacon fat which floated in lumps on the top. The stuff looked disgusting, and didn't taste much better, but Tommy ate regular portions of it. He knew he had to be tough to survive and move on to greater things.

Joe Gess noticed that Tommy was very restless and always wanted to be doing something. He was always ready to move from one pitch to another where there would be new challengers to face. The important thing was that he was learning and improving all the time, and Gess recognised that Tommy possessed a natural intelligence that couldn't have been picked up at school.

Although there were always plenty of men willing to challenge the booth fighters, they were sometimes inclined not to trust the people who actually ran the booths. There were occasions when Joe Gess even had to hand over a pound before a challenger would climb into the ring. If a man was beaten inside the three rounds, he was not entitled to any money, and it was Joe's job to get it back. He usually managed to do so while Tommy and his mates were helping the beaten challenger to recover. He was only ever caught out once by a cheat. On that occasion, he handed money to the challenger, but as he climbed into the ring to introduce the fighters, the man bolted, taking the money and a pair of boxing gloves with him. Much to Joe's annoyance, he was never caught.

Like other booth owners who were cheated in this way, Joe learned from the experience, as he demonstrated one day when the booth was pitched at Garnant near Ammanford. A hefty-looking character with a muffler tied in a knot at the side of his neck and the peak of his cap covering one eye challenged Farr from the crowd. 'I'll fight the big stiff,' he yelled as Gess was introducing Tommy from the platform, 'but what about the dough?'

Joe told him the rules, but he said he would only go into the ring if the money was handed over to his mate beforehand. Joe therefore took the precaution of posting the other fighters on either side of the man holding the money. Tommy finished off the big husky in quick time, and his mate was quickly relieved of the pound.

The months passed by and Tommy's physique developed. His weight shot up to just over 11 stone, and he rapidly gained in experience and became more competent. As opponent after opponent was battered to the floor, so his reputation spread, and eventually it became very difficult for Gess to get challengers for him.

There was only one occasion Joe Gess could recall when Tommy actually cost him money. It was one night at Pontycymer, when none of the normal rough types who frequented the booths seemed interested in fighting, and it looked as though some 'gee' fights would have to be arranged between the booth fighters.

Suddenly from out in the crowd, a voice called out, 'I say there, old top. I fancy a go with your Mr Tommy Farr. Yes indeed, I shall jolly well take him on.' To the complete amazement of everyone, a young man wearing a high silk hat, a cutaway morning coat, pink stripped pantaloons and a silk cravat stepped forward. He wore chamois gloves and carried a gold-headed cane, and hardly looked like someone who frequented the boxing booths.

The crowd stood in complete amazement, but quickly burst into laughter when Tommy yelled, 'A poof. Bring the bleeder on up here.'

The man stepped up on to the platform and carefully started removing his clothes. He set his hat carefully down on the floor, and grouped his gloves, cane, cravat and shirt on a chair. He then indicated to Joe Gess that he was ready to commence action.

'Knock his English noggin off, Tom,' whispered Joe.

'Right, boss,' replied Tommy, and the action commenced.

As they squared up to each other, it looked like another formality for the rugged Farr, but he was about to get the shock of his life. Not only did the stranger take every blow without flinching, but he proceeded to give Tommy the biggest hiding of his life. He was knocked to the floor 16 times during the three rounds, and was thoroughly relieved when time was up.

Joe Gess admitted that it was one of the most astonishing displays he had ever witnessed in all of his 50 years in the booths. When it was all over, the stranger, showing no emotion, casually got dressed, and then quietly walked away. He even refused to accept the prize money. Nobody ever found out who he was or where he came from.

Tommy never forgot the hiding he got that night, and recalling the incident years later, he remarked, 'That poof was a Jim Corbett, Bob Fitzsimmons and Kid McCoy all rolled into one. I've never seen him since. All I do know is that somewhere out there, the champion of the world is walking around at large.'

This was one of many fights Tommy had in the Joe Gess booth which would never appear on any record or in any newspaper report. He fought miners, farmers, labourers and many men who were unemployed. All were tough and willing, desperate for extra money.

Eventually the time came when Tommy decided that he had learned as much as he could from the booths. He was determined to strike out on his own and go for the real fights. When Tommy told Joe Gess, the booth owner had been expecting it for some time.

There weren't many men around with the experience of Joe

Gess. He had seen fighting of every possible description, from the sawdust rings out on the mountainsides where men fought with bare knuckles to the resin-covered canvas rings beneath bright arc lights. He knew Tommy had it in him to go all the way, although he expected it to be at middleweight.

Joe was sorry to see Tommy go because the youngster had a way about him that made him popular wherever he went. At Pontardawe the local boys had presented him with a dressing gown, and at Garnet he had been given a cigarette case. Such incidents were rare in the booth game, but demonstrated just how much the sportsmen of the west of Wales appreciated Tommy's ability and personality.

'He could make friends as easily as he could knock them over,' Gess once remarked. There were occasions when the booth boys were put into lodgings by Joe in villages they happened to be visiting. 'I never received a single complaint from people with whom Tommy Farr stayed,' said Joe.

As Tommy finally walked away from the booth, there was a tinge of sadness in his heart. Despite the hardships and the primitive existence, the booth had been his home for well over a year, and Joe Gess almost his dad.

The booths were without doubt the breeding grounds which set Tommy Farr off on the road to a professional career. That road would eventually lead him all the way to a fight for the heavyweight championship of the world. In later years Tommy looked back on those days, thankful for the existence of the booth and men like Joe Gess, although his biggest reward for a single fight was 7s 6d and his lowest about half a crown. 'Then one night, a kindly booth owner handed me half a sovereign and I walked home with the air of a Rothschild,' he remarked.

Despite their primitiveness, the booths helped get Tommy away from the pits which had seemed to be his destiny, and they gave him an apprenticeship. Farr always insisted there was no better breeding ground for any aspiring young pugilist, and once described them as being 'crunching, smashing, cracking things, often primitive and bloody beyond belief'. Taking on all comers prepared him for every eventuality in the ring. The experience he gained as a youngster amid those surroundings could not have been bettered anywhere. Without the booths he would never have learned the guile and defensive skills that would help him in the years to come. He learned to look after himself when the going got tough, especially when challenger after challenger saw him as just a frail kid who must be an easy touch.

It was Tommy's superlative boxing skill that carried him through his many battles in the booths against grown men much bigger and heavier than he was. As he recalled many years later, 'You never knew where the punches were coming from. Sometimes they came from their boots, so you had to think quickly to measure your man.'

Tommy also described how, apart from learning the cunning and techniques of boxing, he discovered how to pick up money from the floor of the ring with his gloved hands. Known in the fight game as 'nobbins', money was often thrown into the ring by appreciative spectators at the end of a really good fight, and in the booths it was encouraged by the owner. 'You damn well had to learn how to pick it up,' said Tommy, 'because every penny was the difference between a square meal and a crust of bread.' In fact, he became such an expert at it that he often doubled his weekly pay.

4

LONDON AND BACK

Although Tommy had enjoyed his time in the booths, he had become more dispirited with life in general. These were extremely depressing times, and he had seen conditions, particularly in the South Wales coalfields, getting steadily worse all the time. Poverty stretched right the way across the Rhondda Valley, and there was no money to be earned in Tonypandy other than in the pits.

Even as a youngster, Tommy was a lad with a very strong will and a mind of his own. He had a big heart and tons of courage, and was convinced that if he was to get anywhere in the fight game, he had to make his way to London. He was convinced that once he reached the capital, work would be easy to find and there would be plenty of fights. He believed that in no time at all he would be earning a good wage, not just the few shillings he had been picking up in South Wales.

'I was naive, I suppose,' he said, years later, 'just a boy, but I was determined to make something of myself.'

He set off from home one morning with just a crust of bread and a hunk of cheese stuffed into the pockets of his tattered, worn-out jacket, carrying just one spare shirt. He had no idea how long the journey would take, but his feet got some respite when a kindly lorry driver stopped and offered him a lift for a few miles. Then, after trudging about 20 miles, he was worn out, so he climbed over a gate into a field and lay down under a haystack. Within a few minutes he was sound asleep and didn't awaken until daybreak. He spent the second night wrapped in newspapers under a hedge on the main Gloucester Road. It was a night he would remember for many years to come.

Because of the time he had spent down the mines, darkness held no fears for Tommy. But on this particular night, out in the

41

open air, miles from anywhere, he suddenly became scared to death. He was dozing when he suddenly heard a rustling in the hedge behind him. Then he heard footsteps which slowly got nearer, and then to his horror the branches behind him began to move. He lay there terrified, with sweat pouring down his face and his heart beating rapidly. With a yell he suddenly leapt out into the road, and as he turned round he saw the huge white face of a cow staring at him in the moonlight.

Although he was extremely relieved, he got no more sleep that night, and as soon as it was light he took to the road again. He walked all day and then, as darkness fell, he bedded down again under another hedge, this time just outside Gloucester. That night he was suddenly awoken by the sound of footsteps, but this time he recognised they were definitely human. Again he was scared stiff, but plucked up courage to call out 'Hello'. The footsteps suddenly stopped, but there was no answer, just an eerie silence. Just as Tommy was about to turn and run, the mystery person called back, 'Hello'. Immensely relieved, Tommy climbed out of the ditch, to discover that it was a farm bailiff doing his rounds.

Over the next few days Tommy continued his hike towards London without further event. He quickly found out where the boxing gymnasiums were and walked several extra miles to reach them. He hadn't considered the possibility of being rejected, but that is exactly what happened. As he trudged from one gymnasium to another, disappointment followed disappointment because nobody had heard of him. Even when he told promoters he was a fighter and had been in the booths, they refused to give him any fights. They saw him as a scruffy-looking kid who didn't look strong enough to punch his way out of a paper bag, let alone go into the ring with hardened professional fighters.

Tommy had arrived in London cold, thirsty, half-starved and extremely footsore, and as door after door was slammed in his face he wondered if leaving Tonypandy had been such a good idea after all. As he walked around the streets amid pouring rain, with water squelching through the soles of his cracked boots, he began to think that the whole world was against him. Great bitterness was building up inside him, but it was turning him into one of life's determined fighters, and it would play an extremely big part in his ring battles in the future.

He knew he had no choice but to tramp the streets until he found something, and so for day after day, he did just that. He ate whatever he could find, and slept rough on many occasions. He did manage to find the odd job as a labourer, hotel boot cleaner and marker in a billiard hall, but they were for only a day or two at a time, and the money he was paid was never enough to pay for regular lodgings.

Tommy quickly discovered that although London was a huge place, it was just as hard to find work there as in the Rhondda. He didn't know his way around and had no friends, so he became extremely lonely. One of his greatest anxieties was having only one pair of boots, and they had seen their day. There was nothing worse than tramping the streets in boots which caused blisters and let in water every time it rained.

His first spot of good fortune since leaving home came when he discovered that a large house in Cricklewood was being taken down brick by brick in order to be shipped to America. The contractor needed workers and gave him the break he desperately needed. Although he didn't earn a lot of money, Tommy was able to afford three square meals a day for the first time since arriving in London. He also had enough left over to buy a new pair of boots. Unfortunately, the job lasted only a couple of weeks, leaving him to walk the streets again in search of something else.

One rainy evening, cold and soaked to the skin, he arrived outside the Savoy Hotel in the Strand. At the side of the building was a huge vent which pumped hot air into the street, and after watching London's rich folk for a while, Tommy snuggled against it for warmth. Later in the evening he ambled down Savoy Hill to the River Thames, and with a pennyworth of chestnuts for his supper, made his way along the Embankment. There he met a friendly night watchman who gave him a hot drink and some of his supper.

The watchman gave Tommy shelter for the night, and the following morning directed him to a barge owner who was looking for someone to work aboard a vessel moored along the Thames. He got the job without any problem but soon realised why nobody had taken it before him. The vessel turned out to be a filthy, rat-infested rubbish barge, but Tommy decided that he had no choice but to get stuck into the work.

Tommy slept on the boat, and the first night was like nothing he had experienced before. He couldn't sleep because of the roaring wind, and he was terrified that the creaking ropes which held the boat to its moorings would snap, leaving him to drift alone down the Thames to a watery grave. He also had to contend with scores of rats which scampered over his bunk and occasionally nibbled at his feet. It reminded him of the huge rats which frequented the pits back in South Wales, and he began to wish he was back there.

Although conditions were appalling, Tommy stuck at the job, shovelling coal into the stoke hole whilst stripped to the waist and pouring with sweat. He suffered from terrible blisters on his back, caused by boiling water which dripped from leaking pipes as he toiled away. His reward for the slaving and sufferance was a mere 30 shillings a week, but he flatly refused to give up just because the going was tough.

He soon got used to the residential rats, the sound of the lapping water and the creaking ropes, and the Thames barge remained his home for almost three months. Then one day he could stand it no longer, and quit. He headed towards Paddington and found lodgings in the Edgware Road, just round the corner from the station. There he had a fluke win whilst playing cards with a number of other young men which netted him seven pounds.

Tommy had sworn that he would never return to Tonypandy unless he was a rich man, but by now he was convinced it was time to swallow his pride and make his way to Paddington Station in time to catch the last train to Cardiff.

At the station he bumped into a man who also happened to be Welsh. He wanted to know Tommy's name, where he was from and what he was doing in London. On hearing the whole sorry story, the stranger gave Tommy his return ticket to Cardiff. Recalling the incident years later, Farr said some people regarded the Welsh as being impetuous and impulsive, 'But that was the most impetuous and impulsive Welshman I ever met.'

Tommy caught the Fishguard Express, and once settled in his seat was happier than he had been for months. He left the train at Cardiff and walked all the way to Tonypandy, where he told anyone he met that he had made a lot of money in London. Unfortunately, his ragged clothes told another story.

With some embarrassment, Tommy poured out the whole story to Job Churchill, particularly about the extreme loneliness he had experienced so many miles from home. Job listened intently, then told him to forget all about it and put it down to experience. 'It's all part of growing up, my lad, and you will be all the better for it.'

Tommy knew that Jim Driscoll and Jimmy Wilde, who also came from deprived areas of Wales, had built a better style of living by fighting, and had started in the booths. 'Job, I've got to be a fighter or nothing,' he insisted. 'Get me the fights and the rest will be easy.'

'Not as easy as that, Tommy Farr,' warned the old saddler. 'I wouldn't be your manager even if I wanted to be, which I don't. The most I can do is help in launching and steering the boat. We'll get caught in many a squeak before we reach dry land.'

Years later, Tommy often recalled his desire to become a fighter. 'Want, you know, eats into you,' he remarked. 'I was subjected to strife and tribulations of poverty. It necessitated positive thinking. I knew what I wanted and went after it.'

Tommy's biggest fault was that he was headstrong and believed that once he started fighting again, his troubles would be at an end. He didn't consider the possibility of anything going wrong, or what he would do if things didn't work out. Fortunately, Churchill was an extremely cautious character who considered every possibility. He recognised that Tommy badly needed some education, so he fed him with books and spent time teaching him to read and write properly. He even sent him to evening school, where he learned about the hotel trade he had enjoyed so much during his summer holidays.

Hungry for action, Tommy issued challenges through the *South Wales Echo* to local men, including Charlie Bundy, Dai Benyon and Ashton Jones. Churchill, meanwhile, got him into a proper training routine at the Gethin Hotel at Penygraig. It had been with Job's blessing that he had gone to Joe Gess in the first place, and it was at his suggestion that he sought him out again.

The Joe Gess Travelling Pavillion went on throughout the year all over south and west Wales. The veteran showman put on at least one show a week, whatever the weather. The contests he staged were good value, and during the 1930s it was estimated that between 400 and 500 licensed fighters got work through his booth in the course of a year.

Many good men, including Owen Moran, Jim Driscoll and Frank Robson, travelled with Gess or boxed for him at some stage of their careers. Robson, who was British featherweight champion in 1906–7, and claimant to the title from 1907–10, worked for Joe for seven years. Even after retiring from the ring, he fought up and down the country in booths until he was over 60. It was solid characters like Robson who kept the booths alive, and indirectly Farr picked up their skills, which were passed down the line.

Joe Gess had recognised Tommy's potential long before he left the booth, so when the youngster approached him again, he agreed to match him in fights for decisions. This was to Joe's advantage because by arranging an attractive contest in advance, he would advertise it and draw a good crowd into the booth.

In August 1932, with the booth pitched at Tredegar, Joe matched Tommy with the experienced Ashton Jones of Trealaw, who two years earlier had fought for the Welsh lightweight title. Although it was Tommy's first serious contest for 15 months, he put up a spirited performance to earn a draw over ten rounds.

Gess was delighted to have Tommy on his shows because he knew he would never be in a dull contest. Six days later, the youngster boxed another ten-round draw with Bunny Eddington at Pontycymer, and then on a Saturday evening two weeks later, dropped a 12-round decision to Albert Donovan at Tredegar. The following week he got a much-needed victory when he outpointed Bob Jarrett (Cardiff) over ten rounds at Aberavon.

Every night, the booth was packed, and when they were scheduled to visit Clydach Vale, Gess matched Tommy with Hopkin Harry (Pontardawe) in a much-talked-about fight which would never appear in any record book. The day of the contest, however, turned out to be a disaster for Tommy. Early that morning, whilst on their way to the Rhondda, the lorry carrying the booth equipment broke down, and Tommy had to walk almost five miles to get petrol.

Hopkin Harry was a heavy puncher, but Tommy was more than holding his own until the fifth round, when he sustained a nasty cut over his left eye. Gess immediately pulled him out of the fight because he had already matched him to meet the vastly experienced Tiger Ellis at Ystrad just four days later.

The fight with Ellis was a big step up in class for Farr because his opponent had won and lost the Welsh welterweight title earlier that year. Ystrad was also Ellis's backyard. With his eye patched up, Tommy boxed at long range for the first two rounds, trying to get the measure of his man, but in the third, Ellis's experience began to tell. Farr was floored for a count of four, and in the fourth, the wound over his left eye reopened. Although he fought back gamely, the injury worsened and the fight had to be stopped in the fifth round. It was a particularly nasty cut, and within a few days inflammation set in and caused Tommy serious problems. He had been due to box a return with Bob Jarrett at Garnett on 14 October and meet Hopkin Harry at Pontardulais on 4 November, but the injury did not heal and Gess had to cancel both contests.

It was late November before Farr was fit to box again, and when he faced Bert Mellin of Neath at Pontardulais, he boxed with great caution to take a ten-round decision. With his confidence restored, he challenged Jerry Daley, Glen Moody, Albert Donovan, Young Ellis and Bunny Eddington, but none showed any interest. That became immaterial, however, when Gess made a fight for Tommy which really brought him to attention in the west of Wales.

Jim Wilde of Swansea was preparing to box in a competition and invited Farr to face him in a try-out. After it was over, Tommy told Gess that he fancied meeting Wilde for real over a distance. The booth owner duly obliged, and matched them over 12 rounds at Pontardulais. Wilde weighed about 13 stone at the time, but, having met bigger men in the booths, Tommy was unconcerned about size or weight. Despite his physical advantages, Wilde couldn't fathom out Farr's style and the Tonypandy boy won comfortably on points in a good fight. It was probably his most notable success to date because Wilde was being talked about as a good heavyweight prospect.

Gess was convinced that Tommy's confidence improved tremendously after beating Wilde. He recalled that although he had always expressed great belief in himself, there had been occasions when he went into the ring lacking confidence. 'Once he found out how good his opponent was, and they got down to the real stuff, he was all right,' recalled Joe.

Tommy's booth days ended very abruptly one night when his brother John unexpectedly turned up at the Gess Pavilion. 'Tommy, I've been trying for months to get you a real fight,' said John, 'and now I think I've done it.' He had managed to persuade local matchmaker Rees Henry to give Tommy a chance. He was always looking for new talent and knew that Tommy had grown tremendously since leaving home to join Gess, and he had heard about his performance against Jim Wilde. He therefore agreed to match him with experienced Jerry Daley of Penygraig in the main event at the Judges Hall, Trealaw, on 30 December. Win, lose or draw, Tommy's purse was £4, representing untold riches to the youngster who had been grafting in the booth for just a few bob a week.

Although Farr had the determination to become a successful fighter, the contest with Daley was a tremendous step-up in class. Apart from being Welsh middleweight champion between 1929 and 1932, he had met good men including Len Harvey, Jock McAvoy and 'Cast Iron' Jack Casey. He had also been a regular sparring partner to Jack Petersen. Jerry was expected to be too strong and experienced for the youngster, and was a 10–1 on favourite in the pre-fight betting odds.

Billed as 'Kid' Farr of Clydach Vale, Tommy was so hard up that he couldn't afford the food necessary to build him up for such a fight. His last meal before going into the ring against Daley consisted of just a kipper.

The Judges Hall was packed on the night because Daley from neighbouring Penygraig was a local hero. He was obviously expecting an easy night because he had agreed to fight another of Petersen's old sparring partners, Charlie Bundy, at Treherbert the following evening. Farr, however, even as a youngster, held no fear and had no respect for reputations, and to the surprise of many knowledgeable Rhondda boxing followers, he put up a tremendous performance. At the end of the 12 rounds the referee gave a draw, but many onlookers considered Tommy very unfortunate not to get the decision.

Tommy's showing against Daley really brought him to notice in South Wales. Although he allowed Jerry to make the pace, he was always quick to counter and frequently scored with sharp left leads. Often disregarding defence, Daley kept storming after the youngster, but with advantages in height, reach and speed, Tommy used these to the full. By the end of the fight, Daley had a bad cut over his left eye, and would be in no condition to meet Charlie Bundy the following night. Farr, on the other hand, was almost unmarked, and jumped at the chance to take Jerry's place when the promoter offered it.

The big Saturday night crowd at the Tynewydd Labour Hall at Treherbert saw a fight which, although being far from a classic, contained plenty of hard hitting. Farr put up a magnificent performance in the experienced Bundy's backyard, standing toe-to-toe with him from the opening bell. Many blows were wild and there was little science for much of the fight, but the crowd loved it. Bundy was the master at close quarters, but Tommy used a sharp straight left which landed constantly with devastating force. He jolted the local man's head back with monotonous ease, although Bundy stormed back during the tenth, eleventh and twelfth rounds. In the final three rounds, Farr boxed with great maturity and ran out a fine points winner.

Tommy had returned to the professional ring grimly determined to succeed, and had gone the distance with two tough, experienced campaigners on consecutive nights. He had shown just how much he had learned in the booths, and was never in serious trouble in either fight. He was developing physically all the time, and was ready to move up from middleweight to light heavyweight.

5

PROGRESS TO A TITLE

Not being able to afford to travel far, Tommy confined himself to taking fights within a radius of about 25 miles of Tonypandy. This also suited his faithful band of about 100 supporters, most of whom were miners, who followed him to the arenas of South Wales. It enabled him to live at home, where he was under the watchful eye of Job Churchill, who accompanied him to all his fights. Purse money was not good, but Job was a shrewd gambler, and by sensible betting on the fights, he and Tommy picked up quite a lot of extra cash.

Although he was challenged to a return by Charlie Bundy, Tommy's first fight of 1933 should have been a return against Jim Wilde. They were due to meet in the main event at the Tonypandy skating rink in early February but the bout was cancelled at the last minute when both men refused to fight because the attendance was too small.

Tommy returned to action in mid-February against Billy Thomas of Deri over 15 two-minute rounds at the Bargoed Coliseum. Although he boxed brilliantly at times, he lost the decision, which was met with a very mixed reception. Thomas went on to challenge Welsh middleweight champion Glen Moody two weeks later, only to lose on points. Three days before that fight, Moody faced Farr in a try-out at the Ruperra Hotel, Pontypridd. Tommy was so confident he could beat him in a real fight that he was at ringside when Moody met Thomas, and before the fight issued a challenge to the winner. Moody won, but never gave Farr a chance, and it was his first taste of top-class men avoiding him.

Three weeks later, Tommy met Bunny Eddington in a return contest at the Judges Hall, and had all kinds of trouble for the first three rounds. His booth experience, however, served him well, and a perfectly timed right to the jaw changed the course of the fight. For the next six rounds he used his left to good effect, and in the eleventh had Eddington almost out on his feet. At the end of the 15 rounds Tommy was a clear winner. It showed how much he had improved since drawing with Bunny the previous summer, and earned him his first headline: TOMMY FARR'S FINE WIN.

After knocking out Dai Benyon (Merthyr) in two rounds at Gorseinon, Tommy issued a challenge to any middle or cruiser-weight in Wales. He particularly wanted to meet Welsh champion Randy Jones over the full championship course, but said he was also ready to fight Glen Moody (Pontypridd), George Smith (Tonyrefrail) or Dave Norris (Clydach Wales). He asked that any replies be sent to him care of the Cross Keys Hotel at Tonypandy.

When Farr and Jerry Daley drew at Trealaw in December, there was a great deal of controversy over who should have got the decision. Shrewd matchmaker Rees Henry knew he would be guaranteed a full house, so he decided to match them again. This time Tommy was given plenty of notice, and his purse, which was doubled to £8, was by far the largest to date.

By this stage he had taken on Tom Evans, a Welsh miner, as his trainer, and together with Job Churchill and Tommy's brother John, they went to great lengths to get him ready for the fight set for the Judges Hall on 21 April. In the weeks leading up to it, they embarked on a strenuous training routine and fed Tommy up with plenty of steaks.

Farr and Daley were both confident of victory and agreed to put up side stakes. With both being local, interest in the fight was tremendous. It intensified on the eve of the contest when the boxers met Mr W. E. Phillips, Secretary of the Welsh Area of the British Boxing Board of Control, and agreed to increase their side stakes to £20. They also agreed to weigh in at 12 stone under a £10 forfeit.

Once the fight got under way, Tommy quickly showed that his performance in the first contest was not a one-off. Again it was a tremendous fight with no quarter given, and there were thrills in every round. The outstanding feature was Tommy's left hand, which he threw with speed and accuracy. In one round it landed 14 times to Daley's face without reply. There were times when he hammered Jerry around the ring, and only Daley's tremendous courage and ability to absorb punishment prevented Farr from winning inside the distance. At the end Tommy was extremely tired, but this was the first time he had boxed over 15 three-minute rounds.

When he drew with Daley back in December, Tommy impressed many people, but this time he did more than that. He served notice that he was a young man with a great future ahead of him provided he was brought along properly. His performance brought praise from William E. Allen, Boxing Editor of the *South Wales Echo*, who in a report headlined CRUISER OF BIG PROMISE – KID FARR IMPRESSES, wrote:

> Cultivate this Farr, and I predict a big future. In the first five rounds, I thought here is the second best man in the principality. First of course we put the British champion Jack Petersen. Farr in this period boxed, and indeed fought, like a champion.

In the audience was Joe Gess, and he was watching Tommy fight for the first time since they parted company. Afterwards he remarked, 'He showed tremendous improvement. I am convinced he will be a champion one day.'

Farr's progress was rewarded with a fight with Randy Jones of Ammanford at the Merthyr Labour Club on 6 May. Jones, the Welsh light heavyweight champion, represented a step-up in class for Farr. Some people believed he was ill advised to meet Jones at this stage of his career. Others who saw him beat Jerry Daley a couple of weeks earlier, however, were of the opinion that he had an even-money chance of winning, and the contest brought about some hefty betting.

Jones obviously thought he was on to a good thing, because his chief second didn't even bother to accompany him. As usual Farr was confident, and in the build-up Evans and Churchill mapped out a curious training schedule for him. They cut out orthodox sparring, kept him working on the heavy bag, and in addition made him wrestle with them for periods every day in order to build up his strength. The tactics worked, because Tommy caused a mild sensation by flooring Jones four times before forcing him to retire at the end of the seventh round.

Despite conceding quite a lot of weight, Tommy gave an impressive display and had the Welsh champion on the retreat from the opening bell. Stiff accurate lefts set Jones up, and a crashing right to the jaw put him down as early as the second round. His left eye was cut in the third by heavy rights, and towards the end of the round he was floored again for a count of seven. From this point Farr was a fighting fury, tearing into his more experienced opponent and smashing home double hooks to head and body. He was fighting like a champion, but became

51

careless in the fifth, taking a wicked left hook to the jaw which would have floored most men.

They felt each other's punches in the sixth, and both were spoken to by the referee following a series of clinches. Jones held his own in this round as he met Tommy head on in a toe-to-toe slam. In round seven, Farr was again brilliant, and straight lefts to the face followed by heavy rights to the body made the champion give ground. Midway through the round, Jones was sent crashing to the floor for a count of six, but on rising was limping badly, having apparently twisted an ankle. He went down again shortly afterwards and was still on the floor when the bell saved him with the count at six. It was no surprise when the towel fluttered from his corner, and afterwards it was revealed that his right ankle was badly sprained. By this time, however, Randy was being well beaten by a man now considered by some experts to be the best light heavyweight in Britain outside Petersen.

Just seven days later, Farr was in action again against old foe Charlie Bundy at the Bargoed Coliseum over 12 three-minute rounds. It was the main event on a Saturday evening show before a packed house. He gave another wonderful display rated by many followers of Welsh boxing as the best of his career so far. Now billed as Tommy 'Kid' Farr, his left was like a piston and his defence superb. Much the superior boxer, he used his height and reach advantage to the full.

Bundy realised that to try and box Farr was out of the question, so he changed his tactics and began wading in, throwing punches from all angles. He attacked the body to try and slow Tommy down, but as the fight wore on he became more erratic. Farr, meanwhile, persisted with his jab, backed by the occasional heavy right, and Bundy took a lot of punishment. Charlie, though, was as tough as they come and took the youngster all the way. At the end Tommy was a good points winner of a fight generally thought to be the best seen at the venue for some years.

Tommy was thrilled by his results since returning to regular action; they confirmed his belief that he really could succeed in the fight game. But he knew that if he was really to progress, he had to get fights in London. It didn't matter how good he was or how many fights he won in the little mining towns of South Wales, he would never get any recognition if he didn't fight in the capital.

Still resentful of the fact that when he was in London no promoter had given him the chance, he was suddenly offered a fight on a show being promoted by Sydney Hulls at the old Crystal Palace. Hulls was one of the leading promoters in London and had matched Phil Scott's young prospect, Eddie Steele of Nor-wood, with Randy Jones. Having sustained a damaged ankle in his fight with Farr a week earlier, Jones was forced to withdraw. Hulls was desperate to keep the show alive, and although he had never heard of Farr, he was persuaded to use him as a substitute. In doing so he was confident he would not unduly trouble Steele.

Tommy travelled to London just two days after his fight with Charlie Bundy. With four straight wins in the space of six weeks, he was full of confidence and knew that a win over Steele could really be the turning point for him. To celebrate the occasion he bought himself a new gumshield, something he had never previously been able to afford. Foolishly, he did not take the precaution of checking that it fitted properly.

Although desperate to impress in his first appearance in a London ring, the outcome could not have been worse for Tommy. Not only did he take part in a terrible fight in which there was no real action, but he also ended up a loser amid the most unusual circumstances. The fight was marred by persistent holding and slapping, which brought both men repeated cautions from the referee. The crowd soon became restless and throughout the contest showed their disapproval with bouts of stamping, slow handclapping and booing.

Steele, who had been out of the ring for some while, was heavier than the Welshman, and in the sixth round landed the only solid blow of the fight when he sent Tommy to the floor for a short count. The bout ended unexpectedly in the seventh when Steele threw what appeared to be a moderate blow, catching Farr in the region of the throat. Tommy immediately stopped boxing, vaulted over the ropes and ran up the aisle towards the dressing rooms. Everyone watched in complete amazement, not knowing what he was doing. When he returned to the ring shortly afterwards, he discovered that the referee had awarded the fight to Steele, believing the Welshman had retired. When told of the decision, Farr became extremely angry and quickly convinced himself it was yet another instance of everyone being against him.

It was later discovered that Tommy's strange behaviour had been caused by the new gumshield. It did not fit properly and when the blow from Steele landed, the shield dislodged and slipped into his throat, causing him to choke. He had leapt from the ring in shear panic, and on reaching the dressing room persuaded one of the other boxers to thump him on the back. This knocked the gumshield back into his mouth, and once he could breathe freely again, he returned to the ring, naively expecting the referee to allow him to continue.

Tommy's anger turned into a mood of complete devastation. He had been longing to fight in London, and having finally got the chance, he had completely blown it. He turned to Job Churchill in his corner, expecting some sympathy, but instead was told he was 'a blasted young fool' for leaving the ring. Churchill was in fact so angry with Tommy that he hardly spoke to him over the next few days.

Farr was completely unknown in London and his performance did nothing to enhance his reputation. Although not of championship class, the fight attracted plenty of publicity because of the ending. Tommy was convinced he would never get the chance to box in London again, and returned to Wales a very dispirited young man. Churchill knew that the only way to get his mind right was to get him another fight as soon as possible. So just three days after the Steele fiasco, Farr climbed through the ropes at the Judges Hall to try and avenge the defeat Billy Thomas had inflicted in February.

Job's tactics worked to the full because Tommy gained sweet revenge over Thomas in a thrill-packed 15-rounder, at the end of which he was a good points winner. In the early rounds he was made to miss badly and was mainly on the defensive. In the fourth, however, he changed tactics and staged a good old-fashioned punch-up, during which a wicked left hook to the jaw rocked Thomas. From the sixth onwards, Tommy forced the fight and a couple of times sent his opponent reeling across the ring. Midway through the tenth, Thomas's left eye was split by a powerful right. Blood streamed into his eyes and he looked in a bad way, but fought bravely to keep Farr off.

Tommy continued to force the pace and often had his man in trouble. The closing rounds were fast, bitter affairs, with Farr attacking strongly and Thomas fighting back gamely. At the end it was close but Farr fully deserved the decision and it was well received by the packed house.

Four days later, Tommy was in action again, this time at Pontypridd Town Hall against Tony Arpino, a London Italian who had acted as Jack Petersen's sparring partner. He was considered by many people to be the cleverest boxer Tommy had faced. Although conceding ten pounds in weight, Farr's left hand picked up the points from the opening bell. He was superior in every department and boxed his way to another good decision.

In the space of 17 days Tommy had engaged in five fights, and the two wins back in Wales had pushed the Steele defeat to the back of his mind. Job Churchill had done his work well but wanted to keep Tommy active. So on 3 June he faced George Smith of Tonyrefrail at the Merthyr Labour Club. Although he had quite a big weight advantage, Smith was no match for Farr, who won the 15-rounder easily. George was floored in the fourth for a count of five, and again in the seventh for six. In round ten, Farr was brilliant. Smith was sent to the floor for two counts of eight and was in a bad way when the bell rescued him. In the eleventh he sustained a badly cut left eye, and in the fourteenth was floored again. The count had reached nine when the bell come to his rescue. Tommy was so in command during the final round that shouts of 'stop the fight' and 'throw in the towel' came from the audience. To his credit, Smith was extremely tough and game, and lasted out to the final bell.

Farr was improving with every contest, and on the Jack Petersen–George Cook British Empire title bill at Cardiff three weeks later, he forced Gunner Bennett (Windsor) to retire after eight rounds. Five days later he took on the experienced Tiger Ellis at Tredegar before a huge crowd on a promotion organised in connection with the local hospital week. Using his left hand brilliantly, Tommy took a clear decision over 15 rounds. It was a fight described as being one of the best ever seen in north Monmouthshire between men from the heavier divisions.

The following week, Tommy was back at the Merthyr Labour Club, where he took a close decision from Ernie Simmons of West Bromwich. The victory earned him another striking headline, FARR'S GREAT VICTORY, in the *South Wales Echo*. Despite the erection of a new stadium, poor weather conditions kept the attendance down, but those who did brave it got their money's worth. Simmons proved to be one of the toughest men Tommy had met and was full of confidence, having just beaten Jack Casey, 'the Sunderland Assassin'. He stormed after Tommy, catching him with heavy blows to the stomach. There were thrilling moments in the eighth and ninth rounds when they engaged in heavy toe-to-toe slugging and Simmons appeared to be the heavier puncher of the two. By the thirteenth his aggression had made it a close affair, but in the last two sessions Farr's left hand took him to victory.

At the Welfare Hall, Ebbw Vale, seven days later, Tommy confirmed his superiority over Bunny Eddington in another contest described as being one of the most exciting seen at the venue. He boxed like a real champion, and after the fight it was announced he would meet Randy Jones for the Welsh title at the Empire Theatre, Tonypandy, the following Friday.

Tommy was the natural contender for Jones' Welsh light heavyweight title, having convincingly beaten him just two months earlier. Apart from the defeats by Billy Thomas and Eddie Steele, and the controversial draw with Jerry Daley, he had won his other 11 fights in grand style since embarking on his new campaign just seven months earlier. He was rarely in a poor fight, and Welsh boxing enthusiasts were starting to sit up and take notice of him. Local press coverage of his fights had been good, and he had received his share of the headlines.

Both men trained extremely hard and when they weighed in at the venue at 2 p.m. on the day of the fight, both looked extremely fit and tense. Two thousand fans crammed into the Empire that evening, the large majority of them behind the local boy Farr. Ringside seats costing 5s 9d, and stalls and circle at 3s 6d had been sold out well in advance. Many people, particularly the locals, expected Farr to dominate Jones just as he had in their previous fight. This one, though, turned out to be a totally different affair.

The ring had been erected on the theatre stage, and few people realised that it sloped upwards away from the footlights. Because adjustments weren't made, the back of the ring was about two feet higher than the front. This meant that the boxer facing out into the audience enjoyed a clear advantage over the one with his back to it. One moment Farr was towering over Jones, and the next minute the roles were reversed. There was therefore a constant psychological battle for the 'top of the hill'.

The fight started slowly, but by the second round it was clear that Farr's left hand was the better weapon. In this round he sustained the handicap of a cut left eye, but nevertheless dominated the first four rounds with his left. In the fifth, Jones got home with his best punch of the fight so far, a crisp left hook to the jaw, and from that point onwards Tommy did not look so comfortable.

In the sixth Jones called on all his experience and brought his left hand into play, puzzling his young challenger. The seventh saw Tommy get back on top again, and he boxed brilliantly in the next three rounds. By this stage he was dictating the exchanges with his immaculate left hand, and in the ninth the champion experienced his worst period of the fight. Farr hit him at will and every punch he threw landed. Jones' left eye was badly cut, and on two occasions he became so frustrated at not knowing what to do that he just stood still in the centre of the ring with his hands on his hips.

In the eleventh, Farr appeared to tire and Jones came back into the fight. A big left swing caught Farr flush on the chin, but he took it well and moved around the ring to keep out of danger. He kept using his left but by now it was more of a prod than a solid punch. In the fourteenth, Jones again caught Tommy with dangerous rights, which kept the crowd on the edge of their seats. During the last minute of the round, however, Tommy staged a big rally which won him the round.

Jones came out for the last round and joined in a toe-to-toe punch-up despite blood again pouring from his damaged left eye. It was his last hope of hanging on to his title, and for a while it looked as though he just might succeed. Farr, however, still had plenty left, and once he was out of trouble he coasted the rest of the round. At the end he was the clear winner, and when referee Billy Morgan walked over to him he leapt into the air with delight. Great sportsmanship had been shown throughout the fight, and Jones' manager was the first person to congratulate Tommy on his victory.

Tommy Farr was light-heavyweight champion of Wales at the tender age of 20. It was an outstanding achievement for one so young, and by beating Jones he had done much to restore the prestige of the Rhondda in Welsh boxing. His only regret was that his father had not been alive to see him do it. George Farr had died on 5 May 1932 at his home at 59 Court Street from hemiplegia and cerebral haemorrhage. He was just 56.

Victory was sweet, and Tommy was bursting with excitement. He felt he could win a world title straight away without any trouble.

There was to be no resting on laurels, and just seven days later Tommy travelled to Belfast to meet the former middleweight champion of Ireland, Jack O'Brien. Again he gave a splendid exhibition of boxing to beat an experienced opponent, and once more it was his stabbing left hand which was his most potent weapon. Tommy used it to great effect as he strove to get to close quarters, and the Irishman was given a real battering. The end came in the sixth round when his corner threw in the towel.

Tommy's success over the past six or seven months had turned him into a local hero in the Rhondda, but as so often happens, his achievements attracted great rivalry. At the beginning of August, he was suddenly challenged to a fight by Dave Norris, another local light heavyweight who fought out of Clydach Vale. Norris was born less than a mile from Farr, and for some while rival supporters had watched the progress of the two men and made the inevitable comparisons.

Once Tommy became Welsh champion, individuals close to Norris issued a challenge of £25 a side. In doing so they stated they would lodge their money with the *South Wales Echo* or any other reputable source, if Tommy was prepared to accept the challenge. There was tremendous local interest in the prospect of such a fight, and opinion was divided as to who would be the likely winner. Farr had been much busier than Norris, who although very impressive in the gyms, had been described as suffering from stage fright when he fought Charlie Bundy at Trealaw. He had also been beaten in seven rounds by Scottish champion Jim Winters at Glasgow. Nevertheless, the prospect of a 'Rhondda Derby' was mouth-watering for the fans.

A couple of weeks later the two boxers and their backers met at the Pandy Hotel in Tonypandy under the chairmanship of Mr W. J. Phillips, Secretary of the Welsh Area of the British Boxing Board of Control, to see if terms could be reached for a fight. The two men arrived looking very grim-faced, and the atmosphere was electric.

'Well, what about it?' snapped Farr, as soon as everyone was seated.

'I want fifteen two-minute rounds,' growled Norris.

'I want fifteen three-minute rounds,' retorted Farr.

'I'll give you winner-take-all and other conditions if you will give way on the question of fifteen three-minute rounds,' said Norris.

'I'm firm on three minutes,' replied Farr, 'because I consider two-minute rounds to be no distance at all.'

'Well,' said Norris, 'you have boxed often enough over no distance.'

Farr ignored the taunt. He just sat and stared at Norris, waiting for the next remark.

'Well,' said Norris after a short pause, 'there is nothing left for me to do but box Randy Jones and a few others, and then meet you for the cruiserweight title.'

'Suits me,' snapped Farr, who got up and left the table. It was clear for all to see that there was no love lost between the two, and there was no attempt at a handshake from either man as they parted company.

A few days later Tommy claimed that he was disappointed he and Norris had failed to agree terms, but insisted that his main objective was to be recognised as a contender for the British light heavyweight title. By this time, Len Harvey was champion, having beaten Eddie Phillips of Bow on points at Olympia in June. Tommy was ranked behind Phillips, Laurie Raiteri (Stratford), Bob Carvill (Bridlington) and Tommy Tucker (Bamber Bridge).

Farr said he was willing to meet any of the men ranked above him for a worthwhile purse, and hoped that offers would be made by the Tonypandy, Merthyr or Llanelli promoters. 'My aim is to reach the top,' he said, 'and I hope those gentlemen can get me the right fights on Welsh soil.' Tommy even went to the lengths of advertising his services and invited promoters to contact him at 59 Court Street with their offers.

As the new season commenced, Tommy was matched with Tom Benjamin of Duffryn and London, who was thought to be a very dangerous opponent. He had been boxing in London and had met leading men in the upper divisions, such as Raiteri and Archie Sexton so he was regarded as more experienced than Farr.

As he had been out of action for two months, Tommy trained hard and then took the unusual course of having a public workout at the Hibernian Club and Institute in Tonypandy four days before the contest. He went through a total of nine rounds against his three sparring partners, one of whom was Jerry Daley.

A crowd of about 1,200 packed into the Judges Hall, Trealaw, and saw Tommy beat Benjamin much more easily than had been anticipated. They were considered to be the best two men in Wales at the weight, because Jack Petersen had by this time moved up to heavyweight. Yet it was not an attractive fight, because they seemed to have too much respect for each other. It was only in the twelfth and thirteenth rounds that Benjamin forgot his caution and set about Tommy in an attempt to land a knockout. As usual, Tommy's brilliant left hand saw him through and he finished a long way ahead on points.

During the next two weeks Tommy took on two more strong experienced men in Charlie Chetwynd of Leicester and Jack Marshall of Accrington, and beat them both. Against Chetwynd he softened up a strong but clumsy opponent with left jabs, then gradually brought heavy rights into play. By the seventh the Leicester man had a badly damaged nose, and in the ninth Farr was going all out for a spectacular finish. In this round Chetwynd went down for a count of nine, but struggled up and fought back bravely. Farr, however, could not miss him, and after he struggled back to his corner at the end of the round, Charlie's seconds threw in the towel.

Jack Marshall was said to be one of the strongest men in the North of England, and had a reputation for possessing a big punch in his right hand. The big crowd at the Merthyr Labour Club expected fireworks from Marshall, but despite his physical advantages, he was no match for the brilliant Welshman. Tommy's fast left jab completely baffled Marshall, and he was driven all round the ring in the first round. Tommy brought heavy punches into play in the second and Jack was in serious trouble when a right put him down for a count of seven. Only the bell saved him from being knocked out. By the fifth Marshall's left eye was almost closed, but he stood toe to toe with Farr and exchanged heavy punches. First one would back off, then the other, but by the end of the round the man from Accrington looked sold out. As Tommy came out for round seven, he looked as fresh as when he started. He threw punches with both hands from all angles, and a cut appeared on Marshall's cheekbone. As he fought back bravely, Tommy caught him with a tremendous right over the left eye which split it so badly that the referee immediately stepped between them and stopped the contest. The crowd had turned up expecting fireworks, and they certainly got them from the Welsh champion.

Three weeks later, Tommy convincingly beat Seaman Harvey of Chatham on points over 15 rounds at Trealaw, and then the following week took on Steve McCall of Scotland, who was remembered for his magnificent contest with Frank Moody. He had also fought Len Harvey for the British middleweight title in 1930 and given him a hard fight until having to retire in the ninth round. McCall had held the Scottish middleweight title for three years, the light heavyweight title before relinquishing it, and fought for the heavyweight title at the beginning of 1933. Having recently knocked out Jack Marshall in the first round, he was thought to be Tommy's supreme test.

The Scotsman took plenty of supporters with him to Merthyr, and cries of 'Come on, Steve' could be heard all round the stadium. Tommy Farr held no fear for reputations, and as soon as the opening bell sounded he set about McCall. He boxed like a real champion, with speed, accuracy and versatility, and his performance against the vastly experienced Scotsman left many old-timers at the ringside amazed. His immaculate left leads found McCall's head time and time again, round after round. In the fifth, a left-right combination sent McCall's gumshield flying across the ring, but he fought back like an enraged tiger. Farr, though, controlled him and built up a big points lead with his left. By the ninth, old injuries had opened up above both men's eyes, and these became targets for left jabs. Farr's was the finer weapon, and by the end of the tenth, McCall's left eye had closed. Farr tried to end it in the eleventh, and drove the battered Scotsman all round the ring. He tried to fight back, but when the bell sounded, he literally staggered back to his corner and fell onto his stool. His seconds worked frantically, and as he came up for the twelfth he was very weak. There was no respite, and the vicious Welshman pounded McCall with both hands.

Suddenly it was all over, as the towel came in from Steve's corner just as he himself turned away, raising a glove in surrender. Tommy Farr had passed his supreme test with flying colours, and after the fight he was described as the best light heavyweight, apart from Jack Petersen, that Wales had seen for many years.

It says much for the times, because despite sustaining some injuries, Farr travelled to Blackpool the following day, and just two days after his gruelling battle with McCall, took on Ernie Simmons of Birmingham over 12 rounds. Tommy was clearly not himself, and after six rounds he was well behind, but then he picked up the pace and levelled matters up. Simmons staged a big rally in the last minute of the final round and was awarded the decision, but it was very unpopular with the crowd.

In reality Tommy should not have taken the fight at such short notice, but he had beaten Simmons at Merthyr in July and was convinced he could do it again.

After a break of four weeks, Tommy outpointed Leo Evans of Buith and London in Merthyr at the beginning of December over 15 rounds in a very close, punishing fight. Tommy was in trouble in the thirteenth and fourteenth rounds but recovered well to win the last round easily. At the end Evans was only just able to walk to his corner. It was Tommy's last contest of 1933, although he did return to Belfast to box a return with Ernie Simmons on 13 December, only to find that the man from Birmingham had failed to show up.

Nevertheless, 1933 had been an exceptionally good year, one in which Tommy's reputation had spread rapidly throughout the towns and villages of the Rhondda. In Merthyr, the promoter billed him as 'the wrecker of champions' before his fight with Leo Evans, because of the good men he had beaten.

Tiger Ellis had been Welsh welterweight champion in 1932, Jerry Daley middleweight champion of Wales from 1929 to 1933, and Randy Jones Welsh light heavyweight champion during 1933 until Tommy beat him. Jim Winters was Scottish light heavyweight champion during 1933, whilst Steve McCall had been middle-weight and light heavyweight champion of Scotland between 1929

61

and 1932. During the past 12 months or so, young Tommy Farr had beaten them all, and in doing so had managed to earn as much as £15 for some of his more recent fights. Less than 12 months earlier, he hadn't been able to command half that amount.

During 1933, Tommy had fought on 28 occasions, losing just three. In less than a year, he had risen from being a booth fighter to light heavyweight champion of Wales and a genuine contender for the British title.

Most of Farr's early fights went the distance, which was due largely to the fact that he was more concerned with earning his pay than risking injury to himself. Whilst he was always willing to stand and have a toe-to-toe slog, he always did so on his terms, and when the going got tough, he used his considerable boxing skills to get himself out of trouble.

Tommy wasn't interested in making a name for himself by running up a string of quick wins against unknown opposition, and much preferred the safety-first approach against better-quality opponents. The experience he gained in the booths had taught him good basic skills, and as a result he was rarely in serious trouble. At this stage of his career, he was fortunate that he sustained very few serious injuries, but again this was due largely to his skill and ringcraft. This enabled him to fight on a regular basis and earn reasonable money.

By this stage, Tommy's earnings were far greater than he had picked up in the pits, and with the astute Job Churchill's guidance, he learned to save quite a lot. It was not long before he could afford to buy the little terraced house in Court Street where he had been raised, and it became one of the proudest moments of his life. The fact that he was able to do it for his brothers and sisters meant that at last they had the security of knowing there would always be a roof over their heads. When they were children, there was the constant fear that they would be turned out into the streets, but now those fears had evaporated for ever.

Because most of his fights went to decisions, nothing much was heard of Tommy outside Wales. He was not considered an exciting prospect, and consequently he rarely got offers to fight elsewhere. Apart from the Steele fiasco, the only other occasions when he had ventured away from the Rhondda were when he travelled to Belfast and Blackpool to meet O'Brien and Simmons. Tommy knew, however, that now he was a title contender, it was crucial that he boxed further afield. He had developed into a good, competent fighter, and Job Churchill and Tom Evans were confident that he could look after himself wherever he fought. Like Tommy, they knew it was time to spread his wings.

When he was invited to return to Belfast to box Kid Scott of Sheffield on a Sunday evening in January 1934, Tommy jumped at the chance, mainly because he loved Ireland. The good-natured people of Belfast had spoiled him with their kindness when he boxed there the previous July, and Tommy admitted that he had been very close to tears when it was time to say goodbye.

The fight itself lasted just 90 seconds, during which time Tommy put Scott down for the full count with a tremendous right to the jaw. Afterwards the young Welshman went back to his lodgings and to his amazement found a turkey dinner with all the trimmings waiting for him. It had been specially prepared by his landlord to celebrate the occasion. Tommy was speechless as he sat at the table because never before had he experienced such generosity.

Tommy's two fights in Belfast had both been staged by Jim Rice, whom he described as being the most open-handed boxing promoter he had ever met. 'Gentleman Jim was quite unlike any other promoter I knew,' he remarked years later. Apart from his purse for the Scott fight, Rice also gave Tommy a present of £25, which was a huge sum of money to a 20-year-old from the stricken mining region of South Wales. The promoter even sent a taxi to meet the boxers off the boat, and Tommy recalled that win, lose or draw, Rice always made sure it was available to take them back to the quay afterwards.

Despite the fact that he had progressed considerably since the Steele fight in London, the memory of it still needled Tommy. It was one of a number of incidents which occurred during his early days that made him very bitter and believe that everyone was against him. He was certainly a youngster with a chip on his shoulder, but all of the hatred that had built up inside him was turning him into a grimly determined young fighter.

It was at this time that, with the help of the famous boxing referee Moss Deyong, Tommy suddenly got the chance to reappear in a London ring. One day during the early part of 1934, when Deyong was preparing a bill for a charity show, he was approached by Sam Russell, another promoter who put on shows at the Holborn Stadium. Russell also managed a number of fighters, including Eddie Phillips of Bow, one of the leading light heavyweights in the country. Russell asked Deyong why he didn't use his fighters on the charity shows, whereupon Deyong said they would cost too much.

However, Russell said Phillips would be prepared to fight for a purse of £100. This interested Deyong immensely because Phillips would make an attractive top of the bill, although a good opponent would have to be found to bring in a big crowd. Suddenly Deyong remembered that when he was in Wales some months earlier, he had seen Tommy Farr box. Whilst he hadn't considered him to be championship class, he had been sufficiently impressed to believe he would beat a lot of good men.

Russell had never heard of Farr, but agreed to use him, and so the match was made. When Deyong offered Tommy the fight, he explained that as the show was for charity, he couldn't offer him a very large purse. That didn't bother Tommy in the slightest because here was the chance for him to return to a London ring. Furthermore, he knew that Eddie Phillips was one of the best light heavyweights in Britain, having taken Len Harvey to a points decision the previous June. It was the opportunity he had been waiting for, to show the fight buffs in the capital just how good he was.

Phillips had advantages in height and reach; but as the fight opened, Farr ignored these as he went after the Londoner. His blows were so well placed that Phillips was floored twice in the opening round from swift rights to the jaw. Tommy won the first six rounds, the difference being that he found the target with ease whilst Eddie frequently missed. Phillips became very frustrated, and at the end of the third round, struck Farr after the bell with a heavy right to the head. Tommy was clearly very angry and turned on the Londoner, and it looked for a moment as though there would be an ugly scene. Sensibly, though, Tommy hesitated, turned and walked quietly to his corner. Phillips, however, started to follow him, and had to be forcibly restrained by the referee and led back to his corner.

The crowd were extremely angry with Phillips and there was uproar throughout the interval. Before the start of the fourth round, Moss Deyong, who was the referee, called both men together in the centre of the ring and gave them a stern lecture. They shook hands and the bout continued without any further bad feeling.

The seventh round was the turning point in the contest as Phillips finally got to grips with Tommy's style. A left hook floored the Welshman, but although he was up quickly, his left eye was badly cut. Phillips gained in confidence and forced the pace to make up the points deficit. In the final round he fought like a tiger and had Tommy reeling against the ropes, and at the end he took Moss Deyong's decision.

As he left the ring, Tommy received a wonderful ovation from an appreciative audience, and Moss Deyong confirmed afterwards that Phillips had only just won. Tommy was happy because the Steele fiasco was now behind him.

In the audience that night was Ted Broadribb, an influential man on the London fight scene. Apart from having a strong stable of active boxers, he was also the matchmaker for the Royal Albert Hall shows. He was impressed by Farr's showing and saw great possibilities for him. As a result he spoke to small hall promoter Jim Wicks and suggested he matched Farr with Phillips in a return contest and put it on at one of his shows at Wandsworth Stadium.

Meanwhile, Tommy returned to Wales, and after a break took on Scottish champion Jim Winters at the Greyfriars Hall, Cardiff, on 26 March in a fight which was billed as a British title eliminator. Nobody had ever extended Tommy as the Scotsman did, and time and again the Welsh champion's head was jolted back by heavy right hands. Things were made more difficult for Tommy when he damaged his right thumb as early as the second round, and he rarely used his right from then onwards.

By the eighth round there was very little in it, and this prompted heavy betting at the ringside. A number of punters placed large bets on Tommy at odds of 5–4 on.

In the eleventh, Tommy had a particularly bad time for over half a minute as the Scottish champion drove him round the ring, scoring with tremendous rights. Farr's courage and stamina were unquestionable, but how he remained upright was a miracle. In the later rounds Tommy scored well with his left jab as Winters chased after him, and at the end there could have been very little in it. Farr got the decision, but it was very close and there were a number of people who were critical of the referee.

Afterwards, amid the booing, referee Jack Hart said, 'I had no hesitation in giving the verdict to Farr because he punched the cleaner.'

The Scottish champion was very disappointed. 'I thought I was a good winner. My opponent did nothing but paw me with his left hand.' Winters said he would like to meet Farr again, and he didn't mind where.

Tommy was naturally happy with the decision, although his right thumb, which he said he damaged on Winters' head, was painful and swollen. 'He did not hurt me one little bit,' he said, 'not even with that terrible right hand of his. I agree I did not box

65

like I have been doing in my training, but I am sure I did well enough to earn the verdict.' Later, however, in the cold light of day, Tommy confessed that it was the worst exhibition he had ever given to the public, and said he could give no reason or make any excuses for his poor showing.

6

AWAY FROM THE RHONDDA

Tommy's run of success in South Wales, particularly his win over Jim Winters, attracted the attention of Newcastle promoter John Padgett, who offered him two fights in quick succession at the St James Hall. The first was against local hero Jack Casey on 23 April, and the other two weeks later against Canadian Charlie Belanger, both over 12 rounds.

Casey, a real tough professional, was nicknamed 'the Sunderland Assassin' because of the way he hammered his opponents to defeat. By the time he met Farr he had engaged in 201 fights, including losing on points to Len Harvey for the British middleweight title in 1932. Everyone in the Welsh camp was aware of Jack's big punching reputation, but they weren't worried because life in the booths had toughened Tommy.

Casey had a reputation for keeping his opponents waiting, so just before they were due to go into the ring, Job Churchill made an excuse to go to Casey's dressing room. 'Would Jack oblige the Welsh party by ducking under the ropes on time to enable us to catch the night train home,' growled Job.

'Don't worry about your train,' snapped one of Casey's seconds. 'Jack will see that the fight is over in good time for you to catch it.'

Job didn't hang about to argue, but shot straight back to Farr's dressing room. Tom Evans was furious when Job told him what had been said. He went to the door and shouted loud enough for the opposition to hear, 'To blazes with the train. Casey will never put Tommy down.'

'Not unless he kills me on my feet,' added Tommy for good measure.

The remarks had certainly stirred up feeling between the two

67

camps, and the scene was set for a right set-to once they got into the ring.

During the first three rounds, Farr scored repeatedly with his left as he used his reach advantage to the full. He landed some good rights as well, and for a while Casey was very puzzled. Jack knew only one way to fight, and that was to storm forward, and once he found a way inside, he punished the Welshman heavily about the body.

At the end of the fifth, Farr asked Job Churchill how he thought things were going. 'On tonight's form,' said the old saddler with an enthusiasm that Tommy had never known before, 'you've got a chance of a championship someday.'

By the sixth, though, Tommy was looking very tired and groggy. He had landed some tremendous rights on Casey but they had had no effect, and this appeared to make the Welshman lose heart. Although he resorted to his orthodox boxing, he couldn't keep Casey out for long. In the ninth Jack drove Farr round the ring with a heavy two-fisted bombardment which had the crowd on the edge of their seats. The fight swung one way and then the other. Tommy's stamina was incredible, and despite the punishment he was taking, he always recovered well between rounds and finished the final round like a winner.

Tommy and Job Churchill were both convinced they had won, as were many people in the crowd. There was a mild demonstration when Casey was declared the winner, and Tommy was loudly cheered as he left the ring. Afterwards Churchill insisted that it was one of the fiercest fights he had ever watched, and the following day it was written up in a number of newspapers as the best fight seen in the North for years. It was certainly one from which both men emerged with a great deal of credit.

Tommy was very angry at not being declared the winner, and claimed it was yet another case of him being robbed of a decision. Referee Murphy had taken some time to add up his score card, and this caused Tommy to believe that the fight was close and had therefore been given to the local man.

The following day *Newcastle Evening Chronicle* sports reporter 'J.G.O' admitted he had expected Farr to receive the decision.

[Murphy] and I will therefore agree to differ on one of the toughest heavy-weight battles that has been seen in Newcastle since the memorable meeting between Casey and Harvey. I would have given the verdict to Farr for his immense superiority and sound left leading and connecting.

When Tommy climbed back into the ring at St James Hall two weeks later to meet Charlie Belanger, it was one of the few times in his entire career that he actually felt apprehensive. The fight was made at catchweights, which meant that neither boxer went to the scales. When the Canadian stripped off his dressing gown, the normally fearless Welshman was horrified. Belanger looked huge, and it was estimated that he weighed almost 13½ stone compared with Farr's 12 stone.

Job Churchill sensed the fear in his fighter, and reminded him that he had not been knocked out since he was a boy. He insisted that win, lose or draw, he was on his feet at the end.

Belanger had a punch of iron; every time he landed, Tommy was hurt. Between rounds Job and Tom Evans worked hard to keep their man going, but he was in pretty bad shape. Every round he tried but found he was up against something he had never encountered before, and something against which his normally immaculate left hand was totally useless.

By the end of the ninth round Churchill and Evans knew that Tommy could never win by boxing the Canadian, so they changed their battle plan. Between rounds, Churchill yelled, 'Tommy, you've got to take a chance. Chuck the boxing and go in and fight. Punch your weight into him, and if he gives ground, pile it on all you can.'

Job sent his boy out for a do-or-die effort, and Tommy had the courage to give it a go. He summoned up every ounce of strength left in his body, which had once been described as a bag of bones. The battle which ensued had the crowd on their feet as Farr tore after his opponent like a madman. He hit Belanger good and hard, and for the first time in the fight saw him back away. Up until this point, Tommy had been boxing to Job's orders but to no avail. Now he was fighting and making some progress, but every inch of his head and body was aching, and he was experiencing pain he never new existed. Tommy Farr was a young man of extreme courage, and responded to every scream of 'After him, after him,' which came from his corner.

Belanger was a good, seasoned professional, and he ducked and dodged his way out of trouble. At the end of the contest he got the decision. Tommy had done everything asked of him in those last three rounds, and the people of Newcastle loved him for it. Unfortunately, by the time he changed his tactics, it was too late.

The journey home to Wales after the fight was an absolute nightmare for Tommy. His arms and chest were black and blue, his eyes cut and swollen, and his lips were split. His throat was puffed out to the level of his chin, and he felt terribly weak. Time and again he asked himself what on earth had he been hit with. Job told Tom Evans to fix the cushions in their carriage so that Tommy could lie on his back, but even so every jolt of the train sent pain shooting through his head and body. They tried to force some food into him but he couldn't take it, and in the end they had to give up. Then one of them suddenly had the bright idea of putting a straw into some milk so that Tommy could gently sip it. But even that was an effort.

The next day, the *Newcastle Evening Chronicle* reporter again gave Tommy's latest fight in the North-East space in his column:

As he did against Casey, the Welshman again revealed a wonderful left lead, but he did not overcome the heavy body attacks that came from Belanger once they got to close quarters...I got the impression last night, that Belanger is not as good as I thought he was the other day when I saw him punching the ball and bag at Seaman Watson's gym. He simply shook the building with the power of his blows, but he must have been delivering them wrongly last night as he pounded away at Farr's body, or the lesser man must surely have gone to the floor. As it was, all the swinging blows which the Canadian brought over with both hands from behind his back, had little effect on Farr.

The reporter obviously didn't know what a tough man Tommy Farr was, and in a way his remarks were a tribute to the Welshman's condition.

Tommy took probably the worst hammering of his career that night, but fortunately he was young and very strong. Back home he soon began to recover, and it was not long before he was training again and hungry for work. Back in London, Jim Wicks had succeeded in matching him in a return with Eddie Phillips, and the fight was to go on at the Wandsworth Stadium. In the meantime, Tommy reached an agreement with Ted Broadribb that he would handle his affairs when he boxed in London. Ted had been impressed by what he had seen of Farr previously, and asked the British Boxing Board of Control to recognise the fight with Phillips as a final eliminator for the British light heavyweight title.

Job Churchill took no chances once the contest with Phillips was signed, and sent Tommy off to his farm at St Athan, a pretty little Glamorganshire village. There he trained hard for several weeks, putting in hard work on the land as well as in the ring in an attempt to harden and thicken himself up. The plan was to win the fight by a knockout so that there could be no argument, and on the day before the fight Tommy looked in perfect condition as he left Wales for London. 'I am certain I can reverse the last decision,' he said as he boarded his train.

On the day of the fight, Churchill and Evans went on a sightseeing tour of London, while Tommy rested in his hotel room. He slept like a log, and it was only when Job and Tom returned that they all realised it was almost time they were due at the stadium. They grabbed the few things they wanted and rushed to Wandsworth, where they were met at the gate by the anxious-looking whip. 'They're waiting for you, Farr,' he yelled angrily. 'You're on next.' They all dived into the dressing room, and Tommy had never stripped so fast in all his life.

The stadium was packed with a crowd of over 20,000 expecting a top-class contest, and Phillips, having been the chief sparring partner to Len Harvey, was a firm favourite. Farr had the better of the first round, in which he was the aggressor. Phillips took no chances and boxed carefully, but Tommy managed to score with several stiff lefts to the face.

In the second, Phillips went on the retreat and prevented the Welshman landing the big punches he had planned. The best punch of a fairly even round was a right under the heart from the Londoner.

As the third opened, Tommy scored with some good lefts which were troubling Eddie, and generally at this stage Tommy was the master. Suddenly he landed a punch to the stomach which brought a caution from the referee. This seemed to unsettle him, and after a few more left jabs, he threw a tremendous left to the stomach which had all his weight behind it. Phillips was hurt and heading for the floor when Tommy cracked home a right to the jaw for good measure. As the Londoner hit the canvas, Farr turned away and saw the referee approaching him, he thought to stop the fight. To his amazement, he was promptly disqualified for a low blow.

Churchill and Evans immediately jumped into the ring and appealed vigorously but to no avail. The appeals turned to yelling and arguing, and Churchill was eventually ordered out of the ring.

Phillips lay on the floor for quite some time, and when he did eventually get up and leave the ring, there was tremendous booing. There were tears in Tommy Farr's eyes as he walked across the ring to shake hands with Eddie. He felt humiliated

71

because he had trained harder for this fight than ever before. His hopes and ambitions had been blown sky-high by one reckless punch.

'Don't cry, Tommy,' said Churchill as he stood beside him. 'The day will come when you will get him.' The sympathy of the crowd was with him as well, and they cheered him loudly as he left the ring.

On the homeward-bound train that night, Tommy was a very angry man and could not sit down. For four hours he paced the corridors, fuming with anger. He was convinced that he had been robbed, and now he had to begin all over again.

The connections in London had seen enough from Tommy to offer him more work, and six weeks later he was back at Wandsworth Stadium to face old foe Ernie Simmons. It turned out to be Tommy's first success in the capital because he managed to get a draw. It was a well-contested fight, and although both men scored with some good punches, there was never any likelihood of a knockout blow being landed.

Since losing to Charlie Belanger at Newcastle, Tommy had thought of little else but revenge. He badly wanted to meet the Canadian again because he felt certain he could beat him at a fixed weight. Job Churchill, however, had said that he would never allow Tommy back in a ring with the Canadian to take another hiding like the one he got at St James Hall. When he received an offer from London to meet Belanger at Wandsworth two weeks after the Simmons fight, Tommy was more than willing. However, he made the stipulation that the Canadian would not weigh in at more than 12 stone 9, and that the promoter dealt exclusively with him. Job Churchill must not know the fight was taking place.

Tommy let Tom Evans into the secret, and they agreed to keep the details strictly to themselves. As it was to be just a supporting contest, there would be nothing in the daily newspapers, so Job wouldn't find out. The fact was that few people outside Tonypandy really cared whether Tommy won or lost the fight.

Evans put Tommy into a training routine of sorts, but adequate preparation was out of the question because most of the days and nights were spent dodging Job. Early on the day of the fight, Farr packed a little bag and ambled off to the station, where he met Evans, who had casually done the same. They took the train to London, but every time it stopped at a station, they expected Churchill to poke his head through the carriage window. They were on edge all the way, and when they were just a few miles from their destination, there was a sudden loud slam of a corridor door. 'That's him,' whispered Evans. 'That's him, all right,' replied Farr. Then to their relief, the carriage door opened and in stepped a friendly ticket inspector.

The two men were no more relaxed once they had left the train at Paddington, and decided against using their usual hotel in London. Instead they went straight to Wandsworth and told one of the groundsmen of their fears. The man offered to take them to his own home, which was only a short distance away. Once there, he showed Tommy to a bedroom where he could rest for a few hours. Evans, meanwhile, mounted guard outside his door.

Evening came, and to the surprise of both Farr and Evans, there was still no sign of Job. After arriving at the stadium, Tommy stripped quickly and almost ran into the ring to face Belanger. Although there was a good deal of hard hitting during the fight, there was also a lot of holding, which marred the exchanges. It was scrappy in the early stages but warmed up considerably as the fight wore on, and both handed out considerable punishment.

Farr had the better of the long-range exchanges and concentrated on good body attacks. Every time he drove home his right, he clenched his teeth and muttered under his breath, 'that's another one for Newcastle.' At the end, Tommy was awarded the decision, which was not only sweet revenge for the previous hammering at the hands of Belanger, but it also marked his first victory in a London ring.

Tommy had still found the Canadian a tough opponent, and he was relieved to hear the final bell. Belanger himself was all in and badly battered, but had still managed a smile as Farr was declared the winner, and was quick to walk over and congratulate him.

As soon as he had dressed, Tommy ran to the nearest telephone and called Job Churchill in Penygraig. 'That you, Job?' he asked casually when the phone was answered.

'This is me, Tom,' was the reply. 'Where are you, down in Cardiff?'

'No, in London,' yelled Tommy excitedly, 'and listen, Job, I've just given Charlie Belanger a hiding as good as the one he handed me. He was very nearly out in the seventh.' Tommy was proud and excited, and would loved to have seen Job's face.

To his amazement, the old saddler was thrilled and wanted to know where, when and how it had all happened. Then before the money ran out, he insisted, 'Well, mind you don't stay in London. Come straight home and keep your money in your pocket.'

Tommy returned to Wales a very relieved young man. He had

got revenge over the man who had given him his worst ever hammering in the ring, and achieved his first success in five fights. He was pleased with his performance and, confident that the bad patch was over, agreed to meet another hard-hitting Canadian, Del Fontaine, at Swansea two weeks later.

The man from Winnipeg was a real tough guy who had fought all over Canada and America before arriving in Britain during the early part of 1932. In less than two and a half years, he had crammed in more than 40 fights and won 21 inside the distance. He was no stranger to Swansea, having beaten Billy Thomas and Les Ward both in five rounds back in August 1932, and in the build-up to the fight he was described as 'the Petersen of the cruiserweights'.

Farr had challenged any cruiserweight in England for £200 a side. The fight with Fontaine promised to be a thriller and there was tremendous enthusiasm amongst fans in the west of Wales. The venue was the Mannesmann Hall on a promotion staged in connection with the Swansea Sportsmans Hospital Bed Appeal. A large crowd even assembled at the weigh-in, at which Fontaine scaled 12 stone 4, despite going on the scales fully clothed in plus fours and boots.

The fight lived up to expectations and was one of the most thrilling seen in the west of Wales for years. Although Farr got the decision, many people considered the Canadian unlucky, because he attacked throughout the first eight rounds. At the end, Farr was the stronger but there were several occasions when he was literally out on his feet. Fontaine tried all he knew to add him to his list of knockout victims, and the Welshman was cut over his right eye in the fourth and over the left in the eighth.

The tenth was a terrific round in which Farr was a fighting fury. He landed four solid uppercuts to the Canadian's jaw but could not put him down. It was the same in the final round, and Fontaine, although almost out on his feet, fought as though by instinct. The fight was so vicious and gruelling that the *Swansea Evening Post* described both men as being 'punch drunk and exhausted at the end.'

Farr finished with both lips badly split. In his rush to get to Swansea, he forgot his gum-shield and paid the price.

Despite the intensity of the fight and the attention it attracted locally, it was quite incredible that it would never appear on the records of either fighter in the years to come. The following year, Fontaine appeared at the Central Criminal Court charged with the murder of his girlfriend, and in his defence it was claimed that he was insane due to being punch-drunk. Details of his terrible beatings were given to the court, but didn't save him from the gallows. Del Fontaine was executed at Wandsworth Prison on 29 October 1935.

Despite the gruelling battle with Fontaine, Tommy quickly signed to defend his Welsh light heavyweight title against old foe Charlie Bundy at the Judges Hall, Trealaw, just two weeks later. In view of their previous encounters, a record crowd turned out, and as Tommy had progressed considerably since then, he was expected to win easily. It didn't turn out that way, however, and was a hard slogging battle from start to finish.

Bundy caused Tommy plenty of trouble throughout the 15 rounds, and there was no stage during the fight when he could afford to relax. Although he landed pile-driving rights throughout, they had no effect on the man from Treherbert. 'A man of iron' and 'a human sponge' were just a couple of ringside descriptions of Charlie, a real tough guy of the ring, as he continued to soak up the punishment.

Farr had an anxious time during the ninth round when he was caught by a tremendous right to the stomach, and he had to hang on for all he was worth. He weathered the storm, and his superior ringcraft and sharp left hand eventually won him a good points decision. It was the third time these two had staged a tremendous fight, and the appreciative crowd gave them standing ovations as they left the ring.

Although he had engaged in yet another gruelling battle, Tommy showed what tremendous powers of recovery he possessed. Just five days later he returned to London to meet Dave Carstens of South Africa in the main event at Wandsworth Stadium. It was an open-air show, but conditions were appalling. Rain poured down throughout the entire programme, and spectators sat beneath umbrellas whilst the master of ceremonies and cornermen worked wearing mackintoshes. Although the boxers got some respite because the ring was covered by a huge tarpaulin, the canvas was still very wet and slippery.

Carstens, an Olympic Games gold medallist at Los Angeles in 1932, was unbeaten in five fights in Britain, none of which had gone the distance. Against the tough Welshman, however, he made very little impression. There were times when Tommy looked rather jaded, as though the effects of his war with Charlie Bundy had taken their toll. Nevertheless, he boxed skilfully and appeared to have won comfortably. The referee, however, gave the decision to Carstens, causing an uproar which lasted several minutes. Farr was furious, convinced that yet again he had been robbed of a decision.

Tommy's next fight took place a month later at Llanelli Working Men's Club on a show organised in aid of the Gresford Colliery Disaster Fund. Pit disasters were all too frequent in this part of the world, and the boxing fraternity were always amongst the first people to give whatever help they could.

In the Gresford disaster of 22 September, a total of 265 men had died, including three from a rescue party. Tommy knew from bitter experience what it was like to be without parents, and when he was offered the chance to appear on the show, he readily agreed to do so for expenses only.

Although Tommy was now recognised as being one of the best light heavyweights in the country, the bill was topped by a contest between world featherweight champion Freddie Miller of America and Cuthbert Taylor of Merthyr. Farr faced ex-seaman Harvey of Chatham in the chief supporting contest. They had met a year earlier, with the Welshman winning on points. Harvey was probably one of the most experienced heavyweights in the country at the time, and the previous week had boxed a draw with Jim Wilde of Swansea. He had taken part in more than 150 contests and met such men as Marcel Thil, Len Harvey and Harry Crossley.

On the night of the fight, the hall was packed to capacity with more than 4,000 fans. They were there partly to aid the Disaster Fund and partly to see the fine bill of fights that had been lined up. Had the police not closed the doors in the interests of safety, there would have been double that number trying to squeeze in.

The contest between Farr and Harvey was a disappointing affair and finished at the end of round nine when Harvey retired with a badly damaged thumb. Up until that point, he had been out-boxed by the Welshman, who might have won the contest sooner had he not shown some restraint.

Although hard to come by, money meant everything to Tommy at this stage. Whilst Tom Evans and Job Churchill did everything possible to get him fit and strong, it was an expensive process because to maintain his strength a special diet was essential. Tommy therefore never refused a fight, and two days after beating Harvey he travelled to Bradford and outpointed Eddie Pierce over 12 rounds.

Farr's last fight of 1934 was at the Judges Hall against Pat McAuliffe of Belfast, a contest in which he completely shattered the views of critics who persistently said he didn't possess a knockout punch. He tore out of his corner at the opening bell and set about the Irishman with some ferocious two-fisted punching. McAuliffe was clearly hurt on a number of occasions, and when the second round opened, it was obvious that Farr was looking for an early night. A left to the jaw staggered the Irishman, and when Tommy crashed home a right which travelled no more than 12 inches, he went down heavily with no hope of beating the count. Pat was badly hurt, and it was several minutes before he was able to leave the ring.

Tommy had lost just one of his last seven fights, and although not his manager, Ted Broadribb was keeping a close eye on his progress. At this stage they had an agreement whereby Ted would handle Tommy's affairs in London, whilst his contests elsewhere were generally arranged by Evans and Churchill. Broadribb was convinced that Farr was now a genuine championship contender, and pressed his claims for a fight for the vacant British light heavyweight title.

Len Harvey won the title in June 1933, but that November also won the heavyweight title by beating Jack Petersen. Although Jack regained it in June the following year, Len had continued to campaign amongst the heavyweights. Anxious to keep the light heavyweight division alive, the Board of Control therefore declared the title vacant.

Broadribb was an influential figure, and the Board duly supported his claim on behalf of Farr by matching the Welshman with Eddie Phillips for the vacant title. Promoter Bernard Marcus won the bidding and announced that the contest would be staged at the Mountain Ash Pavilion. Contracts were drawn up at a Tonypandy hotel, and guaranteed Farr just £50 compared to Phillips' £250. Public reaction was incredible, and the promoter was inundated with requests for tickets.

Elaborate alterations were made to house what would be the biggest crowd ever to attend this famous venue. The platform where many famous bands and choirs had performed concerts was temporarily removed and a gallery erected in its place. Another huge gallery was built on the opposite side to accommodate standing viewers, and both stretched from floor to ceiling. As two permanent galleries already existed, a basin was formed around the ring, and by utilising every piece of available space, it was possible to house more than 10,000.

The promoter adopted a democratic attitude towards the pricing of seats, with ringsiders at 10s 6d and many others available at half a crown. Although it was the first British light heavyweight title fight to be staged in Wales, it was also thought to be the first time that a British title fight could be seen indoors for half a crown.

As soon as the prices were announced, there were applications for blocks of 50 and 100 seats, from Londoners as well as from Pontypool in the east of Wales and Haverfordwest in the west. In order to accommodate the large numbers of people expected to travel, many private companies laid on special transport, whilst the Great Western Railway Company put on extra trains. It was even agreed that the licensing hours in the area could be extended from 10 p.m. to 10.30 p.m.

As soon as the contest with Phillips was fixed, Tommy Farr set up his training camp at the Swan Hotel at Penygraig under the watchful eyes of Churchill and Evans. He trained as hard as ever and first thing every morning he would run between six and eight miles on the Penrhys mountain. He was usually accompanied by Dave Norris, the Clydach boxer who had been engaged as one of his sparring partners. During the course of the outing each morning, they would stop and engage in a 20-minute bout of wrestling, which was part of the strength and stamina-building programme designed by Churchill and Evans.

In order that Tommy remained relaxed and got plenty of fresh air, he took up playing golf. Every day, along with promoter Bernard Marcus and a group of others, he played at least one round at the Rhondda Golf Club.

During early January, Tommy received an invitation to spar with Jack Petersen, who was training in Cardiff for his contest with Walter Neusel at Wembley on 4 February. Tommy refused the offer, saying, 'When I meet Petersen it will be for real with his title at stake.' Ironically it was Eddie Phillips who spent a few days sparring with Jack instead.

Tommy was well into his preparations for the title fight when he agreed to meet Arthur Novell of Notting Hill at the Judges Hall, Trealaw, on 11 January. Churchill was intent on keeping him in touch with the real thing and believed the contest would sharpen him up and give him a useful workout. It didn't last long because Farr literally tore out of his corner at the opening bell and pounded the hapless Londoner with a series of heavy punches to the body. He was completely devoid of science, but it was soon obvious that Novell was no match for him. With the fight just two minutes old, Farr ended hostilities with a tremendous left hook to the jaw, which put the Notting Hill man out for the count.

As he worked towards his peak, Tommy was joined in the gym

by Jack Marshall of Accrington, and they engaged in some very rough sessions. With just a week to go before the fight, Tommy reached a condition that he had never attained before. 'Critics who say I have no punch should be here to see me,' he remarked at the end of one session. 'And they should see the state of my sparring partners at the end of the afternoon.' Jack Marshall confirmed that even with 20-ounce gloves, the Welshman was hitting much harder than when they met 15 months earlier.

Just as everything looked to be going according to plan, disaster struck with just four days to go. When punching in earnest one afternoon, Tommy crashed his right hand against a sparring partner's elbow. An agonising pain shot up from his wrist to the shoulder and he had to stop boxing. He went over to Churchill and Evans, who took off his glove. Although there was no obvious damage, Churchill was worried and sent Tommy straight to Porth to see Bill Cheyne, a respected bone specialist. He immediately diagnosed a fractured metacarpal, one of the five long bones in the hand between the wrist and the fingers.

Although there were just a few days left before the fight, there was no question of Farr pulling out. He was too concerned with his future and felt sure that he could outbox Phillips with just one sound hand. Apart from that there was the matter of a £100 forfeit if he failed to comply with the articles of the contract. To the 21-year-old Welshman, that was a tremendous amount of money. Secret attempts were therefore made to repair the damage, including injections of cocaine and incessant painful manipulation by Bill Cheyne.

Restricted to light work in the gym with just the left hand, Tommy's weight began to creep up. The situation was closely monitored by using the gym scales which had supposedly been properly tested. However, on the eve of the contest there was considerable anxiety because when Tommy walked into the local store owned by the father of Welsh Rugby international Cliff Jones and stepped onto his scales, the needle swung round to 12 stone 12. This meant he was five pounds over the championship limit.

Tommy left the store, and immediately set about some hard and continuous exercise to try and get the surplus weight off, but by the next morning he was still three pounds overweight. Tom Evans then suggested a series of hot baths, and this worked. At the weigh-in at 2 p.m. Tommy was three-quarters of a pound inside the limit. The problems were a closely guarded secret and only those people very close to him knew the true position.

As the two boxers shook hands at the scales, Phillips said, 'I am fit and confident, but if Farr should beat me, I will be the first to congratulate him.'

Once again Eddie Phillips proved to be Tommy's bogeyman by taking a points decision after 15 rounds. Farr seemed to box without confidence and only rarely showed the brilliance which had won him the title shot. The fact was the weight-reducing process had left him without the strength required to become champion.

Tommy had the better of the early rounds, particularly in the third and fourth, when he hurt Phillips with heavy punches to the body. In the fourth he caught his man with a good right to the jaw, but the excruciating pain shot up his arm again. The effects of a pain-killing injection given to him before the fight had worn off already, and there were still 11 rounds to go.

Tommy knew from that moment he had a mountain to climb, and to make matters worse he was badly cut over the right eye in the fifth round. Blood streamed down his face and proved to be a severe handicap. From that point onwards he was having to use his damaged arm for defence while he attempted to score points with his left.

Phillips completely dictated the fight from the seventh round onwards as he picked his punches well. Farr looked worn out as the Londoner hit him with tremendous punches, but he wouldn't be put down. The decision in favour of Phillips was a correct one, and referee Jack Smith was surprised when he heard booing from a section of the crowd.

To Farr's credit he made no excuses other than to say, 'I boxed sadly below form and I attribute that to the fact that my right hand gave out. I shall have to see a specialist about it.'

As he left the ring, Tommy's loyal supporters gave him a great ovation, but it was little consolation. He was a very dejected young man. With the advantage of the fight being on home soil, he had been confident of victory, yet despite the huge vocal support of his many Welsh fans, he had been beaten by Eddie Phillips for a third time.

To make matters worse, he had his first serious disagreement with Job Churchill shortly after the fight. The old saddler was so disappointed at Tommy's failure to become British champion that he got it into his head Tommy had not trained thoroughly. In the end Tommy packed a bag and set out for London, to be on his own for a few days.

At first he was bad-tempered and disgusted with himself over his defeat. He was clearly at the crossroads of his career, but by

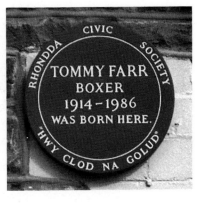

Left: The miners cottage at 3
Railway Terrace, Blaenclydach,
where Tommy was born

Above: The Rhondda Civic
Council plaque which hangs
above the front door

Left: Tommy with Job Churchill
on the steps of Penygraig Labour
Club where he boxed in 1930

Early picture of Tommy
before he moved to Slough
in 1935

The Dolphin Tavern, Slough, where Tommy lived and trained between 1935
and 1937

Farr (left) meets Tommy Loughran at the weigh-in for their fight in London on 15 January 1935. Ted Broadribb looks on

Tommy was presented with a lucky horse-shoe by a two-year-old girl as he trained at the Star and Garter, Windsor to fight Ben Foord

Farr and Ted Broadribb have breakfast at the Green Man, Blackheath the morning after beating Max Baer

Farr receives congratulations after beating Neusel. Evans holds his glove aloft while Rinty Monaghan pats his stomach

Max Schmeling (front left), and Farr agree to meet for Sydney Hulls (centre).
Back row, left – right: Max Machon, Colonel Wilson and Ted Broadribb

Farr and Joe Louis shake hands after signing contracts in New York on
2 August 1937

Left: Some of Tommy's relatives listen to the commentary of the fight with Louis (at Slough)

Below: Farr attacks Joe Louis with a classic left lead in their fight on 30 August 1937

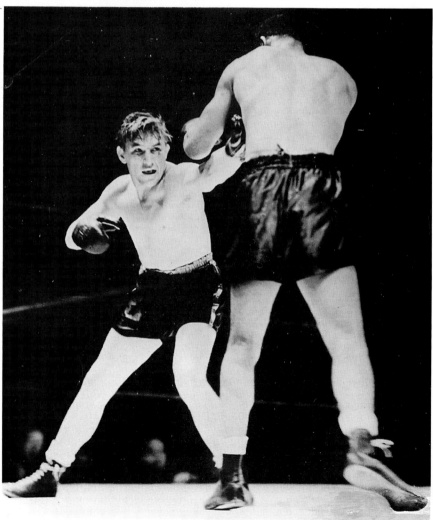

Louis appears apprehensive as Farr pushes forward

Farr and Tom Evans wave to fans at the quayside as the Queen Mary docks at Southampton in October 1937

Tommy Farr standing in an open-topped car being cheered by crowds at Aberdare Carnival Sports day in June 1937

With musician/songwriter 'Doria' who helped Tommy compose the song 'Maybe I'll find Somebody Else' which he recorded in November 1937

being alone, he calmed down and thought more clearly. The fact was that without boxing there was no future for him or his family. There was nothing for it but to return home and start all over again.

7

BROADRIBB TAKES OVER

Despite having had more than 100 fights, Tommy was still only 22. He held the Welsh title, and was convinced he could become British champion, and possibly go on to greater things. To achieve those ambitions he needed proper guidance on a regular basis, but first and foremost he had to get his damaged hand fixed.

The break-up between Farr and Churchill didn't last very long, and they were soon good pals again. Churchill agreed that Tommy now needed a full-time manager, and Farr was convinced that Ted Broadribb was the man he should turn to. He recognised Broadribb's ability as a matchmaker and manager; more importantly, Tommy knew Ted had the right connections, especially in London.

His chance to approach Broadribb was not long in coming. In early March 1935, Ted travelled to Wales with one of his fighters, George Daly of Blackfriars, who was matched with Boyo Rees in a British lightweight title eliminator. The fight was taking place at Mountain Ash, and Broadribb and his party were booked in at the Carpenters Arms public house at Aberdare. When Tommy discovered this, he decided to wait no longer, and went and found Ted on the day of the fight.

Broadribb was sitting in the bar talking to the landlord, Bill O'Reilly. Suddenly the door opened and in walked Farr, accompanied by Tom Evans. He walked straight up to Ted. 'Mr Broadribb, you know a little about me. I want you to manage me because unless you do, I shan't get anywhere.'

From previous experience, as well as stories he had heard from other sources, Ted knew Tommy could be a real handful. He knew all about his moods and his belief that everyone was against him. In the short time they had been associated with each other

82

in London, there had been a number of disputes over a number of things. If he became his manager, Ted knew that as soon as something went wrong, he would get the blame for it.

Broadribb had enough problems from being the matchmaker for promoter Jeff Dickson's shows at the Royal Albert Hall without taking on any more. Yet as Tommy stood in the bar nursing his broken hand, Ted saw him as a lonely, nervous boy who lacked confidence as a person. He knew that both of his parents were dead, so rather than rejecting his request out of hand he adopted a somewhat sympathetic attitude and told Tommy he would need time to think about it.

At this point Ted left the bar. Tommy turned to Evans and said, 'Tommy boy, we must not let Broadribb go back to London without agreeing to look after me. If I am to become champion, he's the one to help me to the top.' Evans agreed, and they decided to stay in the bar until Broadribb reappeared.

When Ted failed to reappear Tommy asked the landlord to call him down. Ted was somewhat surprised to find Tommy still there, but agreed to sit and discuss matters with him. Tommy insisted that although he had lost a few fights, he had never been stopped. Broadribb agreed that such a record would make him a good promoter's man, and took the view that although Tommy was not a world-beater, he would always be in there trying, and most likely still be on his feet at the end of a fight no matter who he was up against.

Ted knew that he and Farr could make money, so he agreed to make a fresh start and become Tommy's manager. He insisted on the so-called American contract, in which the manager agreed to earn the boxer no less than a certain sum within one year. A normal British Boxing Board of Control contract would have compelled Farr to stay with him for five years but Ted clearly didn't fancy being tied to Farr for that long.

Ted knew that Farr had great potential as a fighter and that his style would pull him through. The problem was to get the Welshman national recognition. At this stage of his career he needed to be matched with opponents who were names within the fight game.

Although he was somewhat cautious about taking Farr under his wing, Ted Broadribb did have some understanding of the young Welshman's predicament. Born at Walworth in south London in December 1888, the son of an old bare-knuckle fighter, he too had been brought up amid poverty and he too had done many man-sized jobs when just a small boy.

Ted began boxing in 1909, and showed so much promise that within a year he was being talked about in the same breath as some of the best bantamweights around. At the time his brother was boxing as 'Snowball of Walworth', a name given to him by the locals because he had a patch of white hair on the back of his head. Ted was therefore known as 'Young Snowball'.

The highlight of Ted's fighting career was in 1910, when he travelled to the Wonderland in Paris and stopped Georges Carpentier, who ten years later became light heavyweight champion of the world. In his biography, the great Frenchman admitted that Snowball beat him as completely as any man could ever do. It was the only time that Carpentier was beaten inside the distance by a British boxer.

Broadribb's career in the ring was sadly brought to an abrupt halt in 1911, when he suddenly developed eye trouble. However, he soon took to promoting shows at local halls in south London, starting at the famous Manor Place Baths at Walworth.

A few years later, Ted moved into management, and then having built up a large stable of boxers, into matchmaking.

To know the standard of as many boxers as possible, Ted attended shows all over the country. He was at Moss Deyong's charity show at the Holborn Stadium on 1 February 1935 when Eddie Phillips was given the decision over Farr, and he liked what he saw from the young Welshman.

At that time, Ted considered Jack Petersen, another Welshman, the answer to his box-office prayers. As Ted watched Farr develop, he recognised that in time he just might push Petersen to the limit.

Broadribb knew that if their partnership was to have any chance of success, the Welshman must live nearer to London. It was therefore agreed that Tommy should move to Slough, an overspill town in Berkshire with a huge Welsh population.

Broadribb chose Slough because he wanted Tommy to train at The Dolphin, a famous boxing hostelry used by a host of top-class fighters. Apart from the Star and Garter at nearby Windsor, The Dolphin was probably the best-known boxing gymnasium in the country. Situated on the Uxbridge Road just a few hundred yards from the main A4 London Road, it was ideally sited for boxers who wanted to train away from London. The main Paddington-to-London railway line passed through Slough, and The Dolphin was just a five-minute walk from the station.

The Dolphin holds a place in the history of Slough because it was built in the late 1860s as a replica of the old Dolphin Hotel which once stood a quarter of a mile away on the Bath Road. Surrounded by fields, and situated on the eastern boundary of the parish until it was demolished in 1869, the old hotel was the first building travellers came to as they approached Slough from London.

In 1914, the Dolphin had been taken over by George Bennett, a keen sportsman. He built a ballroom at the back, and a cricket pitch came right up to its windows. In 1928, he built a greyhound track in the grounds, later called the Slough Greyhound Stadium. In 1932 Mr Bennett opened a gymnasium and training camp for boxers, and it was not long before top fighters from Britain and abroad travelled to Slough to train.

George Bennett agreed to give Tommy lodgings, and The Dolphin became his home for the next 18 months. He settled in quickly, and wasted no time getting down to the serious training. He showed his willingness by offering to assist any man who needed a sparring partner, and soon showed he was no pushover. He often spent the best part of the day in the gym, and if he was not training, he was watching others who were.

Recalling his move to Slough some years later, Tommy admitted, 'It was at The Dolphin that I started training seriously.' He also recalled the day that he explored the town centre and came across a branch of Lloyds Bank. 'Oh goodie, a Welsh bank, I thought. So I went inside and put all my money into an account.' Tommy in fact deposited his entire life savings of £19.

During the period between losing his fight with Eddie Phillips at Mountain Ash and signing up with Ted Broadribb, Tommy had been matched with Jim Wilde of Swansea for a purse of £60. When Broadribb discovered this, he promptly broke the contract and paid the £10 forfeit. He considered that the purse Tommy was to receive was totally inadequate for a contest between two of the best big men in Wales at the time.

Once Broadribb was satisfied that Tommy was fit and ready to go, he started fixing up fights for him. Their boxer-manager partnership kicked off in London in May 1935 when Farr took two fights in the space of five days. The first was against the coloured Scotsman Manuel Abrew, whom he beat at the White City, and then he fought Canadian Eddie Wenstob before a packed house at the Stadium Club, Holborn.

Tommy attacked Abrew relentlessly, flooring his man for a short count in the second round, and for nine in the sixth. Abrew was in such a bad way at the end of this round that he retired.

The fight against Wenstob was a completely different affair, with

Farr using his immaculate left hand to win clearly on points. The Canadian had in fact injured his right hand in training a few days earlier, but refused to withdraw from the fight because the show, promoted by Sydney Hulls, was in aid of the Greater London Fund for the Blind.

Farr agreed with Broadribb that if he was to get to the very top, it was essential that he boxed at venues around the country, particularly the big ones in London. If a suitable opportunity arose, he should also be prepared to travel abroad. It was also important that Tommy remained active, and under Ted's guidance he had boxed on no fewer than ten occasions by the end of the year. Apart from appearances in London, he also fought in Leicester, Cardiff, Bristol and in Paris. More importantly, he remained undefeated in those contests.

Broadribb's idea was to give Tommy as much exposure as possible without taking unnecessary risks. He travelled to Paris in June and beat an Italian, Presida Pravesi, on points on a promotion in which Jeff Dickson was involved. He returned in November and went one better, knocking the Italian out in the fourth round.

Ex-Nottingham policeman George Brennan was outpointed at Leicester in July and again in October. On the second occasion, the former European Police heavyweight champion had Larry Gains in his corner, and advice which he gave Brennan during the course of the fight incensed Farr. As early as the second round, George was floored and in all sorts of trouble. Gains climbed on to the apron of the ring and yelled, 'Stay down, Bill.' When the count reached nine, he shouted, 'Get up and claim him.' Brennan got up and hung on for dear life and survived the round. This went on throughout the fight and every time Brennan went to the floor or was in trouble, Larry yelled instructions to him. Farr became so angry that at one stage he leaned over the ropes and shouted down at the former British Empire champion, 'I can lick you.' The good-natured Larry smiled back and shouted, 'You couldn't lick me if I was a lollipop.' After the fight, Farr went looking for Gains, and when he found him issued a challenge. He forgot one thing, that Ted Broadribb now chose his opponents, and he didn't think Tommy was quite ready for a man of Larry's calibre.

The two most significant contests for Tommy during 1935 were against fellow Welshman Frank Moody. Their first fight was at the Welsh White City at Sloper Road, Cardiff, and after a hard 15-round slog, the decision was a draw. There was so much controversy surrounding the result that there was a rematch on 21 December the same year, this time at the Greyfriars Hall, also in Cardiff.

When the first contest was made, Farr's Welsh light heavyweight title was to have been at stake. However, despite London promoter Jeff Dickson putting up a purse of £1,000, both Farr and Moody claimed that it was insufficient for a contest of such importance. Eventually, Farr decided to relinquish his title, and it was agreed that the contest would go ahead as a non-title event for the same purse – believed to be the largest in Britain for a non-title contest.

The fight was one of the most talked about in Wales for a very long time. Farr and Moody were considered to be the best two light heavyweights in that part of the country. Frank was a veteran of nearly 200 fights and had been a professional for almost 20 years. He began boxing at the age of eight, started his professional career as a flyweight, and fought his way up as he grew. He had been a great favourite in London, and back in June 1923 was the first opponent in Britain for Larry Gains, whom he beat in five rounds at the Ring, Blackfriars. Frank had campaigned in the United States for four years and was regarded by many experts as the best British boxer sent there since the First World War. Although Frank retired from the ring in 1931, he had embarked on a successful comeback just a few months earlier. In his preparations for the contest with Farr, he took on one of Tommy's old spar-mates, Dave Norris, to assist him.

Although Farr had been around a few years himself, he was very much the up-and-coming young prospect. He was 14 years Frank's junior, and this was thought to be a good fight for him at this stage of his career.

As early as the first round, it was clear that Moody was still a superb craftsman, and Farr was unable to land a telling blow on him. During the first five rounds, Frank used his left hand cleverly to build up a slight points lead. In those early rounds, Farr tried rough-house tactics and wild swings, but the cagey veteran had little trouble in avoiding them and tying up his younger and more eager opponent.

There was no real incident until the seventh round, when suddenly Farr caught Moody with a chopping right which split the flesh above his cheekbone. It was a terrible injury, which spurted blood, and most men would have quit there and then, but Frank Moody was as tough and game as they come, and if the injury hurt him, then he certainly didn't show it. The eye filled with blood, and no sooner had Frank wiped it away with his glove than it filled up again. Seeing victory within his grasp, Farr chased the wounded veteran around the ring. Using all his defensive skill and ringcraft, Moody managed to keep away from the heavy punches and survived the round. When the bell came to his rescue, he was in a bad way, with his face and chest a sea of blood.

Most ringsiders expected the corner to retire their man, but it was Frank Moody who made the decisions, and he didn't know the meaning of the word quit. As he came out for the eighth, the wound was still bleeding and he looked like a sitting duck. Farr hammered away to head and body as he tried to end the fight, but he couldn't put Frank down. Suddenly the pendulum swung as Moody landed the best punch of the fight, a solid right to the jaw, which shook Farr to his boots. He was in serious trouble, but the veteran from Pontypridd just hadn't the strength to follow up. Farr hung on and his youth saw him through to the end of the round.

The blood from Moody's injury eased by the tenth, and he seemed to get a second wind. Although Farr was by now scoring all the time with his left, Frank gave almost as good as he got in rounds 11 and 12. There were occasions when Tommy tried wild rights, but he was made to miss badly by Moody – much to the enjoyment of the huge crowd, estimated to be almost 16,000.

Twice in the later stages of the fight, referee Mr C.B. Thomas went to Moody's corner to speak to the seconds. Firstly he severely warned the chief second for shouting instructions during the fight, and then between rounds 12 and 13 he examined a liquid that was being poured over Frank's head. When he discovered that it was champagne, Mr Thomas walked away smiling.

Although he was extremely tired, Moody refused to give up, and in the fourteenth round he sent Tommy hurtling across the ring from a perfect right to the jaw. In the final round, both men set about each other with vicious two-fisted attacks. Both survived because Moody was too tired to finish his younger opponent, and Tommy hadn't the experience to tag the skilful veteran.

At the final bell, referee Thomas astounded nearly everyone by calling it a draw, when it appeared that Farr was a clear winner. If courage counted for anything, then Frank deserved his share of the decision, and he was the hero in the eyes of the crowd. At the end, hundreds of fans swarmed around his corner yelling, 'Good old Frank', and 'Well done, Moody'.

Frank just sat on his stool semi-blind, too weary to appreciate the ovation. It was more than ten minutes before he was able to stand up, and by this time Tommy Farr had left the ring almost unnoticed. He looked stunned by the decision when it was given, and slumped back in his corner with tears in his eyes. It was yet another occasion when Farr was convinced he was a victim of an injustice in the prize ring.

Moody was also unhappy with the drawn decision, and after he had recovered said, 'I gave him a boxing lesson, and had he not luckily cut my eye, I would have beaten him. When I went up for the last round, I thought I was ahead on points.'

Back in his dressing room, a number of stitches were inserted in Frank's gashed cheekbone. Once the damage had been patched up and bandaged, he said, 'Fight him again? I'll fight Farr for two hundred pounds a side, but at twelve seven. I mean that.' He had a point to make, because on this occasion Tommy had been several pounds heavier.

The referee attempted to justify his decision. 'It was a good fight. Moody won points on his defence. The last round might have decided the fight. There was no decision possible other than a draw.'

Farr, who didn't have a mark on him, soon got over his disappointment and paid tribute to Moody. 'What a grand old fighter,' he said graciously. 'Although I do not agree with the verdict, I am glad that he gained a draw. It will do him good. If ever I have a big fight for which to prepare, I would love to have him coach me.'

Farr had always recognised Frank Moody as one of the finest men in the fight game; in fact he had been one of his childhood idols. During the later rounds of the fight, it was noticeable that Tommy didn't play on Frank's injured cheek, believing that he was winning clearly on points. This had been well and truly noted by Job Churchill, who gave Tommy the short end of his tongue when they got back to the dressing room.

Although the fight had captured the imagination of the public in Wales, it was something of a disappointment, and the hard truth of the situation was admirably summed up by *Boxing* reporter Ted Scales:

> It is never really pleasant to see youth opposed to age in the boxing ring. It does not seem to me to give either side a fair chance. Age knows too much for youth, but youth is too active and forceful for age.

There followed the inevitable arguments between the rival groups of supporters over who was the better man and who should have got the decision. Not since the days of Jim Driscoll and Freddie Welsh had there been so much controversy over two Welsh boxers.

After the fight, Tommy Farr returned to Slough, and not much was heard about him in Wales during the next few months. His fights with George Brennan in Leicester and Presida Pavesi in Paris received little or no publicity there.

However, Tommy's position was the subject of comment by the Editor of *Boxing* on 30 October 1935.

> For some reason or other, Farr has been overlooked by promoters. This sturdy Welshman is an honest fighter who is always out to do his best, and at this time when so many people are bemoaning the dearth of home talent, it is too bad to leave Farr on the shelf.'

All sorts of rumours started to circulate, prompting William E. Allen, Boxing Editor of the *South Wales Echo*, to write a small piece about Tommy. He mentioned the rumour that Farr had become just a punchbag up at The Dolphin for his fellow boxers, and as a result he had lost his form. It wasn't long before Tommy heard about the story. He was angry and wrote to Mr Allen, making his position very clear:

> Just a line re your remarks in last Saturday's article. It's a terrible thing to put such a remark in. You call me a punch bag. Ask Pancho Villa, Obie Walker, McCorkindale, Roy Lazar and others if I'm a punch bag. I am unlucky if anything, but still undaunted. I haven't a scratch on me since I've been up in Slough. If I had the press behind me like Petersen and Harvey, I would be having just as much money for my fights as they do, and fighting a lot more often. I am being pulled down, and you by making those remarks, are not giving me a fair crack of the whip which is all I want. If anyone deserves to get on, it's me. I lead a clean life and do good by everybody. For example, since I have been in Slough I have found work for 63 Welsh unemployed, and if you would like me to write and confirm it let me know. Would any of the big noises do it? If Petersen wants a sparring partner for his fight with Harvey, you get him to offer me decent terms and I will come down.
>
> *Tommy Farr*

The truth of the matter was that as soon as the return fight with Frank Moody was signed, Tommy went into serious training at The Dolphin. He was extremely popular in Slough, particularly with the big Welsh contingent there, and many turned up at the gym daily to see him train. His sparring partners included Don McCorkindale and Americans Obie Walker and Roy Lazar, who were training for fights in Britain. Tommy was reported to be punching faster and harder than at any time in his career, and he was repeatedly told by Job Churchill to forget any feelings he had for Moody. 'There's no room for sentiment in this game,' said Job. 'If you want to get to the top, you set out to destroy your opponent. That includes Frank Moody, and I don't care how much you admire him.' Tommy knew in his heart that Job was right, and in his training he worked to increase his punching power, hoping that he could use it to good effect when he met Frank for the second time.

Tommy was confident he could beat Moody, and issued a statement that once the contest was over, he would be prepared to challenge any light heavyweight in Britain for a side stake of £200.

Meanwhile Farr kept in trim by taking two fights within a fortnight. He beat Eddie Wenstob on points in a return over ten rounds at the Ring, Blackfriars, and then travelled to Bristol, where he outpointed Dutchman Rhenus De Boer over 12 rounds. On this occasion, he stood in as a substitute for Wenstob. The contest was just five days before he was due to meet Moody.

The twenty-first of December 1935 was a big day for sport in Wales, particularly in Cardiff. During the afternoon the national Rugby Union team historically beat the All Blacks 13–12 at Cardiff Arms Park. In the evening another big crowd gathered expectantly for the return fight between Farr and Frank Moody.

In the dressing room before the fight, Job Churchill went out of his way to impress upon Tommy the importance of victory. 'There must be no beg pardons this time, Tommy,' he said as he tugged on the gloves.

'All right, Job,' said Tommy, 'I promise.'

There was a hint of sadness in his voice, but Tommy knew a knockout would be the only satisfactory ending. Apart from the importance of advancing his career, Tommy had another reason to make sure that he beat Frank. One of his closest friends, Ted Bryant, had laid substantial bets on him, and he didn't want to let him down.

As in their first contest, Moody's experience showed in the opening round as he made Farr miss, time and again, although towards the end of the round Tommy did get home with several telling rights. In the second, the pattern was the same with Farr doing all the attacking and Moody boxing defensively and looking to counter. In the third, Farr looked concerned as Moody boxed better than he had at any stage during their first fight. He was beginning to look like the Frank Moody of old.

Then, just as everybody was expecting Frank to carry the fight to his opponent, Farr got into his stride. The end came dramatically in the fourth round. Moody shook Tommy with a good left hook to the face, but was totally unprepared for the counter. Farr cleverly manoeuvred him into a defenceless position and then smashed a right hook onto the veteran's jaw with terrific force. Moody didn't see it coming, and crashed to the floor, where he lay flat on his back. The count was a mere formality, and it was fully five minutes before he recovered.

True sportsman that he was, as soon as Frank got to his feet he went straight across to Tommy and congratulated him on his victory. Despite the crushing defeat, Moody was as popular as ever, and the crowd cheered him all the way to the dressing room. In an interview, he conceded that he had taken one fight too many and should not have met Farr a second time.

Tommy gained no personal satisfaction from the victory and later said that he was sick of the whole business and wished the return contest had never been made. While the referee was counting Moody out, Tommy had looked around the ringside and seen what appeared to be the entire Moody family: father, mother, four brothers, sisters, wife and two charming daughters. 'The grief on their faces depressed me more than ever before,' said Tommy. It was something he remembered for a very long time. 'Frank Moody was a grand and gallant opponent, and a supreme sportsman in defeat,' he commented. 'I wish I could forget the whole thing.'

However, Job Churchill would still not allow Tommy to be sentimental over Moody. 'He's a professional, Tom,' he said. 'He would have knocked your head off if he got the chance, and then said sorry afterwards.'

8

STEP-UP IN CLASS

Although fight fans in some parts of Britain were at last beginning to take notice of Farr, he still hadn't impressed those in London. The big promoters weren't clamouring for his services, and the Board of Control weren't interested in him either. They refused to nominate him for title eliminators because they didn't consider him to be a good enough box-office attraction. This infuriated Farr, adding to his belief that everyone was against him.

Ted Broadribb, however, was still convinced that the Welshman had the potential to become a champion, and was more than satisfied by his performances since coming under his guidance. Although the quality of opponents Tommy had met during 1935 was solid, Ted knew he must be stepped up in class and matched against men who would bring the best out of him. Furthermore, he needed to beat 'named' opponents if he was to impress the fans.

The chance Ted was looking for came when Jeff Dickson, the London promoter, brought former world light heavyweight champion Tommy Loughran to Britain for a series of contests. The promoter's intention was to build him up towards attractive fights with Jack Petersen and Larry Gains.

Loughran had already boxed twice for Dickson, outpointing Maurice Strickland in London and sharing the honours with Andre Lenglet in Paris a month later. Dickson now intended using the American to top his bill at the Royal Albert Hall in January 1936, and told Broadribb to find him a suitable American opponent. Ted promptly offered the services of Farr, and Dickson eventually agreed that the Welshman would make a good opponent.

Tommy Loughran had won the world light heavyweight title in 1927 and defended it six times before giving it up in 1929 to campaign as a heavyweight. He then faced quality men including Max Baer, King Levinsky, Ernie Schaaf, Johnny Risko, Paulino Uzcudun and Jack Sharkey. In 1934 he was matched with the massive Primo Carnera for the heavyweight title but had to give away an incredible 86 pounds, and lost on points. Loughran was 34 when he came to Britain. Recognised for his unique style and wonderful boxing skill, and as one of the finest boxers around, he was considered to be approaching the end of his career.

Whilst the American had been fighting heavyweights for some time, Farr had only just moved above 13 stone, and this would be his first contest in the top flight. Loughran was a firm betting favourite because his brilliant stand-up style of boxing, which helped him outpoint the likes of Georges Carpentier, was thought to be too much for Farr.

The Welshman was delighted to get the chance to meet Loughran. 'I am certain I shall be able to give Loughran more to do than he did against Strickland and Lenglet,' said Tommy when the match was made. Farr and Churchill were sufficiently confident to take advantage of generous betting odds, and placed a number of heavy bets that Farr would win.

Farr recognised it was his chance to break into the big time, and before the fight remarked, 'I don't want to be boastful, but I think that when we finish tonight Loughran will have greater respect for myself and British boxers as a whole. This is my chance and I am confident I can give some people a surprise.'

During the first three rounds, however, the American made Tommy look very amateurish. He was made to miss time and again, and it looked as though the bookies had got it about right. Farr was not overawed by his opponent's reputation, but although he carried the fight to him during these rounds, it was the American's skill that was winning the points.

Tommy put even more effort into his work in the fourth and fifth rounds, driving Loughran from corner to corner. However, even when he was backing away, the former champion showed masterly control, and his experience appeared to be the telling factor.

In the sixth, Loughran was cautioned for hitting with the open glove, and from this stage in the contest Farr seemed to take over. At the start of the round, Job Churchill had whispered to Tommy in Welsh, telling him to put a pre-arranged plan into operation. The American was certainly in all sorts of trouble in this round, and one right under the heart sent him into a half-spin.

During the next couple of rounds, Farr tried to muddle

94

Loughran out of it, and then in the ninth set up a whirlwind attack. He threw punches from all angles, and the American showed clear signs of tiring. The last round was Tommy's best of the fight as he stormed forward from the bell. Leading with his left and crossing his right, he drove his man to the ropes and banged away for almost a minute, taking nothing in reply.

There was complete uproar when the Welshman was given the decision. The next contest had to be delayed, and the protests continued long after it had begun. As the referee raised Farr's hand, Loughran merely shrugged his shoulders. Then in the sporting manner for which he was known, he walked across and congratulated his conqueror. His manager Joe Smith, however, normally a quiet, well-mannered American, jumped out of the ring and rushed round to where Colonel Myddleton, Chairman of the British Boxing Board of Control was sitting. 'I demand to see the referee's score card,' he yelled.

'That is not possible,' replied Myddleton. 'In Britain the referee's decision is final.'

Smith then politely asked if the decision could be set aside.

'I see nothing wrong with the verdict,' responded Myddleton, advising Smith that any protest should be made in writing to the board.

As Jeff Dickson stood in the centre of the ring his face told the whole story. He had banked on Loughran winning, but now the lucrative fights he had planned with Petersen and Gains had been thrown away because an unknown Welshman had ripped up his programme. Hiding his disappointment, he congratulated Farr on his victory. Now he had to decide if Tommy was a big enough draw to top future Albert Hall promotions.

After the fight, Loughran was subjected to a barrage of questions from the press. 'I never expected to get such a bad break,' he said back in his dressing room. 'I thought I won at least seven rounds, and when the referee gave Farr the decision, I was the most surprised man in the Albert Hall.'

The American claimed that as early as the first round he had realised Farr had tremendous ability and amazing pluck. 'I could have knocked him out at one stage,' added Loughran, 'but that would have done untold harm to a boy who had every chance of becoming a champion. So I merely contented myself with out-pointing him.'

Loughran was one of the most popular American fighters ever to visit Britain and, despite his remarks, made no official protest at not getting the decision. He soon won the admiration of everyone

95

who met him. After losing to Farr, he had two further contests, beating Jack London at Bristol, and losing to Ben Foord in Leicester.

Farr was not unduly concerned about the reaction of Loughran or the crowd to his victory. As far as he was concerned, he had won well and claimed the scalp of a former world champion. To have gone ten rounds with a man of Loughran's experience was far more beneficial than scoring half a dozen quick wins over mediocre opposition. The one thing that did make him angry, however, was when Loughran later told a *News of the World* reporter that he had allowed Farr to win the last round 'to encourage the boy'.

The verdict in Farr's favour received scathing criticism in the press. Most reporters agreed with the fans that the American had won clearly. A few conceded it had been a close affair, but nobody was convinced Farr deserved the decision.

In his autobiography years later, the eminent sports writer Peter Wilson remarked, 'If I were on my death bed and under oath, I would still swear that Loughran won the fight.' Wilson was covering his first big fight for the *Daily Mirror*, and was convinced that the antics of Ted Broadribb had influenced the referee.

According to Wilson, Ted jumped into the ring at the end of the fight, shouting, 'Well done, Tommy, you won every round. I didn't know you could be so great. You skated it.' Expecting Loughran to get the decision, the reporter recalled thinking there's no harm in trying. Wilson claimed that Wilfred Smith, officiating in his first major contest, checked his score card and started to walk towards the American's corner. Then he suddenly changed course, made an adjustment to the card and went to Farr's corner and raised his arm.

In view of the crowd and press reaction to the decision, Farr said he would be happy to meet Loughran again. 'I think I could beat him easier the next time,' he remarked, adding that his priority, however, was to get a fight with the German Walter Neusel, who had just returned to Britain. 'To succeed over Neusel,' said Tommy, 'would emphatically put me in line for a fight with my countryman Jack Petersen, which is the ambition of my life.'

Tommy was becoming obsessed with the thought of fighting Jack, and was convinced that Petersen was deliberately ducking him. 'I think I've got an excellent chance against Jack,' he continued. 'I've had eleven fights in the last nine months, winning ten and drawing one. Petersen has had three in nearly two years and lost two of them.'

Shortly after he was matched with Loughran, Tommy was asked if he would help Petersen, who was training in Cardiff to meet Len Harvey. Farr refused saying 'I've said this before, the only time I'll meet Petersen is in the ring for his title.'

Farr's persistent clamouring to meet Petersen brought a protest from Welsh heavyweight champion Jim Wilde, who accused him of trying to jump the queue. Wilde had won the Welsh title the previous year by outpointing Charlie Bundy, and was annoyed that Tommy considered he was entitled to fight Petersen after just one contest as a heavyweight. 'Who the bloody hell does he think he is?' asked Jim angrily. 'Let him fight me first, then we'll know who should fight Jack.'

Wilde's father even wrote to WIlliam E. Allen of the *South Wales Echo*;

> Farr forfeited £10 to the Welsh Branch of the British Boxing Board of Control rather than meet Jimmy. One of the reasons was that when the offer was made to stage the match in the West of Wales, Farr's manager Ted Broadribb turned it down because he considered the monetary reward was not compatible with the importance of the event.

Farr's win over Tommy Loughran brought him to notice in other quarters, and he received a number of offers for fights. One came from America for him to fight in Boston against the winner of a contest between ex-world champion Jack Sharkey and Tony Stucco. Back home in Wales, old opponent Charlie Bundy issued a challenge for a fight at twelve seven with a £100 side-stake.

After the Loughran fight, Tommy returned to Wales and went to stay with Job Churchill for a few days. Still very much his father figure, the old saddler wanted to be satisfied no liberties were being taken with the boy, and asked Tommy exactly how much he had received from each fight under Broadribb, and made him list every penny, including training expenses and manager's fees.

'They're ripping you off, Tom,' he snapped angrily. 'I'm going to sort this out once and for all.' Without any hesitation he wrote a lengthy letter to Broadribb saying he understood Farr was unlikely to receive more than £125 for the Loughran fight despite having been promised between £250 and £300, and added that Farr had also told him about other purses he had received under Broadribb's management. Job insisted he could get Farr more money fighting in the small halls back in Wales, and threatened to take him out of boxing altogether if the rewards were not higher.

In a lengthy reply, Broadribb stated that he was surprised to receive such a letter especially in view of the progress Farr had made under his management. He explained that although he had experienced headaches, worries and financial loss, nothing had deterred him in his efforts to get Tommy to the top, where he could earn big money. Broadribb warned Churchill that if he and Farr thought they could throw him overboard, he would take legal advice. He could produce evidence to show that Farr received more than any boxer he had fought, with the exception of Loughran, who rightly received a larger percentage due to his international reputation. Ted reminded Churchill that he had never gone after Farr, seeking to become his manager. However, Farr was under contract until March 1938, and until then, he would manage him. Farr's earnings since joining him the previous year had been £772, and he hadn't lost a contest.

Three days later Broadribb wrote to Farr, telling him he regretted that he believed he could break their contract after all that had been done for him. 'What you have to complain about, I do not know, but if you consider that just because you are now in the top line of boxers you can throw me aside, you are mistaken. You have entered into a contract. I have carried out my part of it, and you have got to carry out your part.'

* * *

In his autobiography *Fighting Is My Life* published about 20 years later, Broadribb admitted that this was one of the many storms he had to contend with during his relationship with Farr. He was of the opinion that Farr should have been a lone wolf, and for a great deal of their time together, it was touch and go as to whether they would part company.

Despite their differences of opinion, Broadribb continued to press the claims of the Welshman. In 1936, he even wrote to Nat Fleischer, Editor of *Ring* magazine, asking if he could help to get Farr the recognition he deserved; in his opinion Tommy was the best heavyweight prospect he had ever seen. Tommy knew the fight game inside out, and had everything except the punch of Jack Dempsey. Broadribb said he believed Farr would show his true potential during the next six months.

Farr and Broadribb eventually settled their differences and Tommy was soon back in training at The Dolphin at Slough.

Jim Wilde was booked to meet the Dutch heavyweight champion, Peter Van Goole, at Swansea on 5 March but had to withdraw through injury. Farr agreed to take his place, and at about the same time it was announced that he and Wilde would meet in a long-awaited encounter at Swansea in May. It was a fight they both wanted because there was genuine needle between them over who was the best heavyweight in Wales. They had been due to meet a year earlier, but when Ted Broadribb became Farr's manager he pulled him out.

Ted now managed to negotiate a purse of more than £200 for Farr from promoter Bert James, a much better deal than the £60 Tommy had originally been offered, and Broadribb considered that the £10 forfeit he had paid a year earlier was money well spent.

Against Van Goole, Tommy boxed well below form and not nearly as well as he had against Loughran. 'But what else could you expect?' he said angrily after the fight. 'The man would not fight, and I can tell you it was infinitely harder for me to have to be continuously chasing around the ring than to stand up and have a go. It's impossible to fight a man who runs away.'

To be fair to Tommy, the Dutchman was a terribly difficult opponent. He was a huge man weighing almost 17 stone and carrying rolls of flesh on his shoulders and around his stomach. He looked so out of condition that it was amazing he was able to last the full 12 rounds.

Ted Broadribb was not in the least bit disappointed with Farr's performance, and decided that Tommy was ready for another stern test. He matched him against another former world light heavyweight champion, Bob Olin of New York.

Olin had studied law at Fordham University and worked for a firm of stockbrokers. A successful amateur boxer, he had won Golden Gloves events two years running. He made a small fortune on the stock market but when he lost it all in the Wall Street crash, he became a professional fighter. He won the world light heavyweight title in November 1934 by outpointing Maxie Rosenbloom, but lost it the following year to the great John Henry Lewis.

Farr continued his preparations at The Dolphin, and relaxed by listening to music. He had an extremely fine library of gramophone records, and loved listening to Verdi and Wagner. He also played the piano and the accordion.

Bob Olin arrived in Britain about ten days before the fight and, like his fellow American Tommy Loughran, created a fine impression with the public. He was a smart, well-spoken man with a charming personality, assets which disguised the fact that he was a rugged prize fighter.

Olin boxed a three-rounds exhibition at the Stadium Club in London about a week before he was due to meet Farr. He showed that he loved a fight, and tore into his opponent with such ferocity that at times it looked as though he would knock him out, which was not the intention during exhibitions in Britain. It was rumoured that Olin deliberately adopted these tactics because he had heard that Farr was young and relatively inexperienced, and hoped to unnerve him.

Farr and Olin met at the Royal Albert Hall on 2 April 1936, and it was the Welshman who dominated the opening exchanges. Showing plenty of confidence, he moved around the ring quickly, taking the fight to his more experienced opponent and scoring well with straight lefts to the face. Olin relied mainly on the occasional heavy swing to the body, although in one exchange a good left hook opened a cut above Farr's right eye just before the end of the first round.

Tommy's cornermen did a fine job on the cut, and as he came out for round two, he immediately launched a fierce two-fisted attack and stayed on top throughout the next two rounds. Olin took time to warm up but made the body his main target whenever they were at close quarters.

The fight settled into a pattern, with Farr frequently piercing the American's guard with his straight left while Olin always looked dangerous with his big swinging punches. Tommy had a scare in the fifth when a big left hook to the jaw floored him, but he was up without a count and took the attack straight back to the American.

Farr looked to be in front going into the sixth, but again Olin landed heavy shots to the jaw with both hands. Tommy took them well but by this stage was being made to miss with many of his jabs. It seemed as though Olin's greater experience was at last beginning to tell.

The pace of the fight was extremely quick for two big men. Throughout the seventh and eighth Olin continued to attack, but Farr contented himself with using the left jab to check his opponent as he rushed in. Olin made a tremendous effort in the ninth, tearing into Farr with big punches from both hands. One right went straight through the Welshman's guard, sending him crashing to the floor. Although badly shaken, he climbed to his feet at two, and using his left jab effectively as he backed away, kept out of further trouble.

In the final round, Olin gambled everything on his big punching, but the brave Welshman stood his ground and punched back. They threw everything at each other for the full three minutes with neither prepared to give an inch, and when the final bell rang everyone knew it was close. Referee Charlie Thomas had no doubts and walked straight across to Farr and awarded him the decision.

Many people thought Olin deserved the verdict, and again there was some booing. What mattered to Farr and Broadribb was that another former world champion had been beaten, and ten more rounds of experience were under Tommy's belt. The Loughrans and Olins of the fight game provided more experience than years of sparring in the gym. By the time Tommy fought them, they had taken part in over 200 professional contests between them.

Afterwards, Olin, sobbing like a child and clutching a friend round the waist, said, 'I've fought many a fight. I have lost quite a few, including a world championship, but I did expect in England I would be shown some sportsmanship. I consider I was robbed. Why can't I get a clean break?'

Olin's manager, Paul Damski, who also looked after Walter Neusel, angrily said, 'Olin played with him as a master does with his pupil. It was a dreadful decision.'

Back in his dressing room, Tommy Farr was in no doubt. 'I had no fear about the result. I am happy. Olin certainly caught me with a nasty left hook in the ninth round but apart from that he didn't hurt me a bit.'

When he was told that Olin was in tears and protesting that he'd got a raw deal, Farr said 'I can sympathise with him if that's what he thinks, because I've had plenty of raw deals in the past, but his claims are nonsense.'

Tommy insisted that he now wanted to be matched with Jack Petersen. Promoter Jeff Dickson confirmed that he had offered the Wembley authorities £1,000 to release Petersen in order that he could be matched with Farr. 'Petersen against Farr at the White City would be an absolute money-spinner,' he said, 'and it is our intention to stage the fight in Derby week.'

Although the decision over Olin had been booed, many experts claimed it was not as bad as the one Farr had been given over Loughran. Nevertheless, the following day Paul Damski confirmed that he had written to the British Boxing Board of Control asking that they check the points on the referee's score sheet.

The decisions in Tommy's favour over Loughran and Olin had done nothing to improve his popularity in London, although the fight fans there were at last beginning to talk about him. Against Olin he had displayed a considerable amount of courage as well as good boxing skills, and he was clearly a man who had to be reckoned with.

Financially, Tommy did not fare too well from the Olin contest, receiving little more than £200. As with the Loughran fight, Ted Broadribb had expected receipts to be much higher and advised Tommy to take a percentage as opposed to an agreed purse. Again Farr was very resentful, and at one stage even doubted the honesty of his manager. The truth of the matter was that Tommy Farr was not an attraction in London. Later the same year, Broadribb guaranteed Tommy a percentage of the gate when he met Frenchman Charlie Rutz at the Empress Hall. Rutz was guaranteed a purse of £100 plus expenses, yet Farr ended up with just £20 after all his expenses had been paid.

Having defeated Loughran and Olin, Tommy was convinced that promoters would be falling over themselves for his services. In fact he received no definite approaches, and to make matters worse, the British Boxing Board of Control were still not interested in his claims to recognition. The efforts of Jeff Dickson to get Petersen released from his contract with Wembley authorities were ignored, and instead Jack went ahead and defended his titles against Jock McAvoy.

Farr was extremely annoyed that McAvoy got a shot at the titles, because he was only a middleweight. It added to Tommy's belief that the board were against him and that Petersen was definitely ducking him.

Although he was due to meet Jim Wilde at Swansea on 18 May, Tommy was extremely disgruntled. He left Slough and went to stay with Job Churchill in Wales, but became very lethargic. Training was boring, and as a result he started to put on weight.

Job soon got him moving again. 'You've got a fight coming up, my boy,' he said. 'How do you fancy finishing second best to Jim Wilde?'

As usual, Tommy responded to Job. He did a couple of hard weeks digging trenches to harden up his muscles and hands. At the end he was pleasantly surprised to be handed £5 2s 6d wages. 'Not bad, is it? Getting paid for training.'

He then moved back to his regular training quarters at The Dolphin and got down to hard sessions with Pat Marrinan, Don McCorkindale and Johnny Rice. His extra weight soon came off and he was looking to be back to his best.

The fight with Wilde was creating tremendous interest both in the Rhondda and in Swansea, and promoter Bert James was assured of a sell-out. The venue was the Vetch Field, home of Swansea Town football club. There was room for 7,000 spectators under cover, while arrangements were also made for ringsiders to be moved to a stand in the event of rain. Special train services were laid on from the Rhondda at excursion prices to cater for Tommy's great band of supporters.

There was a sensational opening to the fight as Farr shot from his corner at the bell and launched a terrific attack. He shoved Wilde to the ropes and landed punch after punch on him. The Swansea man was reeling and in serious trouble. It looked as though he must go down, but using all his fighting instinct he managed to get away from the ropes. Suddenly there was a tremendous turnaround as Jim caught Farr with a vicious right to the chin, and the Tonypandy man hit the floor. For a moment it looked as though the fight was all over, but Tommy was made of iron. He climbed to his feet almost immediately; but Wilde tore into him, intent on finishing it there and then. His overenthusiasm was his big mistake because he missed with most of his shots and allowed Tommy to grab and hold on until the bell came to his rescue.

As they came up for round two, Tommy had fully recovered and didn't give Wilde another chance. Jim did win the third and fourth rounds, and also the eleventh and twelfth when he staged a big rally to try and swing the fight his way. Apart from that, Farr was always in control. It was a fight which pleased the crowd, with plenty of big punches landed by both men. At the time it was described as being one of the finest heavyweight fights ever seen in Wales. It was fought in a very good spirit despite pre-fight needle, and referee C.B. Thomas had very little to do.

Mr Thomas did, however, astonish many people in the 15,000 crowd when he declared the contest a draw. Farr, who did not have a mark on him, looked a clear winner, whilst Jim Wilde left the ring with a cut left eye, badly puffed lips and bleeding nose.

Back in his dressing room, Tommy could not hide his feelings when he said, 'I never squeal when I know I've lost, but it is terribly upsetting not to get the verdict when winning as I'm convinced I did tonight.'

Ted Broadribb was equally unhappy with the decision and offered to deposit £200 with the *South Wales Echo* as a side stake for a return provided Wilde covered it.

The result of the fight completely changed Farr's immediate plans. He had been due to sail to the United States aboard the

103

Queen Mary on 27 May, and there was a provisional arrangement that he would fight either Art Lasky or Kingfish Levinsky. Broadribb announced, however, that he had now cancelled the proposed trip.

The drawn decision against Jim Wilde in fact did Tommy no favours at a time when he was struggling to get fights, despite having beaten Loughran and Olin.

There was even more discontentment in mid-June when it was announced that Jack Petersen had agreed to defend his title against the South African Ben Foord in August. Tommy had been convinced that he would get the next shot at Jack and, with both of them being Welsh, it would be a sell-out and bring in the long-awaited big purse. When he heard the news he wrote a letter to the sports editor of the *South Wales Echo*:

> I was surprised to see Foord matched with Petersen. It strikes me that I don't mean a thing when reading your article the other day that Foord had a side-stake waiting to be covered by any of the heavies. My manager Ted Broadribb and I have had £200 waiting to be covered for the last three months for Neusel, Petersen or Foord. I am still ready to fight Petersen when and where he likes for a side-stake, and if I am not there at the end, I will give my end of the purse to charity. I am hoping to be matched with Neusel sometime in August.
>
> *Tommy Farr*

In the hope that Broadribb and Jeff Dickson could arrange a fight with Walter Neusel, Tommy went to Job Churchill's farm at St Athan for a couple of weeks in June to start getting into shape. He was accompanied by the Irish heavyweight Pat Marrinan, who was also managed by Broadribb, and one Saturday evening they boxed an exhibition for Joe Gess at Talbot Green.

Negotiations for a fight with Neusel fell through, but in mid-July Broadribb reached agreement with Swansea promoter Bert James for a return with Jim Wilde at Cardiff in September. Wilde's Welsh heavyweight title would be at stake, and the promoter made application to the British Boxing Board of Control for the contest to be recognised as a final eliminator for the British title. His application was supported by the Welsh Area Council.

When the fight was announced, both Farr and Wilde stated they were prepared to meet Jack Petersen or Ben Foord and put up side stakes of up to £500. Wilde was so enthusiastic at getting the contest, that he spent a considerable amount of money on a new gymnasium which he erected near to his home at St Thomas's in Swansea. He engaged Max Hodgetts, Bill Wainwright, Johnny Summers and Dai Jones as sparring partners, and hundreds of local people gathered daily to watch him train.

There was tremendous interest in the fight throughout Wales. This increased when the Board of Control announced that they would recognise it as the final eliminator for the British title and that Secretary Charles Donmall would attend in the company of Mr W.J. Phillips, the Welsh Area Secretary.

The promoter priced seats very reasonably, with ringsiders costing 15s, and there was a special area reserved for unemployed people at just 1s 3d. There was plenty of heavy betting on the fight, and many people even travelled from the Rhondda to the west of Wales looking to place bets. A lot of money was put on Tommy Farr at evens and 5–4.

Tommy began his training in the sun at Bournemouth before moving to The Dolphin. About a week before the fight, stories began circulating about a romance when an attractive brunette was seen at Tommy's training camp. Pat Hyde was a well-known vocalist and radio singer in London, and every day she watched intently as Tommy went through his training. There was great press interest in their relationship, and when asked about a possible engagement, Tommy remarked, 'Marriage is a very big thing, you know, and I want to make a real success of my career before I ask a girl to share life with me. But if I beat Jim Wilde...'

On the night of the fight, a crowd of more than 20,000 saw a truly professional performance from Farr, who from the start made Wilde look like a novice. He left nothing to chance, and punched hard to knock out the Swansea man in the seventh round to capture the Welsh heavyweight title. The punches that made him champion were a tremendous left hook to the stomach, followed by a right to the jaw which didn't travel more than a few inches.

Both men went to work at the opening bell, and Wilde looked strong as he landed two rights to the jaw. He forced Tommy into swift exchanges, and by the end of the round, Farr's left hand was finding the range.

In the second round, there were some exciting exchanges. Wilde shook Tommy with a couple of heavy right swings, and he was looking dangerous. Farr, however, was scoring with good straight lefts to the face, followed by right crosses, and an ugly bruise came up under Jim's left eye. Wilde could not match

Tommy in terms of skill, and before the round ended more lefts opened a bad cut under the same eye.

In the fourth, Wilde struggled to survive when a good left hook to the stomach sent him to the floor in agony. He looked up appealingly at referee Ben Hardwicke from Tylorstown, and loud protests were made by his cornermen about the legality of the punch. These were ignored by the referee. Jim was up at eight and just about hung on to see the round out.

Rounds five and six contained a lot of infighting and mauling, but again Farr was the more skilful as he made Wilde miss time and again with his right swings.

Early in the seventh, Farr worked his way into close quarters with a series of left and right combinations to the head and body. Wilde seemed unable to fend off the big attack, and after a brief bout of infighting, Tommy let go a tremendous left hook to the stomach. As Jim was about to drop, a vicious right landed on his damaged eye for good measure. His seconds again made frantic appeals to referee Hardwicke, and again they were ignored. The count continued, and although Wilde struggled to his feet at the count of ten, Hardwicke ruled that he was out and ordered him to his corner.

Although most ringside spectators had no doubt that the punch to the stomach was clean and above the belt, pandemonium broke out between fans sitting further back. They clearly thought Wilde had been hit low and was robbed by the referee.

Afterwards both Wilde and his manager Joe Morris stated they intended lodging a protest with the Board of Control, and if necessary were prepared to submit two doctor's certificates confirming that the blows were low.

Throughout the fight, Job Churchill could be heard screaming from behind Tommy's corner, 'Use your gym punch, Tom.' Afterwards Farr revealed that they had been practising the left hook to the stomach throughout training because Job believed it was the punch that would win the fight. 'With the leverage I got behind it,' said Tommy, 'there was no way Jim was going to beat the count. He did well to get up in the fourth when I did him with a similar shot.'

The way that Tommy Farr had dispatched Jim Wilde to become heavyweight champion of Wales he served notice that there was definitely new blood in the heavyweight ranks.

9

RECOGNITION AT LAST

Immediately after beating Jim Wilde, Tommy went off to Blackpool for two weeks' holiday, but when he returned he was not a happy man. Before meeting Jim, he had received a letter from the British Boxing Board of Control stating quite definitely that the winner would be recognised as a contender for the British and Empire titles. When that letter was written Jack Petersen was champion, but on 17 August he was beaten in Leicester by Ben Foord.

Although Ted Broadribb immediately attempted to negotiate with Foord to defend his titles against Farr, he was ignored. Sydney Hulls, meanwhile, announced that Foord and Petersen would meet in a return at Harringay and he would be asking the board to agree that it would again be for the titles.

Broadribb protested to the board that Farr was now the logical contender as he had beaten Jim Wilde in an official final eliminator. On hearing of his protest, Hulls said, 'It makes no difference, the fight will go on and I leave it to the public to judge. It will be under championship conditions over fifteen rounds, and probably take place on the fifteenth of January.'

Tommy was disillusioned and very angry. He had beaten Loughran, Olin and then Wilde in a final eliminator, but for what? 'If this is what professional boxing is all about,' he remarked, 'I would be better off going back to the pits to earn my bread and butter.' Tommy was on the verge of quitting there and then. He was seen in Pat Hyde's company more and more, and it was obvious that he had completely lost interest in boxing.

It was Len Harvey who gave Tommy a glimmer of hope. Len was the matchmaker for Arthur Elvin's Wembley set-up, and had been at Cardiff to see the Wilde fight. Afterwards he approached Tommy and told him that Wembley were interested in matching him with Petersen despite the fact that Jack had lost his titles to Foord. Tommy agreed to be put under contract to Wembley because Petersen was the one man in the world he wanted to fight. It was now very much a personal thing, and to actually get Jack into the ring was more important to him than the titles.

Arthur Elvin made Petersen a substantial offer to meet Tommy, but he turned it down saying he was only interested in winning back his titles. Despite Jack's rejection, Wembley didn't give up with Tommy, but setback followed setback, which did nothing towards ridding Tommy of his complex that everyone was against him. Suddenly on 25 November, there was hope for Tommy when the Board of Control issued the following statement:

> An application by Mr Sydney Hulls, promoter, for official recognition of the Ben Foord–Jack Petersen contest for the British & Empire championships, was placed before a meeting of the Stewards last night. The Stewards in reviewing the contest between Foord & Petersen at Leicester on 17th August, wished to be first assured that Petersen is the logical contender for such titles. They therefore decided not to recognise the Foord–Petersen contest as for the championships mentioned until Petersen has met and defeated Tommy Farr who has already been declared by the Stewards as the official contender for the titles held by Foord.

'I have longed for this for years,' Tommy commented when he heard the news, 'and I am overjoyed. To oppose Petersen to prove who is the best heavyweight in Wales will be my life's satisfaction.'

Jack Petersen, however, disagreed with the Board's decision and remarked, 'Everybody seems to have had something to say, and all I can add is that Farr will have to wait until after the Foord fight.'

A couple of weeks later Farr and Petersen came face to face when they attended a boxing tournament in aid of the Cardiff and District British Legion at the Greyfriars Hall. Farr made a particularly sporting gesture when he bid three guineas in an auction to obtain a pair of Petersen's boxing gloves. He turned to Jack, and with a grin said, 'Now I've got your gloves, Jack, perhaps we can at last get down to the real business.'

By this time, Tommy had moved out of his lodgings at The Dolphin and into a pleasant semi-detached house in Sussex Place. Although his earnings hadn't been as great as he might have hoped, the young Welshman had managed to save enough money to buy his first property. He deliberately didn't move far, because he loved Slough and the people who lived there, and he had become extremely popular.

Situated halfway along a quiet side road off the Uxbridge Road, Heckfield was opposite the Lascelles playing fields and just half a mile from The Dolphin. As soon as the house was his, Tommy called for his sisters Phyllis and Sally to leave Tonypandy and live with him.

Tommy was on a real high because after all his years of struggling in the wilderness, things seemed to be going well for him. Rejuvenated by the British Boxing Board of Control's announcement that Jack Petersen should meet him, he got back into serious training without delay.

He was matched with the French champion, Charles Rutz, at Earls Court on 21 December in a warm-up contest, but for this fight, surprisingly changed his training routine. Instead of doing everything at Slough, Tommy decided to do just his road work there early each morning, then travel down to Hammersmith Stadium for sparring and gym work. He explained that he enjoyed travelling, and there were better sparring partners in London.

Tommy beat Rutz on points but was not at all impressive, and the fight did nothing to improve his relationship with the London fans. The Frenchman conceded about eight pounds in weight and several inches in height, but captured the hearts of the crowd with a splendid display of courage. He left the ring to tremendous cheers, whilst Farr's reception was lukewarm. Tommy later conceded, 'That was the worst exhibition I ever gave in public. I was over fifteen stone and felt as big as a carthorse.'

The history of boxing in Britain shows that in general there are two types of promoter: the small hall man who goes on year in, year out, putting on shows at the same venues, and the big promoter who uses the larger venues such as Wembley, the Royal Albert Hall and, in Tommy's day, Harringay.

Jeff Dickson and Sydney Hulls were big promoters, but Dickson was on the way down, whilst Hulls was rapidly becoming the top promoter in the country. He had been putting on shows at Wembley, but when Harringay opened its doors to boxing in 1936, he began promoting there as well. Hulls travelled to America and signed up former world heavyweight champion Max Baer to appear on a major promotion in London sometime during 1937.

He had originally wanted to match Baer with Jack Petersen, who had been a top attraction in Britain for several years, having originally won the British heavyweight title in 1932. He successfully defended it against Jack Pettifer and Jack Doyle in 1933, before losing it on points to Len Harvey in November the same year. He regained the title in June 1934, stopping Harvey in 12 rounds, then successfully defended it on a further three occasions, one of those being against Harvey. Then in August 1936, he was surprisingly beaten by the South African Ben Foord, who stopped him in three rounds.

In an attempt to break into the big time, Foord took on Walter Neusel in November 1936. Despite putting up a great performance, he was beaten on points, although many critics thought he had done enough to win. Foord was then rematched with Petersen to give the Welshman the chance to regain his titles. Despite the Board of Control ruling that they would not recognise the fight as being for the championship, it was nevertheless scheduled to go ahead at Harringay on 1 February 1937.

A few days before the fight, Foord went down with flu, and Neusel was offered to Petersen as a substitute. Jack jumped at the chance because it would give him the opportunity to avenge two previous defeats suffered at the hands of the German in 1935. He always believed he could beat Neusel, and knew that Hulls had plans to match him with Max Baer. The incentive for him to win was therefore tremendous.

Job Churchill was convinced that Petersen would be beaten again, and probably retire from boxing for good. He therefore convinced Farr that it was in their interests to be at Harringay for the fight. 'It's all about being in the right place at the right time, Tom,' he said. 'Let them know we mean business.'

Despite the fact that Tommy disliked Petersen for persistently ducking him, throughout the fight he loyally yelled encouragement for his fellow Welshman. Alas, the pattern of the fight was the same as their previous two. Despite making a tremendous effort, Jack was forced to retire in the tenth round, after the German had given him quite a beating.

Immediately afterwards, Farr remarked, 'I have been waiting for Neusel to lick him again. I have been challenging Petersen for twelve months. Perhaps he will now condescend to meet me.'

Unfortunately for both of them, Jack would never fight again. He announced his retirement from the ring a few weeks later because of eye trouble. This meant that Jack and Tommy would be deprived of a huge pay day.

Tommy never really forgave Jack for refusing to meet him, and for years he would say so whenever the opportunity arose. 'I always disliked Petersen,' he once remarked. 'Ever since I was a middleweight I wanted to fight that fellow, and he always took on

110

somebody else, even when it came to the title fight in which Foord whipped him. I was kept out of the big purses by Petersen. He would never recognise me or my claims, and simply refused to fight me.'

On another occasion, Tommy angrily remarked, 'Petersen got out of the game with something like $200,000. I wish I had met him for the title and a side stake of that amount. He was the one man I knew I could lick, and maybe he thought the same thing.'

Some years later when he and Petersen met, he told him exactly what he felt.

'You don't like me, do you?' asked Jack with a smile.

'No,' replied Farr bluntly. 'When you had the title, you would never give me a fight, and I don't like anyone who stops me earning my bread and butter.'

Petersen's sudden retirement from the ring meant that Sydney Hulls would have to revise his plans for Max Baer. Ben Foord, as British champion, was not particularly inspiring. He had little international status, and apart from his victory over Petersen and the defeat by Neusel, had done little to arouse the fans. So the promoter decided to match the former world champion with Neusel. Unfortunately, a British Boxing Board of Control ruling prevented a contest between two overseas boxers. Relenting to some extent, the board decided that in the event of Baer defeating the reigning British champion, they would recommend Baer being permitted to meet Neusel.

Hulls decided to give Tommy Farr the chance to challenge Foord for his titles first, then match the winner with Baer, and if all went according to plan, still put Baer in against Neusel later in the year.

The first Tommy knew about this change in fortune was when he received a telephone call from Ted Broadribb. 'There's something doing, Tommy,' said Ted, 'and if it comes off, it's the biggest thing you've tackled so far. I'll let you know about it later.'

Filled with excitement, Tommy paced anxiously around his house in Slough.

Then some five hours later the phone rang again. 'Will you take seven hundred and fifty pounds to fight Ben Foord?' asked Broadribb.

'Why yes, of course I'll fight him,' Farr told his manager, once he had got over the initial shock. The purse offer was not a fortune, but Tommy would have fought Ben Foord for a packet of cigarettes because it was the chance he had been waiting for.

Contracts were signed, and the fight set to take place at

Harringay on 15 March 1937. A few days later, the British Boxing Board of Control issued a statement confirming that the fight would be under championship conditions, and that the first Lord Lonsdale Championship Belt would be presented to the winner. The belt would be a new one, and only the fourth to be issued by the board. The previous ones had been won by Benny Lynch, Jimmy Walsh and Johnny McGrory.

As soon as the arrangements were finalised, Sydney Hulls sailed to New York to meet Max Baer and his manager Ancil Hoffman. He was hoping to persuade them to accompany him back to Britain to be at the ringside for the Farr–Foord fight.

Meanwhile, Tommy Farr had his first fight of 1937 before a packed house on promoter Peter Prince-Cox's show at the Colston Hall, Bristol, on 10 February. His opponent was the Dutch-American Joe Zeeman, making his first appearance in a British ring. Zeeman put up a game performance but could not cope with the heavier punching of the Welshman, who at 15 stone 6, had a weight advantage of almost two stone.

Tommy punched well with both hands, and was in charge from start to finish. He forced the pace from the opening bell, and his aggression won him the early rounds. He did, however, have a scare in the fourth when Zeeman caught him with a tremendous right to the jaw which pulled him up short.

In the sixth, Zeeman went down for a short count, and on rising was given a real going over by the Welshman until the bell came to his rescue. The seventh was another good round for Tommy as he attacked throughout. Then in the eighth, he really set about his opponent, hammering him with heavy blows to the body. As Zeeman slowed, so Tommy switched his attack to the head, and cracked home a right hook to the jaw which ended the fight. The American hit the floor heavily and the count was a mere formality.

Although Tommy's purse for the fight was only £60, he had been given an ideal warm-up for his title fight with Foord. The big money was now in sight.

When Tommy knew he had finally been given the chance to fight for the British heavyweight title, he was very happy and excited. But a sudden feeling of uneasiness built up inside him. It was most peculiar and unexpected from the normally tough and arrogant young Welshman. He'd had his tremendous desire to get to the top from a very young age. Now, as the opportunity approached, he was almost having a touch of the seconds. He couldn't bear the thought of failure, and the consequences.

112

Fortunately for Tommy, he was professional enough to be able to put his thoughts behind him, and he was also fortunate to have Job Churchill close at hand. As soon as the fight with Foord had been signed, Job begged Tommy to return to Wales. He was convinced that the Welsh mountain air was essential to a fighter's training.

'It's good for your wind, Tommy,' Job would say, 'and the mountain slopes will make your leg muscles like steel.'

Tommy knew the old saddler was right. They set up a training camp at the rear of the White Hart, a well-known sporting hostelry in Penygraig, and Tommy got straight down to work.

Job had Tommy running up the mountainsides early every morning and spending lots of time just deeply breathing in the air. The day started at about 8 a.m. with a seven-mile run on the mountains between the mid-Rhondda and Gilfach Goch where Tommy used to romp and play football with other boys.

Tommy also made a point of walking to the local pit each morning to chat with old workmates, and when training was over he spent hours each evening just talking to them, often in local pubs or working men's clubs.

Once the gym was set up, Job Churchill started recruiting sparring partners. Farr himself even travelled hundreds of miles in search of the right men, but despite him offering 30 shillings a round, there weren't many takers. Dave Norris, the Clydach light heavyweight, and Pinkie Jenkins, a 16-stone man from Pembroke Dock, joined the camp, along with several rugged colliers. Members of the local police force occasionally dropped in as well. But it soon became apparent that top-class sparring partners were not available in the Rhondda, so Tommy moved to the Star and Garter, a famous boxing hostelry at Windsor where champions from all parts of the world had trained.

There was disappointment in the Rhondda because the cheaper tickets for the Farr–Foord fight were not readily available. The large proportion had been snapped up by the London fans, and the old complaint that those in the provinces were being neglected was raised once more.

Tommy quickly settled into his camp at Windsor. His chief sparring partner was Alf Robinson from Manchester, backed up by Pat Marrinan and PC Roger Hunter, the giant six foot eight Metropolitan Police champion. Ted Broadribb also brought in capable young welters and middleweights each day to help build up Farr's speed. No expense was spared, and the Welshman quickly improved in both condition and movement.

113

The training was intense, and Tommy shed over a stone. Only a few months earlier he had scaled 16 stone 3 when he met Charles Rutz.

Broadribb said he was so confident of Tommy's chances against Foord that he was going to back him to the extent of £500. 'Anyway, I think that these championship contests should carry substantial side stakes as they did in days gone by,' he added.

Farr was equally happy with his preparations. 'I am confident I shall succeed where Petersen failed,' he remarked. 'I'm feeling grand, and I've got it in my bones that I can beat this fellow. I've seen him box, I've played cards with him, and I believe I understand his temperament, but most of all I believe I know the way to beat him.'

Part of Tommy's leisure time was still taken up listening to records. Church organ music and Handel's *Largo* were amongst his favourite pieces of bedtime music. He had a good voice and often used to sing to himself as part of his relaxation; in fact, he had been heard by certain people in the music industry, who offered him a musical engagement.

Max Baer, meanwhile, arrived in Britain accompanied by his wife, brother Buddy, manager Ancil Hoffman, Sydney Hulls and Jerry Casale, alleged to be an armed guard. After two days in the capital, he and his party also moved to the Star and Garter.

As Tommy Farr completed his final training session, he leaned over the ropes of the training ring and said, 'This is the King's Coronation year, and I mean to make it mine as well.'

Ben Foord took his training just as seriously as Farr. Shortly after the fight had been made, he moved from London to Desborough, a small village in Northamptonshire. There were no distractions as there had been in London when he prepared for his fight with Walter Neusel.

'I do not under estimate the ability of Farr,' said Foord. 'He has a great record as a heavyweight, and I believe it is a fact that he has never been knocked out. Still, I feel so well and have been punching so hard in the gym that I am sure I shall beat him.'

Before the fight with Foord, Job Churchill and Farr decided it was gambling time. They took it so seriously that they held a 'sinking fund' for betting purposes. The Tonypandy syndicate were gambling heavily. Foord was a firm betting favourite, so they were able to lay plenty of bets at odds of 3–1 and 4–1 against Farr, knowing that if Tommy could pull it off, a huge pile of money would be waiting for collection.

* * *

By 12 noon on the day of the fight neither Foord nor Farr had arrived at the Stadium Club for the weigh-in, and there were a few anxious faces amongst the officials. Ben arrived from Desborough just a few minutes late, but Tommy, after the comparatively short drive from Windsor, was some 15 minutes late.

During the week leading up to the fight, there were rumours that Tommy Farr had grown his first moustache. 'I'm glad to see you have shaved Tommy,' said Foord as Farr arrived and walked over to shake hands with him. 'I expected to see you with a beard.'

'But fighters don't wear beards,' replied Farr. 'They belong to painters and poets.'

The two men were well matched physically, and at 14 stone 7, Foord had a weight advantage of just one pound. He was a strong favourite to beat Farr, mainly on the strength of his last contest, in which he took Neusel to a close points decision. Many critics and fans believed he had the more impressive record, because Farr had not long been in the heavyweight ranks.

Both men entered the ring to big ovations, and it was clear from the noise that a very large contingent of Welshmen had travelled up from the valleys for the biggest occasion yet in the ring career of Tommy Farr.

There were plenty of celebrities at the ringside, including Max and Buddy Baer, Walter Neusel and Jack Petersen. In turn they visited the corners of the two fighters and wished them luck. Whilst Foord appeared composed and relaxed, Farr looked dour, vicious and on edge.

Foord had prepared well for the fight, and entered the ring in perfect condition. 'He looks good to me,' whispered Tom Evans as he lightly massaged Farr's shoulders.

'And he looks good to me,' agreed Tommy.

However, Farr remained confident because he had worked out a fight plan back in Wales. His task was to think quickly and keep the South African at bay all the time. Most importantly, he was to keep moving to ensure that Ben didn't land the one big punch which would end the Welshman's dreams. Farr, Churchill and Evans all knew that a fight with Max Baer was a strong possibility if Tommy won. With it would go a great deal of money, so there had to be great caution and no chances.

The fight had hardly begun when referee Jack Hart was in action forcing the two men apart. Foord opened with a sharp left to the face, but by bobbing and weaving Farr got inside and punched away to the body. Ben didn't like it so he grabbed and held on, and the pattern was set for a fight with very few moments of real excitement.

As the champion tried lefts to the head, Farr countered with rights to the body which brought him a warning from the referee, who adjudged them to be low. During another maul, Farr was pushed to the canvas but got up immediately and took the fight to Foord. The round ended with both being warned for holding.

Foord opened the second session with a left and right to the head, but again Farr moved inside and punched away to the body. He then held and clinched, drawing a further warning from referee Hart. The champion also received a warning in this round when he grabbed Farr around the neck with his left arm, having missed with a heavy right.

The contrast in styles made it extremely untidy, and as the holding and mauling continued Jack Hart worked overtime. Farr showed some skill in the third and fourth rounds as he repeatedly made Foord miss badly as he attempted to land his heavy punches. Whilst Ben became frustrated at his lack of success, Farr began to grow in confidence.

As usual, Job Churchill was in close attendance, and when Farr returned to his corner at the end of the third round, he put his head through the ropes. 'Tommy, did you hear them shouting for blood?' he whispered. 'Well, to hell with them. You box, and try nothing you are not sure you can do and you'll win by more points than you can count.' Tommy knew his old pal was right.

The holding continued in round five, and Jack Hart was forced to break them up several times in quick succession. During this round Farr landed his best punch so far when a solid straight left brought blood streaming from Foord's nose. Tommy looked the more determined during the sixth, scoring with good left jabs to the body, but was made to hold again when the champion scored with a solid left to the body, followed by a right to the chin.

Throughout the seventh there was continuous mauling and holding with neither man prepared to take risks and leave an opening. In the eighth, however, the crowd were treated to some of the best action so far. Foord scored with good lefts and Tommy countered with solid shots from both hands. Following one fierce rally, Foord went to the canvas for a count of three, although it was not clear if a punch put him there. On rising he jabbed well, but Farr came on strongly towards the end of the round.

Ben was outmanoeuvred by the clever Welshman in the ninth, but came back in the tenth to score with good hooks to the body and have Tommy holding once again. Farr then showed his grit and courage as he fought back strongly to make the champion grab and hold.

Farr was up quickly at the start of round 11 and looked very determined as he took the fight to Foord. Ben backed away, but when Farr got close he held on yet again. When he did throw his big punches, Foord was made to miss badly, and the Welshman boxed coolly to have his best round so far. Tommy continued to press forward in the twelfth but was forced to take two solid left jabs to the face, followed by a right. He then showed his toughness by taking three rights to the jaw without any obvious ill effect.

During the next two rounds both men appeared to realise the fight was extremely close and still there to be won. There was suddenly much more urgency about their work and although it was rough, crude, mauling stuff, Farr looked much the better boxer. He continually made Ben miss with wild swings as he desperately went for a knockout, but at the same time kept his left jab going to pile up the points.

It was a tribute to Tommy's wonderful condition and spirit that, in the face of the champion's revival, he remained cool and took everything without flinching. This was particularly noticeable in the fourteenth when Foord threw a wicked left hook to the body which landed well below the belt. Surprisingly there was no caution despite gasps and loud protests from the crowd as well as from Farr's corner.

Few were sorry to hear the bell for the final round. Generally, it had been boring stuff, with few of the thrills expected from a heavyweight title fight. Ben made a desperate effort in the final session to land the one big punch that would end the fight, but the skilful Welshman kept his head. He boxed calmly and moved away from danger every time Foord threatened.

Farr was still picking up points and hammering away at the champion's body when the final bell sounded. Without even checking his card, referee Hart walked straight across to Tommy and raised his arm. His dream had come true, and he was now heavyweight champion of Great Britain and the British Empire.

The several thousand Welshman were on their feet and burst into singing the Welsh National Anthem. They cheered loudly for several minutes, and Tommy's eyes filled with tears as he listened to them whilst the Lonsdale Belt was strapped around his waist by Colonel Myddleton, Chairman of the British Boxing Board of Control.

Those fans were his people, and they had cheered him from

the moment he had stepped into the ring, just as the Welsh miners had cheered Freddie Welsh more than 20 years earlier when he won the world lightweight title. As Welsh remarked, 'Their powerful united voices made the rafters ring, and what man could fail.'

Hundreds of miners rushed to the ringside, and as Tommy climbed through the ropes they hoisted him shoulder-high and carried him all the way to his dressing room.

What had promised to be an interesting fight had turned out to be what is known as 'a stinker', described in many quarters as being one of the worst championship bouts of all time. Booing again greeted a decision awarded to Farr in the capital. Neither man had shown anything like the form that was expected of him, and Jack Hart was the busiest man in the ring. By the end of the fight his arms and shoulders ached from continually pulling the fighters apart as they held, mauled and hugged in numerous clinches.

After the fight, Max Baer was non-committal over the decision, but didn't think British heavyweights punched correctly. 'Unlike American fighters, they fail to hit the target by the shortest route,' said Max, 'and they don't punch with the knuckle part of the glove.'

In Tommy Farr's dressing room, it was as much as a dozen policemen and stewards could do to keep the well-wishers from mobbing the new champion. It was a truly wonderful night for the young fighter who had worked his way up from the very bottom with little or no encouragement in the early days.

At Job Churchill's insistence, Tommy returned to the Star and Garter at Windsor immediately after the fight, but the next morning he held a press conference.

'I beat Foord because I knew I was good enough to win,' he said. 'People do not credit me with much chance of beating Max Baer, but without boasting too much, I can tell you that the fight will not lose me any sleep. I do not care whether it is Baer, Joe Louis, or any man breathing. They are all the same, two ears, two eyes, a nose, and two hands. But there is one thing they haven't got, and that is a bigger heart.'

Straight after the fight, Job Churchill persuaded Tommy to return to Tonypandy for a while. 'You're the champion now,' said Job firmly, 'and don't you forget it. They've got to find somebody for Max Baer, so we're on velvet. No more grubbing along.'

* * *

Becoming British champion was the most important thing in his life to Tommy, and when he came back down to earth he went to great lengths to explain his feelings. He said that many of his early contests in the small halls of South Wales were moments of tremendous importance and high achievement.

'They were the little stepping stones on the Welsh side of the river which were to take me over to the boxer's land of promises,' he remarked. 'In winning his first championship, like winning his first fight, every boxer, I suppose, finds himself possessed by a dangerous exultation. Dangerous in the sense that it distorts the perspective and inspires the belief that the top of the hill is only just over the next little hill.' He felt that way when he landed his first knockout in the boxing booths, and the feeling nearly caught him again when he beat Randy Jones to win the Welsh light heavyweight title. 'I felt just as proud at winning that championship as I did the other night when I beat Ben Foord.'

When he returned to South Wales, Tommy was met at Tonypandy station by Councillor Tom Smith in his official capacity as Chairman of the Rhondda Urban District Council. A crowd of more than 2,000 had gathered outside the station, and cheered wildly when the new British champion appeared.

Tommy was anxious not to let success go to his head. 'These people know me for what I am and what I have been,' he remarked. 'Quite rightly, they expect me to be the same Tommy Farr in the sunshine as the one they helped in the shadows. There's a friendship here more priceless than a dozen championship belts.'

He left the station in an open-topped car and toured the streets, which had been decorated with bunting. At least 20,000 excited people lined the half-mile route to Pandy Square, and William E. Allen of the *South Wales Echo* reported that he had never seen such a big crowd in the Rhondda for a sporting occasion.

From the little cottage in Clydach Vale where Tommy was raised, a banner hung across the street, with a picture of the Lonsdale Belt and the words 'Welcome to our own hero'. On another banner was the message, 'You did it to Foord, now slay the Baer'.

A further 10,000 people gathered in the square at Penygraig, where Tommy made a short speech. Then his car was escorted by the Tonypandy Silver Band and the Llwynpia Fife Band to the home of Job Churchill.

That evening Tommy was the guest of honour at a reception at the Judges Hall, Trealaw, when he was presented with an inscribed gold watch.

Tommy had been back in Wales for little more than a week when Ted Broadribb telephoned with the news that Farr and Churchill had been waiting for. 'You're fixed to fight Max Baer,' he said.

Farr told Hulls exactly how much he wanted. He made it clear he wouldn't fight for a penny less, giving Hulls the first taste of the fact he would not be short-changed. Although the shrewd Welshman never publicly announced the exact details of his purse, he did say more than once that he received more for that fight than for all of his previous ones put together.

The fight was set for Harringay on 15 April. In making the official announcement, General Critchley gave some indication of Farr's stand. 'There has been some difficulty as regards Farr,' he remarked, 'but now he's definitely fighting because we have offered him an additional inducement that if he beats Baer we will release him from his contract with us for other fights.'

Shortly after the fight was announced, the New York State Athletic Commission lodged an objection with the British Boxing Board of Control. They claimed that as Baer had walked out on his contract with Madison Square Garden, he should be banned from boxing in Britain. The board called a hasty meeting and heard evidence from all parties concerned. At the conclusion of the enquiry a statement was issued saying that in their opinion the New York State Athletic Commission had no claim against Baer. They would therefore not interfere with his proposed fight with Farr.

10

WORLD CLASS SCALPS

Max Baer was a tremendous attraction in the ring in any part of the world. A great character, he was totally unpredictable and had all the antics of a comedian, clown, actor, magician and fighter rolled into one. He was quite properly known as the 'glamour boy of the ring'. He fought out of Nebraska, weighed around the 15½-stone mark, and was six feet two and a half inches tall. As a fighter he was rough and strong, and possessed one of the hardest right-hand punches of all time.

He won the world heavyweight championship in June 1934, knocking out Primo Carnera in the eleventh round, but lost it to James J. Braddock on points in June the following year. Then in September the same year, he fought an up-and-coming young Joe Louis, but was knocked out in the fourth round. He was so dismayed by his performance that he soon announced his retirement form the ring. But he missed the glamour of the ring, and in June 1936 embarked on a busy comeback campaign, taking part in 18 fights in only 4 months. With the exception of a six-rounds points defeat at the hands of 'unknown' Art Oliver, it was a complete success, and he was ready to meet world-class opposition again.

The people of London really took him into their hearts as they discovered what a natural man he was. Max was genial and witty, and they loved his wisecracking. He was also a reporter's delight, and the newspapers gave him great coverage. No American fighter, past or present, with the exception of Muhammad Ali, has ever attained such a high degree of popularity in Britain as Max Baer.

Ted Broadribb decided that Tommy should train at the Green Man at Blackheath, considered the finest gym in London by many followers of boxing.

121

The proprietor was Seaman Jim Lawlor, himself a more than useful professional fighter, who was also the gymnasium instructor. The gym had originally been a dance hall, and still housed a concert piano which had been used by Charlie Kunz. It contained full-length wall mirrors and a 15-foot-square ring, and overlooked spacious heathland for the daily running.

The British champion and his party moved in almost immediately, and Seaman Jim hung a huge banner over the front entrance to the hotel: TOMMY FARR TRAINS HERE DAILY. Farr soon became quite friendly with Jim Lawlor, and together with trainer Tom Evans, they often went to the cinema on afternoons off. They sparred together on many occasions, even though Jim weighed only 10½ stone and Tommy was well over 14.

One day whilst he was training, Tommy was visited at the Green Man by Gilbert Odd, later to become Editor of *Boxing News*, and arguably the finest British boxing writer of all time. He was then a young reporter with *Boxing*, and he presented Farr with a Certificate of Merit awarded to him for his victory over Ben Foord. The Welshman was thrilled, and said it would give him an even greater incentive when he fought Baer.

The Editor of *Boxing* had prepared a poster for the issue due to be published the day before Tommy met Baer. It read TOMMY FARR CAN BEAT MAX BAER. Tommy's reaction was simple: 'Sure I can,' he remarked, and took the poster and hung it on the gymnasium wall. Within a few minutes, the inside and outside of the Green Man were decorated with the posters. Tommy told Gilbert Odd that after the fight, he was on a glass of champagne with him.

'But you're certain you're going to win,' said Odd. 'What about having the champagne now?'

'Oh no,' replied the cautious Welshman. 'I'm going to win all right, but you can't always rely on a referee. When I get the verdict, you get the champagne.'

For this fight, Farr trained as he had never trained before, using middle and light heavyweight sparring partners. Emphasis was put on speed, in the hope that if he could keep the heavy-punching Baer at bay, he would be in with a great chance.

Although the routines were rigid and strict, Tommy knew that he had to be in a relaxed frame of mind, so on the Saturday before the fight he left his camp for a day with his family in Slough. 'We have a grand family meeting like this before every big fight,' he said. 'What we do, we do together.'

Amongst the many visitors to the Blackheath training camp was

Jimmy Wilde, who apart from being President of the growing National Union of Boxers, was also a columnist for the *News of the World*.

Although Tommy was looking good in training, general opinion was that he didn't have a chance against Baer, who was reported to be in magnificent shape. Jimmy Wilde, like Tommy, was an ex-booth fighter, and he didn't go along with the majority.

'Baer may hit too hard for the British champion, and may also prove to be too strong,' wrote Wilde. 'Despite that, I think that if Farr can last six rounds, he will have a great chance of winning. Farr is no fool with his fists, and is very game.'

Farr was no fool, and appeared to have done his homework well. During the last few days of his training, when he was working with French champion Charles Rutz, it was noticed that he was concentrating on his defence to a left hook as though he expected Baer to make liberal use of such a weapon.

Another visitor to the British champion's training camp was Jack Petersen, who by this time was writing a boxing column for the *Sunday Chronicle*. Although it had been widely predicted that Jack would never fight again, the official announcement of his retirement had not been made until about a week beforehand.

Dressed in a pair of old baggy plus fours and a faded football sweater, Farr was watching his sparring partners playing darts when Petersen walked in. When their eyes first met, Petersen realised that they were two men of clashing personalities and temperaments. He knew exactly what Tommy was thinking, and was convinced it was not hostility he read in Farr's eyes as he narrowed them. Nor was there any jealousy. What he did read, however, was resentment at the bad luck which had robbed him of the chance of fighting the one man he had always longed to meet.

'I was a heavy-weight. I had been champion, and I was a natural foe,' wrote Jack in his column the Sunday after his visit to Blackheath.

As the two big men eventually came together, they shook hands and exchanged pleasantries. Suddenly and abruptly, Farr said, 'Jack, I'm sorry you are leaving the game.'

'Thanks,' replied Petersen, but there was something in Farr's eyes that made him suddenly wonder if that was the right answer.

'I'm sorry because if there is one man in the world I would like to take a crack at, it is you. I have always wanted to fight you, Jack,' said Tommy dourly. 'I was always wanting to get at you, and you never gave me the chance, and now the chance has gone.'

123

Listening to Farr, and looking at him, Jack realised that Max Baer was going to have a much harder fight than many people believed. 'If Tommy thought that about me,' he wrote, 'how must he feel about Baer who has enjoyed the glamour and limelight, and the big money, during the years while Tommy has been struggling. Perhaps it's because I'm another Welshman, and Tommy regards me as an especially irritating obstacle. If so, let me say now that I wish him all the success that good fighting can bring. I saw in him all the stubbornness of a typical Welsh fighter. Never have I seen such earnestness and such determination to win.'

There was no hint of animosity in the enthralling story Jack wrote after his visit to Blackheath, and for the first time ever, he openly expressed his feelings about his fellow Welshman, and gave readers an insight into Tommy's background.

'Luck had no part in Tommy's rise. He has had to fight every nick of the way, and you can read the struggle in his face. Although we were neighbours as boys, I hardly spoke three words to Tommy until I met him yesterday. When I saw Farr working out, I was as sorry as he was that he and I never fought. It would have been an interesting contest.'

The sports pages of the nationals were generally full of stories about Max Baer, who had set up his training camp at the Ace of Spades on the Kingston bypass in Surrey. Crowds flocked there daily to watch him train, and there were always plenty of pressmen and photographers there as well.

The interest that everyone was showing in Baer angered Tommy immensely, and he launched a bitter attack on the public for flocking to see him. He also criticised the press for the massive coverage they gave Baer and his antics. 'They know nothing about the fight game,' he angrily told one reporter, 'and I'm sorry, but I will have to lambast their American boyfriend, mark my words.'

Very few newspapers gave Farr any chance of beating Baer, and several were convinced he wouldn't last the distance. He was totally unconcerned with opinions of the critics because he was used to being the underdog, and generally fought better when the odds were stacked against him. They certainly were on this occasion, with some bookies laying 10–1 against him.

During the first week of training Tommy had given Job Churchill £1,000 to lay bets on him. The crafty old saddler nosed around and got plenty of bets at odds of about 4–1. The day before the fight, Tommy gave him another £100, and again generous odds were obtained.

Twelve thousand fans packed into Harringay Arena. Baer was clearly the main attraction, and when the crowd saw him enter the arena, they went wild and the noise was deafening. Dressed in a dazzling gold dressing gown, Max strode down the aisle, sparring jauntily. Pausing in a corner, he rinsed out his mouth and then climbed the ring steps to become the first ex-world heavyweight champion to fight in a British ring since the First World War.

Max really did his stuff, circling the ring flashing a smile towards the Society ladies seated at ringside, bowing to the rows of celebrities and shaking hands with anyone who was within range. Max was a real showman, but he did nothing to impress the grim-faced Farr, who was standing quietly in the opposite corner. Some years later Tommy admitted that this was the only occasion when he went into the ring hating an opponent. He also admitted that Max had done nothing to provoke that attitude, and it was completely unjustified.

Baer was an inch and a half taller than Farr, who was six foot one, and at 15 stone 1½ outweighed him by almost a stone. Tanned by the Californian sun, Max looked a magnificent specimen. He appeared full of confidence, and was anxious to create a good impression on his first visit to Britain.

As the bell sounded for the start of round one, Max shot from his corner, threw a tremendous right under the heart of the Welshman, and then stood back smirking as though expecting him to fall. It took more than one punch to floor Farr, and instead of dropping to the canvas, he moved inside, planted a stiff left jab into the American's face and then another. A third solid left smack on the nose followed, and then as Baer angrily lashed out with big punches, so Tommy hit back with a vicious right which split the American's left eyebrow. On seeing how badly the eye was cut, Max's brother Buddy screamed from the corner for him to quit.

Max realised it was a bad cut and threw a barrage of heavy punches to the British champion's body, but Tommy was too quick. He moved out of range and replied with two sharp lefts to the face as the bell ended an exciting opening round. The crowd cheered Tommy loudly as he strode back to his corner, and at last he appeared to have the London fans behind him. He had won the opening round, and having looked at Baer, knew he could beat him.

Baer's manager, 'Pop' Hoffman, talked fast and anxiously in the corner during the interval, urging his man to get stuck in and make a fight of it. 'You've got the punch,' he screamed. 'Get out there and use it.' Max stormed from his corner at the start of round two, punching with both hands, but found Farr equal to everything that was thrown at him. Even this early in the fight, Max knew he was in for a tough time. Every now and then he would resort to clowning by standing back, hitching up his trunks and letting out a yell like an Indian brave as he tried to unnerve Farr.

The Welshman was unmoved, and whenever Baer charged in, all he did was to impale himself on the end of Tommy's left jab. Max had his best success with short hooks thrown from either hand when they were in close, but whenever he tried the big right he was famed for, Tommy was out of range.

In the third, Baer charged at Farr, throwing lefts and rights to the head, but the Welshman broke up the attack with his immaculate left jab, which was emerging as one of the best in the business. Max threw some terrific punches in this round, and had any of them connected, Tommy would have been lucky to survive. Fortunately, his fine boxing skills enabled him to block or avoid the shots, adding to the frustration of the rugged American.

In the fourth Baer drew blood from the Welshman's nose when he hammered him into a corner with a barrage of heavy punches. Again Tommy kept calm and broke up the attack with counter-punches to the American's head, but as they stepped back from the exchange Farr was seen to be bleeding from a cut beneath his left eye. Baer had much more success in this round and at the bell swaggered back to his corner with the air of a man who believed he could finish the fight whenever he liked.

Round five began with Farr fighting out of his now familiar crouch. The American tried several uppercuts but was out of range, and when Tommy smiled, Max was enraged and savagely drove in vicious hooks which hurt. Farr sensibly reverted to the left jab to the head to pile up the points. The big Welsh contingent who had made the journey to London could sense an upset, and they cheered Tommy's every move. Frequent render-ings of *Land of My Fathers* echoed around the arena from the cheaper seats at the back.

Unconcerned by Baer's advantages in height and reach, the British champion took the attack to his opponent in the sixth. Whenever Max swung his powerful right, which he had developed whilst working in a slaughterhouse back in the States, Tommy's chin was nicely tucked behind his shoulder. In this round, Baer's curly head constantly jolted back on the end of the British champion's accurate left hand. Then a flashing right crashed down

126

on Max's damaged left eye to bring the blood streaming again. Stung into action, and noisily urged on by his brother, the former world champion punched back viciously. 'Fight him, Max,' screamed Buddy, 'you've got him for sure.'

Max hadn't got Tommy at all, because although his big attacks were still dangerous, they were becoming ragged from the constant attention of the British champion's brilliant left hand. It was a soul-destroying weapon of the finest calibre, and becoming a fight winner. All the speed training he had done in his preparations was paying off handsomely.

It was at this stage of the fight that Farr and Tom Evans sensed the strength was going out of Baer's punches. Although the muscular American posed and threatened, he was having little success. Farr, however, still felt as strong as when he climbed into the ring, and as the fight progressed so his confidence grew. During the interval between the sixth and seventh rounds, Job Churchill leaned through the ropes and whispered, 'You've got him now, Tom. Go after him.'

During the next three rounds Baer tried all he knew to try and put Tommy off his guard. Although his antics amused many people in the crowd, they did nothing to disturb the concentration of the dour, determined Welshman. Farr stuck to his job magnificently and showed his critics just how well he could fight. In the eighth he caught Max with a flashing left, causing further damage to the injured left eye, and by the end of the round the American was again in urgent need of repairs.

Ted Broadribb and Tom Evans realised that Baer was too tired to seriously hurt the British champion, and again urged Tommy to go out and fight. He did just that, and as they clashed in the centre of the ring, both connected with straight lefts. Farr then waded into Baer, catching him with a solid right to the head. As Max backed away, the excited Job Churchill jumped to his feet shouting, 'After him, Tom, after him.'

Baer then hit back and they stood toe to toe, punching away at each other with short, rasping hooks which were all landing. Suddenly it was Farr's turn to back off, but in doing so he returned to the left jab. Twice he caught the American full in the face, but Max replied with a vicious right uppercut, shaking the Welshman to his boots. Tommy was in the peak of condition, and his fitness saw him through as he took punches that would have floored most other fighters. The action and noise were so intense that neither man heard the bell. They continued swopping punches until their cornermen jumped in and pulled them apart.

There were some anxious faces in the American corner because Max was a long way behind, with the handicap of the badly damaged left eye. Farr, meanwhile, was still looking fresh and showing no signs of slowing down. Hoffman knew Max had to get his right hand on target, so he gave him an ultimatum, 'Knock this guy out or blow the fight.'

Throughout the tenth and eleventh rounds, Baer tried all he knew but to no avail. Although the desperate American fought savagely, bringing blood streaming from Farr's left eye, the skilful Welshman ducked, weaved and sidled his way out of trouble. There were occasions when it seemed that Baer's tremendous strength must wear Tommy down, but the left hand kept him out of trouble. This was his night and he was boxing better than at any stage in his career. Baer could punch like nobody he had met before, but Tommy knew victory would be his provided he kept his head and did nothing stupid.

As they shook hands at the start of the final round, Max smiled and beckoned Tommy towards him. 'Come on, Tommy, have a fight,' he leered. To his surprise, Farr nodded and leapt straight in with a two-fisted attack. The astonished American soon hit back with vicious swings, bringing the crowd to their feet. It was a non-stop round, and Farr, with his left eye almost closed, gave as good as he got. When the bell ended one of the most memorable heavyweight contests ever seen in Britain, Baer threw his arms around Tommy and planted a kiss on his cheek. Without as much as a glance at his score card, the referee walked straight to Farr and raised his arm.

Being the great sportsman he was, Baer went straight to Farr's corner and congratulated him. His damaged eye was shut tight, his lips were puffed and torn. 'Well done, Tommy. I guess you licked me fair and square.' The remark was an accurate assessment because although his aggressiveness had excited the crowd, Max never seemed to get going until the closing stages. By that time he was too far behind to get the decision.

It was in the last two rounds that Farr showed the hallmark of a real champion as Baer made his desperate bid for victory. Although he was a long way ahead on points, Tommy didn't just sit back, content to take a decision. Some of Baer's punches went in hard and deep. Despite this, Tommy rarely resorted to defensive tactics, and the harder the American tried, the more Tommy got stuck in and hit back. At times he boxed rings round Max. He fought savagely, right up until the final bell, against one of the hardest punchers in the world. His spirit amazed the

London fans, who prior to this fight had not been excited by his performances. Tommy not only confounded the critics but put British boxing well and truly back on the map and restored prestige within the heavyweight division.

It was a well-earned victory, and the crowd cheered wildly. They waved programmes and handkerchiefs, hats were thrown into the air, and the excitement couldn't have been greater if Tommy had just won the world title.

Charles Donmall, Secretary of the British Boxing Board of Control, was one of the first to congratulate Farr. 'You have done more for British boxing than any boxer has done for years,' he said. 'The stewards of the board are extremely proud of you.' And referee Mr C.H. Douglas later went to Tommy's dressing room, not only to congratulate him, but to thank him for a clean fight.

It was during the course of this fight that Ted Broadribb realised something special about Farr: his arrogant determination to prove people wrong was turning him into a much better fighter.

As he left the ring, Tommy was mobbed by hundreds of excited fans all wanting to slap him on the back or pat him on the head. He savoured the occasion, nodding and smiling as he shuffled slowly back towards his dressing room behind a posse of policemen battling to clear the way. The scenes were incredible, and the tough ex-booth fighter was later forced to admit there were tears in his eyes and a massive lump in this throat.

Land of My Fathers was sung loud and clear by the large Welsh contingent. This time, the Londoners in the crowd also got involved, and although very few knew the words, they hummed along to the tune. Those fans who had frequently booed Tommy in the past gave him a standing ovation because never before had a British heavyweight champion handled a top American with the confidence he showed against Baer.

Long after he was safely back in his dressing room, Tommy could hear the uproar continuing. Dozens of fans tried to reach him to take him off to celebration parties, but to no avail. Suddenly there came a sharp bark of 'Home, my lad.' Tommy looked up to see the imposing figure of Job Churchill, with Tom Evans at his side, nodding in agreement. The three of them slipped quietly away from the temptations of champagne to the comforts of their Blackheath training quarters. Their only celebration tipple was a pot of hot tea.

The attendance at Harringay was about 12,000, and Sydney Hulls reported that receipts were around £17,000. Baer received a purse of £4,500 free of tax, whilst Farr, who had privately negotiated with the promoter, was believed to have received between £3,000 and £4,000. Tommy was now a big attraction, and Hulls wasted no time in lining him up to top his next Harringay bill, scheduled for 15 June.

Attitudes towards Tommy changed dramatically after his victory over Baer. Many people in Britain suddenly became more boxing conscious because in a single fight he had suddenly emerged as a genuine world-title contender. The press reporters in particular changed their tune because a British sporting hero could always be guaranteed to sell newspapers.

The victory over Baer also seemed to change Farr's personality. Although he remained somewhat arrogant and aggressive, the bitterness in him seemed to thaw and he became much more mellow. His natural wit and the philosophy he had learned from Job Churchill, together with a hidden charm and dry sense of humour which had been bottled up inside him for years, suddenly began to emerge. As the chip-on-the-shoulder attitude of the old Farr began to disappear, he became more popular.

Back in the Rhondda, a group of Tonypandy miners celebrated Tommy's victory over Baer by burning an effigy of *Daily Express* columnist Trevor Wignall, who had predicted that Baer would thrash Tommy.

Wignall, however, put the record straight. Under the headline TOMMY FARR – I WAS ENTIRELY WRONG he commented, '... he is an infinitely better fighter than I have given him credit for in my recent references to him.' There was no animosity from Tommy and he gave the reporter an exclusive interview. He revealed that in the immediate future he wanted to have a holiday, do some more fighting and earn some more money. He added that he also wanted to get married. 'But not immediately. Let's get the fighting over first.'

* * *

The win over Max Baer had turned Tommy into a major attraction, and suddenly promoters were clamouring for his services. Within an hour of his victory, two big offers were received for him to fight in the United States. One came from Ellwood Rigby, a promoter in Pittsburg, who cabled Farr with an offer of $25,000 to meet John Henry Lewis in July. The other was in a cable to Ted Broadribb from Madison Square Garden matchmaker Jimmy Johnstone. 'Congratulations,' it read, 'will you consider Farr with Schmeling early in June? Cable immediately.'

'I don't think we shall consider going all the way to Pittsburg to fight John Henry lewis,' said Ted. He did, however, disclose that their next objective was in fact a fight with Max Schmeling, but it would not be in America.

With his new popularity, Tommy was offered contracts for variety and vaudeville work all over the country, and just three days after the fight, he appeared at the Palladium. Although he was given a wonderful reception, the occasion seemed to give him stage fright. In response to shouts of 'speech', the young Welshman muttered nervously into the microphone, 'I thank you very much,' and started to walk off. The audience wanted more, and after some coaxing he returned and added, 'I hope to beat Schmeling.' He then beat a hasty retreat. A few moments later there was a tremendous cheering and laughter as Tommy led a pony across the stage and into the wing. 'I would sooner fight any day,' he remarked later.

Tommy also agreed to appear in a production *Hugh the Drover* at the Sadlers Wells Theatre in London. He loved opera and had a good voice, and when he attended a dress rehearsal, members of the company, many of whom were Welsh, gave him a warm welcome. He was to referee a three-round fight in one scene, and gave advice to Welsh singers Tudor Davies and Redvers Llewellyn, the two contestants.

In addition to his London engagements, Tommy made appearances at Birmingham and Cardiff. He had an act which lasted about 20 minutes, and the critics believed it would add to his popularity.

When news of his stage appearances reached the Rhondda, many people there feared Tommy would not return home. But they didn't have long to wait because within a few days the Welshman decided he needed a break. As soon as it was known he was coming home, arrangements were hurriedly made for a reception in his honour.

The Rhondda people were so proud of Tommy that a number named their children after him. A few days after he beat Baer, a Llwynpia child was christened Tommy Farr Jones.

On his way up the valley from Cardiff, Farr decided to call at Job Churchill's house at Penygraig. The old saddler was thrilled when Tommy insisted he accompanied him and Tom Evans to the reception at the Empire, Tonypandy. They arrived to a thunderous welcome and it was as though the whole community had turned out. Some 5,000 people broke through a police cordon as men, women and children rushed forward to grab their hero's hand.

Tommy loved children, and to a group of schoolboy admirers he said, 'Call me Tommy and we shall be pals. Call me mister and we are going to have a few rounds.'

The highlight of the ceremony came when Tommy was presented with an inscribed silver salver by Rex Willis, a 12-year-old pupil at Llandrass Cathedral School, on behalf of his parents, Captain and Mrs W.E. Willis, proprietors of the Empire Theatre. 'Tommy,' said Rex, 'we are proud of you.'

Before leaving the theatre, Tommy said, 'I am more touched by the kindness of my pals than by any of the other fine receptions I have had, though at one place they were so enthusiastic they tore the door off my car.'

As the news of Tommy's defeat of Max Baer spread, so offers for his services poured in from all parts of the world. Sydney Hulls, meanwhile, realised that Farr had a real chance of beating Walter Neusel. It was a fight the public wanted to see, and he and General Critchley were desperate to put it on because they knew it would be a guaranteed sell-out. The big German had been the scourge of British heavyweights for five years and was undoubtedly the best active heavyweight in Europe. Although his countryman Max Schmeling was regarded as Europe's number one, he had been inactive for some time whilst trying to secure himself a world title fight.

A growing number of people believed Farr was the man who could avenge the long list of victories over British heavyweights. Should he succeed, he would climb into the top three or four in the world ratings. Hulls therefore contacted Broadribb with a purse offer of £3,250, which Ted immediately accepted. Although it was announced that contracts had been signed and the fight was set for Harringay on 15 June, the matter was far from settled.

Farr was extremely unhappy when he heard of Hulls' offer, and, backed and advised by the shrewd Job Churchill, insisted that he wanted £5,000 plus £200 by way of training expenses or he would refuse to fight. Although he wanted to fight Neusel more than anyone else, he was certain that if he held out long enough he would get what he was asking for.

Tommy decided to go to Churchill's farm at St Athan for a break following the strenuous programme of engagements he had undertaken since the defeat of Baer. Before leaving London for St Athan, the Welshman went public about his stance over the Neusel fight, saying; 'The fight may be fixed allright but we haven't settled, signed, and sealed the terms yet.'

On his way to St Athan, Tommy stopped off in the Rhondda

and paid a surprise visit to Joe Gess, who had his boxing booth pitched at Pontypool. They spent a couple of hours in Joe's palatial caravan reminiscing over old times, but it wasn't long before people realised Tommy was there. Suddenly the caravan was surrounded by hundreds of people wanting autographs.

By this time Farr was a national hero guaranteed to draw crowds wherever he went, so the organisers of the Pontypool Hospital week contacted him and asked if he would act as a judge at certain events. A group of Rhondda sportsmen who were planning a big boxing show in aid of Porth and District Hospital, also requested his attendance. Tommy was always anxious to help charity events and agreed to help the Porth event, subject to his training schedule. He made a firm promise that he would attend the Pontypool Hospital week events, and appear in Joe Gess's ring on 19 June. 'Come rain, hail, or snow, I shall be there. It was in Joe's school that I learned all I know.'

Job Churchill had arranged for a number of sparring partners to go to St Athan in order that Farr could begin light training. Tommy soon got back his interest and early each morning made the trip to the Rhondda for a climb up the mountains, just as he had done for the Baer fight. Then it was back to St Athan for the rest of the day. Apart from his normal training routine, Tommy also engaged in heavy trench digging, wood chopping, mixing concrete and laying paths, all designed to harden him up after the period of good living.

Churchill also introduced an unusual extra into the training when he handed Tommy a pair of six-pound dumb-bells, and for the next three weeks he supervised the British champion as he hung halfway out of a bedroom window and engaged in strenuous muscle-building exercises.

After they had been at St Athan for about a week, Farr and Churchill suddenly made a trip to London to try and sort out the purse-money problem.

Progress was not easy and matters were only finally resolved on 14 May at a meeting at the Board of Control offices. It was later discovered that Farr and Churchill stood firm and succeeded in getting every penny of the £5,000 they had been demanding.

The demand for tickets was tremendous. In Wales notices appeared in local newspapers advertising trips from Cardiff to London to enable fans to see the fight, and every seat was taken within a day or so of the announcement.

Some weeks before contracts for their fight were signed, there was an incident between Farr and Neusel when they met by

133

chance at the Star and Garter at Windsor. The German happened to walk into the restaurant where Farr was having a meal in the company of two attractive young ladies. He recognised the Welshman and tried to humiliate him by chatting to the ladies. To Farr's annoyance, Neusel suddenly pretended to discover him sitting at the table.

'Why, Tommy Farr!' said Neusel. 'You of all people. The man I most want to meet.' He boasted about his defeats of Jack Petersen, and then virtually issued a challenge to Farr. 'Now it's your turn,' he sneered. 'When are you going to fight me?' Farr was seething with anger but managed to control himself because he didn't want to cause a scene in front of the ladies.

'Listen Neusel,' he said quietly but firmly, 'this is hardly the place to talk shop. There's ample room out in the car park. We'll go quietly out there. I know the ladies will excuse us. It won't take me more than five minutes.' Realising that he had aroused Tommy's temper, Neusel shook his head, and, with a silly grin on his face, remarked, 'You are a funny man, Tommy Farr.' With that he turned and walked out of the restaurant.

As soon as he had disappeared, Tommy brushed the incident aside saying, 'I just wanted to get his goat, but we'll fight one day alright, if I have anything to say about it, and when we do, put your small change on Tommy Farr.'

Farr never made any secret of the fact that he was confident of beating Neusel, and his view was shared by William E. Allen, boxing editor of the *South Wales Echo*. In one of his columns shortly after the fight was announced, Mr Allen wrote:

I have a hunch that way as well. Indeed I should fancy Neusel is made for the Welshman. With his fast-moving body and piston-like left hand, he should find no difficulty in winning points from the ponderous, slow-moving German. That Neusel hurts when he hits, we all agree, but I think Farr will be clever enough to dictate the fight at long range.

They were bold words by Mr Allen, but he had tremendous faith in Tommy as had most sports writers for the *Echo* and *Western Mail* newspapers. Unlike their counterparts from the nationals, they were more accurate in their predictions, and always gave him good press.

* * *

Born at Bochum in Germany in 1907, Neusel was six years older than Farr but didn't turn professional until 1930, having won the German Amateur title the previous year. Standing 6 foot 2½ inches tall and weighing about 15 stones, he was a solid puncher and had won 35 contests before suffering his first defeat. He made his British debut in 1932, stopping Bobby Shields in three rounds, and became a regular visitor, particularly to London. His other victims included Gunner Bennett, Reggie Meen, Jack Pettifer, Eddie Steele, George Cook, Henry Crossley, Ben Foord, Gipsy Daniels, Larry Gains, Maurice Strickland and Jack Petersen, whom he beat three times. The only men to come close to beating him were Len Harvey and Don McCorkindale, with whom he drew, although McCorkindale did beat him on a disqualification.

Neusel was managed by Paul Damski, and their relationship was similar to that between Farr and Job Churchill. The two men were friends before boxing became their way of life, and when Walter was an amateur he worked in a chemist's shop during the day. One day Damski arranged for him to box an exhibition with a leading German professional. When it was over he handed Neusel a cheque, saying, 'Here is your pay, you are now a professional fighter.' From that point they became fighter and manager, and when Damski was forced to leave Germany, having been denied the rights of citizenship because he was a Jew, Neusel followed him.

Known as the 'Teuton Terror', Neusel fought in France, Belgium, Austria, America and Britain as well as Germany. By the time he agreed to meet Farr, Max Schmeling was the only world-rated fighter to have beaten him on a night when Damski was absent form his corner.

Damski was largely responsible for the way Neusel managed to beat Petersen in their third meeting at Wembley in early 1937. Walter was on the verge of being stopped in the ninth round and was only rescued by the bell. Although he was almost out on his feet, the attention and advice of Damski ensured that he went out for the tenth capable of turning the fight around.

The German set up his training camp at the Star and Garter several weeks before he was due to meet Farr. Among his sparring partners was Joe Zeeman, who had been beaten by Tommy at Bristol in the February.

Farr, meanwhile, moved back to the Green Man, where he trained rigorously with sparring partners Bert Ikon, Alex Bell and Max Hodgetts, all of whom had previously worked with Petersen. As training became more intensive, Monmouth heavyweight Nelson Park was recruited, along with Bob Scally and Seaman

135

Rowles. They sparred with 20-ounce gloves known as 'pillows', but inside Farr's was a special attachment designed by Tom Evans in the form of a mitten. Pads were attached and set so that it was only possible to hit with the knuckle part of the glove, eliminating the risk of damage to the hands.

Although he suddenly broke training one day to make a flying visit to the Rhondda to attend a charity function, Tommy left nothing to chance. He mixed speed with aggression in his build-up to the fight, much to the discomfort of the spar-mates. There was also tremendous determination on the part of Tom Evans, who spent hours massaging Farr's stomach muscles. 'Not only does this treatment assist to increase his speed and punching power,' said the trainer, 'but it will also render him more immune to those terrible body blows that have really been responsible for the German's triumphs.' Evans also succeeded in increasing the Welshman's chest measurement by a full inch.

Bouts of wrestling became a regular feature of the training programme. It was a strength-building process Evans strongly believed in, and when he first introduced Farr to it, Evans was able to throw him about with ease. Now it was different because Tommy was much stronger.

Tommy knew that Neusel would be the stiffest opponent of his career and couldn't afford to take him lightly. The preparations for Baer had been hard but these were even tougher, and throughout the long, sweltering afternoons, Tom Evans really put him through it.

In the pre-fight betting, Farr was once again the underdog. Although he was now recognised as a fine boxer, the bookies and fans were convinced that Neusel would be too strong for him. This suited Tommy down to the ground because he always fought better when he was the outsider. However, despite his confidence about the outcome of the fight, Tommy was still concerned about his popularity, especially in London. Although he knew he had won the hearts of many fans by his magnificent showing against Baer, he was still not convinced it would last. The events of previous years had given him a terrible inferiority complex and turned him into a very suspicious man.

He was so obsessed with being popular with the fans that a few days before the fight he telephoned the respected sports journalist, James Butler. 'What can I do to make myself more popular, Jim?' he asked.

'Knock out Walter Neusel as quickly as you can,' was the direct reply.

Tommy knew that very few people believed he could win yet alone knock the German out, but he was convinced he could do exactly that.

* * *

By the eve of their fight, Farr and Neusel were both in peak condition. The German had trained hard under the expert eye of hired British trainer Snowy Buckingham. His manager Paul Damski said, 'Walter is better than he has ever been. He will win. He doesn't say so, I say so because he don't talk. He don't say anything. Frankly, I cannot see Farr lasting more than four or five rounds.'

Farr was unconcerned about the task he faced, and after his final workout left his Blackheath training camp to go yachting on the Thames.

Confident of victory, Farr and Job Churchill laid out more than £1,000 in bets, many on Tommy to win by a knock out.

On the morning of the fight, it was after 9 a.m. before Tommy climbed out of bed, and he did very little apart from relaxing. The weigh-in was at the Stadium Club at Holborn, but by the scheduled time of 1 p.m. there was no sign of the Welshman. Neusel became increasingly impatient, and after 15 minutes said he had waited long enough. He stripped off and demanded to be weighed. His official weight was given as 14 stone 8¼.

He was about to leave when Farr and Tom Evans walked in. Tommy immediately apologised for being late, explaining that they had been held up in heavy traffic on their way from Blackheath. He had in fact been driven to Holborn in a new £700 car given to him by one of his rich admirers. Scaling 14 stone 7¾, he was just half a pound lighter than the German.

The fight was a tremendous attraction, and Harringay Arena was once again packed to capacity. Ringside seats were occupied by people from politics, society, stage and screen, and all classes of sport. Boxers included Max and Buddy Baer, Ben Foord, Len Harvey and Arno Kolblin, who was introduced as the official heavyweight champion of Europe and Germany. Also at ringside was Jack Petersen, who received the most wonderful reception when introduced from the ring. The Chairman of the German Boxing Federation, Dr Metzner, had travelled to London, not only to see the fight but also to try and persuade the British Boxing Board of Control to recognise Max Schmeling's claims for a world title fight. He stated that if Farr beat Neusel he would press for him to be matched with Schmeling. Max himself was seated alongside Herr Von Ribbentrop, the German Ambassador in Britain, and a number of other officials from the German Embassy.

When Neusel entered the ring he gave a straight-arm National Socialist salute in the direction of Von Ribbentrop, who acknowledged with a call of *'Heil Hitler'*.

The moment the crowd spotted Farr making his way towards the ring, massive cheering broke out and he was given the finest welcome he had ever known. It continued long after he was in the ring and there was a short delay before the introductions could be made. As he prowled around the ring, Farr looked down and saw Von Ribbentrop and Schmeling looking extremely cocky. He was already very fired up, but their expressions angered him even more. 'I'll show you,' he muttered.

Back in his corner, Tommy leaned through the ropes and told Job Churchill to go and bet another £100, this time on him to beat Neusel inside the distance.

The fight had aroused such passions that Sydney Hulls arranged for the introductions to be made in three languages. Walter Rothenburg, the Berlin promoter, did so in German, Sydney James from Swansea in Welsh, and regular Harringay MC Pat Regan addressed the audience in English. Whilst the introductions were being made, Neusel sat in his corner looking extremely glum, which was strange for a man with his record against British fighters. A few moments later when he and Farr met in the centre of the ring to receive the referee's instructions, he stared blankly at the floor.

Neusel started the first round in a crouch and tried to club Farr around the body but in doing so received an early warning from referee Jack Smith for holding with his left whilst trying to hit with the right. Farr started quickly and was soon shooting his immaculate left jab into the German's face. He followed with a cracking right to the ribs, causing Neusel to grab and hold – only to hear the referee shout 'break'. As they stepped back, Farr fired a stiff left into the German's face, catching him just below his right eye. A following right only just missed his unprotected chin.

The British champion was already throwing his right more than in previous fights and was grimly determined to stamp his authority from the start. Throughout the opening session he dictated the long-range exchanges with his left, and even outfought the German at close quarters. Although Walter tried his familiar rough stuff, Tommy's confidence was growing rapidly. Then as he drove a powerful right to the solar plexus, he noted a twinge of pain on Neusel's face. Going straight back at his man, Tommy feinted a left to the stomach but instead slammed two solid left hooks to the chin. As the round ended, the German received another caution, this time for hitting with the heel of the glove.

Tommy had won the first round easily, and as he returned to his corner at the bell, the crowd, who had got right behind him from the start, gave him a tremendous ovation. He had shown Neusel that he was not afraid to take the fight to him.

The German was out quickly for the second but was halted by Farr, who looked prepared for anything. His left jab smacked into the German's face, causing the blood to stream from his nose. Again Tommy feinted with a left to the body and when Neusel's guard dropped, he shot over a solid right to the chin. Although the German tried to be the master in the clinches, Farr was having none of it. When Neusel swung a big right to the head, the Welshman moved inside and countered with a beautiful right of his own which shook the German from head to toe. Heavy rights to the ribs made Neusel gasp, and just before the bell two tremendous rights had him staggering back on his heels. Had the bell not ended the round at that point, Farr would probably have finished it there and then.

The big crowd were loving every second of the action, and their cheers were a tremendous spur to the grim-faced Welshman, who won that round as clearly as he had the first.

Tommy was confident that the German's fate was sealed. He was making him look like a clumsy novice, and Neusel had shown he was hurt when the body punches slammed home. Between rounds the kill was quietly discussed, but it was Broadribb who had the final word. 'Let him think you have fallen inside to cover,' he instructed. 'Stay in close during the rough stuff and take care not to give him too much rope.'

At the start of the third the Welshman was off his stool and straight cross the ring at Neusel. Taking him completely by surprise, he smashed home a solid right to the body. The German was confused and shaken, and his face was soon smeared with blood which again streamed from his nose. Yet he responded in the only way he knew, using his ox-like strength to try and wear Tommy down with hefty hooks to the ribs. Farr, though, was unlike any of his previous British opponents because he was just as strong.

Undeterred and unhurt, he stormed back, and a slashing right opened a nasty gash on Neusel's right cheek, causing more blood

139

to stream down his face. Tommy stalked the German around the ring with the air of a man who knew he had the fight in his pocket. Three lefts to the stomach sent Neusel reeling into a corner, to bring the crowd to their feet screaming for the kill. Tommy tore into his man with savage punches containing all the power built from the strength-building exercises and hard graft which started weeks earlier back at St Athan.

Neusel had nowhere to hide and a big right to the jaw made his knees buckle. With his face smeared in blood, he looked in a terrible state. He was badly hurt, but Farr was in no mood for sympathy, and at that point showed that he possessed the killer instinct to go in and finish the job. A solid left to the mouth followed by a perfect right to the chin sent Neusel crashing to the canvas, his face twisted in pain. The crowd could hardly believe what was happening and again rose almost as one, cheering wildly as the previously invincible German sprawled on the canvas.

Thumping on the ring, Paul Damski screamed at his fighter to get up, but Neusel was like a man stricken with paralysis. Eyes glazed, he pushed himself into a sitting position as the count reached four, but could only shake his head as he pointed towards his knee. He never looked like getting up, and when the count reached ten he was only on one knee. Damski immediately went to the aid of his stricken fighter, who had to be helped back to his corner.

Pandemonium broke out because Farr had achieved the impossible in completely destroying the seemingly unbeatable German. Hundreds of fans from the poverty-stricken Rhondda had been saving their shillings since the fight was first announced. This was the moment they had dreamed of, and they gave their man the greatest ovation he had ever heard.

Farr was the only person who appeared to be in control of himself, seemingly as unconcerned as if he had just completed a sparring session. Job Churchill recognised that dangers could loom from the result, and as soon as Tommy returned to his corner he muttered, 'Don't get any ideas, Tom. As soon as we can, we'll all go back to Blackheath for a nice cup of tea and then off to bed.'

Nevertheless, Tommy savoured the moment and his eyes gleamed as hundreds of fans flocked around the ringside trying to shake his hand. Photographers crowded into the ring, and the familiar sound of *Land of My Fathers* echoed around the arena, bringing lumps to the throats of many hardened ringsiders. Tommy was besieged by reporters anxious to hear his comments.

'It was just the way I wanted it,' he told them. 'I am very pleased and hope everybody else is.' It was a marvellous night for British boxing, and for Farr and Wales in particular. Not only had he done the job he set out to do, but had also avenged the defeats of Jack Petersen and the many others who had suffered at the lethal fists of Neusel.

After he beat Ben Foord, Tommy had said that if he could ever get Neusel into the ring he would do what Petersen had failed to do. The manner in which he did it sent his stock soaring and put him in line for a crack at the world title. He looked every inch a champion from the start, never allowing the German to settle, and never fearing his reputation. He had taken just 7 minutes 55 seconds to become the first man to put the big German down for the full count, and succeeded in doing what Schmeling and Primo Carnera had never managed.

As he prepared to leave the ring, Tommy cast his eyes down to the ringside seats which Von Ribbentrop and his party had occupied but saw they were empty. The fact was, the German Ambassador, his face black as thunder, had stormed from the ringside as Neusel was counted out. His party, including Schmeling, followed shortly afterwards.

The journey from the ring was even more difficult for Tommy than it had been two months earlier after he beat Baer. Even when safely inside the dressing room, there was no peace because the place was crowded with excited reporters bombarding him with questions.

'I knew I could win,' he told them. 'Everything went according to plan. And lads, I'm not going to California in the morning, I'm staying right here.' Then suddenly he wanted to be left alone. 'All right, lads,' he shouted, 'that's enough for tonight. Once out of this dressing room, it's over the hills and far away for me.'

Outside in the arena there was absolute chaos as crowds of excited fans pushed and shoved their way through the corridors towards the dressing room. Those who got through almost hammered the door off its hinges. Although Tommy was with them in spirit, Job Churchill was still in command and had masterminded a way of escape. Very quietly, a car was driven to the rear exit, and at a prearranged signal, he, Farr and Evans made a dash for it. They had barely got into the car when some of the crowd spotted them, and before they could drive away, they were surrounded by cheering fans. Only when the mounted police came to their rescue were they able to drive off to Blackheath and that favourite cup of tea.

141

11

MEN BEHIND THE CHAMPION

A few days after the fight Tommy revealed that he had recently been to see a numerologist who assured him that his lucky number was 15. 'The corroborative evidence is that I have had wins over Food and Baer on the fifteenth day of the months, my year of birth, 1914, totals fifteen by adding the figures together. When I beat Neusel last Tuesday, it was also the fifteenth.'

There had been nothing lucky about the way he beat the German because he had pulled off what had seemed, before the fight, an impossibility.

Neusel was obviously embarrassed by the outcome of the fight. 'A cartilage in my right knee gave way owing to an old injury,' he told reporters. 'I was off my balance and took a hard punch. I didn't mistake the count when I was on the floor. The leg hurt me and I knew it was no good going on.'

Fleet Street heaped praise on the Welshman, and every national paper in the country devoted pages of coverage to the fight. These accounts reflected on the sheer brilliance of Farr's performance, showing just how feeble Neusel's leg injury excuse was. A minority thought Neusel could have got up, but had this really been the case, there would have been a storm of booing.

The morning after the fight Neusel was still not prepared to admit he had been beaten fairly and squarely by a better man. At his London hotel he said he would probably need an operation on the cartilage of his right knee before he could fight again. Sooner or later every fighter meets his match, but the unsporting German could not bring himself to admit having met his. 'It was a pure accident which beat me,' he said, 'but I will come back. You have to take this kind of setback in boxing. It's all in the game.'

Despite the excuses he offered, Neusel was always remembered by true fight fans. In later years it was claimed he fought mainly in Britain and France because he hated the system in Nazi Germany, and for many months made Paris his home. This may well have been true because he certainly kept faith with Paul Damski during the Hitler era and refused to be parted from him. When Neusel was drafted into the German Army, he joined as a mere soldier and never attempted to avoid duty as many other top sportsmen apparently did. One of his proudest moments would have been seeing his son win a gold medal in the Tokyo Olympics in 1964, albeit not for boxing, but sadly he died one week beforehand.

* * *

To keep going the way he did, especially as a youngster, Farr showed that he had unlimited courage as well as plenty of natural ability. Yet no matter how good a man is, or how much determination he possesses, he will always need help along the way. Meeting up with Job Churchill when he did was sheer good fortune. The old saddler had always been interested in the top boxers in Wales, and in his younger days boxed dozens of rounds with Tom Thomas, who was British middleweight champion between 1906 and 1910. Thomas was another ex-booth fighter, and many of the things which made him a champion were passed on to Farr through Churchill.

Job had also handled other good fighters, including Jerry Daley, who was Welsh middleweight champion between 1929 and 1932, and Penygraig fighters Billy Moore and Gordon Cook, both of whom won the Welsh lightweight title. It was when Farr beat Daley in April 1933 that Churchill realised he had the potential to become a great fighter.

Churchill was a unique character, at one time known as a pugilistic terror in the Tonypandy district. He belonged to an old school of mountain knuckle fighters and had a tremendous knowledge of all types of fighting. He knew all the tricks of the trade, and apart from personal successes in the rough-and-ready rings formed on the mountainsides, he had a reputation throughout the Rhondda of being the finest trainer of his time. He specialised in building up stamina, and had prepared men for contests lasting as long as 70 rounds.

As Tommy Farr found out, Job was not prepared to take on just anybody. Twice as a youngster he had begged the old saddler to take him on, but only when he went back a third time did Job agree. Years later, Tommy asked why he had been so reluctant in the first place. 'I wanted to find out for myself whether you had the right temperament,' Job explained, 'because temperament is as important as fists to a man who wants to make a name in the ring.'

Churchill recognised that even as a young lad, Tommy had the right temperament. Although he could be extremely arrogant, he knew exactly what he wanted. Intent on becoming a great fighter, he would do all that was required of him to make it. Job always remembered the day when Farr first asked him to teach him how to become a top-class fighter, explaining that he knew what he did for Tom Thomas. It impressed Churchill because Thomas had been champion before Tommy was born, yet he had taken the trouble to find out everything he could about him.

The relationship became so strong that the young fighter wouldn't go into the ring unless Job was seated in his corner. If the going got tough, Tommy was confident Job would know a way out, which he invariably did.

In all Tommy's early fights, Job entered the opposition camp to get an idea of what to expect and so work out tactics for the fight. Never once did he let Farr down, and on fight nights always sat in the corner, dictating the course of the fight. 'Do this, Tommy, do that Tommy,' he would yell in Welsh. Years later, Farr confirmed that Job's instructions were invariably correct.

Churchill was always ready to back his man if he fancied his chances, and was recognised as a very shrewd gambler. This was clearly demonstrated by the way he and the Tonypandy syndicate placed dozens of bets on Farr when he fought Loughran, Foord, Baer and Neusel; they really took the bookies to the cleaners. Although he had backed Tommy in many of his early fights, Job did not have a bet on him the night he fought Charlie Belanger at Newcastle in 1934. Although Farr was not boxing at his best at the time, it was nevertheless another example of Job's astuteness.

Away from boxing, Churchill was a man of exceptional foresight and business instinct, and as Tommy's career developed, he was always there to advise him. 'He became my guide and philosopher, and then my Chancellor of Exchequer,' remarked Farr. 'Every penny I earned had to be properly used and accounted for. Irksome though he was at the time, I found Job's assistance of the greatest benefit in later years.'

As a youngster, Tommy knew nothing about the value of money, and was unconcerned so long as he had some cash in his pocket. He recalled an occasion when he topped a bill outside Wales, and after the fight the promoter had paid him in large and small silver. 'I felt like a walking Bank of England going to the train,' he remarked. When they were alone, Job demanded to have a check-up. A dozen times he counted all the silver coins and never twice did he obtain the same result. 'We're three half-crowns short, Tom,' he claimed angrily. All the way back to Tonypandy, Job remained angry about the deficiency, convinced they'd been cheated.

There was, however, another side to Churchill's character. He loved to play practical jokes, as Tommy found out on more than one occasion. On his first visit to Job's farm at St Athan, Tommy spotted a bird rise from the undergrowth. In his eagerness to have first shot, he wrenched the shotgun from Job's hand and quickly took aim. The bird dropped into the grass and Tommy jumped over a hedge to recover his prize. Proudly holding the plump pheasant aloft, he expected to have praise heaped on him, but instead Churchill hobbled up to him with a stern look on his face. 'Now you've done it,' he said. 'That's my daughter's prize cockerel.' Tommy fell for it, and was worried sick. Several hours elapsed before he learned the truth.

There were plenty of amusing tales about Job. Before having a proper artificial leg fitted, he used to stomp around on a wooden one. At the time, he owned a motor cycle combination, and one night set out on it to attend a boxing promotion. One of the wheels flew off and Job was thrown into the road and down an embankment. He found, much to his embarrassment, that the leg had snapped clean in the middle. Although otherwise unscathed, he couldn't walk, and in the end rode back to Tonypandy on a rag-and-bone cart without seeing Tommy that night.

Job had a tremendous liking for motor cycles and in his younger days won solo and sidecar races. He came from a sporting family, and his brother John was one of the finest track cyclists Wales has ever produced.

Tommy Farr never forgot the help he received from Job, and throughout his career, and for many years afterwards, was quick to praise him in interviews. 'For as long as I can remember,' he once remarked, 'Job limped up against the ropes and bent over them to watch me. He's the grandest man alive.'

At the receptions in the Rhondda following his defeats of Foord, Baer and Neusel, Tommy was quick to pay tribute to all the people who had helped him, particularly Churchill and Tom Evans. He also made special mention of Job's sister-in-law, Lily Evans of Penygraig, who had been his cook.

Tom Evans had been sports crazy since he was a schoolboy,

and played Association Football for seven years. In his youth he was a tremendous sprinter and won many prizes on the South Wales tracks, although he didn't quite reach national standard. He became interested in the methods used to train athletes and studied massage, which formed a significant part of his preparation of fighters when he became a boxing trainer. It was unusual, yet tremendously creditable, that a working miner could baffle doctors with his uncanny skills and theoretical knowledge of the human body.

One of the best tributes to Evans' skill came indirectly from a Harley Street specialist when he examined Farr the day before he met Max Baer. 'Whatever happens to you tomorrow night,' said the specialist, 'you will strip the finest specimen I've seen for many a long year.'

The relationship between Churchill, Evans and Farr was summed up by Tommy: 'Tom Evans is the best trainer in this or any other country. Like Job, he has seen me grow up from a kid. Between them, Job and Tom have been a kind of joint father to me, looked after me, and encouraged me. They put me right when I was in danger of going wrong. Everything they did, they did it for me.'

Joe Gess also played a special part in developing Farr. Without the experience gained in Joe's booth, he would never have learned his tremendous skills and craftiness. It was there he developed his famous bobbing and weaving style as he learned to dodge the rushes of crude allcomers.

The caravan in which Joe travelled had been his home since the day he was born, back in the 1880s. It had been the auditorium where countless stories of great fights, fighters and hardships were told over the years. Joe first became involved in the booths with his brother Frank who was in charge. He did the 'housework' while Frank fought most of the leading men in Britain at his weight. Between them they had over 50 years' experience in the booths, and at one time or another, most of the top boxers in Wales worked for them.

Despite constantly organising shows and fixing up plenty of good fights, Gess struggled to make a living for several years due to the tremendous unemployment rate in south and west Wales. Farr recognised this, and when he left promised that once he became a champion he would not forget the booth. He was true to his word, and when in Wales, always looked Joe up if he had time, and sometimes boxed an exhibition for him.

There was one occasion when Tommy had to let Joe down.

Gess was extremely angry when Tommy didn't turn up and the next time they met gave him a real roasting. Tommy apologised, and a couple of months later visited Joe's booth and took on six challengers. He was British champion by this time and it gave Gess one of his best nights for a couple of years. Afterwards Joe tried to settle up but Tommy wouldn't hear of it. Recalling the incident some years later Gess remarked, 'Under that tough skin, Tommy has a very warm heart. He can be a good pal or a nasty enemy.'

Joe was delighted when Farr won the British heavyweight title. 'I knew he would do it,' he declared. 'I've watched that lad grow from raw. He's gone from a tough kid into a polished boxer.'

* * *

The morning after beating Neusel, Tommy ordered a copy of every national newspaper he could think of, and sat over an early breakfast proudly studying reports of his achievements. He was an extremely happy man because no matter how big his complex had been beforehand, he knew he was now a national hero. Completely unmarked, he sat smoking a cigarette and joking with Tom Evans, and proudly announced that later in the day they would set off for Wales in his new car, which he had still not driven.

Tommy publicly thanked all his well-wishers, and made special mention of an unnamed priest who said prayers for him before the fight, an ageing woman who sent him a crucifix, and a housewife who supplied enough Welsh cakes to feed a multitude. Then in typical sporting fashion he said he wished he could find the right and adequate words of sympathy for Neusel.

Accompanied by Tom Evans and wealthy hotel owner Tom Crofts, Farr travelled to Wales later that evening and booked into an hotel in Cardiff. The next morning when he arrived in the restaurant for breakfast and prepared to have some photographs taken, a waitress asked if he would like some flowers on the table. 'No thank you,' said Tommy, 'but I could do with all the food you can bring. Give the flowers to Walter Neusel.'

Tommy left his Cardiff hotel for Aberdare on the first stage in a hectic series of engagements. The Fête Committee had organised a luncheon in his honour, and thousands of excited people waited patiently for over an hour in Victoria Square to greet him. Tommy had to park his car some distance away in Market Square, and he and Tom Crofts walked the rest of the way to The Boot Hotel where the luncheon was to be held. All along the route, excited fans gave him a tremendous reception. Not expecting such a turnout, Tommy was clearly quite embarrassed.

After lunch he accompanied officials to Aberdare Park for the official opening of the fête. Whilst there, Tommy accepted an invitation to Pontypool Hospital Carnival Sports Day the following Saturday. The crowd was more than 35,000, and his attendance was largely responsible for all records being broken, and more than £500 was raised for the hospital fund.

After leaving the fête, Tommy went to Pontypool hospital, where he visited all the wards. He shook hands with many of the patients and promised everyone an autographed photograph of himself. That evening he kept his promise to Joe Gess and visited his Boxing Pavilion, which was pitched at Pontypool Park. Joe had arranged an attractive programme of fights, and with news that Farr would put in an appearance, the place was packed out and many people were turned away.

Amongst his other engagements over the next few days, Tommy visited the Bristol Rovers football ground at Eastville, where he presented a trophy and cheque for £250 to the owner of a winning greyhound. He also agreed to a sudden request from the matron of a convalescent home called The Rest to visit the patients there whilst he was in Wales. Tommy readily accepted and spent more than an hour chatting to patients, most of whom were Rhondda people. They welcomed him by singing *Cum Rhondda*, and sang the Welsh National Anthem before he left.

One function which Tommy was extremely sorry to miss was a reception in his honour at Penygraig. He had suddenly to return to London the previous day after receiving an urgent telephone call from Sydney Hulls.

* * *

Tommy's rise to fame dramatically changed the lifestyles of his sisters Phyllis and Sally. Less than a year earlier they were still living in the grimy little miner's cottage at 59 Court Street at Clydach Vale, where their only entertainment was the local cinema and concerts at the village hall.

The wife of miner Richard Evans, Phyllis had been working from dawn to dark, cooking, mending and washing. It had been just the same some years earlier when at the age of 15 she had been a mother to Tommy and her other brothers and sisters. She had been a domestic servant from the age of 13, and went on to become second kitchen maid in Lord Lonsdale's household.

After moving to Slough to live with Tommy, Phyllis and Sally were suddenly able to make shopping trips to the big stores in the West End of London. They visited luxury theatres and cinemas, were invited to big parties, and spent leisure hours at the Savoy Hotel. Phyllis became very fashionable and dressed in luxury clothes, whilst Sally became a sophisticated and modern young lady. Yet not 18 months earlier she had not travelled more than a few miles from Tonypandy.

Although Tommy's own good fortune had provided his sisters with a new life, Richard, his elder brother by nine years, was content to stay in the Rhondda. With a wife and four children, the youngest just a few months old, he resisted Tommy's persistent pleas for him to move to Slough. His wage as a miner was just £2 10s a week, of which 15 shillings went on rent, but he wanted to stay with the way of life to which he was accustomed, and retain his independence.

* * *

Despite the differences between them, Farr knew that the guidance he received from Ted Broadribb had been essential in his climb to the top. The victories over Baer and Neusel had pushed him into the top of the heavyweight rankings alongside Max Schmeling. There was by this time considerable speculation about a meeting between them in what would be a logical world title eliminator.

It was, however, as a result of a complicated situation which had developed across the Atlantic that Tommy would challenge for the world title much earlier than expected. He was soon to emerge as the central figure in a promotional battle between Mike Jacobs in New York, and Hulls and Critchley in London.

12

THE SCHMELING AFFAIR

The situation in America involved the world's three leading heavyweights: world champion James J. Braddock, Max Schmeling, the legitimate contender for the world title, and Joe Louis, an outstanding prospect and the world's hottest box office attraction. For two years a power struggle had developed between Mike Jacobs, a New York promoter, and Jimmy Johnston, promotional boss of New York's Madison Square Garden, for control of the world heavyweight title.

During 1935, Louis, a young black fighter from Detroit, was being carefully steered up the heavyweight ladder. He had beaten such quality opponents as Primo Carnera, Max Baer, King Levinsky and Paulino Uzcudun. In June 1936, however, his bubble burst when Schmeling knocked him out in 12 rounds.

A former world champion, Max had lost just 7 of his 59 fights. He won the title in 1930 by beating Jack Sharkey, but lost it when Sharkey outpointed him in a return in 1932. The following year the German was knocked out in 10 rounds by Max Baer, but had come back with good wins over Neusel and Uzcudun. Although he was still a top class heavyweight, Jacobs considered him to be passed his best and matched him with Louis, believing he would become another name fighter on Joe's already impressive list.

The win over Louis put Schmeling right back into title contention, and most critics shared his view that he was now the official challenger for the title held by Jim Braddock.

Known as 'The Cinderella Man', Braddock got his nickname from the story of his background. He had met his manager Joe Gould by chance whilst living in poverty and trying to support his three children. When Jim beat up-and-coming prospect Corn Griffin, Gould let the world know they were after the title.

Braddock was an unemployed stevedore when he met Max Baer for the title in June 1935, but was given no chance of winning. Despite odds of 20–1 against him, he turned the form book upside down by beating Max. In just a year he had risen from an almost unknown fighter to champion of the world.

Mike Jacobs made no secret of his ambition to control heavyweight boxing but was being prevented from staging a fight between Braddock and Louis by the terms of an agreement Braddock signed before he beat Baer. It stated that in the event of him winning the title, his first defence would be under the promotion of the Madison Square Garden Corporation.

The Garden were in financial trouble and if Louis were to win the title they would lose their last asset in the battle against Jacobs. After Schmeling's defeat of Louis, Johnston therefore quickly signed him up to fight Braddock for the title in September 1936. On 18 August, however, Braddock made application to the New York State Athletic Commission for the contest to be postponed because he had developed arthritis in his right hand. His request was granted by the Commission but created a desperate problem for Johnston and the Garden.

The delay was just what Jacobs needed because he knew that if he could get Louis back into the title reckoning, he could take the play away from the Garden. In the months that followed he matched Joe with mediocre opponents to ensure there were no further slip-ups.

Once Louis was back on the winning trail Jacobs offered Schmeling $300,000 for a return, but Max refused to be tempted. Although he had been inactive awaiting Braddock, he knew the champion would be an easier proposition than Louis.

Jacobs then approached Braddock's manager, Joe Gould, who was realistic enough to know that Jim was likely to end up a loser whether he fought Louis or Schmeling. With Louis being such an attraction he knew the rewards would be substantially greater. Like Tommy Farr, Braddock knew all about poverty and needed all the money he could get.

Braddock was offered $500,000 or an option of fifty per cent of the gate plus half the movie and radio rights. Jacobs also offered him a ten per cent cut of all Joe's purses for subsequent defences should he win the title. The deal far exceeded that guaranteed by Johnston. After months of negotiation, a contract was signed making Louis the first black man to challenge for the heavyweight title for 29 years.

The Garden Corporation immediately filed a suit with the

151

Federal Court alleging that Braddock's contract bound him to the Garden, and his fight with Schmeling should proceed. The Federal Court ruled that the contract binding Braddock to meet Schmeling before Louis 'placed an unreasonable restraint upon his liberty'. The Garden's application was refused.

The Garden appealed against the ruling but in the meantime went ahead and set a Braddock–Schmeling fight for 3 June 1937. They even had tickets printed and put on sale.

On 3 June the New York State Athletic Commission persisted in holding a farcical weigh-in ceremony but it came as no surprise when Braddock failed to turn up. Everyone knew he was training to fight Louis. The Commission held an immediate enquiry and Braddock and Joe Gould were each fined $1,000 for violation of Commission orders. Braddock was also suspended from boxing in the state of New York.

Mike Jacobs anticipated the situation perfectly and had arranged to stage the Braddock–Louis fight in Chicago outside the jurisdiction of the New York Commission. Schmeling was furious because, despite complying with the terms of his contract, he had lost about $25,000 in travel and training expenses. He decided to seek support of other European countries in his claim to world title recognition, and London was his first stop. He arrived on 13 June and had discussions with the British Boxing Board of Control. He also met Sydney Hulls and General Critchley, stating that he was anxious to fight Tommy Farr.

Max was accompanied by Walter Rothenburg, a German promoter, who had already cabled Farr with an offer of £10,000 provided he beat Neusel. The Welshman ignored it but before leaving London the morning after Tommy beat Neusel, Rothenburg increased his offer to £15,000. Farr was still not tempted. It was a wise decision because had he allowed himself to be lured into a fight in Germany, he would never have been allowed to win.

Louis duly won the world title by knocking out Jim Braddock in the eighth round at Chicago on 22 June, but was well aware of public opinion that he should not have got a title shot ahead of Schmeling. At a reception in Chicago the following day he said, 'I don't want to be called champion until I've licked Schmeling.'

When asked about the possibility of a world title fight, Tommy said: 'I am a fighting man. I leave the fixing of my fights to Mr Hulls, and although he has told me I'm going to fight the Louis–Braddock winner, I'm going to take Schmeling first. As I've said, it is too complicated a situation for the fighting man, though one thing is certain, I will fight for the world championship. According to present arrangements it is to be in London with the Louis–Braddock winner. That is all I know.'

Tommy had become a national hero, and everywhere he went he was mobbed by cheering crowds. When he did manage to escape to more peaceful surroundings he spent hours dealing with huge quantities of fan mail, cables from all over the world, and making countless telephone calls. His success had also attracted the attention of a number of companies and he received offers to advertise their products. The cash incentives were good, and with the support and guidance of Job Churchill, several deals were struck up over the next few weeks.

Advertisements appeared in newspapers for products Tommy had agreed to endorse. The most striking appeared in the *South Wales Echo*. Measuring five inches by fifteen, and apart from his signed endorsement of Bulmer's cider, it contained cartoon drawings of Tommy, his car and a trophy.

Newspapers, including the *Daily Express, News of the World, Sunday Chronicle* and *Reynolds News,* all ran stories about his life and rise to fame.

Tommy decided to spend a few days at Job Churchill's farm at St Athan, but his break was brought to an abrupt halt by a telephone call from London confirming that he was to meet the winner of the Louis–Braddock fight. He was bathing at Porthcawl when he heard the news, and the announcement came as a complete surprise because he was convinced that he would have to beat Schmeling before getting a shot at the title. Mike Jacobs, however, had given an undertaking that either Louis or Braddock would travel to London to fight Tommy at the White City on 30 July on a percentage of the gate. As both were tied to Jacobs, it didn't matter who won. Farr was thrilled once the news sank in because it would be the first heavyweight title fight in London for almost 30 years.

Jacobs, however, was a greedy man. Despite having reached a tentative agreement with Hulls and Critchley for Farr to meet either Braddock or Louis, when the time came he demanded ridiculous terms.

Eventually, after lots of haggling and indecision over the long-distance telephone, Critchley got fed up and instructed Hulls to go ahead and match Farr with Schmeling. The promoter wasted no time, and invited all parties to attend a meeting during the afternoon of 22 June at his Shaftesbury Avenue offices just hours before the Braddock–Louis fight in Chicago.

Once the business at Shaftesbury Avenue had been concluded, Farr, Schmeling, Hulls, Broadribb and others crowded into a Rolls Royce and sped to Critchley's office at Pall Mall. As soon as they arrived, Critchley announced to the waiting reporters that terms had been agreed for a 15-rounds contest between Farr and Schmeling to be staged at the White City on a date still to be decided in August or September. He added that application would be made to the British Boxing Board of Control for the contest to be recognised as being for the world title.

After further lengthy discussions it was agreed that the fight would take place on 30 September. Although it was set to become the biggest heavyweight fight to take place in Britain for many years, no official statement was made about the purses the two men would receive. This was very unusual, but the reason behind it would soon become abundantly clear.

Hulls duly applied to the British Boxing Board of Control for the fight to be recognised as being for the world title. It was generally expected that the board would only recognise the Farr–Schmeling fight as an eliminator for the world title, and nominate the winner to meet Louis. It therefore came as a complete surprise when they announced that they would approve Hulls application, and their decision was strongly criticised in many quarters.

However, one thing was now very clear. The agreement between Sydney Hulls and Mike Jacobs for Louis to meet Farr in London would surely go by the wayside.

* * *

The contest between Farr and Schmeling had been arranged with precision timing on a day when everyone in the United States was preoccupied with the Louis–Braddock fight. Jacobs was taken completely by surprise and the first he heard of the activity in London was from Trevor Wignall of the *Daily Express.*

Although he was angry, Jacobs called Ted Broadribb as though nothing had happened. 'Louis has won,' he said, 'and we are ready to come over for the fight with Farr on 30 July,'

'It's too late,' replied Broadribb, 'I've signed up with Schmeling.'

Jacobs was furious so he cabled Wembley promoter Arthur Elvin asking if he was still interested in staging a world title fight involving Louis. Elvin responded with an offer of a contest with either Len Harvey or Jack Doyle. Determined to get his own back on Hulls and Critchley, Jacobs provisionally agreed to accept terms on behalf of Louis.

As news of the Farr–Schmeling fight spread, there were reports from the States suggesting that if Schmeling got the chance to meet Louis, he would walk out on Farr and head straight for New York. Tommy was warned that Max was not to be trusted and was only going along with Hulls and Critchley to put pressure on Jacobs to offer him a title shot.

Jacobs was determined to block the proposed London fight and immediately cabled Schmeling inviting him to return to the States for a fight with Louis. To his annoyance, Max ignored him. Jacobs then telephoned the New York Boxing Commission and persuaded them to send a cable to Schmeling offering him a title fight in New York. Again the German refused to respond.

In desperation, Jacobs sought help from Nat Fleischer who had travelled to Britain and Europe on many occasions and was well respected there.

'How close are you to Tommy Farr and his manager?' asked Jacobs.

'I am very friendly with both, especially Broadribb,' replied Fleischer, 'why do you ask?'

Jacobs explained the situation whereupon Fleischer agreed to contact Broadribb and find out exactly what the position in London was. It was agreed that once they knew how much Hulls had offered Farr, they would raise the offer for him to fight Louis in New York.

Over the next few days there were a series of phone calls between Fleischer and Broadribb. When Ted stated that Hulls had offered Farr the equivalent of $30,000 to fight Schmeling, Jacobs offered to double it for him to meet Louis in New York for the title.

Anxious to protect their own interests, the Americans were desperately trying to force Broadribb into pulling Farr out of the fight with Schmeling. They knew that if it went ahead as planned, and the German won, it would have a disastrous effect on New York's monopoly of the heavyweight title.

It was, however, not pressure from America, but unexpected events in London which would be responsible for another dramatic change of events. The next day, details of purse money due to be paid to Farr and Schmeling were published in a London newspaper contrary to an agreement made when the initial negotiations took place. Farr was furious when he discovered that Schmeling was to receive £15,000. He had no idea how much the German had been offered until he read it in the paper. He felt betrayed and let down by Broadribb, and considered he was worth every penny as much as Schmeling. Tommy's purse was set

155

at £7,500, and he blamed Broadribb and told him he would not fight under those terms.

It wasn't long before the press got wind of the problem, and Broadribb angrily explained the position to a group of reporters: 'It seems quite unfair that Tommy Farr should receive £7,500 and Schmeling £15,000. We turned down a better offer for the fight in Germany, and also one from America for a match with Joe Louis before we made this provisional arrangement with Syd Hulls. I understand it is not Syd's fault, and if he stages the fight outside the present arrangements, we'll come in. Unless he does, we will withdraw and Tommy Farr will next fight in America.'

Broadribb admitted that he had been approached by Mike Jacobs for Farr to meet Louis, and added: 'After seeing Syd Hulls this morning, I am cabling Jacobs accepting his proposal. After the Board of Control's decision, the Americans will be only too pleased to have the chance of making Louis undisputed champion of the world.'

Jacobs told Broadribb that Farr would be guaranteed $60,000, plus 25 per cent of the movie and radio rights, and four round-trip tickets. The contracts would protect them against any subsequent court action.

Broadribb accepted the offer without a moment's hesitation because the guarantee to Farr was more than double the purse offered by Hulls and Critchley for him to meet Schmeling, and therefore couldn't be refused.

The next day, Farr personally telephoned Nat Fleischer and thanked him for his part in making the arrangements, but expressed concern over a story from Germany which suddenly appeared in British newspapers. It claimed he was a fool for agreeing to fight in America because New York was the only state to recognise Louis as champion. Tommy insisted that he was only interested in fighting the official world champion.

Fleischer insisted that the story was untrue, and within a few hours arranged for the National Boxing Association to cable the various press agencies in Britain confirming that 31 states controlled by the NBA recognised Louis as the champion. When he read the story in the newspapers, Farr was satisfied.

* * *

Sol Strauss was a brilliant contract lawyer, and had set sail from New York just before Jacobs made his offer to Farr. His original mission was to sign up a fight between Louis and either Len

Harvey or Jack Doyle in conjunction with the Wembley authorities. Now the plans had changed, so Jacobs cabled him, and advised him to offer Farr the terms disclosed over the telephone to Ted Broadribb.

Strauss arrived at Southampton on 4 July but refused to discuss any details until he had spoken to Arthur Elvin and Broadribb. Elvin raised no objections when told of the new proposals, and agreed that as British champion, Tommy Farr was entitled to fight for the world title. Wembley would not stand in his way.

Strauss and Broadribb then set off for Eastbourne where Farr was staying for a couple of days. He had entered his car, a 1926 Lammas Graham, in the annual Concourse d'Elegance and won first prize in a group for closed-top cars. Tommy was staying at the Cavendish Hotel and when he returned after the competition he was called into the lounge by a page boy. There, he was surprised to see Broadribb and a group of other men, but when introduced to Strauss the position became clear.

'I am here to represent Mike Jacobs,' said the lawyer, but before he could continue Tommy whisked him away to the privacy of his bedroom insisting that any conversation between them should be strictly private. Only when he was satisfied that he would be paid exactly as Ted Broadribb had been told over the telephone did he agree to sign contracts to meet Louis on 26 August.

* * *

When Sydney Hulls arrived back in London from Germany he claimed to be astonished to hear of Farr's withdrawal from the Schmeling fight. He insisted that contracts in his possession were binding on both boxers. Hulls and Critchley hurriedly arranged a meeting with their lawyers and a few hours later issued a statement confirming that legal action would be taken against Farr.

Farr's withdrawal from the fight became a major talking point in the boxing world, and received extensive media coverage in Britain, America and, in particular, Germany. German leaders were said to be extremely angry because this was the second time in a matter of just a few weeks that Max had been badly let down. All of this came on top of their other humiliation when Walter Neusel was destroyed at the hands of Farr, and now it seemed that they would be unlikely to get their revenge over the British champion.

Schmeling himself was furious when he heard the news. He immediately flew to England and was met at Croydon Airport by Hulls and his lawyer. Hulls knew that he had to act quickly so he instructed his solicitors to bring an action against Farr to prevent him from meeting Louis.

On 8 July an application was made before his Honour Mr Justice Bennett in the Chancery Division of the High Court for an injunction 'to restrain Farr from boxing publicly without written consent of the plaintiff Sydney Hulls before the date of the proposed contest with Max Schmeling agreed upon in a contract in writing dated 22 June 1937, made between Farr and Hulls, and signed by Farr, his manager Ted Broadribb, and Hulls.'

A writ was issued and the case listed for hearing on 13 July. Sol Strauss had anticipated such action and immediately put a pre-arranged plan into play. When he knew that Hulls was seeking an injunction, he persuaded Tommy that he would be better off in Paris away from the action.

Strauss chartered a light aircraft, and early on the morning of Sunday 11 July, he and Farr took off from Croydon Airport and headed across the Channel, where they would remain until the High Court action was resolved.

Proceedings in the case listed as Sydney Hulls (promoter) versus Tommy Farr (boxer), commenced on Tuesday 13 July before Mr Justice Bennett. Counsel for Hulls stated that a contract was agreed for a fight between Farr and Walter Neusel, and on the same day there was a further contract which provided that in the event of Farr beating Neusel he agreed to box Joe Louis under the promotion of Hulls. In the event of Louis being unable to fight Farr, the contract arranged for him to fight another opponent to be selected. If the opponent was other than Louis, the financial arrangements would be agreed upon by Hulls and Ted Broadribb, and the fight would take place between 15 July and 1 August 1937.

Counsel argued that on 22 June there was the contract referred to in the writ in which Farr agreed to meet Schmeling at the White City on a date to be agreed. Hulls agreed to pay Farr £7,500, and in the event of the gate receipts exceeding £30,000, the promoter agreed to pay the boxer in addition, 30 per cent over £30,000, and 22½ per cent of any sum received from film rights or broadcasting and TV rights.

There was a verbal agreement that Farr would call at Hulls' office the next day to sign the requisite contract. Counsel submitted that there was a clear obligation that Farr's next fight would be against Schmeling. Affidavits of Hulls and Schmeling were read to the court.

Counsel for Farr read an affidavit of the Welshman in which he denied having agreed to call at Hulls' office on 23 June to sign the document. When the contract was entered into there was no suggestion that it should contain any prohibition against him boxing Joe Louis before the date of the Schmeling contest. Farr claimed that if Hulls had inserted such a prohibition as suggested he would not have signed the contract unless he received some consideration for being prevented from earning money in the intervening period.

Farr was willing to meet Schmeling on 30 September as per the terms of the contract, but after he had boxed Louis. An affidavit of Ted Broadribb supported Farr's claim.

At the conclusion of his summing up, Mr Justice Bennett said, 'The defendant is not bound to bind himself not to fight publicly so many days before the date of the contest if he is not willing to do it in the period which the plaintiff desires he should agree. I see on the materials before me, no term of contract by which Farr has bound himself not to fight in public before the fight with Schmeling in September. In my judgement there is no foundation for this motion and it is dismissed.'

Immediately after the case was over, the Stewards of the British Boxing Board of Control called a special meeting to consider their position, then issued the following statement:

The Stewards of the British Boxing Board of Control, view with concern the statement made in the High Court today, and afterwards published in the newspapers, that they recognise Max Schmeling as the heavyweight champion of the world. At no time have the Stewards made such declaration. When they discussed the application for the Tommy Farr–Max Schmeling contest to be officially recognised as for the heavyweight championship of the world, they declared at the meeting that they considered the title vacant.

In a previous statement, the board had stated that in their opinion James J. Braddock had broken his contract to meet Schmeling for the title, and as a result he was suspended in New York. Therefore he was not the champion when he fought Joe Louis, and the Stewards considered that their contest was only for the American championship. They argued that the title was therefore vacant, and Schmeling and Farr were entitled to fight for it.

The court ruling was a defeat for Hulls, and left Farr free to sail for New York the following day as arranged. Ted Broadribb was delighted, and as he left the court, he paused to say, 'I'm just going to ring up Tommy with the good news. We're off to New York tomorrow.'

13

AMERICA HERE WE COME

It came as a great disappointment to the large crowd of well-wishers who gathered at Waterloo Station on the morning of 14 July, when they heard that Tommy was in France. They included Sir Noel Curtis-Bennett, John Harding, and boxers Don McCorkindale and Johnny Curley. Some had been waiting since daybreak to wish him luck as he set off on the first stage of his journey across the Atlantic. However, the crowd were good-humoured, and their disappointment soon turned to cheers when Ted Broadribb told them, 'We are going to bring the title back to Britain. I have waited twenty-seven years for this.'

Scottish light heavyweight Bob Scally and lightweight George Daly from Blackfriars, along with journalist Charlie Barnett and Farr's trainer Tom Evans, made up the party. There were warm handshakes for all of them as they stepped on to the boat train for Southampton, where they would later board the Cunard liner *Berengaria*, and head for New York.

The first part of the journey passed without incident, and they boarded the liner on time. Farr and Strauss, along with Jeff Dickson, joined it at Cherbourg as arranged.

The first difficulties were encountered just two days out into the Atlantic. Broadribb made an advance of wages to one of the boys, but when Farr found out he complained so bitterly that somebody remarked, 'I feel like giving myself up to the first recruiting officer I come across, or should I get out and walk back?'

Farr hardly spoke a word to Broadribb for a while, and there were plenty of hard looks and a terrible atmosphere. Eventually everyone sat down and had an open talk. They agreed that they all had a common purpose of trying to win the world heavyweight title for Britain. Although Tommy was a prickly character, they knew that their attentions should not be diverted no matter what internal squabbles developed. Years later, Broadribb would admit he was convinced that the dissension which arose made the task ahead much more difficult, and may well have affected the eventual outcome.

The *Berengaria* was an elaborate liner with a well-equipped gymnasium, and the British party put it to good use. Tommy trained daily, doing mainly long stints of skipping, but when Jeff Dickson got him exercising with a medicine ball, Tom Evans was furious and put a stop to it.

Soon after the liner reached quarantine outside New York harbour on 21 July, more than 30 reporters rushed aboard seeking interviews. There were also newspaper photographers and others making cine films, and the clamour for attention was like nothing Tommy had ever experienced before. He stood up to the press bombardment much better than his manager had expected, and with his relaxed, easy chat created a good impression with the newsmen meeting him for the first time.

Smartly dressed in a tan suit, green shirt, polka-dot tie, brown and white shoes, and pork-pie hat, he amused his audience when he revealed that his London agent had telephoned him with a film offer. 'I've told them they can keep their movies,' quipped Tommy, 'I'm no matinee idol.'

He then served notice on America that he fully expected to take the world title back to Britain. 'Joe Louis is just a man with two arms, two legs, just like me, and I hope to win by a knockout,' he said, smiling confidently. 'He's a good fighter, but Schmeling has shown me that he is easy to hit. So indeed has Braddock, who, after all, is a fairly old man.'

Farr and his party were escorted ashore by Nat Fleisher and Jack Dempsey. At the quay, Mike Jacobs smart limousine awaited them. The welcome was incredible, and all the way to the customs barrier people wished Tommy luck. Even traffic cops stopped to shake his hand.

The programme for the day was extremely hectic. First the party was escorted to the New York Hippodrome, where a reception had been organised by Mike Jacobs. Tommy met the American promoter for the first time, and was told that he could have anything he wanted. Jacobs suggested that he spent a few days having a look around and settling into the American way of life before getting down to serious training.

The party were treated to a real English tea, after which Tommy had to strip off and do a spell of skipping, shadow boxing and bag punching for newsreel cameramen.

The next step was Radio City, where Farr, Broadribb and Dickson all spoke over the air. It was then on to the Alamac, where the party would stay until Tommy moved to his training camp at Long Branch at the weekend. After freshening up, they sat down to a dinner organised and paid for by Jacobs.

Later that evening, Jacobs took his guests to Jack Dempsey's restaurant, and then to a new restaurant which had been opened by Benny Leonard. Tommy was overwhelmed by the welcomes he received, and it seemed an age away from the days when he thought everyone was against him. By the end of the day, he was extremely tired and returned to his hotel ready for a good night's sleep.

News of the Welshman's arrival appeared in every New York newspaper. Caswell Adams of the *Herald Tribune* was particularly impressed when he met him. He claimed that people were surprised that Farr was not offensive or cocky, just supremely confident of winning the world title. Many people were apparently intrigued by Tommy's scars, prompting particular comment by Adams; 'Farr is the most scarred fighting man ever to arrive in this country. His face is a field of scars, and he has long ugly streaks on the calves of his legs and along the back of his hands.' According to Adams, Farr's cauliflower ear was as a result of too much scrumming when he played in a Rugby team back in Wales.

Tommy was horrified to learn that critics and fans alike were convinced he would be an easy touch for Louis. The American opinion of British heavyweights was pretty low, and the phrase, 'horizontal British heavyweights' was on the lips of almost every American fight fan. In the past there had been poor showings from Phil Scott, Joe Beckett and Bombardier Billy Wells when they met good American opposition. Consequently, Farr was seen as just another English lamb being led to the slaughter. Despite this, the welcome he received could not have been warmer.

Tommy's training camp was set up at Long Branch, a small seaside resort on the Atlantic coast in New Jersey, about 50 miles from New York. A big crowd, some waving flags, greeted the British party when they arrived at the weekend, and there were plenty of offers of help. The town band was playing, and a huge streamer with the words WELCOME TO TOMMY FARR hung across the street.

Tommy was greeted by the Mayor, Alton Evans, a man of Welsh ancestry with a brother living in Wales, and was presented with a key affording him the freedom of the town. Ted Broadribb was so taken back by the welcome that he said if Tommy did beat Louis, he would finish up as Mayor of Long Branch.

People Tommy met included Bob Evans, who 15 years earlier had kept the Dunravin Hotel in Tonypandy, and Dai Williams, an ex-boxer from the Rhondda. Tommy was handed a letter from another Welsh-born mayor, Stanley Davies of Scancton, Ohio, who said that nothing short of the end of the world would stop him being at ringside for the fight.

The living quarters for the British party were in a beautiful mansion set in spacious grounds with a drive on either side. It had 14 rooms, overlooked the seafront, and contained a swimming pool and luxury gymnasium far superior to the sweatshops Tommy was accustomed to back home.

Mike Jacobs ensured that Tommy lacked nothing by way of facilities, expenses and minders. Jerry Casale, a character known in New York as 'Jerry the Gun', was assigned to act as Farr's personal bodyguard, chauffeur and general helper. Casale was a real tough guy who could perform any task required around the training camp, and he and Tommy soon became close friends.

Two American heavyweights, Abe Feldman and Joe Wagner, were recruited to act as extra sparring partners to Bob Scally, who was only a light heavyweight. He would be used for speed because Broadribb knew this would be as important against Louis as it had been against Baer and Neusel.

Broadribb recruited an old friend, Babe Calnan, to act as his American adviser, and Ken Barker, an English chef who had once cooked for the King, to ensure that Tommy received a stable diet. Barker, a native of Manchester, was a survivor when the Belgian relief ship *Mont Blanc* blew up in Halifax harbour, Nova Scotia, in December 1917. He went to live in America in 1919, and had worked in the kitchens of most leading hotels in New York.

Although Mike Jacobs had suggested Tommy took a few days to settle in, Tom Evans was having none of it. They did spend one morning sightseeing before moving to Long Branch, but as far as Evans was concerned, that was enough. Farr had barely settled into his quarters when the trainer ordered him to start roadwork. Evans didn't want any distractions, and decided that the sooner his man got to work, the better.

The daily schedule commenced at 8 a.m. with an eight-mile run followed by an hour of recreation. At 10 a.m. Tommy moved to a greyhound stadium about a mile from his living quarters for basic gym work. After a light lunch, sparring commenced at 2 p.m.

Once Tommy had settled into the camp, he said he would love

to have a Welsh dragon flying on the roof alongside the Union Jack and the Stars and Stripes. On hearing this, the *South Wales Echo* made arrangements for one to be flown to him. 'Isn't that grand,' said Tommy as soon as the news reached him, and promptly sat down at a piano and played the Welsh National Anthem.

The following day, an Imperial Airways flying boat named *Cambia* flew from Foynes in Ireland to Botwood, Newfoundland, on to Montreal, and finally to Port Washington, Long Island, in America. It was only the second time that an Imperial Airways flying boat had crossed the Atlantic, and, piloted by Captain G.J. Powell, a native of Cardiff, it was appropriate that it carried a small brown paper parcel addressed to Tommy, containing the national flag of Wales.

The official presentation to Tommy was delayed for about a week to allow a group of Welsh miners travelling from the Rhondda to be present. The Mayor of Long Branch, Alton Evans, proudly told Tommy that it would be the first time a Welsh flag sent from Wales had flown there from a boxer's training camp. Then Dai 'Nippy' Davies, an old Rugby full back from Treherbert, jumped into the ring and invited everyone to join in the singing of the Welsh National Anthem.

Back in Wales, arrangements were being made for another memento to be conveyed to Tommy. This time it was a red dragon, the size of a handkerchief and woven from silk. It had been worn by Freddie Welsh on his trunks the night be beat Willie Ritchie in 1914 to win the world lightweight title. Afterwards, Welsh had given the dragon to his good friend Mr Gwyllum Seaton of Pontypridd, and it was Mr Seaton's wish that Farr should wear it in his world title bid. Mrs Suzannah Edwards, a sister-in-law of Job Churchill, was travelling to America for the fight, so Mr Seaton asked her to take the dragon with her and sew it on Farr's dressing gown. Mrs Edwards sailed from Southampton on 11 August aboard the *Queen Mary*, but the following day, Seaton died from a heart attack. His last wish was carried out to the full.

Few British boxers have received a welcome from the American people like Tommy Farr's. After arriving in the States, his quiet confidence and modesty won him instant popularity, and there were plenty of people who wanted to become his friend. Tradesmen offered him clothes and food without charge, and a dog track syndicate offered him a huge guarantee to fight Max Baer after Louis. Film director Victor Jory invited him to star in what was described as a million-dollar picture, and two separate film offers were cabled from London. One was for a part in *Fast and Furious*, the other for *From Pauper to King*.

Farr's guest appearances were varied, but once he was in strict training, Broadribb insisted they be kept to a minimum. One Sunday evening in early August, however, a concert was given in Tommy's honour at the mansion at Long Branch. Among singers to perform at the concert were Alice Morley of *Hit the Deck* fame, and little Patsy Donovan, a niece of Don McCorkindale, a heavyweight with whom Tommy had sparred many times at The Dolphin in Slough.

Tommy was also a guest of Clem McCarthy, a noted radio sports announcer, in a nationwide broadcast about his career. 'He has come up from nowhere in practically no time,' McCarthy told his audience. Referring to Tommy as the 'Cinderella Man' of British boxing, he added, 'A year ago I don't think any boxing writer in America had ever heard of Tommy Farr, but now they are all writing about him.'

The broadcast lasted about half an hour, and gave a chilling insight into the terrible hardships the Welshman had endured as a youngster. Tommy recalled his days in the booths, and told how he went to bed hungry if his boss had to pay a pound to any challenger he had failed to knock out inside the three rounds. Asked by McCarthy about his plans for the future, Tommy replied, 'I plan to keep right on boxing until I have enough money to last me for life.'

* * *

Once the serious training got underway, Tommy showed that he was very confident and sure of himself, and caused Mike Jacobs a few anxious moments by refusing at first to use a headguard or mouthpiece. Eventually he saw sense and gave in to the persistent pleas of the promoter.

Generally things went along smoothly during the early stages. Tommy was relaxed and looked impressive, prompting some critics to describe him as the best British boxer since Jim Driscoll. Ted Broadribb's confidence grew in leaps and bounds, but the calm between him and his fighter was to last for only seven days. Farr suddenly became very edgy at having to train in front of hundreds of highly critical Americans. He was loudly referred to as a 'bum' who wouldn't last more than a few rounds with Louis, and his anger made his gym performances less impressive.

During one particular session, Tommy was repeatedly caught

with left hooks to the jaw from Abe Feldman. A small boy in the audience loudly asked, 'Can't Farr fight better than that?' He was quickly hushed, but some observers believed he had innocently voiced the general view that Tommy would have to improve considerably if he were to be any match for Louis.

When Ted Broadribb commented that Tommy looked bad in training, he got a mouthful from the angry Welshman, who didn't realise that Ted was merely trying to gee him up at a time when he was getting very low.

The newspapers were also writing Tommy down, and the amount of criticism was on a scale he had never experienced before. Things were getting to Tommy to the extent that his moods and temper occasionally spilt over during interviews, and he threatened to punch one reporter on the nose and have another thrown out on his ear.

Broadribb was convinced that the criticism was preventing Tommy from concentrating on his training, and tried everything he knew to calm him down. He suggested that he should handle the mail and newspapers to help Tommy concentrate more, but this just angered the Welshman further, and he deliberately spent even more time studying the critical reports.

During the first few days of sparring, Broadribb worked in the ring with Tommy, acting as trainer and referee. Consequently, he appeared in many of the films and photos that were taken. This irritated Farr, who accused him of getting too much publicity. At one stage, their relationship was so bad that conversations were conducted through a third party.

The situation was becoming almost unworkable, so Tom Evans suggested Broadribb should stay outside the ring during sparring. Although his feelings were deeply hurt, Ted reluctantly agreed. As a mere spectator outside the ropes, he became convinced that Tommy was getting slower. Ted had difficulty in controlling his frustration at wanting to yell advice, and at one stage threatened to quit the camp altogether. Only George Daly and Jerry Casale were able to talk him out of it.

No matter how hard he tried, Tommy couldn't get going for several days. It wasn't tiredness or laziness, but the change in climate which was the cause. Since arriving at Long Branch, it had been hot and oppressive, and he failed to adapt to the conditions, which were like nothing he had experienced before. In training he was puffing badly, and having a pale skin, had to wear a shirt to protect his body from the sun. At night, it was hot and humid so he was unable to recover his lost energy.

166

Tom Evans, however, was unconcerned. He rescheduled the daily training programme so that there were no long spells of hard work during the morning, and no sweat baths of sparring in the afternoon. Instead, he got Tommy out on the road during the late evening, jogging, sprinting and walking. They did this for three consecutive nights, covering many miles of road. During the daytime, Tommy just lazed about relaxing.

Evans' tactics worked wonders and turned Tommy around completely. When they got back into the gym, the power came back into his punching and he looked like his old self again. In one session, Basher Dean, a hefty negro from New Jersey who had also been recruited to the camp was knocked cold.

* * *

A week after arriving in the States, Tommy was summoned to the New York State Athletic Commission offices for the signing of contracts. He was a picture of confidence as he extended a hand to greet Joe Louis when he arrived. 'Hello, my boy,' he said. 'How are you? Glad to know you.'

'Hello. I'm glad to know you too,' muttered the champion as he limply shook the Welshman's hand.

After posing for photographers, they stripped off and were examined by Dr William Walker, official physician to the commission, who pronounced both fit to box. Louis couldn't take his eyes off the scars on the Welshman's pale body. 'Tahmmy, what's dee cuts about you?' he asked.

'Oh them,' replied Tommy casually, 'I used to wrestle tigers when I worked in a circus years ago, and sometimes we both got a bit rough.'

'Gee, they told me you were a tough guy,' said Joe in amazement. 'You're sure tough all right.'

Interest in the ceremony was so great that it was broadcast over a radio link-up for the benefit of people unable to get into the commission offices. General John Phelan, Chairman of the State Athletic Commission, introduced the boxers, but the crowd were so noisy that he kept having to shout for order. Amid the confusion, he referred to Ted Broadribb as 'Mr Drawbridge', and addressed Louis' trainer, Jack Blackburn, as 'Mr Washburn'.

Articles for the fight stipulated that Louis would receive 40 per cent of the gate, and Farr was guaranteed $60,000. Mike Jacobs and the two boxers were each required to deposit $5,000 with the commission as evidence of good faith.

After the reading of a clause allowing the boxers as much soft cloth and tape as required for binding their hands, the contracts were ready to be signed. Farr, however, hesitated when he noticed an item referring to an amount of $1,000. Believing it to be the sum he would be paid for the fight, he angrily refused to sign. It was explained that the item was contained in every New York State boxing contract to guarantee a boxer a minimum of $1,000 a year for his services. Tommy smiled and duly signed the contract, but the Americans had been warned he was not a man to be short-changed.

A further problem arose a few minutes later as Broadribb attempted to deposit their British boxer-manager contract with the Commission. Although it was valid until 1 March 1938, General Phelan insisted that it must be on the New York State Athletic Commission's own document, and run for one year from the date of issue. Farr and Broadribb were not happy, and for a while refused to sign a new document. The sweet talk of Mike Jacobs however saved the day, and a new contract valid for a year was eventually signed. It was later reported that before doing so Tommy and his manager struck a private agreement that he would still be released on 1 March 1938.

* * *

Tommy had been in the States a couple of weeks before he realised why he was finding the pressure so difficult to handle. Whenever there had been a crisis back home, he always had Job Churchill to turn to. So without further ado, he cabled Job telling him he needed him by his side. The old saddler made immediate arrangements to travel from Southampton aboard the *Queen Mary*.

Job's arrival at Long Branch cheered Tommy up no end. 'You'll do, Tom,' Job said, after looking his man over and checking his condition. 'I believe you are good enough already, but we have to keep you where you are for the next fortnight.'

Churchill had a strong personality, and his influence helped improve the strained relationship between Farr and Broadribb, and Broadribb eventually worked in the ring again. He was convinced that each session got better, but years later would remark that he believed that the ten or twelve days of argument, misunderstanding and stubbornness probably made all the difference to the eventual outcome of the fight.

Tommy's confidence in his own ability won him many friends

in America, one of whom was former champion Jack Dempsey. Mike Jacobs originally wanted the Welshman to go to Jack's restaurant and spar with him as a publicity stunt, but Tom Evans refused to allow it. He wasn't prepared to have their strict training schedule disrupted, so it was agreed that Dempsey would visit Long Branch while Tommy was training.

Tommy was thrilled when he saw Jack arrive, and through the corner of his eye saw him watching intently as he sparred with Feldman and Wagner. It encouraged him to put on a good display because Jack had been his boyhood idol, and he recalled a time when he wrote to him asking for an autograph.

'Hello, Tommy,' said Dempsey, smiling, as soon as the session was over. 'That was fine, just swell. Can I tell you something?'

'Sure,' replied Farr.

'Well, son,' continued Jack, 'you are going to have a big chance with Louis, but keep that left of yours just a little bit higher.' As he raised his massive fist to demonstrate what he meant, Tommy cut him short.

'Jack, I'm obliged for your advice,' he said, 'but I'm going to fight my own way according to the needs of the moment.'

'Some guy,' said Dempsey, turning to a group of watching reporters. 'I like him, he believes in himself. He's in fine condition, and I wish him well.'

As he was leaving the camp, Jack invited Tommy to dinner at his restaurant. It was an offer the Welshman couldn't refuse. He duly went along together with other members of his camp. The one person missing was Ted Broadribb, who was said to have stayed at Long Branch attending to business matters.

The previous day, it had been revealed that fight manager Al Weill had offered Ted $35,000 to buy Farr's contract. Some observers believed it confirmed that relations between Farr and his manager were still very strained. Others, however, were convinced it was a shrewd publicity stunt to help boost the sale of tickets, which had been very poor. Whatever the truth, all was forgotten within a few days, and reports were that Farr and Broadribb were being civil to one another.

In training, Tommy continued to impress, and there was no better judge of his ability than his principal sparring partner, Abe Feldman. 'Tommy is all deception,' said Abe. 'He is a lot better fighter in the ring than he appears from outside the ropes.'

As the training intensified, Tommy's hours of leisure were cut to a minimum. There were some breaks which helped him relax, and none better than an occasion when he was invited to dinner with Mike Jacobs and his wife at their massive country mansion at Fairhaven in the exclusive Runison Colony in New Jersey. Jacobs had become almost a dictator in boxing circles, and when he signed up a champion for a title defence, he invariably obtained options on the challenger's services for at least one fight. It protected his interests if things went wrong.

* * *

By the time he left Britain, Tommy had become accustomed to good press. Before beating Baer and Neusel, however, he had been subjected to all kinds of criticism, but he was convinced those days were behind him. It therefore came as a shock when the American reporters began writing him down so heavily. Part of the problem was that Tommy didn't understand their boisterous wisecracks and took certain remarks too personally. The remark which annoyed him most was, 'Farr stands about as much chance of beating Louis as Shirley Temple.' The writer was never identified.

When Job Churchill arrived at Long Branch, he didn't escape their jibes. He became known as 'Job Lots', and was described by one journalist as:

a quaint character who must have been plucked right out of Dickens. He sports a scraggy moustache, one lone tooth, a peg leg, and a multi-coloured flannel shirt which he'll turn inside out for special occasions like Sundays and holidays.

Tommy became so fed up with the reporters' sarcasm that he eventually complained bitterly to Mike Jacobs, and said he wanted them all banned from Long Branch. The promoter just laughed. 'So long as they keep you in the news. Take on a thicker skin,' he remarked.

* * *

Meanwhile, back in Slough, the newspaper headlines about Farr were suddenly unconnected with boxing. SLOUGH GIRL SUES TOMMY FARR one read. It related to a case which appeared in the list at Windsor County Court. When Tommy didn't answer to his name, the case proceeded in his absence.

Mary Margaret Crowley, a 16-year-old Slough schoolgirl, had sued Farr for damages following a road accident at Sussex Place.

She told the court that at 8.30 p.m. on 12 February 1937, she was cycling home when a car hit her back wheel. She was thrown to the ground and knocked unconscious. She sustained cuts to her head, arms, and legs, and was detained in Windsor Hospital for a week. Miss Crowley claimed that after being discharged, she still suffered pain and could not sleep at night. The accident prevented her from working for five weeks.

Miss Crowley's father told the court that Farr went to see him the day after the accident and apologised for what had occurred.

Finding in the girl's favour, the judge awarded her £35 costs.

* * *

In London, the Administrative Stewards of the British Boxing Board of Control caused something of a surprise when they issued a statement on 31 July declaring that they would not recognise the contest between Farr and Louis as being for the world title. They would only recognise it as a final eliminator, with the winner meeting Max Schmeling for the title.

In response to the board's announcement, the National Union of Boxers strongly disagreed with the decision. They made it clear that British boxers, in common with the rest of the world, would recognise the fight as being for the world title.

Farr and Tom Evans had joined the union back in May, and whilst he was in the States, the British champion went to great lengths to promote it. He discussed its purpose with Mike Jacobs, and suggested that a similar body be set up out there. Throughout his training at Long Branch, Farr wore trunks bearing the inscription *NUB*, and took great delight in explaining what the letters represented.

Although he refused to comment on the Board of Control statement in London, Tommy was furious when he learned that the same body had declared his Welsh heavyweight title vacant on the grounds of his failure to defend it. 'I'll meet any opponent the board likes to name,' he retorted angrily. 'I've never barred anyone. The reason I haven't defended my title is because no suitable challenger appeared.'

The board's action was somewhat insensitive and came at a time when Farr was under tremendous pressure. Not only was there ongoing bad feeling between him and Ted Broadribb, but also a series of incidents disrupted his training and concentration.

There was an occasion one hot afternoon in late July when Max Baer unexpectedly turned up at Long Branch driving a cherry-red car. Tommy was about to commence sparring with Abe Feldman, but Baer's arrival created such a disturbance that they couldn't begin. Accompanied by his brother, Max strode jauntily towards the ring to great applause from the many onlookers. Everyone forgot about Farr as Max stopped every few feet or so to sign autograph books and anything else that was thrust towards him. He kissed the cheeks of pretty ladies, shook hands with many admirers, and within seconds had literally taken the place over.

Stopping by the heavy bag, he threw a few punches, and followed up by doing some physical jerks. The act was typical of Baer, and the crowd loved it. When he reached the ring, Max vaulted over the ropes, then walked around blowing kisses to the audience.

By this time, Farr was seething with anger at the nerve of the man who had invaded his training camp, interrupted his sparring and taken all the attention. At first Max ignored Tommy, but when he eventually walked across and extended his hand, the furious Welshman turned his back.

'You've got a crust coming here after all those things you said about me,' growled Farr.

'Don't believe everything you read in the papers, boy,' Max told him.

The word 'boy' inflamed Farr even more, and he stepped forward menacingly as though he was about to strike Baer. Max then turned to the crowd and roared, 'He can't punch at all.'

For a moment it looked as though an ugly scene would develop, but Ted Broadribb and other members of Farr's camp jumped into the ring and kept them apart.

Once Baer was out of the ring, Tommy and Abe Feldman got down to work and ignored the American's play acting with the audience. Tommy was still angry, and once he finished sparring, called out, "All right, now where's that guy? Bring him up here and I'll take care of him." Broadribb eventually persuaded Tommy to calm down and shake hands with Max, and shortly afterwards the Baers followed the Welshman to his dressing room where they all posed for photographs.

Some people thought the whole incident was a well planned publicity stunt. If it was, then Farr and Baer played their parts to perfection because nobody else in the camp knew about it. In the years to come neither man would ever claim that it was staged.

The newspapers continued to get at Tommy, and he was particularly angry at reports of a romance between him and a 19-year-old-French cabaret singer. Speculation began when Miss

Jeannette Menet arrived in New York with her parents, Monsieur and Madame Dufoss, aboard the liner *Normandie*. It was known that during her journey across the Atlantic, the girl had spoken to Tommy on the ship's telephone on a number of occasions, and word got around that she was more than just an admirer. Speculation grew even greater when Miss Menet and her parents booked into an hotel at Long Branch, and later visited Farr's training camp.

News spread quickly, and the camp was soon invaded by a host of women journalists, fashion experts, beauty and society columnists, all anxious to ask questions about the relationship. Jeannette and Tommy had been chatting as he prepared for a sparring session, and she was at his side when the journalists began arriving. 'You won't hear any wedding bells here,' snapped Farr, 'only the boxing gong. Isn't that right, Jeanne?'

'The only plan Tommy has is to beat Louis,' said the girl, blushing.

Tommy insisted that there was no truth in the rumours of an affair. He and Miss Menet had first met when he was in Paris with Sol Strauss, and they became good friends. 'She is both charming and very talented,' remarked Farr. 'We get along very well together, and that's all there is to it.' He explained that the girl's parents were keen fight fans and had broken their journey to Hollywood in order to see him box Louis. He claimed that they had booked into a Long Branch hotel to avoid the extreme heat of New York, and not, as the press were claiming, to enable the singer to be close to him. 'Busybodies have mistaken a friendship for something else,' he continued angrily. 'Emphatically the only women in my life I left behind in England. They are my sisters.'

More pressure was heaped upon Farr, when with just six days to go before meeting Louis, he sustained a cut on his right cheek in training. The bleeding was quickly stemmed, and Tommy resorted to skipping and bag punching, but when the vibration caused the wound to re-open, training was suspended for the day.

Although the cut was well away from the eye and not particularly dangerous, a cloud of gloom settled over the camp. As a matter of course the New York State Athletic Commission were informed. The following day, the commission physician, Dr William Walker, visited Long Branch and examined Tommy's injury in the presence of the Acting Chairman, Bill Brown. 'Why, it's only a scratch,' he declared. 'It will be all right in twenty-four hours, and should be completely healed by the time Farr meets Louis.'

Farr treated the whole affair with indifference. 'I knew it was all right all the time,' he said, shrugging his shoulders.

There was one spot of light relief within the camp when a group of Welsh miners unexpectedly arrived. Some had worked with Tommy at the Cambrian pit, and they presented him with a lump of genuine Rhondda coal as a good luck souvenir. Countless other good luck messages poured into the camp.

* * *

As the day of the fight drew nearer, Tommy became more relaxed. His confidence was now showing in everything he said and did, and there were signs that people were beginning to take notice of him. There was suddenly a softening of opinion by the American press, and another indication of the sudden feeling for Farr's chances was reflected in the betting odds. The best were now 4–1, despite all the early talk of Louis being a 7–1 on favourite.

When Tommy sent his final message to the *South Wales Echo*, he said, I feel confident I shall beat Louis with greater ease than I beat Max Baer ... I aim to hit Louis harder than he's ever been hit before ... with so much at stake, how can I help not putting my best foot forward?'

It was raining when Tommy did his final workout. He wore a woollen jersey to protect himself against the unseasonable weather, and he trained under cover for the first time.

On the morning of the fight everyone except Farr was awake early, and on edge. Tommy had to be woken by Tom Evans shaking him vigorously at around 9.30 a.m. Then after a bath and quick breakfast, he was driven to New York for the weigh-in. Huge crowds lined the streets as he approached the State Athletic Commission Offices in Worth Street, and Tommy was thrilled at the reception he received as his car moved slowly through the streets, escorted by a posse of police cars with their sirens blaring.

Louis arrived flanked by three large minders, trainer Jack Blackburn, and managers Julian Black and John Roxborough. They were escorted by two state troopers carrying heavy revolvers on their hips.

Inside the commission offices there was absolute chaos as cameramen, reporters, officials, boxers, managers and plain onlookers jostled for positions. Tommy had arrived just ahead of Louis, and when they came face to face, he smiled and said, 'Hello, Joe, how are you?'

'Good', was the champion's tense reply.

Farr was first onto the scales and his weight was called as being

174

207 pounds (14 stone 11). Louis followed and weighed in at 198 pounds (14 stone 2), giving the British champion an advantage of 9 pounds.

The boxers were then given a stern lecture by General Phelan about butting and fouling. Staring at Farr for most of the time, Phelan warned that if either man butted or used any foul tactics, he would be disqualified and his purse withheld. Farr was extremely angry at being spoken to in this way. 'I've never lost a fight for butting,' he snapped. 'I'm a fair man, both in the ring and out of it. I won't butt Louis, and they needn't be looking for it.'

Ted Broadribb was amazed by the lecture because he had been told the fight would be under the no-foul rule. The only logical reason had to be that the people who mattered were concerned that Farr's infighting skills could upset the champion. It was another topic about which Broadribb would comment strongly in years to come because he was convinced that the rule was deliberately changed to benefit Louis.

As Phelan and Brown were about to leave the commission offices, Mike Jacobs rushed in and engaged them in a hurried conversation. Then to everyone's amazement, he announced that due to overnight rain, the fight would be postponed until the following Monday, (30 August). People were astounded, because the rain had stopped and the indications were that the weather would be fine and settled. There were some nine hours to go before the boxers were due in the ring, and to many people it seemed a feeble excuse to cause the first ever postponement of a world heavyweight title bout.

Louis just shrugged his shoulders when he heard the announce-ment, and started putting on his clothes. Farr looked puzzled, but when asked for his reaction said, 'I was keyed up for the fight but it doesn't make any difference. I would rather be sure of having a good crowd. I have had too many fights to worry about a little thing like this.'

The postponement would in fact be to the Welshman's advantage, so there were no complaints from either him or his manager. Although he was already in peak condition, he was a few pounds over what Broadribb considered to be his best fighting weight. The delay would therefore give them time to get it right, and give the cut on Tommy's cheek extra time in which to heal.

It soon became clear that the real reason for the postponement was nothing to do with the weather. Despite tremendous publicity, there had been indications some ten days earlier that the contest threatened to be a financial flop. The sale of tickets had been

175

disappointing, and it was thought doubtful whether the Yankee Stadium would be more than half full on fight night.

Jacobs was in a quandary because Louis was on 40 per cent of an anticipated gate of $250,000, whilst Farr was guaranteed $60,000. If ticket sales didn't reach a certain figure, an unprecedented situation could arise whereby the Welshman would earn more than the champion.

Farr's chef, Ken Barker, provided some light relief. He had been granted facilities at one of New York's biggest hotels to prepare a special meal of roast chicken with all the trimmings for Tommy to sit down to after the weigh-in. When the news came that the fight was off, everyone's spirits were suddenly deflated, and without saying a word, Barker pulled off his white chef's hat, white coat and apron, grabbed his other hat, and made for the door.

'Where are you going?' cried one of the staff.

'I'm going back to Long Branch with Tommy,' replied Barker.

'But what shall we do with this beautiful meal?' he was asked.

'Eat it,' replied the chef as he shot out through the kitchen door, 'and wish Tommy luck next Monday.'

As soon as he arrived back at Long Branch, Tommy went to work with a skipping rope. He was determined that by the new date he would be in even better shape. 'The postponement is a gift from above,' he remarked. 'It will bring to the ring a Tommy Farr that Louis can't whip nohow.'

During training over the next three days, Tommy wore thick woollen under clothes and went through a strenuous programme which included six miles of roadwork, four rounds of sparring and five rounds of skipping and bag punching. He was in a very mean mood, but during the first session of sparring suffered the humiliation of going to the floor whilst working with Abe Feldman.

As soon as the sparring was over, Farr was confronted in his dressing room by a number of reporters. 'I slipped to the floor, and now I suppose you fellows will say I was flat on my back,' he growled. 'By this time tomorrow, mark my words, you will be saying I was down for a count of nine. If ever I get into the movies, I will make sure I get an American newspaper man as my press agent. They have the most vivid imaginations.'

Although some people were prepared to dismiss the incident as an accident, it duly received the coverage Tommy expected. 'Feldman floored Farr with a clean right to the chin,' claimed the *New York Daily News*. Tommy was furious at another story, which claimed that Feldman either pushed or deliberately tripped him.

He was in a foul mood when he commenced training the

A left lead from Farr is blocked by Jim Braddock during their fight in New York on 21 January 1938

Farr with his fiancee Eileen Wenzell, meets British actor Bruce Lester at Hollywood Studios on 2 April 1938

Farr and Max Baer weigh-in for their fight in New York on 11 March 1938

Farr and Jim Braddock (right) congratulate Joe Louis after his first round knockout victory over Max Schmeling in June 1938

Tommy carves a goose for dinner at the home of Job Churchill at Penygraig on 17 March 1939 while Mrs Churchill looks on

Tommy shakes hands with Arthur Bateman, captain of Brentford Football Club at Griffin Park in 1938 before the 'Bs' match with Manchester United

Farr (right) on the attack against Burman at Harringay on 13 April 1939

Tommy lunches with Joe Louis in London on 9 March 1948. Joe was appearing at the Health and Holiday Exhibition at Earls Court and wanted to meet Tommy socially

With wife Monty at the ringside at Earls Court in November 1950 when Bruce Woodcock lost his British heavyweight title to Jack Gardner

Training at the Crown and Anchor, Brighton, in September 1950 for his first comeback fight

Farr with Dave Edgar (right), Bill Daly (with glass), and American heavyweight Pat Comisky at the Cafe Royal in 1950

Mobbed by autograph hunters at Cardiff Central Station as he arrives in Wales for the fight with Jan Klein, 27 September 1950

Farr shakes hands with Klein at the weigh-in for their fight at Pontypridd on 27 September 1950. Promoter Albert Davies (centre) looks on

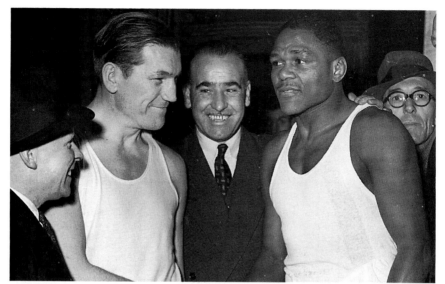

Tommy meets Lloyd Marshall (USA) before their fight at Carmarthen on 4 December 1950. Albert Davies (centre) and Snowy Buckingham (far left) look on

Farr on the attack against Gerry McDermott at Harringay on 24 February 1951 which Farr won on points

following day and took it out on his three sparring partners. As though he was getting the anger out of his system, he knocked them all over the ring, driving in heavy, vicious punches. Against Abe Feldman, he was particularly severe, and Job Churchill was heard to shout, 'Easy, lad. Abe ain't Louis.'

During the evening of 29 August, Farr and his handlers travelled from Long Branch to New York by train, and stayed at an hotel close to the Yankee Stadium. The next morning Tommy got up at 8 a.m. and went for a brisk walk in Central Park before returning to his hotel for breakfast. He spent the morning relaxing until it was time to set off for the weigh-in ceremony, which the New York State Athletic Commission had insisted be conducted all over again.

The Welshman's weight was given as 204½ pounds (14 stone 8½) which Ted Broadribb believed was very close to his best fighting weight, and would make him faster and sharper.

Wearing dark glasses and perspiring freely, Louis looked tense and stern as he stepped onto the scales. He weighed 197 pounds, (14 stone 1), revealing that, like Farr, he had shed weight since the previous Thursday.

Farr was oozing confidence as he faced the reporters. When he was asked how he felt about fighting away from home for the first time, the Welshman replied, 'I honestly think I can beat Louis. I have not come all the way from Wales to pick up the loser's end. I am here to win the world championship, and be the first Welshman to do it.'

The British party then adjourned to the Plaza Hotel. After a good meal, Tommy had a few hours' sleep and generally relaxed until it was time to set off for the arena.

As was their custom before a big fight, Tommy and Job Churchill had gambled heavily. They had laid out about £1,500 in bets at various odds on the outcome of the fight, but just after the weigh-in they decided to wager another £200 that Louis wouldn't stop Tommy.

The atmosphere in the British camp was one of confidence, and the general opinion was that the only real danger of Louis scoring a chance knockout was in the early rounds. Job Churchill was in no doubt about the outcome. 'I have never seen Tommy fitter,' he remarked. 'I do not see how he can lose.' And Tom Evans concluded, 'Farr is in the prefect frame of mind to beat Louis.'

The rugged Welshman had gone to America confident of victory, and despite all the pressures that were heaped upon him, that confidence remained undaunted. With the hard training over, he was in a mean mood and ready for the task ahead.

14

FIGHT OF A LIFETIME

Despite all the adverse comment about Farr's capabilities, there were people in the States who believed that Mike Jacobs was pushing Louis into fighting again too soon after winning the title. The fact was, Mike wasn't doing the pushing, but Joe's managers Julian Black and John Roxborough. Both were shrewd businessmen who were convinced that as Joe was the first black man to hold the title since Jack Johnson lost it 22 years earlier, he had to prove himself that much more.

Louis set up his training camp at Pompton Lakes under the watchful eye of Jack 'Chappie' Blackburn, an ex-pro with experience from more than a hundred fights. He had lost only three, and fought men such as Sam Langford (five times), Joe Gans, and Philadelphia Jack O'Brien. Blackburn was recognised as one of America's greatest light and welterweights until he was sent to prison in 1909 for manslaughter.

In January that year he got involved in an argument during which he pulled out a gun and shot three people, one of whom died. Blackburn was subsequently sentenced to 15 years' imprisonment. He was a model prisoner, and his term was eventually reduced to one of four years and eight months. He was paroled on account of his good behaviour in 1913. On release from prison, he took up a position as director of physical culture, but in 1920 at the age of 37, couldn't resist the temptation to return to the ring. Jack still had plenty of skills, and continued boxing until 1923, when he finally conceded that he was too old. He turned his hand to training, and amongst his successes were Sammy Mandell, who won the world lightweight title, and Charles 'Bud' Taylor, who became bantamweight champion.

Blackburn first became involved with Louis during the summer

178

of 1934. He was at his gym in Chicago one day when Julian Black and John Roxborough walked in and asked him to train Louis who they regarded as a future champion. Jack agreed, and he and Joe stayed together until Jack died in 1941.

Joe once recalled, 'Chappie would make me work in the gym hour after hour, and he was rough on me. He just let me make the same mistake twice, and if I did he would scream, "Now boy, that ain't the way, and you know it. You gonna be a bum fighter or a champ boy?"'

The Louis camp knew very little about Farr other than he was the same age as Joe, had worked in the pits since he was a boy, and had a reputation of being extremely tough. In preparation for the fight, Blackburn took no chances, hiring sparring partners to cover every possible type of style.

Louis was the grandson of a slave, and had been raised with 12 other children in a sharecroppers' cabin in Alabama. At the age of 20, he became Golden Gloves heavyweight champion, and as a professional had been developed into a perfect fighting machine, thanks mainly to the skill of Jack Blackburn. When he began training to meet Farr, he was already in good condition following his preparations to meet Braddock. Everything therefore came easy to him.

* * *

Unlike in the United States, interest in the fight in Britain was tremendous, and Tonypandy not surprisingly was Farr crazy. On every street corner, amongst every group of unemployed at the Labour Exchange, and on waste ground where the whippets ran, the name of Tommy Farr could be heard loud and clear. People talked about what he ate and drank, what he wore, and what he did as a boy. It was as though the town was Tommy's own special property.

In the main street, a large photograph of him was displayed in a shop window. It gave heart to countless mothers of small boys because they knew that Tommy had also tasted the depth and bitterness of poverty in this grim valley of the coal mines. The women adored Tommy. 'He never ate two square meals in a day and now look at him,' was a frequent remark. They all knew his story. He had set an example to their own grubby little urchins who spent hours rolling on the pavements of the narrow streets black with coal dust, with just bread and dripping in their bellies.

People throughout Britain respected Tommy for the way he

had beaten Baer and Neusel to become a genuine heavyweight title contender. He had captured the imagination of the public and would keep thousands from their beds in the middle of the night. As the hours ticked away before he faced his supreme test, the folks of Tonypandy prayed for him. They remembered his kindness to children and hospitals, and he was their hero.

To satisfy the thirst of the British fight fans, the BBC made arrangements for a commentary of the fight to be relayed from the States by means of a GPO radio-telephone system. Programme announcer David Lloyd-James together with two engineers reported for duty at 2.30 a.m. In the *News Chronicle*, Fred Dartnell reported that the BBC were treating the fight like a national emergency because never before had they started up a transmitter at such an early hour.

The fight was the most exciting event in the lives of many folk living in the Rhondda, and irrespective of the outcome they intended making it a night to remember. A huge bonfire was erected on the mountain side at Clydach Vale; when lit it would be seen 30 miles away. Tommy's brother Richard had supervised its erection, and was to light it just before the fight began.

Many people were determined not to go to bed and made elaborate arrangements to pass away the hours whilst awaiting the broadcast. Bands were engaged to play at dances at various centres in the town from midnight onwards. Many parties were planned, and those people with wireless sets invited neighbours and friends to join them. Food and drink was stocked up to cover the long wait until the commentary began at about 3 a.m. Singing was a traditional part of Welsh life and would occupy many hours as well.

Local courts received numerous applications for licensing extensions. At Caerphilly Magistrates' Court an application was granted to keep Abertirdwr Working Men's Hall open from midnight until 4 a.m. to enable members of the public to listen to the fight.

There had been tremendous disappointment when news of the postponement was received, but life soon reverted to normal and arrangements put into place for the new date.

Special consideration was given to the miners on night shift at the Cambrian Pit, where Tommy had worked as a boy, and 100 men were permitted to work from 7 p.m. to 2 a.m. so that they could hear the radio commentary – about a third of the night shift – and names were drawn from a hat.

Many of these men had grown up with Tommy and worked

with him when he was a collier boy. They had a special interest in his progress, and those left below were not forgotten. Bulletins of the fight were to be phoned down the pit shafts and updates chalked on the sides of wagons which travelled to the coal face.

It was not just the miners of Tonypandy who received special treatment. The Marconiphone Company joined forces with the *News of the World* to ensure that pit men in many parts of Wales heard the commentary on the company's latest all-wave sets at miners' welfare halls.

From early evening on 30 August 1937, Tonypandy and the surrounding areas went into the grip of fight fever. There was a genuine belief that not a man, woman, or child went to bed there that night. The air rang with songs and excited chatter, and by 3 a.m. some 500 miners and their wives crowded inside the Assembly Hall at Clydach Vale, where the commentary was to be relayed over huge wireless speakers. A further 5,000 gathered outside in the streets where loud speakers had been installed. At the Judges Hall at Trealaw, the scene of many of Tommy's early fights, more than 1,500 crowded in. It seemed as though everyone in the valley wanted to hear the broadcast.

* * *

Despite the intense pressure he had been put under, Farr remained calm during the final hours leading up to the fight. He arrived at the Yankee Stadium at 8 p.m. local time, and was shown to his dressing room. There, Ted Broadribb carefully applied an extra coating of Carpenters Wax to Tommy's injured cheek. It had proved useful in training and the injury responded well to it.

By the time the fight was due, the ringside was crowded with celebrities, including James Roosevelt Junior, Douglas Fairbanks Senior, Al Jolson, George Raft, Gar Wood, holder of the world speedboat record, Mayor La Guardia of New York, Noel Curtis Bennett and the Marquess of Queensberry.

Tommy was called to the ringside some 20 minutes before the fight was due to commence, and made to sit there whilst a four-round preliminary bout took place. The incident was widely reported in the British press because it was thought that it had been a ploy by the Americans to upset the British champion. Many people back home were convinced that is exactly why it was done, but Ted Broadribb later went to lengths to explain that Louis had also been called out early and made to wait.

Whether it was intended to unnerve Tommy or not doesn't

really matter, because he remained perfectly calm as he sat in a ringside seat between Job Churchill and Tom Evans beneath the clear New York sky.

At last they were called up into the ring, and Tommy ducked through the ropes first. Ted Broadribb, Tom Evans and Babe Culnan went into his corner with him. At Tommy's insistence Job Churchill was also in close attendance; he remained outside the ring, but close to the corner.

Louis entered the ring shortly afterwards, and as they stood there beneath the sweltering arc lights, the largest ever assortment of champions past and present, as well as other well-known fight personalities, were introduced by ring announcer Harry Balough to the crowd of 32,000.

Thunderous cheers went up as each was introduced and took his bow, and it was indeed a memorable sight. There was the great Jack Johnson, the last black man to hold the world heavyweight title, and he appeared to confirm rumours that he and Louis didn't get on when he pushed past the champion's corner without as much as a handshake.

Max Schmeling was introduced, and received a good reception although it was sprinkled with a few boos and hisses. There were former heavyweight champions Gene Tunney, Jack Sharkey, Max Baer and Jimmy Braddock, all of whom were well received by the crowd, and idols from the lower weights as well.

During the introductions, Farr remained calmly in his corner with a grim but determined look on his face. Louis prowled about as the nerves jangled and the butterflies in the stomach worked overtime. At last it was their turn to be introduced, and both received good ovations.

Then referee Arthur Donovan called them to the centre of the ring and gave his final instructions. Then Broadribb asked, 'What corner does Farr go to if he knocks Louis down?' It was the British champion's first contest in America, so Ted insisted that the referee explained the position. 'OK,' said the surprised Donovan with a shrug of his shoulders, whilst a surprised-looking Joe Louis stood by.

They returned to their corners, and as the ring was cleared and the lights dimmed, Farr turned to Job Churchill. 'It's now or never,' he remarked grimly. The press had been picking the round that the champion would finish the job, but Tommy had other ideas. Stern-faced, with chin tucked behind his left shoulder, he strode from his corner and took the fight to Louis.

With all the confidence in the world, he attacked the champion as though he was a sparring partner. He used his left beautifully, and punched away with both hands when the openings allowed him to. He moved quickly and confidently around the ring, and what punches Louis did land had no effect on him. Tommy looked pleased with himself as he sat down at the end of the opening session, which he appeared to have won clearly. Turning to Churchill he said, 'Job, I can box better than Louis, and I'll take him places he's not been before.'

Louis attacked more in the second, and a sharp uppercut reopened the cut on Farr's right cheek. Although it was well away from the eye, the sight of blood spurred Louis on. Although he had another good round, the Welshman knew the cut had given the champion a psychological advantage.

The injury soon reopened in the third, and although Tommy was still proving to be an elusive target, Joe was finding the range. His left jabs were hitting the target, and further cuts opened up under both the Welshman's eyes. It was not a good round for Tommy, who also put a finger on his right hand out of joint, and by the end of the round, blood was streaming down both sides of his face.

The Welshman was more cautious in the fourth, but showed his immense skill as Louis grew in confidence. Several heavy rights caught Tommy, but on landing one, Joe damaged his right hand.

The fifth opened with Farr again appearing somewhat cautious, but when Louis caught him with a two-fisted attack, he slammed back immediately. Another right caught Tommy flush in the face, sending him reeling into a corner. To the amazement of the crowd, he not only stayed on his feet, but came back off the ropes to catch Joe with two sharp lefts followed by a heavy right. It was an action-packed round, and at the end there was tremendous cheering, especially for the courage shown by the British champion, whose eyes were again in urgent need of repair.

Showing plenty of confidence, Farr was off his stool at the start of the sixth, launching an attack before Louis could get into his stride. A thumping left bounced off the champion's temple, and another only just missed. Two sharp left hooks followed, the second of which had Joe reeling. Louis was bemused by the Welshman's speed as he tried to counter, and, urged on by the crowd, Tommy drove the champion across the ring. When Joe did hit back, Farr stood his ground, and for a full half-minute they lashed out at each other in an old-fashioned free-for-all which had the crowd roaring.

The action continued right up to the bell, with both men

landing heavy shots. Overall, Farr was the more aggressive, and he returned to his corner smiling because he knew he had won the round in style. The Louis corner were worried, and the champion received a tongue lashing during the interval, particularly from Jack Blackburn, who recognised that Farr was a tough proposition.

Joe looked deadly serious as the seventh round commenced, and pumped a series of left jabs into Farr's face, bringing blood streaming from the cuts. Three murderous left hooks had the Welshman spinning, and a wicked right brought more blood dripping onto his chest. The champion's right hand, however, was giving him pain, and he would later admit that this punch probably hurt him more than Farr. The Welshman was as tough and game as they come, and spitting blood from his mouth and thumbing it from his eyes, he waded forward trying to land his own shots.

Although Louis was now fighting like a true champion, none of his previous opponents, including Baer, Carnera, Braddock, Sharkey, Uzcudun and Levinsky, had been able to withstand the punishment he was dishing out to Farr. Towards the end of the round, Joe landed with several vicious left hooks which had Tommy hanging on. Bleeding badly from the cuts around his eyes, he was driven into his own corner by more big hooks which had him dizzy. As he tried to duck out of trouble, he went the wrong way into a pile-driving right followed by a big left hook. His knees went, but instead of going down, he clutched the ropes for support. As Louis stood back expecting Tommy to fall, so the bell ended the worst round of the fight for the Welshman, but he returned to his corner amid thunderous cheers.

There was great concern in the British corner as the eyes were patched up, whilst on the opposite side of the ring the champion's handlers were urging him to go out and finish it. Ringsiders were convinced that Farr couldn't recover from the battering of the previous round, but to their amazement he was off his stool and taking the fight to Louis as the eighth round began. He looked surprisingly fresh and showed no obvious signs of distress.

The Welshman shook off Joe's opening attack by walking straight through a hail of blows. Before Louis could recover from the astonishment of his resistance, he was nailed by several right hooks to the head, which had the crowd roaring. Using all his skill and speed, Tommy took the fight to the champion, but as Louis pecked away with his own jabs, the facial injuries started to bleed again. The tough Welshman, however, was unperturbed, and just smiled through the red mask covering his face. By forcing the pace and throwing a steady rate of punches, he stole the initiative, and as the round wore on Louis realised that his chance of a knockout had gone.

Just before the bell, with blood streaming down both cheeks as well as from his nose, Farr launched a sensational attack. The crowd were frantic with excitement as the gallant British champion drove tremendous punches into the champion's body. It was a great round for Farr, and he won it convincingly.

Tommy came out for the ninth again looking fresh, and forced Louis to the ropes with shots from both hands. Throughout the round, however, he again bled profusely from the left eye, and it was becoming increasingly difficult for him to see because both eyes were beginning to close.

Louis appeared to be running out of ideas, and a left hook from Farr shook him up and caused a lump to come up above his left eye. The crowd were right behind the Welshman as he drove Joe across the ring and into the ropes with superb punching. Then, using all his strength, Tommy punched away with both hands. A right hook jolted Joe's head back as they traded shots at close quarters. Then as they broke away, Louis was seen to be cut above the right eye, but the bell sounded before further damage could be inflicted.

At this stage many spectators believed that Joe might have shot his bolt and be in real danger of losing his title. He was clearly demoralised because Farr had taken his best shots and survived the onslaught of the middle rounds. Louis had a worried look about him at the start of round ten because he was not used to being in this position. Normally if he hit opponents as hard as he had hit Farr, they were finished. He knew that if he was to win this fight, it would now be a real test of his character, requiring patience as well as pressure.

Although Tommy landed a good right to the stomach, he was soon at a disadvantage because his corner had failed to stem the bleeding from the cuts around his eyes. As Louis kept pecking away, so the injuries worsened, and in modern times the contest would most probably have been stopped by this stage.

Farr didn't know the meaning of the word 'quit', and somehow kept going. As the round drew to a close, Louis caught him with a left hook to the jaw which shook him badly and had him very unsteady on his feet. It was the champion's best punch for three rounds, and he followed up with a heavy combination which made the British champion hang on grimly, and he was in serious trouble as the bell ended a strong round for the champion.

Once again Farr showed his amazing powers of recovery as he rushed from his corner at the start of round 11 and peppered Louis with left jabs. There were more good exchanges in this round, and the Welshman's ringcraft was again superb. He proved an elusive target, and his courage and gameness earned him a share of the round.

The twelfth was a quieter round, although a tremendous left hook had Tommy reeling backwards. Yet again he recovered quickly and came back with shots of his own, but his battered, bleeding face made him look in a far worse state than he was. Although Louis now looked in command, he was not having things all his own way, and he too was bleeding quite heavily from his injured eye.

Round 13 lived up to its reputation of being unlucky for some, as Farr was on the end of a terrible assault from the world champion. He at last found the range, and his accurate left hand didn't miss very often. Farr was literally eating punches, and his face, a raw red mass, continued to bleed heavily.

As Louis took complete control in this round, so every heart in the crowd went out to the gallant Welshman. He stood there taking vicious punches which would have floored and finished many an opponent. His task was being made harder by the fact that the swellings around his eyes were making it increasingly difficult to see the punches coming. One tremendous uppercut to the jaw visibly shook him from head to toe, and years later he would comment that it was the hardest punch he ever took in his entire career.

'If I had been made of rubber, I would have starved to death bouncing,' he remarked. 'Everything was in that right hand short of murder. It sent red-hot needles into my throat and I feared I would suffocate.'

A few seconds after landing that punch, Louis caught Tommy with another, which crashed against his forehead. The effect was clear for all to see, and it appeared that the Welshman must surely fall to the canvas. Somehow he remained upright and hung on, and later told reporters, 'I feared my spine was broken.'

It was a miracle that Tommy survived the thirteenth round, but he did, although even after the minute's interval, he still looked ready to be taken.

Louis came out fast at the start of the fourteenth, determined to continue where he had left off. His left jabs soon brought blood flowing from Farr's injuries, and a good right had the Welshman reeling backwards. Louis drove him around the ring and forced him into a corner, but again Tommy's superb ringcraft took him away from serious trouble.

The Welshman threw the occasional desperate right swings, and it was noticeable that Louis was somewhat apprehensive of them. There had been occasions throughout the contest when he backed away from such shots as though afraid to take one on the chin. He was described by some reporters as being 'gun-shy', because the memories of Max Schmeling still lingered in his mind. Towards the end of the round, Farr became the aggressor again, but didn't do enough scoring to take the round.

As they came up for the fifteenth and final round, the crowd were well and truly behind Tommy. He had stood up to the champion's murderous punching, and made most of the critics eat their words. Now with just three minutes left, he came off his stool as hostile as ever, and was in the centre of the ring all of ten seconds before the bell. To show that he was still full of fight, he danced around. He even had a smile on his face, and his legs seemed as strong as when he had started almost an hour earlier.

Yelled on by the crowd, the Welshman produced a grandstand finish by going out fighting just as he had come in. He was so full of fight that he appeared reckless as he went after the champion. He believed that he had taken everything Joe had to offer, and there was no way he could be stopped now. Refusing to give an inch, Tommy stood with the champion, trading punch for punch, swing for swing, in what seemed like an endless stream of leather. It was all Farr now, and despite the blood that seeped from his wounds, he kept moving forward and forced the exchanges.

Ignoring the jabs that were coming from Louis, he threw caution to the wind as he made a great do-or-die effort to snatch victory. A long left grazed the champion's chin, and then a fast right caught him on the side of the jaw. Louis hit back savagely with shots of his own but they couldn't halt Farr as he slammed in two more rights to the head which had the champion reeling backwards.

The crowd were going wild with excitement as Tommy stormed forward with both arms swinging and drove Louis to the ropes, where they engaged in a free-swinging rally. It was a fantastic last round and a fitting climax to any championship contest. The Welshman showed his remarkable strength and stamina, and frequently broke through the champion's defence and shook his

187

confidence.

When the final bell sounded, it was Louis who looked relieved. Both were bleeding quite badly, but as they touched gloves at the end, there was plenty of mutual respect. Despite his cuts and bruises, a broad grin stretched across Farr's face as though he had enjoyed every minute of the fight. The two fighters then returned to their corners to wait, for what would seem like an eternity, before the verdict was announced.

Around the ringside, there was great excitement and speculation, with many spectators and pressmen believing that Farr would be declared the winner. Those thoughts were fuelled when referee Arthur Donovan suddenly walked across to the Welshman and shook him firmly by the hand. Then there was a sudden hush as the master of ceremonies collected the score cards of the referee and two judges, and people settled down awaiting the verdict.

Louis was duly declared the winner on all three cards, but the announcement was partly drowned by a mixture of booing and cheering. General opinion was that the decision was fair and just, and although at first he looked shocked, Farr accepted defeat gracefully. He went straight across to Joe's corner to offer his congratulations, and it was a very relieved champion who greeted him. He knew that he had beaten a man with far more courage than anyone he had met before.

There was a great deal of confusion afterwards surrounding the referee congratulating Farr. But that was exactly what he did: congratulate him on a wonderful performance, not a winning one. Donovan's scoring of the fight also brought about a great deal of comment because incredibly he made Louis the winner by thirteen rounds to one, with one even. The two judges were more realistic, with William McParland scoring it 9–6 in favour of Louis, and Charles Lynch 8–5 to the champion, with two even.

Donovan was the top American referee of his time, having taken control of a dozen world title fights prior to this one. He had refereed all Joe's contests in New York, and this was to be the first of 12 of his title fights in which he would officiate. Nobody who knew Donovan would seriously challenge his integrity, but for him to have given Farr just one round was beyond comprehension, and was a real smack in the face for New York's claim of efficiency in the scoring of fights. Even Louis disagreed with Donovan's account, and afterwards there were many calls from American fight fans demanding that more opportunity be given to other top referees.

After the fight, Farr and Ted Broadribb were interviewed in the ring by radio commentators and asked for their comments on the verdict. 'The people here tonight have given us a wonderful hand,' said Broadribb. 'Farr fought a wonderful battle, but Louis won.' Tommy made no comment about the decision, and merely said that he had done his best. In the years to come, he would never claim to have won.

In recognition of his victory, Louis was presented with a magnificent gold challenge belt donated by the National Sporting Club in London. The presentation was made by the club manager, John Harding, who, together with some 30 other members, including the Marquess of Queensberry and Sir Noel Curtis Bennett, had travelled to New York aboard the *Queen Mary* at the beginning of August.

After Louis had been declared the winner, many people fought and struggled to get to the ringside to mob him. The majority were hysterical black supporters of the champion, carried away by the excitement of his victory. The renowned New York riot squad went into action with truncheons drawn.

Before the fight there had been a fear of race riots because Louis was defending his title for the first time against a white man. As a precaution at least one thousand policemen had been on duty in and around the Yankee Stadium. Elsewhere, in areas including Harlem, patrols were trebled in case trouble flared up.

Black boxers had proved to be very popular in Britain, and in contests with white men there had been no serious consequences. In America, however, such fights had only served to enflame passionate hatred between people of opposite colour. The fight between Jack Johnson and Jim Jeffries at Reno in 1910 was a classic example.

As soon as order had been restored in the stadium, the boxers left the ring, and it was Farr who got the cheers. He was a winner with everyone in the arena except the officials, and the ovation he received as he made his way back to his dressing room was absolutely tremendous. For 15 pulsating rounds he had made a mockery of the familiar 'horizontal British heavy-weights', and his country could be justly proud of him. He had been the first British heavyweight champion to fight for the world title for nearly 30 years, and now he left the ring with his head held high.

Tommy had fought a courageous battle when his back was against the wall. Having faced adverse newspaper comment for six weeks, he had had the determination and guts to put that mental handicap out of his mind. Once he was in the ring, he went for

Louis from the opening bell, and by the end of the fight had captured the hearts of the American people. He may have lost the fight but his courage had made America his for the asking.

* * *

Back home, the people of South Wales were solidly behind Tommy. There was tremendous excitement and cheering as the voice of Canadian commentator Bob Bowman shouted across the air waves, 'Tommy Farr is putting up a wonderful show.' When they heard how well Tommy had begun the third round, one or two wags shouted, 'Stop the fight.' It was that sort of night, with tremendous happiness and good humour. There were moments of anxiety, too, especially when the commentators described Farr's facial injuries and the pressure Louis was applying.

The fight sounded extremely close, and there was great disappointment when the decision was announced. It was received with an outburst of boos and hisses because many people were convinced Tommy had been robbed. Their greatest thrill was when they heard Tommy's voice on the radio sending good wishes to everyone at home. He said he had done his best but his eyes had let him down. 'If Louis says I'm a tough guy,' said Farr, 'that's because I'm a Welshman.'

Although he had lost, Tommy had made the people of Tonypandy extremely happy, and crowds stood in the streets singing *Land of My Fathers* long after the fight was over. At high points along the mountain range, bonfires flared. Many were still glowing hours later.

The feelings of the South Wales people were conveyed to Tommy by Mr G.J. Williams, Chairman of the Rhondda Council, in a cablegram immediately after the fight: 'Heartiest congratulations on your courageous and magnificent fight. We are proud of you and confident that you will yet gain the world title.'

Tommy later admitted that he was very moved when he received it.

The people of Slough were also extremely proud of Tommy, especially the thousands of Welsh folk living in the Manor Park district known as 'New South Wales'. There was scarcely a house that didn't contain groups in their night clothes, huddled around wireless sets listening to the broadcast. As in Tonypandy, many families held parties which went on all night.

Apart from the Rhondda, there was nowhere in Britain where news of the fight was more anxiously awaited. At The Dolphin

Hotel, which had once been Tommy's home for some 18 months, licensee George Bennett organised an invitation dance specially for the occasion. It was attended by about 200 guests, and four loud speakers relayed the commentary to the hotel ballroom.

Tommy's elder brother John and his wife were among the guests and listened intently to every word. They showed no emotion until the final round, when it sounded as though the Welshman was going all out for victory. The cheering was deafening when the final bell sounded because most people believed he would be declared the winner. Others were just proud that he had fought so courageously and survived the distance.

During his stay at The Dolphin, Tommy had made many friends and become an extremely popular figure in Slough. Several people wept unashamedly when they heard his voice on the radio assuring them he had done his best.

In a little house not far away in Salisbury Avenue, Tommy's younger brother Doug, sister Mrs Margaret Short and other relatives and friends listened to the fight on a brand-new radio set presented to them by McMichael Radio Limited, a local company in Slough. In fact, every member of Tommy's family huddled around a wireless at one address or another. His sisters Phyllis and Sally and nephew Aneurin were with their aunt Clarrie and a group of friends at a flat in Piccadilly.

When the decision was announced, everyone was stunned and disappointed because they were convinced Tommy had won. Suddenly there were tears of joy as they heard Tommy's voice on the radio speaking particularly to his family and friends in Tonypandy. Once the disappointment had passed, everyone began cheering. Phyllis, Sally and young Aneurin proudly clasped leeks in their hands as aunt Clarrie led them in singing the Welsh National Anthem.

In many parts of the Rhondda the celebrations carried on into the next day. It was as though Tommy had won the title, and to mark the occasion many people decided to take a day off. Special thought was also given to the hundreds of children living in the vicinity of Court Street, where Tommy had lived until moving to Slough. Irrespective of whether he won, a tea was to be given, just as had been done for the Coronation. On that occasion he had sat down with about 500 youngsters and in fact paid for their treat. The kids loved him. He was their hero, and the tea in his honour marked the respect which local people had for him.

Whilst thousands of people stayed up all night to listen to the fight, the actions of one young fan actually brought about a strike.

Tommy Milligan was a millman at the Tynewydd Tin Plate Works at Montnewydd, and on the night of the fight took a radio to work. During the commentary, all the other millmen stopped work and listened in. The management objected and suspended Tommy from work for a fortnight. His workmates promptly called a strike, and as a result three mills stopped working when the afternoon shift refused to take over. Between 60 and 70 men were idle and would not be allowed to restart work until the following week. Their stoppage had been unconditional and unconstitutional, and they were punished for breach of a trade union agreement.

The commentary of the fight had been relayed through the national transmitter at Droitwich in Worcestershire. There was so much interest in the fight that edited editions were broadcast from Droitwich at 6 a.m. and 7 a.m. and also from all regional transmitters. At 9.20 p.m. the same evening, a further edited version was broadcast nationally.

Interest in the fight generally was colossal, and it was established that some 2 million people listened to the commentary in Britain; in London alone over 2,000 asked to be awoken by telephone at 2.30 a.m. According to the GPO it was one of the greatest number of 'sack' calls ever made. At electric power stations, engineers watched in amazement as indicator needles suddenly swung to a point expected at normal switching-on time. Gas board workers noticed that their huge storage tanks were being emptied as if it were daytime as all over Britain electric lights and gas stoves were being turned on.

* * *

Back in his dressing room, Tommy Farr sat on the rubbing table usually reserved for the New York Yankees. Bloodied and bruised, his sturdy legs dangling wearily over the edge, he faced a dozen or so reporters who crowded round him. 'I have no alibis,' Tommy told them. 'Louis earned the decision.'

'Louis is the best and cleanest fighter I ever met,' he continued. 'And he hits harder than all of them put together. But I would like to fight him again, and I would like to meet Schmeling too.'

There were many people in the arena who thought Farr had won the fight, but that was not the view of the Welshman or his manager. 'I think Louis won and do not hesitate to say so,' confirmed Broadribb. 'I gave Farr five or six rounds, but had he not had his eyes bunged up, he would have done much better.'

Any hopes that Tommy had of returning to London to meet Schmeling were quickly dispelled by Broadribb. In answer to questions from reporters about the future, he said, 'We are not fighting for anyone but Mike Jacobs. He has been fair to us, and we keep to our contracts.'

The fact was that when the contracts were signed, Jacobs took out an option on Farr's services for at least one more fight in case things didn't turn out according to plan. The Welshman's performance amazed him, and he knew he had found another meal ticket.

Surrounded by reporters immediately after the fight, Joe Louis wearily admitted, 'Tommy is one of the toughest men I ever fought. It was the hardest fight I ever had. Farr fooled me; I thought I had him, but he wouldn't be finished.'

Jack Blackburn added his tribute to Farr's performance. 'Louis hit Farr with shots that would have dropped, yeah, flattened most other fighters in the world. Farr is a real tough man, and he has got an awkward style. He is a better fighter than people give him credit for.'

Ed Winchell, the respected American commentator and broadcaster summed up Tommy's performance when he told listeners, 'Those who said Farr wouldn't last three rounds, were very, very wrong. I don't think I have ever seen a gamer fighter in the prize ring. All credit must go to the Welshman.'

During the course of the many debates after the fight, it was argued that Farr's lack of a big punch probably cost him the title. Max Schmeling made that very point afterwards when he remarked, 'Tommy fought a brave fight, but you cannot win only on a brave fight. If he could only punch!' In a few words, Max had summed up the thoughts of every fight fan in Britain.

Tommy's wonderful performance stemmed very much from self-belief. He always believed he would win, and repeatedly said so, much to the annoyance of many Americans. The press boys laughed, but Tommy fought as he had never fought before, and his display made him a hero for life. One of his outstanding characteristics had always been that criticism brought out the stubborn, arrogant streak in him. He ignored the mud-slinging of those newsmen who persisted in trying to belittle him, and their insults just fired him up making him grimly determined to prove the 'know-alls' wrong.

The pre-fight troubles between Farr and the American press had arisen partly because libel laws didn't exist in the States as they did in Britain. Some journalists freely admitted to giving their readers tarted-up stories in order to provide good reading. It was a very different situation to that which existed in Britain, and one which Tommy couldn't understand.

The Welshman's bad feeling, however, was soon forgotten, and most of the press warmed to him and wrote complimentary reports of the fight. In the years that followed, he did not have a single enemy amongst them, and even to this day, he is recognised as one of the finest British ambassadors of the sport since the days of Jimmy Wilde.

There was tremendous coverage of the fight back in Britain, and whilst reporters paid tribute to Tommy for his wonderful effort, they were divided as to who they thought won. Generally, the British press didn't question the decision, and there were very few claims that Tommy had been the victim of a home-town decision.

Shortly after the fight, there was an interesting claim by American sports writer Ed Sullivan that the crucial seventh round, in which Louis came close to scoring a knockout, was allowed to run for half a minute too long. When they heard about his allegation, the New York State Athletic Commission summoned Sullivan to their offices to hear his story. He duly attended, but the result stood.

In Britain, there were plenty of tributes for Ted Broadribb, Tom Evans and Job Churchill, but although there were many references to Tommy having been a booth fighter, nobody referred to Joe Gess, the man who really set him on his way. Joe was entitled to share in the praise because there were no better judges of fighters than travellers like him, and he deserved to be more than just a Cinderella of the fight game.

* * *

As often happens in boxing, solid friendships are formed between contestants following a big fight. This was the situation between Farr and Louis, and for the rest of their days they would pay tribute to each other. There were many interviews, and on one occasion some years later when Tommy was asked if he thought he had beaten Joe, he replied, 'Louis was a far superior puncher to me. I can still feel two right-handers.'

Although Tommy never once claimed he had won the fight, he often produced a spot of dry humour when asked about it. A typical example was some 20 years later when interviewed on radio by Peter Wilson of the *Daily Mirror*. Wilson brought up the subject of Louis, and quick as a flash Tommy cracked, 'I wish you'd stop writing about him, Peter bach. Even twenty years later, I've only got to read his name and my nose starts bleeding again.'

Louis once remarked, 'Tommy was a real smart guy, nobody's fool. I didn't carry nobody, I just couldn't catch up with him.' Years later, Joe said that in his opinion, Farr was the best-conditioned heavyweight ever to come out of Britain. 'He was tough and had a lot of heart. He took a punch as well as anyone I ever met.'

15

HERO IN DEMAND

After the fight with Louis, Farr returned to Long Branch under a heavy police escort. The third and fourth fingers of his right hand were bandaged, and his thumb badly swollen.

That night Joe Prendergast and his sisters, who owned the West End Casino at Long Branch, threw a party in Tommy's honour. Governor Hoffman and many other famous personalities attended to pay tribute to the gallant Welshman. Surrounded by them, he recalled the occasion some five years earlier when he had tramped all the way from Tonypandy to London without food, and used the roadside as his bed. He had come a long way since then, and was eternally grateful.

Tommy's performance against Louis had won him about £3,000 in bets. Job Churchill was due plenty as well, and collecting their winnings was high on their list of priorities. Tommy was also anxious to speak to members of his family in Slough to assure them that he was OK, and just a couple of days after the fight put through a call to his home at Sussex Place.

As he recovered from the effects of the fight, Tommy discovered that everyone wanted to become his friend. Over the next few days he became very sought after on both sides of the Atlantic. Numerous letters, messages of congratulation, and presents flooded into his hotel room, and he was invited to a multitude of places by people he had never heard of.

Broadribb, meanwhile, had discussions with Mike Jacobs about Tommy's future, especially as the promoter had an option on his next fight in the States. After considering the situation for a couple of days, Ted announced that the Welshman would return to Britain at the end of September, but go back to the States during the winter for further fights to be staged by Jacobs. Some

196

newspapers carried a story that contracts had already been signed for a return with Louis, but this was denied by Broadribb. 'We would welcome the opportunity of a return bout,' he remarked, 'but Mike Jacobs holds the option on Farr's services, so we will fight any man he selects.'

Back in London, General Critchley announced in a press release that he had decided to release Tommy from the contract requiring him to fight Schmeling at the White City at the end of September:

> I have had a telephone conversation with my New York representative, and told him that I am prepared to release Farr from his contract with us. I propose to take no action in view of the British champion's magnificent show against Louis. It would be almost unpatriotic to do so. Farr will be informed that if he comes back, he will be very welcome so far as we are concerned, and if he decides to fight for us, all well and good.
>
> Farr declared in an affidavit before leaving, that he would return and fulfil his contract, and has made repeated statements to this effect since. But I am quite happy to release him. Anyhow, I have been informed that he is not in a condition to fight at the White City in the period stipulated.

Shortly after Critchley's announcement, Max Schmeling was asked if he would be willing to fight Tommy in the United States, to which he replied, 'My man is Louis. When I beat him, I will fight Farr in England according to our contract.'

Ted Broadribb, meanwhile, was informed by the Press Association that there was a report from London claiming that Sydney Hulls was willing to drop his suit for breach of contract against Farr if he agreed to fight Schmeling in London later in the year. 'We have no intention of ever boxing again in London for Syd Hulls,' retorted Broadribb angrily.

* * *

In view of Tommy's courageous show against Louis, Mike Jacobs knew the public would flock to see him wherever he fought. He therefore intended hanging on to him for as long as possible. As a sweetener, he invited Tommy to spend some time with him at his country home at Fairhaven in New Jersey. The Welshman jumped at the opportunity.

Jacobs told Tommy that if he remained in the States, he would make him a very rich man, adding that if all went well, a return with Louis was a possibility in the not too distant future. Jacobs advised him that in the meantime he should cash in on his new-found popularity by making public appearances which would guarantee him thousands of extra dollars.

The promoter arranged appearances for Tommy at the Steel Pier in Atlantic City on 4 and 5 September, and he also took part in a vaudeville programme with bandleader and radio star Rudy Vallee which was broadcast across America. At Atlantic city, massive crowds paying a dollar a head gathered to hear Tommy do a talk about the fight, and they loved him.

After the final show, Farr, Tom Evans, Babe Culnan and Jerry Casale collected a large amount of cash and started to make their way back to Long Branch by road. Unfortunately, Tommy's earning capacity had not gone unnoticed, and when they reached Hammanton in New Jersey, a car containing five rough-looking men tried to force them off the road. The vehicle, bearing a Pennsylvania licence plate, had trailed them for five miles, and robbery was clearly the motive. The quick thinking and driving skill of Casale saved the day, and they were able to escape. Casale immediately summoned New Jersey state police officers, and they escorted Tommy and his party all the way to Long Branch with the money intact.

A few days after this event reports were received back in Britain of yet another row between Farr and Ted Broadribb.

An angry Tommy Farr made his feelings known to James Butler of the *Daily Herald* in a transatlantic phone talk:

I am definitely through with Ted Broadribb as my manager. In future I shall do my own business. I'm completely fed up with the way I have been mismanaged. The sorry affair started on the night of my fight with Joe Louis. I went to the Yankee Stadium with a split under my eye three quarters of an inch long, and very deep. Soap was smeared over the wound so I could pass through the weigh-in without raising suspicion. You see, if the cut had been spotted by officials, hell would have been raised. Then before the fight, a preparation known as Carpenters Wax was spread over the wound by Izzy Klein, Max Baer's trainer. This seemed to me to be a wise precaution, but to my amazement, Broadribb made one of my seconds take it off. Broadribb then put on a wad of cotton wool. Well, during the first round, Louis caught me with a smashing blow on the damaged eye. The pad was knocked off. Then another punch split my lip. There was no astringent in the corner to stop the blood I was losing. The lack of attention made me furious because in all my fights in England and Wales, Job Churchill was always prepared with a bottle of tincture of steel to stop the blood flowing as a result of a cut. I blame Broadribb for sending me up round after round without attempting to patch up the wounds on my face. It was an awful experience.

Tommy was very bitter in his criticism of Broadribb, yet he failed to mention that the cut had been examined by Dr William Walker, the New York State Athletic Commission physician, who pronounced him fit to fight. Farr made no protest at the time about the severity of the injury, but now levelled considerable blame on his manager and claimed the injury was deep.

Farr's remarks about Broadribb having put a wad of cotton wool over the cut, and of Louis having knocked it off, reeked of fabrication. Not only would this have been forbidden by the referee, but had Tommy actually started the fight with the injury covered, the press would have said so. The fact that there were no such reports tends to cast grave doubts on what James Butler was told.

In his autobiography some years later, Broadribb gave a totally different account about the application of the Carpenters Wax. He claimed it was he who treated the injury in the dressing room before the fight because he had used the wax in training and found that the injury responded to it. He made no mention of Izzy Klein having been involved. If Ted's account was accurate, then Farr was not being truthful with Butler.

It was well known that Tommy could be a very prickly character, and his rows with Broadribb were extremely bitter ones. There are always two sides to a story, and the disputes between these two were no exception. Invariably each blamed the other for what had occurred, and the whole truth was rarely known.

On reflection, it was perhaps sad that after putting up such a wonderful performance against Louis, Tommy should suddenly see fit to publicly accuse his manager of failing to attend to him properly. It sounded like sour grapes, and he came out of it with little credit.

Although at first it was not clear what was happening, one report from the States did confirm that Farr and Broadribb had split up. An arrangement had been reached whereby Babe Culnan would take over the handling of Tommy's affairs in America, whilst Broadribb remained his general manager.

Culnan, a native of Newark, had in fact been Ted's American agent for some time; they had met many years before when Ted first went to New York. As soon as Farr and Broadribb arrived in the States, he was taken on as their adviser. Now he was apparently handling all Tommy's affairs out there, including some musical engagements both in the States and in Canada.

Meanwhile, Broadribb and his wife broke away from the rest of the party, and stayed at the Douglas Hotel in Newark until they were ready to return home.

The dispute between Farr and Broadribb was attracting much attention in newspapers in Britain, America and Canada. Reports differed widely because nobody knew exactly what the true position really was. When approached by a Press Association reporter, Ted Broadribb remained tight-lipped, saying only, 'It's definitely at an end.'

Farr, on the other hand, had plenty to say on the subject, and in reply to a suggestion that Broadribb had alleged he had tried to punch him on the nose over what the manager had said about the decision in favour of Louis being a fair one, Tommy angrily retorted, 'I want it understood that I never questioned the decision in my fight with Louis.'

'Things came to a head last Saturday [4 September] when we had to make a trip to Atlantic City,' continued Farr, 'and Mrs Broadribb decided at the last minute that she wanted to come. There was not room for her, and Ted wanted me to leave my trainer Tom Evans behind. Tom has been my pal for five years, and I flatly refused.'

Despite Broadribb's remark to the contrary, Farr denied that he and his manager had actually split. 'We've not broken,' he claimed. 'If Broadribb wants it to be through, I'll gladly get rid of him, but I won't take Culnan or anybody else as his choice of manager. All these stories about me being fed up with boxing are tommy-rot. The thing is, I am not going to box again until my contract with Broadribb expires next March.'

Tommy said that once his contract with Broadribb had expired, he intended to manage himself with the help of his trusted adviser Job Churchill.

'I will probably allow Culnan to arrange personal appearances and refereeing jobs for me out here, but that's all.'

The fact of the matter was that Farr was in great demand in the States, and there was a tremendous amount of money to be earned from personal appearances. Therefore he desperately needed somebody to look after his affairs out there, because being in a strange country, he just couldn't handle things all by himself.

Broadribb recognised the tremendous earning potential of Farr, and as his manager would be entitled to 25 per cent of all fees. He took the view that if he continued to try and jolly Farr along, the stubborn Welshman would disagree with his suggestions on principle, and consequently lose them a lot of money. Broadribb therefore suggested that Culnan took over the Welshman's affairs in the States. He had previously managed an American tour for the South African heavyweight Don McCorkindale, who married Ted's daughter, so Broadribb had every faith in his ability.

Farr mellowed to a certain extent, so to make matters legal, a contract was drawn up by local attorney Michael Breitkopf in which it was agreed that Culnan and Broadribb would each receive 12½ per cent of Farr's American earnings. All parties concerned were reported to have signed the contracts at the offices of the New York State Athletic Commission.

Culnan duly went ahead and arranged several engagements for Tommy, and announced that they would leave Long Branch on 10 September for Cleveland, Ohio, where the Welshman would make the first of a series of music hall appearances.

There was one occasion when reporters managed to catch Farr and Broadribb together, and tried to ascertain just what the problems between them were. 'I am paying Broadribb twenty-five per cent of my earnings to stay away,' remarked Farr. 'If he wants to give half to Culnan, that's his business.'

Broadribb said, 'Our differences arose from Farr doing things that he should not do. I was forced to call him down many times. He is like me in that respect, both of us hate to be ticked off.'

Within a couple of days Culnan found out just how difficult Tommy could be to handle. The Welshman threatened not to accept a particular personal appearance, even though he was guaranteed earnings of £1,600.

In Britain, meanwhile, it was revealed that Jack Casey, 'the Sunderland assassin', who had been out of the ring for more than two years, was planning to sue Farr for damages. He claimed that remarks attributed to the Welshman in a New York newspaper were slanderous.

Referring to the night he fought Jack in Newcastle in 1934, Farr was quoted as saying, 'I was fighting him on his own ground, and he had plaster of Paris bandages on his hands. Then to make certain, his manager was the referee, his uncle was the time-keeper, and his sister sat right behind my corner and called me names. They called him "Cast Iron" Casey, and he was so tough that they sold his head to a museum for £50 after he was dead.'

Casey wasn't dead, and he was understood to be claiming £2,000 in damages. In an interview with the *Sunday Chronicle*, Jack said that he beat Farr fair and square. However, he eventually let the matter drop, because as the article had appeared in an

American publication, he was not convinced that Tommy had actually said what was written.

On a lighter note, another story appeared in the *Sunday Chronicle* about a girl whose love for Tommy was so great that it caused her to sing in the street in order to raise enough money so that she could go to America to see him fight Joe Louis.

Phyllis Penworthy, a 26-year-old auburn-haired secretary from Sunderland, had seen all Tommy's big fights. At Harringay when he beat Max Baer, she managed to get his autograph. 'From that moment when he smiled at me, I have been in love with him,' she told the paper. 'I decided that I would follow him to the ends of the earth if necessary.'

When she read that Farr was to meet Joe Louis in America, Miss Penworthy had £40 in the bank, so she bought a third-class ticket to New York. Then a month before she was due to sail, she found herself out of work, and her savings had dwindled to just £10. 'Then I had the idea of singing in the street,' she continued. 'I went to Newcastle where nobody knew me, and I was very successful. I went on to Whitley Bay and Durham, and the money came rolling in. In just over a fortnight I collected £15, and that was enough for my expenses. So I sailed to New York on the *Queen Mary*.'

* * *

Back in the States, Farr cashed in on his tremendous popularity by embarking on a strenuous tour of America and Canada arranged by Babe Culnan. He made personal appearances, refereed fights and also had a musical act which the people loved.

In Boston he acted as referee in a wrestling match before a crowd of about 4,000 at the Boston Arena. The event turned into a battle royal during which Tommy punched one of the warring mat men, Ted Germane, in the mouth. The blow was much harder than he intended and caused quite a bad cut. Germane staggered briefly, but then flew straight back at Farr and floored him. He then dropped on him and was all for finishing him off with a stranglehold. He had both hands firmly around Tommy's throat, and had to be pulled off by other wrestlers.

Although Tommy suffered no serious injury, the incident was real enough, but once peace was restored, Tommy apologised to Germane for the blow which had started the trouble, and they shook hands.

In Detroit, record crowds turned out to see Tommy when he

made personal appearances at local arenas. They surpassed attendances of years earlier when Jack Dempsey visited the city.

It was then revealed that Max Baer had commenced training at Sacramento for a possible fight with Farr at Madison Square Garden in November. His manager Ancil Hoffman claimed they had received a cable from General Critchley asking if Max would meet Tommy in London in December or January. The Welshman was in a fighting mood when he heard the rumours, and told a Press Association reporter: 'I'll fight Baer or anyone else at any time, but I want another crack at Louis right away.'

From Detroit, Tommy flew to Wilkes-Barre in Pennsylvania, where he was interviewed on local radio, refereed another fight and was guest of honour at a dinner given by the American Legion. He then returned to New York to consider more than 70 requests for personal appearances and refereeing jobs.

In an interview with Reuter, he made the point of ridiculing articles that had appeared in British newspapers accusing the American reporters of being unsporting to him before the Louis fight:

> It makes me laugh to read what they're saying in London about the American Sports Writers. It's the London writers who have never given me a break. I was never treated more fairly in my life than I have been by the New York sports writers. They knocked me when I deserved it, and they praised me when I had it coming to me. But those London fellows, they always tore me down, an even when I proved they were wrong, they wouldn't admit it by giving me credit.

Tommy had certainly changed his tune from the days when he chased American journalists from his training camp and tried to get them banned altogether.

From New York, Tommy flew to Montreal, where he was booked to referee a heavyweight contest between one of his former sparring partners, Andre Lenglet of France, and Al McCoy at The Forum. When McCoy pulled out, Eddie Coderre stood in as a late substitute, but the event still attracted a crowd of well over 7,000. Farr was undoubtedly the main attraction and the crowd gave him a tremendous reception as he strode down the aisle towards the ring. He didn't get very far, and it was more than 20 minutes before the contest could get under way because he was besieged by crowds of autograph hunters.

While Tommy was in Montreal, he received a telephone call from Andy Lytle of the *Toronto Star.* 'How are you and Ted Broadribb getting along?' asked the reporter.

'We are not,' replied Farr firmly, and before the reporter had the chance to ask for more details, Tommy spat out his own bitter feelings on the situation that existed between him and his manager. It was the kind of stuff that newsmen love, and Lytle took down every word and turned it into an exclusive in his paper the following day.

'Do you hear me clearly?' asked Farr. 'He is out of my life for ever. It makes me feel sort of ill to talk about him, and actually sick when he comes near me. You see, lad, Broadribb never tried to understand me. He never studied my temperament. He should have shouldn't he? After all I'm the meal ticket aren't I?

'Broadribb was the cause of all the dissension you saw in my camp, and he told terrible stories about me, positively terrible stories. He told them to you and to the other newspaper men. Everybody knows it now, and he's hated in England too. I have letters. We didn't fight. I wouldn't fight with him. I just said, "Carry on by yourself, push off, and go to blazes."

'And listen, I wish you'd say in your paper that he couldn't referee a cat and dog fight. He lost me that fight with Louis he did, with that ruddy stuff he put in my eyes. And he couldn't stop the bleeding. And him in the ruddy boxing game for thirty years. I won't talk about him, it drives me mad to do it.

'There are too many cuts at my earnings,' continued Tommy, 'but once I get finally clear of Broadribb, I'll be my own bloody manager.'

Tommy expressed an interest in travelling to Toronto, and this became of great interest to Canadian promoter Jack Corcoran. As soon as he heard about it, he put through a call to Babe Culnan, who was with Farr in Montreal.

Farr agreed to referee a bantamweight contest on Corcoran's promotion at the Maple Leaf Gardens, between Baby Yack of Toronto and Henry Hook of Indianapolis. In return, he was guaranteed $1,000, plus four tickets from Montreal to Toronto, and from Toronto back to New York the day after his refereeing engagement.

Tommy received a warm welcome as he climbed into the ring at the Maple Leaf Gardens to referee the main event, and an even bigger one when he spoke into the microphone. The Welshman undertook his duties responsibly and proved to be an efficient third man.

Before leaving Toronto, Farr asked Jack Corcoran if he would arrange some fights for Mog Mason, the bantamweight who had held the Welsh title from 1934 until 1936. Tommy considered him to be one of the best bantamweights in Britain. Realising that any protégé of Tommy's would prove an added attraction, Corcoran agreed. Tommy promised to arrange for Mason to travel to Toronto, and even agreed to pay his expenses.

Farr's tour of the United States and Canada took in nine cities, and earned him a considerable amount of extra money. He was able to command as much as £500 for doing two shows in an evening, and £200 for individual personal appearances throughout most of September. That was a tremendous amount of money in those days, and earned in surroundings far less dangerous than the ring. There was a great deal of speculation about the amount he earned, but he was said to have deposited more than £16,000 in an American bank. It was also claimed that he had almost as much salted away back in Britain. In view of the way that Job Churchill had taught Tommy to protect his hard-earned cash, it is very unlikely that the Welshman ever made such a disclosure. However, if those figures were anywhere near to being accurate, it demonstrated the sheer magnitude of Farr's achievements, and his tremendous earning capacity.

What was known was that Tommy had big money assets both in Britain and America from films, and also an advertising revenue for various products. Whilst he was in Canada, he featured in large advertisements for Brylcreem in a number of newspapers. He also had the rights of his fight films, believed to be to the extent of 50 per cent in Britain and 33 per cent in the States.

Apart from travelling and entertaining, Tommy was also having his share of the good life, attending dinners, luncheons, receptions and nightclubs. Life became extremely hectic as people continued to clamour for his company. He received numerous invitations to parties, many from film celebrities. Bing Crosby even invited him out to his house for dinner, and sang a number of songs for his guest. There was one condition, though: Tommy first gave a rendering of *Land of My Fathers*.

The lad from poverty-stricken South Wales had never experienced anything quite like the hospitality he was receiving in the States. As he wined and dined in the best establishments, so he smoked and drank quite heavily. Consequently, he began to put on weight and got generally out of condition. His training schedule for the Louis fight had been intense and disciplined, and before that he had trained almost continuously for the bouts with Foord, Baer and Neusel. Now he was firmly established in the States, he intended to unwind and have some fun.

Tommy returned to New York on 23 September, where he was

a special guest at a big promotion staged by Mike Jacobs, which included world title fights involving Barney Ross, Lou Ambers and Harry Jaffa. He sat at ringside close to Joe Louis, and just before the main event both were called into the ring. As they were introduced, the two great warriors turned and faced each other for the first time since their fight almost a month earlier.

Smiling warmly, they shook hands and exchanged friendly words before waving to the crowd, who gave them tremendous receptions. It was clear for all to see that they held great respect for one another, and as they turned to leave the ring, Tommy stepped forward and lifted up the middle rope to allow Joe to duck under it.

* * *

Back in London, a film of the Farr–Louis fight was shown at the Gaumont in Wardour Street about a week after it took place. Heavily edited, it lasted only half an hour. Apparently this had been done to suit the British viewers, to show Tommy's best work. In doing so, however, the film did not portray the complete story and thereby prevented viewers from drawing their own conclusions. Consequently, many people saw Tommy as a clear winner.

Fight fans in Britain were becoming concerned over the Welshman's future because newspaper reports claimed that he was tied to Mike Jacobs. Many people feared that this would mean he would not fight in Britain in the foreseeable future. The position, however, was that while Jacobs did have an option on Farr's services in America for at least one fight – a common practice which still exists in modern times – there was nothing to stop Tommy returning to Britain for a fight. It was up to the London promoters to come up with an offer that would secure his services. The reality was that he could now command big purse money, and such sums were more likely to come from fighting in the United States.

Job Churchill, meanwhile, arrived back in Penygraig on 18 September. All he wanted to do was get back to the business of repairing saddles. 'I am a simple man who likes simple things,' he said, 'and this is where I belong.' Job was, however, extremely concerned about Tommy's welfare, and within a few days sent him a cable in Welsh saying, 'Don't be daft, come home.' The British champion still had a tremendous amount of respect for Churchill, so without further ado, he made arrangements to travel home aboard the *Queen Mary* during early October.

Ted Broadribb arrived back in Britain aboard the *Berengaria* on 5 October, and said that although he was technically still Farr's manager, he intended having nothing further to do with him personally. He confirmed that he had given Babe Culnan power of attorney to act for him and handle Farr's affairs in the States. He did, however, retain 25 per cent interest in the Welshman's British earnings.

Some reports from the States claimed that a row over money had caused the split between Farr and Broadribb, but Ted stated that trouble broke out between them shortly after training for the Louis fight commenced. The publicity Farr received went to his head, and he resented being told what to do in front of the critics. There were several other incidents, and Farr said some nasty things. Broadribb claimed that after the Louis fight, Tommy threatened to punch him on the nose. He reached a point where he couldn't stand it any longer so they broke up.

Broadribb laughed at suggestions made by Farr that he put a dressing over the injured eye before the first round with Louis, and that he had been unable to see, due to the manager's treatment of the injuries: 'I treated his injuries in the ordinary way, and everyone in America agreed how well Farr came out of his corner after the intervals. Another thing which seemed to annoy Farr was that I said publicly that I agreed with the decision in Louis's favour. In fact, two English judges of boxing thought Louis won more clearly than it appeared from the American standpoint.'

Broadribb's feelings clearly ran very deep, and he wrote in his autobiography: 'I would not be telling the truth if I did not say that I was glad when Farr and I parted company.'

* * *

Tommy sailed for England aboard the Cunard White Star liner *Queen Mary* on 6 October. The previous day, an announcement had been made by the Twentieth Century Sporting Club in New York that he had signed a contract which would give Mike Jacobs first call on his services for the next five years.

When the Queen Mary docked at Cherbourg five days later, reported Edward F. Balloch of the *South Wales Echo* was there to meet it.

Tommy said he was aware that there had been a lot of talk about the financial side of his fight with Louis, and added, 'You can take it from me, I am coming home with £9,000 in my pocket, no more, no less.'

He went on to talk about his break up with Ted Broadribb. 'Ted as a manager may be all right,' said Tommy, 'but the fact is we don't get along together. It was no use carrying on under those circumstances. He says I'm under contract to him until July, and that he will collect his percentage. Let him go ahead and collect, but he can take that whichever way he wants.'

When the *Queen Mary* docked at Southampton later the same day, Tommy received a great welcome from his sisters Sally and Phyllis, who went aboard to greet him in his cabin.

As Tommy left his cabin, he was surrounded by reporters. If they expected him to be the same Tommy Farr who left England three months earlier, then they were in for a shock. He was so full of high opinions of the United States, he had developed into one of the finest ambassadors America had ever had from the world of boxing. Strolling about the decks of the great liner dressed in a brown suit, smartly cut in American style, Tommy gazed down on Southampton Water for his first glimpse of England for three months and talked enthusiastically about his American experiences.

Another change that was noticed in Tommy was that he persistently talked in terms of dollars instead of pounds. He spoke freely about the various big money offers he had received in the States, one of which was for a three-month tour with a professional baseball team which he said would net him $6,000 a week, 'just for fielding'. Although he claimed he couldn't say how much he had earned from his vaudeville, film and other appearances, he did admit that it ran into tens of thousands of dollars.

As Tommy made his way down the gangway with sisters Sally and Phyllis clinging tightly to his arms, hundreds of people who had been waiting for hours to greet him cheered, waving handkerchiefs and hats.

In answer to questions, he said he was free to fight in England whenever he liked, providing he received a good enough offer, adding that he would be happy to fight for Wembley promoter Arthur Elvin. 'You've got to realise that America is where the money is,' Tommy replied when asked how long he would remain in Britain. He added that he expected to return to the States around Christmas, and to earn between £100,000 and £150,000 during the next year or so.

It was not until later that evening that Tommy arrived in Slough driving his smart blue sports car. A few reporters and photographers were waiting patiently on the pavement outside 33

Sussex Place. The Tommy Farr of old would have brushed them aside, but now he was much more accommodating. 'Listen, lads,' he said softly as he lifted presents for his sisters from the boot of his car, 'I'm tired and need a bit of rest. Why don't you come inside for a few minutes?'

The house, named Heckfield, was a pleasant semi-detached with a brightly coloured front door, and ideally sited just off the main A4 London Road. 'This is my home,' said Tommy, 'and it's fine to have somewhere to get away from people.' He called for some tea, and sisters Sally and Phyllis soon appeared with a plate of home-made sponge cake and a pot of freshly brewed tea.

'Gee, it's swell to be home,' said Tommy as he relaxed in an armchair, sipping his tea from a thick blue and white cup. 'America's grand. They're great people over there. I had a swell time, but I just wanted to be back with the folks again.'

At a press conference in London the next day, Farr said he was itching to get back into the ring, and would accept a fight in London provided the terms were suitable. 'I've heard all about these heavyweights who are challenging me,' he remarked. 'One is Larry Gains, who is anxious to fight me for a thousand pounds' side stake. Well, tell him to make it two thousand, find a promoter to give me my wages, and the contest is on.'

The Welshman explained that he had been invited by the Wembley Stadium authorities to discuss terms for a fight in London. The problem was, Tommy was still in trouble with the Board of Control for pulling out of the fight with Max Schmeling. Before he could do business with Wembley or any other promoter, he would have to settle his dues before they would allow him to fight in Britain again.

Some members of the press believed the situation could easily be repaired, and urged Tommy to reconsider his position. They suggested that he made his peace with Sydney Hulls and the Board of Control, and take the sensible course of having his next fight in London. Farr didn't see it like that, and he was not the type of person to go cap in hand to Hulls or the board, and apologise. He was not in the fight game for fun, and had received substantially more from Mike Jacobs for fighting Louis than Hulls had been prepared to offer him to meet Schmeling.

Tommy was still angry that Hulls thought he was only worth half of the £15,000 that was to be paid to the German. Having committed himself to Jacobs, he knew that he would still earn a lot of money, but most importantly knew that Jacobs was the man who could get him a return with Louis. This was probably his biggest mistake because as Hulls was the leading promoter in Britain at the time, it is unlikely that he would have refused to promote Farr after his wonderful performance against Louis. He would have been guaranteed a full house at whatever venue Farr appeared, no matter who the opponent was.

* * *

Tommy's first public appearance since returning from the States was at the world title fight between Benny Lynch and Peter Kane in Glasgow the following day, 13 October. The *Western Mail* and the *Daily Record* had engaged him to report on the contest. A number of American newspaper critics had previously complimented Tommy on his powers of observation and ability to describe events, and on several occasions he had proved to be a willing and interesting speaker.

After a chat with the many friends who had come along to The Dolphin to greet him, Tommy made his way from Slough to Euston Station where, accompanied by George Bennett, he boarded an overnight sleeper train for Glasgow. He arrived next morning much earlier than had been expected, but there was still a large crowd waiting to greet him as he stepped from the train at Glasgow Central Station. He was cheered all the way across the station concourse, and willingly stopped and signed autographs for railway porters.

Many people followed him to the Central Hotel where he was staying, and a large crowd gathered outside waiting for him to reappear. News of Tommy's arrival in the city spread rapidly and by the time he re-emerged from the hotel, the crowd had swelled dramatically. Despite being escorted by a posse of police officers, he was jostled and mobbed by the excited crowds who followed him to the offices of George Dingley, promoter of the Lynch–Kane fight. The British champion took it all in good spirit, and along the route he was cheered as he stopped to sign autographs for dozens of admirers.

That evening, a crowd of over 33,000 gave the Welshman a rousing reception when he was introduced from the ring at Shawfield Park. Benny Lynch retained his title with a spectacular knockout in the thirteenth round, and afterwards Tommy described the fight as the best he had ever seen at any weight.

* * *

Tommy was very much in demand for personal appearances, and to promote various products. One of the most unusual advertisements appeared in the *Daily Express* on 15 October 1937. Headlined TOMMY FARR ADVISES THIN, WEAK, RUN-DOWN, NERVOUS MEN AND WOMEN and measuring nine inches by five, it told how he supposedly gained extra poundage and strength for the Louis fight. A lengthy message from Tommy explained how Vikelp, claimed to be made from an amazing Pacific Ocean plant, put power into his punches. 'Even now, I use it constantly. I recommend it to every man, woman, and child.'

Tommy was a guest at Wembley on 19 October when Walter Neusel outpointed Maurice Strickland of New Zealand in his first contest since losing to the Welshman at Harringay in June. A presentation of a large silver casket was made to the British champion by Lord Westmoreland and Sir Noel Curtis-Bennett, and bore the inscription:

Presented to Tommy Farr by the Wembley Boxing Committee in recognition of his gallant attempt to wrest the world's heavyweight championship from Joe Louis in New York on August 30th, 1937.'

The Welshman received another tremendous reception when he was introduced, and in a short speech from the ring, thanked the Wembley people for their kindness. He also acknowledged the support and encouragement he had received from the British people before his fight with Louis.

Early next morning, Tommy travelled to Cardiff to present trophies to the winners of two Welsh title fights.

He was welcomed at the Greyfriars Hall by Sir Herbert Hiles, the Lord Mayor of Cardiff, and received another rousing reception as he climbed into the ring. The crowd of nearly 5,000 was the largest at Cardiff since Jack Petersen was in his prime, and many people saw this as Farr's official homecoming.

Then Jack Petersen was introduced to the ring, and although the reception afforded to Farr had been warm and generous, it was nothing compared with that which greeted Jack. He turned to Tommy, took him firmly by the hand and said, 'What can I say but well done, Tommy.'

Later in the evening, Tommy was delighted to present the Welsh bantamweight title to his protégé Mog Mason, who knocked out Iory Morris of Ammanford in the third round. Mason, who was trained by Tom Evans, was regarded by Farr and Job Churchill as an outstanding prospect. Tommy had desperately wanted Mason to win because he had fixed engagements for him in Canada and the United States.

From Cardiff, Tommy made the short trip home to Tonypandy the following morning to a memorable homecoming. He went straight to a packed Empire Theatre, where he was guest of honour at a presentation to mark his fight with Louis.

After a few well chosen words, a lot of handshakes and a session of autograph signing, Tommy made his way to Clydach Vale to meet his relatives. He went straight to the home of his brother Dick, still a collier at the Cambrian Pit.

Tommy was delighted to see his brother again, and gave special attention to his four nieces and nephews. It wasn't long before a huge crowd gathered outside the house chanting, 'We want Tommy'. The British champion didn't disappoint them, and appeared at a bedroom window, waving to their cheers.

16

LEGAL MANOEUVRES

Soon after returning to Britain, Ted Broadribb made moves to prevent Farr from boxing publicly without him receiving his managerial percentage. Not only did Ted consult his lawyers about the split between him and Farr, but he also placed a notice in the weekly magazine *Boxing* on 20 October:

> Tommy Farr, British Empire champion, is still under contract to me until July 1938. Any business transaction of any description must receive my approval and signature. Boxers, like guns, must have ammunition which is fired by an experienced gunner if the target is to be hit.
>
> Ted Broadribb, 4, Phelp Street, London, S.E. - (Phone – RODney 3381).

The day that the notice appeared, proceedings commenced in the Chancery Division of the High Court in London. The Judge, Mr Justice Crossman, was told that Farr was due to box in an exhibition bout at Birmingham on 1 November. It was believed his purse would be the largest ever paid to a boxer to appear at the venue. As Farr's manager, Broadribb contended that he would be entitled to his percentage of it.

Broadribb was granted leave to serve Notice of Motion against Farr, and the case was adjourned for a week. When the hearing resumed on 26 October, the Notice of Motion asked that Farr be restrained from taking part in the exhibition at Birmingham until judgement in the action. It also asked 'that he be restrained from taking part in any contest, or otherwise exercising his talent, except with the consent of, and as directed by Broadribb.' An application was also made for an injunction to restrain Farr from

213

allowing his name to be used in any commercial enterprise without first obtaining the permission of Broadribb.

The court was told that Farr was under contract to Broadribb until July the following year. It was Farr's case that the contract had been terminated by mutual consent or justifiable repudiation on his part.

Through his counsel, Ted Broadribb claimed that two contracts were in existence, the first expiring in March 1938, the other in July the same year. The case was one where serious damage or mischief would be occasioned unless the injunction was granted at once.

Broadribb contended that whilst the contract was in force he had the right to make arrangements for Farr's engagements and public appearances. He was willing to do so and did not wish to prevent Farr from giving the exhibition at Birmingham.

Farr and Broadribb were both in court to hear the arguments put forward, but sat well apart and showed no recognition to one another.

An affidavit of Broadribb was read to the court in which he made reference to various breaches of contract by Farr. One related to the Welshman's engagement by newspapers to report on the recent Lynch–Kane fight at Glasgow, and to a radio broadcast which Tommy did the same evening.

An affidavit of Farr was then read. He claimed that the contract of 26 July 1937 was forced upon him by the New York State Athletic Commission before the Louis fight. He only agreed to sign it because Broadribb assured him he would not rely on it after the fight.

Farr made reference to his differences with the manager, and disagreed with a number of allegations about money. Tommy strongly criticised Broadribb's treatment of his injuries during the Louis fight, and alleged that his general attitude affected his (Farr's) performance. Tommy claimed that apart from one letter, Broadribb had ignored him since he returned from America. If an injunction was granted, he would be prevented from earning a living.

On the second day of the hearing, a further affidavit of Ted Broadribb was read in which he refuted Farr's allegations. There were also long legal arguments concerning the validity of the two contracts.

Farr offered to pay any monies due to Broadribb into the court provided the contracts were put an end to. In response, Broadribb's counsel told the Judge:

Mr Broadribb's reputation is at stake. Very serious allegations have been made, mostly untrue, as regards his conduct, and he must be protected in some way. The only way he would consider a settlement is on the admission that both contracts were binding. He will then agree on terms that they should be put an end to.

After a further offer on Farr's behalf to pay money into the court, Mr Justice Crossman stated that he was not prepared to grant an injunction. He would make no order of the motion provided Farr undertook to pay into court 25 per cent of his gross earnings pending the trial, and £500 to meet past sums which might have been received. With Farr's agreement, the case was then adjourned.

On 16 November, a spokesman for Farr's solicitors, Messrs Vivian J. Williams & Co, made a statement to the Press Association.

The provisional terms have been arranged by which Farr would pay Broadribb £3,000, and indemnify him in respect of all costs. In addition, each party has agreed to withdraw the allegations against each other. Under the terms, Broadribb will also deliver up all contracts signed by Farr which would leave the boxer free to be his own manager.

The case had been a long, drawn-out and bitter affair. In the end, Farr was released from his contracts and Broadribb was compensated financially – but it was the lawyers who earned the most.

* * *

On 14 October, just three days after his arrival back in the United Kingdom, Tommy received another nasty shock when he was served with a summons. It had been issued on 13 July on the application of Miss Clarice Mary Switen, aged 23 years, of Fuschia Cottage, New Road, Porthcawl, for an affiliation order in respect of a baby girl.

By the time the summons was issued, Tommy had gone to France with Sol Strauss. As he did not return from the States until 11 October, it had not been possible to serve it earlier.

The hearing was set for Bridgend Police Court on 30 October, and on the day there was immense public interest, with hundreds of people waiting outside in the hope of seeing Tommy arrive. The court was packed to capacity more than half an hour before it was due to sit, but everybody had turned up in vain, because neither Tommy nor Miss Switen attended. Instead, both were legally represented, and the case was adjourned until 5 November.

As it was expected that the case would take the best part of a day, a special court was set aside. Again, interest was so great that buses crowded with people from the Rhondda Valley were arriving in the little market town of Bridgend hours before the proceedings were due to commence. A large crowd gathered outside the court more than an hour before it was due to open, and there was a buzz of excitement as people speculated over what might be said in evidence.

Inside the court, the accommodation was hopelessly inadequate to cope with the huge crowd trying to gain admission. Extra police were on duty at all entrances to the building, and everyone entering the court had to produce some form of identification. Long before the court went into session, every seat had been taken, many by reporters representing newspapers from all over Britain.

Farr arrived wearing a heavy double-breasted overcoat and a trilby hat. Inside the court, he sat between his solicitor and the local police superintendent, and was represented by Mr Joshua Davies.

Opening the case, Mr Daphol Powell said he was making application on behalf of Miss Switen in which she asked the court to adjudge Tommy Farr as the putative father of a female child born to her on 10 June 1937.

In evidence, Miss Switen described how she met Farr at a dance at the Welfare Hall at Kenfig Hill on 4 November the previous year. She was told by a boy named Billy Churchill that Tommy Farr wanted to meet her. Together with her friend, she walked across the dance floor to where Farr was standing. 'We shook hands and had a conversation,' said Miss Switen, who confirmed that she and Farr knew each other as children when they both lived at Court Street at Tonypandy 14 years earlier. 'I think we had about 14 dances,' continued Miss Switen. 'We spoke about our people and old times, and we left the dance at about 12.30 a.m.'

The girl said that Farr drove her home to Porthcawl, and in the car he put his arm round her and kissed her.

The next day, Farr and Billy Churchill travelled to Porthcawl in Farr's car to collect her. They drove to Penygraig, and stopped outside Churchill's garage. She went upstairs and Farr joined her, 'and we sat on a settee where intimacy took place,' said Miss Switen.

216

Miss Switen told the court she met Farr again at 6.30 p.m. the following Sunday (8 November), and they went back to the flat at Penygraig. They stayed there until 10.30 p.m. and again they were intimate.

'About a week later,' said Miss Switen, 'I received a letter from Farr, but I destroyed it so that my mother could not see it.' She claimed that in the letter Farr said he hoped everything would be all right, and was longing to see her again very soon. She said she did not reply to the letter.

Miss Switen said that on 7 May she went to see Dr Hodgekinson, who said she was six months pregnant. At the time she was unemployed. When she returned home, she had a conversation with her mother, and as a result telephoned Farr at Churchill's garage.

They arranged to meet outside Newton's garage in Porthcawl one evening at 8.30 p.m. Her mother and Billy Churchill were also present.

She claimed that Farr said to her, 'What is all this kettle of fish you are bringing on?'

She told him he was responsible for her being pregnant, whereupon he asked her if she had another young man. She told him she hadn't. 'He then told me he was engaged to be married,' said Miss Switen, 'and it would ruin his happiness. My mother then spoke to him and asked him if her daughter had to lie in the gutter because of him.'

Farr allegedly then said, 'Let's get down to business. How much money do you want?'

'I did not reply,' said the girl. 'I was too upset.' She said Billy Churchill then remarked that Farr could not marry her because he was a national figure.

The girl said Farr asked her to see him again, but she was too upset to reply.

Continuing her evidence, Miss Switen said that the following day (10 June) she was taken by ambulance to the Bridgend Infirmary, where at 10.45 p.m. the same evening, she gave birth to a baby girl. She noticed that one side of the baby's face was very red, and the feet and hands were very small and had no nails. The child also had no eyelashes or eyebrows, and the lips were not prominent.

Asked by Mr Powell if there was any reason why the child had been born earlier than had been expected, Miss Switen said she had received a nasty shock the previous day. News came to her house that her uncle had been killed in an explosion at the

217

Cymmen Porth Colliery, although it transpired that he had only been injured and had since recovered.

Miss Switen said that on 11 July she wrote to Tommy Farr, who at that time was living in Slough, but received no reply.

At the conclusion of the case for Miss Switen, counsel for Farr, told the magistrates that Mr Powell had to satisfy the court that it was a seven-month-old baby. If he (Mr Davies) could satisfy them it was a nine-month-old child, then the girl's case must fail. 'I ask you to say,' continued Mr Davies, 'that it is a nine months baby, and that Farr cannot possibly be the father.'

The first witness called on behalf of Farr was Dr David William John, of Bridgend. He said he was called to the girl's confinement at Bridgend Infirmary. He made a thorough examination of the baby shortly after it was born, and found that it was a perfectly normal full-term child. 'It weighed seven pounds three ounces,' said Dr John, 'and I would describe it as a chubby, plump little girl. Everything pointed to it being a fully developed normal child.'

Dr Geoffrey Jones came to the same conclusion as Dr John.

Without retiring from the bench, the chairman of the magistrates said that in view of the evidence which had been put before them, they could see no point in pursuing the matter any further, and the application would be dismissed.

* * *

The hearings in the law courts placed tremendous pressure on Tommy, and there must have been times when he wished he had remained in the States. Considerable time was spent with lawyers in London and Wales preparing his defence to the allegations made against him, yet despite all the travelling, he still found time for other things.

As Ted Broadribb had failed to get an injunction, Farr was free to do as he liked, and 8,000 fans gave him a tremendous reception when he stepped into the ring at Sparkbrook, Birmingham, on 1 November. He gave a sparkling exhibition as he boxed three rounds with Gunner Bennett, after which he was presented with a silver Victorian wine decanter on behalf of promoter Ted Salaman as a memento of his visit. Afterwards, when asked if he had any fights planned in England, he replied, 'Only in the law courts.'

Outside boxing, Tommy made full use of his musical talents by writing two songs, which he recorded on the Columbia label in November. He was accompanied on *Remember Me* by George

Formby playing the ukelele. On the flip side was *Maybe I'll Find Somebody Else*.

Tommy loved song writing, and even suggested he might cancel his proposed return to America to progress it. 'There is a lot of money to be made writing songs,' he added, 'and I am more keen about that idea than boxing at the moment.'

Back in the United States, an article appeared in the Chicago-based magazine *Liberty* in which Joe Louis was quoted as making sensational allegations that Farr had resorted to foul tactics during their fight. This was revealed to the British public in an article in the *Sunday Graphic* on 7 November.

Two articles had in fact appeared in *Liberty* in consecutive weeks. The first, written by Jim Tully and headlined WHY JOE LOUIS WILL NOT BE CHAMPION LONG, gave a lengthy but highly imaginative account of the fight, which was undoubtedly biased in Farr's favour. The end of the article read:

> The great Brown Bomber was a flagrant pop gun. Louis's tragedy is that his jaw is not as stout as his heart. Give it, yes, Take it, no. Tommy Farr lost the decision, but found rifts in the Bomber's armour. Next time there will be a new champion.

The following week, the second article appeared in *Liberty*, to give the champion the chance to answer the charges made the previous week by Jim Tully and Tommy Farr that Joe was doomed to lose his next fight because he was 'gun shy', and telegraphed his punches by blinking his eyes.

The lengthy article, supposedly quoting Louis, included the allegation:

> This Farr was the dirtiest fighter I ever met, and one of the toughest. He deliberately tried to butt me in every round, and he did give me a black eye in the eighth with his head, but in the fifth, he deliberately tried to stick his thumb in my eye, and that made me powerful mad ... I wasn't gun shy when I backed away from Farr, I was head shy. During every rest period, Chappie kept warning me not to let him get in close. 'That guy can use his head like a soccer player'. I had to do some tall and fancy stepping to keep out of Farr's head range.

On hearing what had been written, a statement was prepared by Louis and his managers, insisting that Joe never said any such thing, and that there were never any grounds whatsoever for him to do so.

Mike Jacobs said it was absurd for anyone to say Farr had been guilty of fighting in a dirty fashion. He had been distinctly warned against use of the head by the New York Boxing Commission, and told that if he fought unfairly, his purse would be withheld. 'Tommy, who is undoubtedly a clean fighter under any circumstances, was extra careful in the fight with Joe,' said Jacobs.

When asked for his opinion about the alleged remarks, Farr said he didn't believe for one moment that Joe had said such a thing. He confirmed that their fight had been a clean one from both sides.

At about this time, there was sudden concern amongst the Welshman's fans when it was learned that he had been advised to wear glasses temporarily. Some people feared it could mean that his career would be cut short just as Jack Petersen's had. It transpired that the problem was due to a strain on the optical nerve, and he should wear blue-tinted spectacles when in bright lights.

Tommy was challenged to a fight with Australian heavyweight George Cook, by the boxer's wife. She said that she was prepared to put up £1,000 of her own money as a side stake if Farr would accept the challenge. 'It's all the money I have in the world,' she said.

But it was one of many challenges that Tommy Farr resisted, because the offers he had from the United States were far more tempting.

Job Churchill, however, was strongly opposed to him returning to the United States unless it was for a direct shot at the world title. He was convinced that there was plenty of easy money to be made in Britain by taking sensible fights, and argued that the promoters would be queuing up for Tommy's services once he gave the word. Public demand would make the promoters pay Tommy big money, and he would be guaranteed a hero's welcome in any ring in London or Wales. But Farr held firm.

When Tommy visited the Star and Garter in Windsor at the end of November, he offered his services to Canadian Eddie Wenstob, who was training for a fight with South African heavyweight champion Roby Leibbrant. Although he had been suffering from a cold, Farr gave Eddie such a rough time for a round that he refused a second. Tommy did box two further rounds later with other fighters, and remarked, 'This is the first time I've had the gloves on for weeks, but I feel pretty good after that work-out.'

The following week, Farr accepted an offer from promoter Jerry Welch to appear on a show at Mountain Ash, explaining that he expected to return to America before Christmas. 'I am taking advantage of the Mountain Ash show to have a very serious try-out,' he added.

A crowd of about 2,500 gave the Welshman a good reception when he climbed into the ring, then the audience stood and observed a minute's silence in memory of the late Emlyn Michael ('Hector') of the *Western Mail* who had recently died. As well as being a fine boxing corespondent, he was a former Secretary of the Welsh Area of the British Boxing Board of Control, and a close friend of Farr.

The British champion boxed eight rounds with four sparring partners, three of whom he had brought from London. Against the 21-year-old British Army champion, George Markwick, and Police Constable Dick Power of the Monmouthshire Constabulary, he did not have things all his own way. There were some heavy exchanges as both men went flat out against him. Tommy took something of a chance boxing as he did, because, although he kept it quiet, he was suffering from a heavy cold. Yet it was typical of him, and he went through with the engagement because he was determined not to let the promoter down.

Although he was about four pounds above what he considered to be his best fighting weight, Tommy was satisfied with his performance, and believed he was ready to return to the States for another fight. He confirmed that he was in regular contact with Mike Jacobs, and although arrangements were constantly changing, expected to meet James J. Braddock in New York towards the end of January.

Tommy returned to London immediately after the show, but suddenly arrived back in the Rhondda the following week. He explained that the fight with Braddock was fixed for 21 January, and he was determined to get into peak condition. 'Braddock put Louis on his back,' said Tommy, 'and any man who goes into the ring against him who is not in perfect condition is heading for disaster.'

Although Tommy's latest homecoming had been a well kept secret, a small group of people were waiting outside Job Churchill's house when he arrived just after 1 a.m. He had been on the road for seven hours due to thick fog. Despite the lateness of the hour, however, the first thing he did when he got inside was to walk over to the radiogram and insist that the Churchill family listen to some records he had made.

After a few hours' sleep, Tommy was up early to commence training, and he began with a steady six-mile jog to the peak of the steep Penygraig Gilfach mountain and back. He intended staying in the Rhondda for four or five days to get the benefit of the mountain air as a preliminary to serious training. He knew of no better way to get back into top condition than by intensive running on the mountains.

After completing his run, Farr went to visit his brother Dick, but the main reason was to keep a promise to his niece Ann, and bring her a doll. He also paid a round of visits to some of his boyhood friends before returning to Job Churchill's house. He was just settling down to relax when he received a telephone call, and within a few minutes, got into his car and headed back to London. The reason remained a heavily guarded secret, and when approached by a reporter from the *South Wales Echo*, Job Churchill refused to discuss the nature of Farr's business. He said it was private and personal.

During his stay, Tommy had intended distributing 400 toys he had purchased in London, to children at Blaenclydach and Cwnclydach schools. 'I'm afraid I will not be able to visit the schools myself,' he said before leaving, 'but I want the toys distributed on breaking-up day so that the kiddies can enjoy these gifts from me over Christmas.' His gesture to the children of the hardest hit area of the Rhondda was greatly appreciated, and demonstrated the kindly streak that burned inside this hard but gentle man.

Tommy's sudden dash back to London was in fact due to a cable from Mike Jacobs insisting that he return to the States immediately. As the fight with Braddock was fixed, the promoter wanted him over there in plenty of time to do his training.

Despite being an extremely shrewd character, Tommy had allowed Jacobs to talk him into taking the fight with Braddock on the basis that if he won, he would get a return with Louis. For once he went completely against the advice of Job Churchill, and it was probably one of the biggest mistakes he ever made. In the long term, his judgement would cost him dear.

The Welshman was full of high hopes as he set off for the States on 18 December. Accompanied by Tom Evans and Charles Barnett, he left Waterloo bound for Southampton, where they would board the *Normandie* and head back to New York.

When Tommy arrived in New York, he was only four pounds heavier than when he met Louis. Smiling broadly, he told waiting reporters that he expected to have a successful series of contests in America, but was not underestimating the obstacle that Braddock presented. 'Any man who can floor Louis as Braddock did in the first round has plenty to offer,' admitted Tommy.

The British champion set up temporary quarters at Essex House, and visitors were entertained by phonogram recordings of his favourite crooning numbers which he had made especially for private use. His training camp would be set up at Summit in New Jersey, well away from the centre of New York, where he would commence the hard work shortly after Christmas. In the meantime, he had to attend to the wellbeing of his young protégé Mog Mason, who was apparently becoming very lonely in Canada and consequently losing confidence.

Throughout his journey back to the States, the young bantamweight's loneliness was at the forefront of Tommy's mind. Toronto was a long way from the Rhondda, and having sampled loneliness himself, especially as an 18-year-old in London, Farr knew exactly what Mason must be going through. On reaching New York, one of the first things he did was to telephone Mog and assure him he would be with him within a few days.

17

THE CINDERELLA MAN

When Mike Jacobs matched Farr with Jim Braddock, he promised the Welshman a return with Louis if he won.

Braddock, now 32, hadn't fought since losing his title to Louis the previous June. He was considered to be washed up and over the hill, so victory for Tommy would not realistically make him the number one contender. It was also a dangerous fight for him to take because if he lost, he could kiss goodbye to any chance of a return with Louis.

One line of thought was that Jacobs made the match believing Braddock would win. Farr had come too close to beating Louis for the promoter's comfort, and a return could prove extremely dangerous for his grasp of the heavyweight title.

Jacobs strongly disagreed with this viewpoint, and in an interview with *Ring* magazine some years later, went to great lengths to explain that whatever the outcome of the fight between Farr and Louis had been, it would have made no difference.

> Just as long as I am able to continue along the present lines, and have the challengers as well as the champion signed up, I don't have to worry about who has the title. The champion is the biggest asset.
>
> That is why from the day I started promoting, I always had an option on the challenger for one more fight. That gave me first crack at him if he should become the new champion. Then we went from there.

Whatever the truth was, it was well known that Jacobs had become fanatical over gaining the power to enable him to monopolise the heavyweight scene, and having got it, he had no intention of losing control to another promoter, even on a temporary basis.

* * *

As soon as he arrived back in New York, Tommy telephoned Mog Mason daily before travelling to Toronto on 29 December to see him fight Jim Chapman. He received a thunderous welcome from the 9,000-strong crowd, and his presence was just the boost his young protégé needed.

Urged on by Farr and Tom Evans, Mason stormed to an impressive sixth-round victory. 'One more, Mog, one more,' yelled Farr continuously from the corner as the youngster unleashed jolting uppercuts. As soon as the fight was over, Tommy jumped into the ring and hoisted Mason onto his shoulders.

The Canadian people loved Tommy's warm personality, and he attracted plenty of attention from the media. He confirmed that he was now firmly based in the United States, and would continue with theatrical engagements between fights, not only in New York, but also in Detroit and Miami. Asked about his future in the ring, Tommy remarked, 'I'll knock out Braddock, knock Baer's eyes off when we meet again, and be world champion within a year.'

* * *

Accompanied by Tom Evans and Mog Mason, Farr left Toronto and headed for Summit in New Jersey, where he would train for the fight with Braddock. Driven by Jack Corcoran, they covered more than 140 miles of frozen, snow-covered roads before reaching the American border at Buffalo. There they were stopped by Customs men, who told Mason he was not permitted to enter the United States because his passport was only valid in Canada. Fortunately Corcoran was a man of action with considerably influence. He immediately jumped out of the car, made a telephone call and straightened things out.

Tommy was very relieved because, having persuaded Mason to accompany him to Summit, he couldn't bear the thought of his protégé having to return to Canada alone. He had another fight lined up, and Tommy had promised he could train with him.

Although the serious work for the Braddock fight had to get under way, there were still personal appearances lined up for Farr. The following day (30 December), he was a guest at the Hippodrome in New York where Gunnar Barlund of Finland

outpointed Argentinian Alberto Lovell in a battle of the contenders. Mike Jacobs had arranged for him to start an ice hockey
match between two of America's crack teams, Chicago and New
York Rangers, and he was also lined up to referee two fights, for
which he expected to receive about £500.

The training camp at Summit was in complete contrast to the
grim, cold quarters that Tommy had been forced to use just a few
years earlier. Situated some 20 miles outside New York on the
Lackawanna Railroad, Summit was a high point in the Blue Ridge
Chain, and known as Mountain City. Towering above the town
was Long Hill, and perched at the very top was Fred Welsh's
Health Farm, an attractive white mansion.

It was appropriate that the establishment should become Farr's
training camp. Born at Pontypridd in 1886, Freddie Welsh won
the world lightweight title in 1914, but lost it to the great Benny
Leonard in New York in 1917. After retiring from the ring, he had
remained in the States, and was reported to have travelled from
New York to California in search of his dream home. When he
found it on the hill overlooking Summit, he paid $100,000 for it,
and invested the rest of his ring earnings to turn it into a health
farm. Sadly the venture failed, and when Freddie died in 1927
aged 41, he was totally broke.

Set in 160 acres of rose gardens and woodland, the property
contained every imaginable comfort. The walls were lined with
silky tapestry, sideboards and benches tufted with red Moroccan
leather, and there was a billiard room the size of a club. Upstairs
were a dozen bedrooms with casement windows on three sides,
creating views unequalled anywhere in New Jersey and beyond.
There was a wonderful swimming pool, and a well-equipped
gymnasium was housed in one of two strongly built wooden
shacks situated at the rear of the main building. At one end of the
gym were bedrooms for the sparring partners and staff.

The camp was run by Madam Sidky Bey, an Armenian lady with
a vast knowledge of the fight game. She was very proud of her
association with boxing, and had many good tales to tell,
especially about her favourite, Gene Tunney.

When Tommy first arrived at Summit, he had difficulty getting
sparring partners, but was not unduly concerned. He was
extremely confident and believed he was in good enough shape
to tackle Braddock straight away. Only his reflexes needed
sharpening up a little.

For one reason or another, the Welshman continued to attract
plenty of media attention, and not all of it to do with boxing.

Firstly, it was rumoured that Bing Crosby might become his manager, although that story died off almost as quickly as it had started. There were also reports that Tommy would marry New York society girl Eileen Wenzell before his fight with Braddock. One paper even claimed that he was breaking training to see her.

'That report is false,' Tommy angrily told the Press Association. 'Everyone in my camp knows I've been here in these hills constantly, and in bed before ten or earlier every night. Furthermore, I can tell my friends that I am in the best shape of my career.'

The Welshman had previously been quoted as saying that women and boxing didn't mix. 'I intend to stay in boxing to make enough money to become independent,' he added. 'When I'm through with it, I'll have plenty of time to choose me a life mate.' There was, however, plenty of substance to the reports connecting Tommy with Miss Wenzell, because by this time they were in fact very firm friends.

They first met shortly after he boarded the *Normandie* at Southampton for his journey back to New York. Eileen was returning to America from a holiday, and also boarded the liner at Southampton. She was in the company of Ben Goetz, boss of Metro-Goldwyn-Mayer, and a party of film people including ex-boxer Victor McLaglen. That evening Tommy was invited to join them for dinner, and from that moment onwards he and Eileen saw a lot of each other, and she watched while he trained daily in the ship's gymnasium.

Tommy fell in love with the raven-haired Eileen almost immediately, and saw her as the most beautiful girl in the world. Described as a sensible but somewhat reserved young lady, she had been a member of the Ziegfeld Follies, and was recognised as a talented artiste in the world of movies and theatre. In New York, she had something of a reputation for her taste in stylish clothes.

Two years earlier, while motoring with the son of a brewery millionaire, Eileen Wenzell was flung through the car windscreen and sustained terrible facial injuries. She subsequently brought an action against an insurance company, and during the proceedings it was said that she was recognised generally as an extremely attractive young woman. The jury awarded her compensation equivalent to £18,000, which in those days was a record amount, even for New York.

Eileen underwent delicate plastic surgery which restored her beauty. By the time she met Farr almost two years later, all that could be seen of her injuries was a small scar on her forehead.

On their last night on board the *Normandie* Tommy held a farewell dinner party, and Eileen was his personal guest.

On reaching New York, Tommy and Eileen temporarily went their own ways, but it wasn't long before she contacted him at his hotel. They continued to see each other, and after he had returned from Canada, she made several trips to his camp at Summit. That was when the rumours really began.

A couple of weeks before the fight, Eileen Wenzell made her own headlines when news leaked out about an incredible bet she had made at a party given by Tommy Manville, a multi-millionaire, described as a 'man of extraordinary and unexpected whims'. Manville offered to bet Miss Wenzell $50,000 to $10,000 that Braddock would beat Farr. Although the betting was two to one on Farr, the bet was struck, with both parties convinced they would turn out to be winners.

* * *

The atmosphere at Summit suited Tommy far better than that at Long Branch. He was putting everything into his training, and, accompanied by Tom Evans, he regularly ran seven or eight miles in snowstorms and freezing conditions.

Unlike the days when he was training to meet Louis, Tommy didn't allow the press boys to needle him with their stories and wisecracks. There were no insults now, and everyone treated him with tremendous respect.

One day, Tommy had a spectacular workout before a party of distinguished guests including Mike Jacobs, and hammered his three sparring partners in impressive style. He then complained that his sparring partners were not tough enough, and when the six foot four giant Bill Schloenman and another boxer packed their bags and walked out, it looked as though his tongue had caused him to be left high and dry.

As he left the training camp, Schloenman turned to Tommy and said, 'If it's any good to you, Tom, neither Braddock nor Schmeling ever hit me like you did.'

New York agent Eddie Walker was able to provide new sparring partners – Paul Cross and Mickey Shaw from New York, and Jack Tebo from Edmonton, Alberta, who once claimed the Canadian heavyweight title. All three had previously assisted Schmeling, and they soon got to work, giving Tommy his best workouts since he returned to the States. Bobby Milsap, a fast-moving middleweight, was also engaged, and it wasn't long before Tommy was seen to be speeding up rapidly and developing his left hand. Cross remarked that the Welshman was a better boxer than Schmeling and had a greater variety of punches, a good left jab and a good left hook.

Although Jack Tebo did manage to land several jabs on Tommy, he was of the opinion that the British champion was faster with his left hook than Schmeling, and more aggressive, although he did not have such a good right hand as the German.

Mickey Shaw, however, didn't last long. During the second day, in the middle of a workout, he suddenly dropped his hands and refused to go on after Farr had hit him with a solid punch to the head. There was no alternative but to give him his pay and let him go. He said that Tommy was a rough, rugged fighter who took a punch well, and a better all-round fighter than Schmeling. 'Braddock is in for a very tough fight,' he remarked before leaving the camp.

During training, the emphasis was on speed, because Tom Evans was convinced that when Tommy met Louis, he was beaten to the punch as he attacked. The new team of sparring partners worked him hard, and as he continued to impress in his workouts, so Tommy was made a firm favourite at 4–1 on in the early pre-fight betting.

The fight was set for 21 January, and the last time Tommy set foot outside the training camp was when he went to Madison Square Garden nine days earlier to see a fight between world featherweight champion Henry Armstrong and Enrico Venturi of Italy. From that day onwards, it was strict training for the fight ahead.

Tommy was still convinced that nothing would stop him going forward to meet the winner of the Louis–Schmeling contest, and he was certain in his own mind that he could still win the world title. His friend Jack Corcoran was the proud owner of a beautiful diamond ring, and he had promised Farr the previous September that if he won the world title, it would be given to him as a present. 'Be careful of my ring, Jack,' Tommy reminded him now, 'I'll be world champion within a year.'

As the day of the fight with Braddock drew near, the betting odds eased quite considerably. They suddenly dropped from 4–1 on Farr to 13–8 and 12–5 on. This was partly due to stories which appeared in American papers saying the British champion appeared easy to hit with a left jab, which was one of Braddock's pet punches. Some critics also felt he was leaving his chin too open to punches, something that a boxer of Braddock's experience would be able to take advantage of. At one stage the odds shortened to evens, although by the day of the fight, Tommy was reinstated as a firm favourite at 2–1 on.

Tom Evans was unconcerned by the stories, reminding the critics that Tommy had been careless in sparring at Long Branch. 'He doesn't like to be disciplined by others and told how he should train,' said Evans. 'He thinks he can work out his own plan of getting into condition. I think he is better off that way than under a disciplinarian.'

Over at Pompton Lakes, Jim Braddock looked very solid as he prepared for the fight. He particularly impressed former world welterweight champion Barney Ross. 'Jim's legs look good, and if his legs stand up, he'll beat Tommy Farr,' said Ross. 'He looks better to me now than he did at any stage in Chicago when he was training for his fight with Louis.'

However, another reason for the sudden shortening of the odds was the rumours of further dissension in Farr's training camp. Tommy was known to be upset that Mog Mason's return bout with Baby Yack in Toronto had been put back a week until 17 January. This meant that Farr could not travel with him and be in his corner.

The young Welshman was beaten on a technical knockout in the third round due to a badly cut eye. Tommy Farr was extremely disappointed when he heard the result.

Farr had also upset Mickey Shaw, one of his sparring partners at Summit, allegedly telling reporters that he had floored Shaw with a single punch. Mickey angrily claimed that this was untrue.

At a press conference just two days before Farr was due to meet Jim Braddock, trainer Tom Evans gave no hint of any problems. In fact he said that everything was going well, and he hoped to have the British champion down to a good fighting weight of about 14 stone 11 by the night of the contest.

'Tommy is in the best condition of his career,' said Evans. 'His defences have improved beyond recognition. His stamina amazes me, and if the bout goes the full distance, he is certain to beat Braddock because he has more endurance.'

Dr William Walker, the New York State Athletic Commission physician, did not agree. 'Tommy Farr has done too much work and is in danger of being overtrained,' he remarked. He did concede, however, that Farr was the best-conditioned heavyweight he had ever examined just before a big fight.

In view of problems about low punching in recent contests Farr stated that he intended asking the New York State Athletic

Commission for an official interpretation of the rules. A boxer who struck a low blow was only penalised with the loss of a round, and could not be disqualified. Forcing of boxers to wear what were called 'suitable protectors', had failed, and boxing in New York was being robbed by the commission's referees' inability to prevent low punching.

On the eve of the fight, the opinion of Joe Louis was naturally of great interest because he had beaten both Braddock and Farr in consecutive contests.

'If there is a knockout, Braddock will land it,' said the Brown Bomber. 'Farr can't hit hard enough to hurt, but Braddock can. He hit me, and it hurt.' However, Joe still picked Farr to win, and even had a five-dollar bet on him with his trainer Jack Blackburn.

Tommy left his training camp at Summit at 9.30 a.m. on the morning of the fight, having risen early and eaten a substantial breakfast. He refused to send a message to the British public, saying that his newspaper contracts forbade him to do so.

The weigh-in was at lunchtime at the New York State Athletic Commission offices. Farr was half an hour late, and as he arrived, a man stepped from the crowd and thrust a document into Tommy's hand. It was a writ for libel taken out by Mickey Shaw over the allegation that Tommy had told newsmen he had put Shaw down and out with a single punch in sparring. He was claiming damages of $50,000. A New York newspaper was also being sued by Shaw.

Just as the weigh-in was taking place, Ted Broadribb turned up. Despite protesting bitterly that he merely wanted to pay his respects to Farr, he was refused admission. Broadribb left angrily, claiming that it was due to Farr, but in fact General Phelan, Commissioner of the New York State Athletic Commission, had said that only press representatives would be allowed in.

Tommy weighed in at 207 pounds (14 stone 11), and Braddock at 199 pounds (14 stone 3). It was then announced that the boxers would wear trunks as ordered by the commission. Farr would be in purple, and Braddock black.

General Phelan told the boxers that the no-foul rule would apply during the contest. He said that if either man was fouled and went to the floor, it would be the referee's duty to take up the count. No rest for recovery would be permitted, and it would be up to the boxer to either fight on or quit.

Farr became increasingly annoyed and impatient with Phelan as he went on to warn him and Braddock about the penalties for butting. 'I know, I know,' interrupted Tommy, 'we heard all about that last time.'

Jim Braddock always fancied his chances against Farr, and although his manager Joe Gould had wanted him to stay retired, Jim wanted to go out on a winning note. He had in fact pleaded to be matched with Farr, who had endeared himself to the American public by his gallant showing against Louis.

Braddock was considered by many critics to be an ideal opponent for the British champion. Although he succeeded in flooring Louis, Jim had been knocked out in their title bout. Tommy was nine years younger than Braddock, about half a stone heavier and had a reach advantage of three inches. The veteran was not expected to win, and general opinion was summed up by reporter James Lemore on the eve of the fight when he wrote:

> Braddock has no business fighting Farr. Even if he needs the money, he is foolish to gamble with his health. Jim is through as a fighter.

Born at North Bergen, New Jersey in December 1905, Braddock started his professional career in 1926, the same year as Farr. He progressed moderately, but in 1934, whilst working in the docks, suddenly received a call to box on the Primo Carnera–Max Baer bill in New York.

His opponent was Corn Griffin, an up-and-coming young fighter from whom great things were expected. Jim caused a major upset in winning by a knockout, and after two more winning fights was matched with Baer for the title. He entered the ring as 20–1 underdog, but to the amazement of everyone, decisively outpointed Max to become heavyweight champion of the world.

Like Farr, Jim had grown up amid poverty and known what it was like to be cold and hungry, and without the comforts and luxuries in life. It had been a long, hard struggle, but he had risen from the obscurity of a dockworker to the pinnacle of the boxing world. It was a fairy tale story, and after he became champion, the celebrated columnist Damon Runyon nicknamed him 'the Cinderella Man'.

After losing to Louis, it was generally expected that Jim would hang up his gloves for good, but on a bleak cold January night in 1938, he was off to war again. Although he was a battle-scarred, and apparently over-the-hill ex-champion, he was in a mean mood by the night of the fight.

A carpet of snow had transformed New York City, but as he trudged on foot to Madison Square Garden, 'the Cinderella Man' was in no mood to appreciate scenic beauty. A strong wind whistled down Eighth Avenue, and huge snow flakes danced beneath the street lights. Braddock was a world-class fighter, yet he was walking alone in the freezing cold to an arena for a supposed title eliminator.

He always liked to arrive early for his fights and sit alone in his dressing room to mentally prepare himself for the fight ahead. Although this night was no exception, he particularly wanted to absorb the atmosphere of the nostalgic arena. Jim was practical enough to know that this fight would probably be his last.

Madison Square Garden was packed to near capacity, with fans predominantly supporting Braddock, and as he headed down the aisle towards the ring, they gave him a thunderous welcome. The grim-faced but determined-looking Farr was greeted with only a soft spattering of applause, backed by some loud booing as he climbed into the ring.

At the opening bell, it was Farr who immediately went on the offensive, punching holes through Braddock's defence and scoring sufficiently to win the first two rounds. In the third, the Welshman really opened up with solid shots to the body. When he hurt Braddock with two good left hooks downstairs, referee Johnny McAvoy jumped in and ruled that they were both below the belt. 'They were fair punches, above the belt,' protested Farr bitterly, but the official refused to be swayed. Instead, he deducted a point, which cost the Welshman the round. It would prove to be a drastic ruling from his point of view.

Tommy was seething with anger during the interval, and when the fight resumed he set a tremendous pace. Forcing his way in close, he slammed away at Braddock's body until the sides and stomach were bright red. By the end of the round, Jim was gasping for breath, and he asked for extra smelling salts during the break.

During this round, Tommy sustained a cut over his right eye, but it was successfully patched up by Doc Bagley, who was working alongside Joe Gould and Tom Evans in the corner. Farr had been persuaded to engage Bagley because he was known as 'the miracle man'. After the damage sustained against Louis, the Welshman had every reason to fear a reoccurrence of the injuries. In the days leading up to the fight, Bagley had treated his face with a special fluid to toughen up the skin around the eyes. When the cut opened above the right eye in the fourth round against Braddock, it indicated just how much scar tissue Tommy had.

During the middle rounds, Tommy settled down and boxed

233

well enough to win most of them as he continuously jolted the tiring Braddock. He outboxed and outmanoeuvred Jim so well that by the end of the eighth, it seemed that he had the fight won. Crisp left hooks and heavy rights had continued to pile up the points, and at that stage he was ahead on the cards of all three officials.

By this time, the pro-Braddock crowd had quietened down and given up all hope of him winning. They were convinced that old age had caught up with him, but Jim was far from beaten as he sat in his corner after round eight. Spitting blood from between swollen lips, he turned to trainer Doc Robb and said, 'Doc, I'm going out to do the Big Apple.' This was a dance popular in the States during the 1930s.

As the ninth round began, it was a different Braddock who came out of his corner. When the action commenced, the words of Joe Gould were still ringing in his ears. 'We're behind Jim. You gotta take the last two rounds to win it. Stick him with the left, and wait for the chance to cross the right.' Braddock knew exactly what he had to do.

Up to that point he had been flat-footed, but suddenly he was dancing and unloading heavy punches on the astonished Farr. He punched harder in this round than at any time during the fight, smashing home big lefts and rights to the head, which prompted Joe Louis to remark, 'Only Max Baer hits harder than Jimmy Braddock.'

Farr was completely bemused by the sudden transformation of his seemingly beaten opponent, and it was all he could do to weather the storm. As the Welshman's head snapped back again and again, the crowd were on their feet screaming for Jim to finish it. Using all his strength and boxing skill, the British champion tried to take the play away from Braddock, but was picked off by counterpunches. Just before the bell, he was shoved into a corner and rocked by an overarm right to the head, and at the end of the round, there was a huge grin on the face of the Cinderella Man as he flopped down onto his stool.

Every year, there are great rounds fought in boxing rings all over the world. The ninth round in this fight was one of the very great rounds of all time, and will be remembered as such in boxing history.

Braddock could never have lasted a 15-round fight, but he had three more glorious minutes of fighting left in him, and gave it everything he had in the tenth. After an opening exchange of head punches, he drove Farr across the ring and jabbed him repeatedly with lefts and rights which went straight through the Welshman's guard. Tommy was too far gone to stage a big finish, and was under constant pressure as Braddock continued to bore in with the energy and strength of a man ten years his junior.

The crowd were on their feet throughout the final session, screaming for Braddock to knock Farr out. In the final minute, they tried to blast each other out using every remaining ounce of strength in their bodies. Invariably it was the American who landed the last punch of an exchange, and the action was so intense that neither heard the final bell. They continued to fight on, and had to be pulled apart by the referee and their handlers.

Braddock immediately threw his arms in the air, and smiling broadly walked around the ring acknowledging the wildly cheering crowd. As he posed for a large group of photographers who had climbed up on to the apron of the ring, Farr, who was clearly on edge, angrily accused him of trying to hog the limelight and influence the decision.

Ring announcer Harry Balough collected the score cards, and then after a brief chat with referee Johnny McAvoy, picked up the microphone. The fans, who had cheered themselves hoarse with excitement during the last two rounds of the contest, quietened down and waited for the announcement. They knew it was close, and the big question in the minds of many of Braddock's supporters, was whether his remarkable late rally over the final two rounds had been enough to cancel out Farr's big early lead.

Then came the announcement: 'The winner on a split decision – James J. Braddock.' The Garden exploded with wild cheering, and a thrilled Jim Braddock leapt into the air with delight. In those last two rounds he had given everything he had, and set the famous arena alight. Now there were many sets of damp eyes among hardened ringsiders.

Over in the other corner, Tommy Farr turned round and leaned over the ropes the moment he heard the result. He buried his head in his gloves because he couldn't believe what he had just heard. He was shocked and angry at the decision, and after standing there for a few moments, suddenly spun round, kicked his water bucket through the ropes and hurried from the ring.

Tommy got a lot of bad press over his reaction, and was openly accused of refusing to shake hands with Braddock. Jim had immediately crossed the ring to offer his condolences to the Welshman, but Tommy's mind was so clouded that it is unlikely that as he climbed out of the ring, he even saw Jim approaching or heard his words of sympathy.

He was a tough competitor, but on this occasion a bad loser and he didn't even make a bow to the crowd. Instead, he stormed straight back to his dressing room, and for fully 15 minutes sat there glowering and pondering over the setback to his world title chances.

The Welshman flatly refused to talk to anyone, and the scenes became wild as he tried to prevent reporters from entering his dressing room. When they tried to force entry with a massed rush, he screamed angrily at them, 'Get out, bloody well get out.' One cameraman who tried to take a picture of Farr, had to duck hastily to avoid a punch that was thrown at him by the furious Welshman.

After a lot of wrangling, Tommy eventually adopted a more amenable attitude and agreed to allow the reporters into his dressing room. Nevertheless, he remained in an ugly mood, and both he and Charlie Barnett were threatening towards certain journalists who happened to ask the wrong questions.

'I am dumbfounded,' said Farr. 'I wouldn't like to question it, but I think it's unfair.'

Becoming more dejected, Farr growled, 'I guess I couldn't fight it out. I can't fight. I don't want to fight any more. I belong back in the pits. There's a good living waiting for me there.'

He also alleged that referee Johnny McAvoy had coached Braddock during the fight. He said that towards the end of the last round, McAvoy said, 'Come on, Jimmy, there's only a minute to go.'

Farr said he was sorry that he had snubbed Braddock, but added, 'after they had taken away a fight I had clearly won, what do they want me to do, kiss him?'

Before he left for his hotel, the Welshman's last words were, 'I'll get him again, and the decision won't be necessary.'

Much of what Tommy had said was on the spur of the moment, and made amid the disappointment of losing, because he had in fact fought well. The official scoring indicated just how close the contest had been, with Judge LeCron scoring it 6–4 in favour of Braddock, Judge Lynch calling it 6–4 for Farr, whilst referee McAvoy saw it as a draw. The third man had in fact deducted the third round from the Welshman under the New York State ruling for the alleged low blows, and he therefore cast his vote in favour of Braddock.

The most telling difference between the two men, was that by fiddling his way out of trouble at every opportunity, Braddock was able to conserve some energy. His legs remained strong, and in the grandstand finish he took the initiative away from Farr sufficiently to influence the officials.

Farr's anger after the fight was shared by Eileen Wenzell, who had lost her bet with Tommy Manville. 'That freak decision did me out of a nice little fortune,' she remarked. 'I watched the fight through every second, and there could be no doubt that the rightful winner was Tommy Farr. His consolation, and mine, is that we were both moral winners, but they don't pay over dollars for that.'

* * *

The fight had a huge following back in Britain, and the BBC again arranged to relay a commentary at 3 a.m. Many residents of Clydach Vale and Tonypandy again stayed up all night to listen to the action as described by commentator Bob Bowman.

Although it was not relayed to public halls as for the Louis fight, family parties were again organised in many homes. Those who listened to the commentary were shocked by the decision and amazed at Tommy's unsporting reaction. They knew that it had shattered for the time being any chances of a rematch with Joe Louis.

When the fight was over, people went to tell neighbours without radios, and small groups gathered in doorways of the little terraced houses discussing the outcome.

Miners at the Cambrian Pit in Tonypandy did not forget their old pal in his hour of disappointment. 'Hard luck, keep smiling,' was their message in a telegram which they sent as soon as they knew the result.

* * *

Tommy's amazing behaviour after the contest was the main topic of conversation among the crowds as they streamed away from Madison Square Garden. 'Britain has sent us some queer boxers, but none queerer than this fellow Farr,' was the opinion of one famous sportswriter. Another described him as 'a more embittered and resentful boxer than has seldom been seen.' Jack Mahon of the *New York Daily Star* wrote, 'Farr, stung by what he termed "robbery", put on a childish exhibition of sulkiness.'

The following day, however, it became clear that Farr had no animosity towards Braddock over the way the decision had gone. Both called at Mike Jacob's offices to collect their pay, and as soon as they met, threw their arms around one another and shook hands firmly. Tommy immediately apologised to Jim for leaving the ring without shaking his hand.

Both men smiled broadly, and it was clear that there were no hard feelings on either side. Before leaving the promoter's offices, they posed happily for photographers.

'Good luck, Jim,' said Farr as they parted company.

'Good luck, kid,' replied the veteran.

The next day Tommy made a public apology, paying particular tribute to the Cinderella Man. 'Jim Braddock is the cleanest fighter I've ever met,' he remarked. 'Outside the ring, Jim is the most natural and unassuming man I know.'

Tommy had problems of another kind to resolve; he was going into hospital for an operation on his left hand. Several ligaments had been torn during the fight with Braddock, and the doctor who examined Tommy diagnosed that the soreness in his hand was due to a nervous condition in the tendon of the index finger. It was expected to clear up within a couple of weeks, which was a great relief to the British champion, who had experienced serious hand problems back in 1935 when he met Eddie Phillips.

Tommy announced that he was then going to Miami for a holiday at the invitation of the gold and silver magnet Phil Bernstein. 'I need a rest,' he said, 'but when I get back, I would love to meet Braddock again, this time over twelve or fifteen rounds.' He said he had no intention of retiring from the ring.

Whilst the ringside commentary and cabled reports indicated that the fight had been very close, many experts were convinced that Tommy should have got the decision. A number believed that the referee and one judge had allowed sentiment to affect their judgement and give Braddock the decision.

To the more suspicious-minded of Tommy's followers, there was another aspect to be considered. Did the powerful Mike Jacobs have any influence over which way the decision went? After all, he was the man who now controlled heavyweight boxing, and with it the world title. If Farr had beaten Braddock, could they risk putting him in with Louis again, in view of the way he had pushed the champion the first time?' If Farr were given a return fight, and won, it was possible he might walk out on Jacobs just as he had on Sydney Hulls over the Schmeling fight. If that happened, then control of the heavyweight championship would slip from Jacobs grasp. Although there were never any serious suggestions by the press that the promoter had behaved improperly, it was an interesting theory.

When he lost to Braddock, the bottom fell out of Tommy's world because he knew his chance of a return with Louis had gone. Back home there was plenty of speculation about what the future held for him. Many critics felt that his wisest course, was to pack his bags, return to Britain, and make his peace with Sydney Hulls and the Board of Control. Once that was done, he could defend his titles against either Len Harvey or Eddie Phillips, or even have a big-money return with Max Baer.

If Tommy needed any encouragement to return to Britain, he couldn't have asked for better than a telegram sent to him by Wembley promoter Arthur Elvin: *Don't get down hearted. If you intend to fight next in England, don't forget we want you at Wembley.*

Mike Jacobs, however, announced that he intended staging a return contest between Farr and Braddock in New York in March or April, or offering Jim a fight with Max Baer. 'If a return with Farr materialises,' said the promoter, 'it will be over twelve rounds, which will be an advantage to Farr, who is ten years younger than Braddock. Jacobs said he had turned down an offer from Arthur Elvin to co-promote the contest at Wembley on a 50–50 profit-share basis.

Jacobs knew that he could still sell Farr to the American public by putting him in with big-name opponents. It would assure the promoter of continued big receipts, so he intended hanging on to the Welshman for as long as possible.

A lengthy meeting at Mike Jacob's offices was attended by Braddock, Farr and their advisers. Jim said he was willing to give Tommy a return. However, on 30 January 1938, Braddock's wife decided that enough was enough, and persuaded him to change his mind. That same day he announced his retirement from the ring.

Jim had always wanted to retire as a winner. The fight with Tommy Farr had drawn a crowd of 17,369, and he had been guaranteed 27½ per cent of the gate. It was the perfect time to get out.

Braddock left boxing as one of the sport's most decent and honourable men. He opened a bar at 157 West 49th Street, in Manhattan, which he called Inn Braddock's Corner. Unfortunately it was not a success, and went bankrupt after a short while.

In the spring of 1939 he announced another comeback, and there were plans to match him with Len Harvey in London. Jim, however, could not come to terms with the promoter, and he stayed retired for good. Like many other famous fighters of the time, Jim enlisted in the services in the early 1940s. He rose to the rank of captain in the United States Transport Command during the Second World War. He finally reached the end of the road when he died in his sleep at his home in North Bergen on 29 November 1974, aged 69 years.

18

MAX GETS REVENGE

Tommy Farr's defeat by Joe Louis was the type that brings nothing but glory to the loser. By staying the distance with the great champion against all the odds, he suddenly became a tremendous box office asset to Mike Jacobs. This was clearly demonstrated by the number of people who turned out on that freezing cold night to see him fight the presumably washed-up Jim Braddock.

Although Tommy lost that decision as well, Jacobs regarded him as an important addition to his already substantial string of assets, and the following week sent a messenger to Farr's hotel asking him to attend a meeting. Still angry, the British champion flatly refused to go. He was extremely upset and was convinced that the fight game in America stank. He told Mike Jacobs he was sick of the whole affair, and was packing up and returning home.

Jacobs, however, had no intention of allowing one of his meal tickets to walk away. 'Whatever the verdict, fighters must grin and abide. Tough maybe, but fighting's tough whether in or out of the ring. That leastways is life as I know it and have found it,' he said. 'But get this. You're not quitting America, and I'm not going to throw you over. Neither are the folk here. True you've had two fights here and lost both, but your stock stands as high as it did after you took Joe Louis all the way.'

Remembering everything Job Churchill had taught him, Tommy continued to hold out until Jacobs finally relented, and offered him a rematch with Louis on 1 April.

The next morning, Sol Strauss arrived at Tommy's hotel, bringing not a contract, but an invitation to another meeting. When Tommy arrived, he found Joe Gould and Jim Braddock sitting with Mike Jacobs, all looking very glum and serious.

Without beating about the bush,' Jacobs said, 'More trouble,

Tommy, and it's up to you whether we get out of it. Max Baer holds our contract to fight the winner of your fight with Braddock, and insists on fulfilment. That means we've got to find an opponent for him. Jim has retired, so will you take him on?'

'No,' said Tommy angrily, 'I've beaten Max already.'

'Think it over, Tommy,' Jacobs pleaded. 'If you beat Baer, it's an open road to a championship fight again.'

Tommy wasn't convinced, and refused an offer to sign a contract, on the grounds that he had already beaten Baer convincingly in London the previous year and should not be called upon to do it again to qualify for a return with Louis.

After his meeting with Jacobs, Tommy returned to his hotel and discussed everything with Tom Evans and Charlie Barnett. Eventually, albeit reluctantly, they agreed that if he was to have any chance of another shot at Louis, Tommy would have to go along with Jacobs' suggestion and beat Baer again.

The following day, he returned to Jacobs' office, and after several more hours of discussion they reached agreement. The promoter announced that Farr would meet Baer in a return contest on 11 March at Madison Square Garden, over 15 rounds.

The terms agreed were that each man would receive 27½ per cent of the gate. In addition, Jacobs signed a guarantee of £20,000 that in the event of Farr defeating Baer, he would be matched with the winner of Louis–Schmeling fight, in a contest that would take place in September that year. Tommy had at least some satisfaction from the strong line he took, but Jacobs was an extremely hard man to bargain with.

Faced with the prospect of preparing for another major contest without the guidance of a manager, Tommy had the good sense to approach Joe Gould. He had tremendous respect for Joe, who had been in Jim Braddock's corner the night he beat the British champion. Tommy knew all about how Gould had taken Jim away from the docks and steered him along a course to the world heavyweight title.

Joe didn't need too much persuading because he recognised that, like Braddock, Tommy was a man of tremendous courage as well as natural ability. He was convinced that he could do for the Welshman what he had done for the Cinderella Man.

Things were starting to look up again for Farr, but no sooner had he found himself a new manager than trouble hit his camp once again. This time, it was a row between Tommy and his trainer Tom Evans, who was packing his bags and sailing home. The reasons for the split were not clear, but Dan Parker, boxing correspondent for the *New York Daily Mirror*, claimed it was over financial problems arising from the Braddock fight. Farr and Evans, however, refused to discuss the break-up with the press. There was also a claim that Tom Evans had sold his exclusive version of the affair to a journalist. Whatever the true position was, Evans sailed from New York aboard the *Isle de France*, still refusing to comment on the split.

When he arrived at Plymouth, Evans confirmed that he had parted with Tommy for good. 'I gave Farr the best ten years of my life,' he told a *South Wales Argus* reporter. 'I turned down many fine offers because I would not leave him, and what is the result. Now we are parted. I was his only friend in the early days in America when everybody was against him.' Evans said that he was going home to Tonypandy for a couple of days. 'Then I'm going back to America. I have had a good offer from Mike Jacobs, and in the future I shall work for him.'

With Tom Evans' departure, only Charlie Barnett was left from the original 'little band of hope' that had set sail from Southampton on 14 July the previous year. Bob Scally had returned some time after the Louis fight, and George Daly, having boxed for about five months in the States, returned home with Ted Broadribb. Now Evans had broken away from the British champion, leaving people to believe that they must all have fallen out with Farr at some stage.

The break-up with Evans could not have come at a worse time from Tommy's point of view, because the fight with Baer was only weeks away. Furthermore, he was already having difficulty getting sparring partners.

However, Tommy told Joe Gould that he was convinced he would beat Baer again provided he got a fair deal. 'He's done no real fighting since he stopped Ben Foord in London nearly a year ago.'

Gould shook his head and wagged his finger at his new recruit. 'Now Tommy, you listen to me. Maxie has wakened up. He's a different guy now, dead serious. The leopard has changed his spots. No more gallivanting about for the big boy. The clown that was Maxie is dead.

'Mrs Maxie is responsible,' continued Joe. 'Forget that Baer has been out of the ring all this while. He's never left off working since he came back from Europe. A new Maxie has been born. That's why I'm all for you fighting him. He's your big chance to get another shot at Louis.'

Tommy was determined to beat Baer again, but badly wanted some peace, away from pressmen, interviews and photographers.

243

A few days later, in company with Charlie Barnett, Tommy slipped away from the hustle of New York to a ranch high up in the New Jersey mountains, miles from anywhere. The break was necessary if he was to reach peak fitness for the fight ahead.

Up in the mountains, he ran miles along hard rocky pathways, and up and down steep hillsides. Armed with an axe, he felled dozens of trees in his effort to build his strength. In complete contrast, Tommy turned to fishing and shooting for relaxation, and local cowboys lent him and Charlie their horses as a form of transport. Rudie Von Boun, a tough scout whose father used to be a military attaché in the Austrian Embassy in London, showed them how to catch racoon, beaver and trout. These were new experiences for Tommy.

When Farr returned to New York after about two weeks, feeling considerably tougher and tuned up, he put himself under the supervision of Doc Robb, who had previously trained Gene Tunney, Benny Leonard and Jim Braddock. He had also been in Braddock's corner the night he beat Farr. Tommy's chief sparring partner was Charlie Massera, who had beaten good men such as Maxie Rosenbloom and Bob Olin.

Robb's methods suited Tommy down to the ground. After a couple of weeks training he remarked, 'He's been a revelation in his training methods. I never dreamed that one man could know so much about the boxing game. I feel I have only just begun to learn, and I am still in the first standard.'

As the day of the fight drew near, there were rumours to the contrary, the first of which suggested that Farr had gone stale in his training. It was thought that this story originated because with just a week to go before the fight, he suddenly took a day off. Another source suggested that the Welshman's new handlers, in their anxiety to create a 'new Farr', were destroying his natural skill and confidence.

Joe Gould, however, angrily claimed that both rumours were totally without foundation. 'What has given rise to this talk of staleness is the fact that nobody has ever seen him look so good, and they are at a loss to explain it.' As to the remarks about making a 'new Farr', Joe insisted that all he and trainer Doc Robb had been trying to do was to improve the Welshman's timing, and certainly not to crowd his natural style.

With just a couple of days to go before the fight, Farr confounded his critics when he suddenly brought a sparring session to a spectacular finish by knocking out Charlie Massera. Charlie was the best of the 'aides', but Tommy caught him

244

squarely on the jaw with a right smash that followed up a good straight left. Massera was catapulted several feet through the air before landing flat on his face. Farr, Joe Gould and Doc Robb immediately rushed to his side, and it was several minutes before Massera came to his senses. Tommy was extremely concerned and immediately offered his apologies.

One interested observer at the Welshman's camp was Jim Braddock, who predicted that Tommy would win by a knockout within three rounds.

'He has everything in his favour,' said Jim. 'He's one of the strongest men I've met, and in his present condition, looms as a future champion. He gave me much more trouble in ten rounds than Baer did in fifteen.'

At his training camp in New Jersey, Max Baer wound up his sparring with a four-round session. He reiterated his determination to lick Farr, saying, 'He's the most egotistical thing that ever lived. Farr seems to have plenty of trouble with everyone, and he will have plenty more when he gets into the ring with me.'

By this time, the press and public of New York had become warm and sympathetic towards Tommy. More and more people recognised him as a man of great courage, and in his many public appearances, he had demonstrated that he was a knowledgeable man with a natural wit.

An illustration of how people felt was expressed at a dinner to celebrate Jim Braddock's retirement by Judge Robert Kincaid. In the course of his speech he said, 'Frankly, gentlemen, I am among those who misjudged Tommy Farr. In Dempsey's restaurant last week, Joe Gould mentioned that our party was to be joined by the Britisher. I was immediately interested at the prospect of meeting this young fellow who had put our backs up because of things which, according to the press, he was supposed to have said or done. He didn't fit in one little bit with the description of his critics. A big smiling young man, he came straight up to us, and Gould said, "Tommy, this is Judge Kincaid." I repeat, I had the surprise of my life with the discovery that Farr can be candid, witty and entertaining. Before we parted, I felt we had known each other for years. Tonight I am on his side, and I wish him all the luck America can give him.'

At the same dinner, a telegram that Tommy had sent to Jim Braddock was read out. *As your last opponent in the ring, I take off the gloves to shake your hand. Long life and happiness to you and yours. Tommy Farr.*

* * *

245

Tickets for the return fight between Farr and Baer went like hot cakes. By the night of the fight, a crowd of 18,222 packed into Madison Square Garden, having paid more than $74,000 into the box office.

Excitement spilled over at the weigh-in when a scuffle broke out between Joe Gould and Baer's trainer, Izzy Klein. The matter got so out of hand that police had to be called to separate them.

At 15 stone 2, Baer had a weight advantage of three and a half pounds. Promptly at 10 p.m. he left his dressing room and headed down the long corridor leading to the ground floor of the arena. Clad in a blue robe with gold trimming, he was surrounded by trainer Izzy Klein, his manager, Ancil Hoffman, brother Buddy and Jerry Casale. The big crowd rose to their feet and cheered wildly as Max entered the arena. Their deafening roars got louder as he strode down the aisle towards the ring, about to make his first appearance in New York since meeting Joe Louis more than two years earlier. On that occasion, however, the crowd reaction to him had been extremely hostile. They had jeered and called him a quitter because, after being floored by Louis, he took the full count on his knees whilst appearing to make no effort to get up. Now as he strode out to face Farr, all had been forgiven.

The crowd were so absorbed with Max once he was in the ring that very few bothered to watch Farr as he slowly made his entry. The Welshman was not in the least concerned because, being the true professional, he paid no attention to cheers. He knew his trade and was in the business strictly for financial reasons. There was polite applause as he climbed into the ring because people respected him from the Louis fight, but despite the ringside odds, Baer was the people's favourite.

Once they were in the ring, Baer began playing to the crowd. After circling it several times, he blew a kiss at Farr, who was sitting dourly in his corner being gloved up. He ignored the play-acting, but this prompted Max to stop in the Welshman's corner.

'Tahmmy, this is going to be a fight and some,' he drawled.

'Indeed it is, Max,' retorted Farr. 'Another Harringay, eh?'

'Yep, but I guess the boot will be on the other foot this time,' replied Baer laughingly.

As Max returned to his corner, Tommy smiled at Joe Gould and said, 'Same old Maxie, all bubble and squeak. A great guy, Joe.'

'Yeah, but he ain't the same,' warned Gould. 'He's out for blood, and listen, there'll be no fooling.'

The crowd roared with laughter as Max performed his antics. Then Izzy Klein helped him off with his gown, and the women, who always seemed to be present in numbers whenever he fought, screamed as they saw his fabulous tanned body. Max responded by taking a deep breath and blowing his chest out to the full, and then stood flexing his muscles.

Farr sat quietly in his corner but was not amused by anything he saw. He resented anyone making a mockery of the trade that was brutal and demanded dedication from men not clowns.

Tommy soon found out that Baer was a very different fighter from the one he had met in London 11 months earlier. He was vicious and deadly serious, and had developed his left hand in training. Although he showed tremendous courage, the Welshman lost the first three rounds.

He was floored by a terrific left under the heart in the second, but was up at the count of one. He stormed after the American and they had a real set-to, and at the bell Max smiled broadly and patted Tommy on the head as he returned to his corner. Farr was down again in the third, this time from a big right to the jaw. Although he was up at six, he was badly hurt. He was cut under the right eye and in desperate trouble, but bravely hung on until the bell.

'If I can box him I can win,' he told Joe Gould when he returned to his corner.

Gould disagreed, and shaking his head said, 'Tommy, you can outfight him. Fight where you are strong. I don't say he'll quit, but you'll slow him down if you keep close and bang away at his stomach. That's your target, his middle.'

Tommy knew these tactics were wrong because that wasn't how he had won at Harringay, and this time Max was a tougher proposition. Against the advice of his trainer, he came out for the fourth and used his left jab to good effect, achieving his best round so far.

In the fifth, he shook Baer with good rights but they merely stung the American into action. He chased Tommy, throwing big punches from all angles, and one right made his knees buckle. It was a hectic round, and by the end both were bleeding badly. Max was cut over the left eye, and the injury beneath Farr's right eye had reopened.

Baer hurt Tommy badly again in the sixth, but by the end of the round the American's left eye was closing rapidly. Klein slapped the ice bag on it as soon as Max returned to the corner, and worked feverishly throughout the interval. They were becoming nervous because referee Arthur Donovan had already looked closely at the swelling before the round ended.

The eye continued to swell until Max could no longer see out of it. He pressed forward in the seventh, trying to find the punch that would finish the fight, and by the end of the round, Farr's injured eye was badly in need of repairs. Tommy was in desperate trouble again in the eighth when Baer landed with six consecutive rights, one a vicious shot to the body. The Welshman's knees buckled, but he kept moving to Max's blind side and managed to hold on. At the end of the round, they had a real set-to, with Farr still punching away after the bell.

By the eleventh, Tommy was looking the fitter of the two, as Baer's eye was by now a purple swollen mass. Referee Donovan had inspected it several times, and there was genuine concern in the American camp as to how long he would let Max continue. Although Baer kept throwing desperate punches, Tommy speared him with countless left jabs to which he had no defence. The Welshman was well on top in this round and launched a big attack, driving Max to the ropes.

By the end of the round, Baer's eye was even worse, and the crowd hushed as Donovan followed him back to his corner. He took a close look and told Klein, 'I'm going to stop the fight if that swelling is not brought down.' Izzy tried to humour the official, but Donovan was serious. 'Get it down or else,' he ordered. He had given fair warning, and now it was up to the corner.

Tommy was looking in good shape in round 12, slipping Baer's big shots and scoring with plenty of stiff jabs of his own. There were some fierce exchanges but it was another good round for the Welshman.

Baer's eye was looking like a purple balloon, and in view of Donovan's warning, Klein knew he had to do something quickly. As Max dropped onto his stool, the crafty trainer was ready for him. In an instant he nicked the purple lump under the eye with a razor blade and then sucked out the clotted blood causing the swelling. It was an old trick used back in the days of bare-knuckle fights, and it proved effective. Although the eye was still closed, the swelling was not nearly as bad, and the referee seemed satisfied when he made his inspection.

Max was clearly a relieved man as they began the thirteenth. The eye was less of a handicap, and he attacked freely, catching Farr more easily than for some rounds. The Welshman was dazed by one shot, and by the bell was in serious trouble again.

Farr stormed out for the fourteenth, but was caught by a heavy right. As he hit back, he was sent crashing to the floor by another, but hauled himself up without a count. He went after Baer, and there were some furious exchanges which had the crowd on their feet.

Both were desperately seeking victory as they came out for the final session. Baer immediately attacked but Tommy stood his ground, and they exchanged heavy punches. Then Tommy turned his man and drove him to the ropes, where they stood toe to toe, slamming away with neither prepared to give ground. Farr threw everything he had in this round, and was well on top when the bell ended a memorable contest.

It had been an extremely hard fight, full of vicious punching, plenty of skill and an abundance of courage. Baer had tried in virtually every round to put Tommy away, but found himself up against one of the toughest and most courageous men in the game. Their contrasting styles had made it one of the best heavyweight fights ever seen in New York.

At the final bell, Max turned and grabbed Tommy in a headlock, but the Welshman wasn't in any mood for play-acting. He knew he had been beaten by a better man on the night, and his face told the story as he walked, head bowed, back to his corner. All three officials made Baer the winner: Judge Healy scoring 11–3 with one even, Judge LeCron making it 9–5, one even, and referee Donovan calling it a wide 13–2. The huge crowd thundered their applause, believing that Baer was back as a title contender.

Tommy went straight over to Max's corner to offer his congratulations as soon as the decision was announced. He showed none of the bad feeling that he demonstrated following his defeat by Braddock because he knew that he had been well and truly beaten by a determined opponent. As a gesture of friendship, the two warriors drank out of the same water bottle as they posed for photographers. All the harsh words uttered before the fight were well and truly forgotten.

The Welshman left the ring to a tremendous ovation from a crowd appreciative of another courageous performance. Ringside comment was again favourable towards him because he had once more shown himself to be glorious in defeat.

Farr earned great credit for his courage, skill, and durability, as well as for the mighty effort he made between rounds eight and twelve, and again in the last. A lesser fighter would have crumbled within a few rounds under the sheer volume of Baer's attack. The gallant Welshman ensured that the crowd got value for their money, and only he was a loser that night.

Whilst there was near chaos in Baer's dressing room after the fight, Tommy's was nearly empty. He sat there very dejected, and had little to say. He made no excuses, saying, 'I just happened to meet Max on the best night he ever had. I gave it my best shot, and would like to meet him again.' He refused to comment as to whether he would return home and defend his titles. Joe Gould, however, indicated that it was likely that the Welshman would remain in the States indefinitely.

Tommy had shown that he was a very special fighter, and proved that when he stood up to Baer's punches in London, it was no fluke. He had also stood up to Louis, and now he had faced Baer again and been on his feet at the end of the fight. By taking the shots of two of the hardest hitters in the world, he had proved beyond all doubt that he was one of the toughest men in the world.

* * *

Back in Britain, Tommy Farr's latest defeat was a great disappointment to many people, not least Job Churchill, who was extremely angry at the efforts which had been made to Americanise Farr's style of boxing. He said that in his opinion, Tommy's old style was the best. 'If he had stuck to "hit and get away" tactics, and not mixed it with Baer, he could have won.' said Job. 'I think Tommy made a mistake in going back to America again.'

Joe Gould, like promoter Mike Jacobs, knew a good investment when he saw one. With the promise of good things to come, he convinced Tommy that his future lay in the States. Before making any decisions, Joe suggested that the Welshman took a good holiday, and sent him off to Hollywood with strict instructions to relax and enjoy himself.

There he met a host of celebrities including the child star Shirley Temple. 'Mr Farr, I've been promised I can stay up after my bedtime, and you must tell me all about your fight with Joe Louis,' she said. 'I heard it over the radio, but now you are here, I want the full story.'

The Welshman was speechless, and shrugging his massive shoulders, sat down beside the little girl and began his story. 'Mr Farr,' said the girl when Tommy had finished, 'Louis must have been wonderful, but you were wonderful too. You've made me sorry you lost.' As she spoke, Shirley gazed at Tommy with the eyes that had captivated cinema audiences all over the world, and years later he would admit that he was completely charmed by her.

All good things come to an end, and when he suddenly received a telegram from Joe Gould calling him back to New York, Tommy was brought back to reality. It was time to go back to work, so he reluctantly said his goodbyes. The stars responded in typical Hollywood fashion and laid on a special farewell party for him at the Coconut Grove. Not many fighters from a foreign country who lost three fights out of three received the hospitality Tommy did.

* * *

The defeat by Baer caused a great deal of speculation in Britain and America about Tommy's future, and a real argument was raging over his British and Empire titles. Ben Foord and Eddie Phillips had been matched in a final eliminator, with the winner to meet Farr. As it appeared that Tommy wouldn't be coming home in the foreseeable future, Foord and Phillips argued that their fight should therefore be for the titles.

Suddenly, at the beginning of May, the picture changed quite dramatically because Tommy announced that he was returning home aboard the *Normandie* on 4 May.

Once Tommy was back in Britain, the speculation as to who his next opponent would be started all over again. First came a challenge from Jack Doyle, who had been training for three weeks at Slough. He was looking to return to the ring, not having fought since April of the previous year. A few days later came a challenge from Larry Gains to a fight over ten rounds for a nominal figure, or to an exhibition bout in aid of the Chesterfield Mining Disaster Fund.

The situation suddenly became even more complicated when the British Boxing Board of Control issued a statement concerning the British Empire title. Plans were in the process of being made in Canada to stage a fight between Farr and Maurice Strickland of New Zealand, and application was made by the promoter for it to be recognised as being for Tommy's British Empire title.

On receipt of the application, the Board of Control called a special meeting to discuss it. At the conclusion, they issued the following statement concerning their ruling:

The Stewards decided that such a contest, whether taking place in Canada or any other country, would only be recognised on the following conditions:

251

That Tommy Farr first defends his British title against the winner of the Ben Foord–Eddie Phillips contest.

In this contest, the Empire title held by Farr will also be at stake, but so as to give an opportunity to boxers who are not qualified to box for the British title, but only for the Empire title, the Stewards decided that Regulation 31, para. 6, (granting a champion six months before he can be called upon to defend his title), shall not apply to the Empire title, but only to the British title.

Also, with respect to the Empire title, Maurice Strickland must first meet Larry Gains in a final eliminating contest.

Therefore, the Tommy Farr–Maurice Strickland contest is dependent upon Farr successfully defending his title against the winner of the Foord–Phillips contest, and Strickland defeating Gains for the right to meet the holder of the Empire title.

The announcement put things back to where they started because Foord and Phillips were due to meet at Harringay in June.

As Joe Gould had unexpectedly arrived in Britain, the speculation continued, because it was assumed that he had made the journey from the States because he was planning a fight for Tommy in Britain.

Farr, meanwhile, concentrated on business matters outside the ring, and refused to discuss his future. He kept in shape doing light training at the Green Man, Blackheath. Having avoided most of the Fleet Street lads, he did, however, agree to give an exclusive interview to Frank Mitton of *Boxing*.

Farr told Mitton that he was contracted to four further contests in the States, the first of which was against Al Ettore in Philadelphia. He would then meet Harry Thomas in Chicago, Jimmy Adamick in Detroit and finally Maxie Rosenbloom in California. He said all were big-money fights, and added that he would be at ringside for the Louis–Schmeling contest, and hoped to climb into the ring to challenge the winner.

When asked why Joe Gould had suddenly left for the States to meet Mike Jacobs, Tommy said that a third meeting with Max Baer was a possibility. On leaving, Gould had made it clear that his idea of an opponent for Tommy in a British ring didn't go much further than Jack Doyle, but said the fight would only take place if Doyle deposited £2,000.

The dispute between Farr and Sydney Hulls was discussed by the Administrative Stewards of the Board of Control on 18 May 1938. The allegation was one of breach of contract by Farr, and the meeting was attended by Farr and Hulls, together with their legal representatives. After a further meeting on 2 June, the

Stewards duly found in favour of Hulls and ordered Tommy to pay the promoter £750.

The Welshman was disgusted with the decision and, under the rules of the board, lodged notice of appeal. At the same time, he confirmed that he would return to New York in time to be present at the Louis–Schmeling fight, and this would mean he would not be in Britain when his appeal was heard.

Meanwhile, reports from the States indicated that Joe Gould was going ahead with plans for Tommy to meet Maurice Strickland in Toronto, irrespective of whether the Board of Control recognised it as being for the Empire title.

On 15 June Tommy set off from Waterloo Station aboard the boat train for Southampton, from where he would take the *Queen Mary* across the Atlantic to New York. He took with him two Pekinese dogs as a present for his American girlfriend, Eileen Wenzell. Despite having had a worrying time during his stay in Britain, he was in good spirits as he set off.

Travelling with Tommy was Ben Valentine, the Fiji Islands middleweight champion, who was hoping to get a better break in the States than he had in Britain. He too would be handled by Joe Gould.

The date set for Tommy's appeal against the Board of Control's decision in the Sydney Hulls affair, was 23 June 1938. The rules allowed for him to be represented in his absence, and before leaving for the States he prepared his appeal and arranged to be represented by Counsel. It was an extremely long-drawn-out affair, carrying on into a second day, but after all the evidence had been heard, the Stewards dismissed Tommy's appeal. They upheld the Board of Control's fine of £750, and ordered that Farr pay a further ten guineas towards Mr Hull's costs.

Because of the tremendous public interest shown in the case, the British Boxing Board of Control took the unusual step of allowing details of the decision and evidence to be published. The press were given an extremely full and concise account, sufficient to clear up many doubts which existed beforehand. Never before, had the board released such details of an appeal.

On June 22, 1937, Mr Farr and his agent Mr Ted Broadribb, signed an unconditional contract to box Mr Max Schmeling of Germany in a fifteen three minute round contest at the White City Stadium, London, on a date to be agreed upon in the month of September, 1937. The contract was made with and signed by Mr Hulls as the promoter, and thereby he agreed to pay Mr Farr the sum of £7,500, together with certain additional percentages in the event of the net gate receipts exceeding £30,000, and on the sums received from the film and other rights. Brigadier General Critchley and one of the companies with which he is associated, had some interest in this contract, but what this was never emerged, and was, in the view of the Stewards of Appeal, quite irrelevant. On the same date, Mr Hulls entered into a similar contract with Mr Schmeling to box Mr Farr at the same place on the selected day for a renumeration of £15,000, or 40 per cent of the gross receipts, win, lose or draw.

Within a few days of making this contract with Mr Hulls, Mr Farr signed a contract, according to the admission of his advocate, to box only for Mr Mike Jacobs, of America, for a period of months which was not made clear, but certainly extended far beyond the end of September, 1937. Neither this contract, nor any other contract between Mr Farr and Mr Jacobs, nor any copy of such contract or contracts was ever produced either before the Board at the original hearing, or at the appeal, in spite of the fact that the original hearing was postponed from the 18th May to the 2nd June, inter alia for the very purpose of procuring the production of such contract or contracts. Mr Farr's counsel however, at the hearing of the appeal, not only admitted that such a written contract to box only for Mr Jacobs had been made, but also that it contained no stipulation that Mr Farr should be released for the purpose of fulfilling his contract with Mr Hulls in September. He stated that Mr Farr had asked that such a stipulation should be incorporated in the said contract, but that the agent of Mr Jacobs had refused to insert this stipulation, but had said it should be an understanding that Mr Farr should be free to box Mr Schmeling at the White City. In the light of the subsequent events, the Stewards of Appeal consider that the signing of this contract with Mr Jacobs clearly evidenced as early as the beginning of July, Mr Farr's intention of repudiating his engagement with Mr Hulls at any time if he should consider it to his advantage to do so. The Stewards of Appeal are quite satisfied that the very existence of this contract with Mr Jacobs was unknown to Mr Hulls until long afterwards.

The Board of Control also decided that it was time for Tommy to defend his British and Empire titles. During July, they issued a statement to the effect that promoters and boxers, and/or their managers, had up to and including 5 August to arrange a fight between Tommy and Eddie Phillips. The statement added that if the board did not receive notification by that date that contracts had been signed, then the fight would be put out to purse offers.

By this time, Tommy had settled back in New York, but he was keeping in touch with the situation. In a series of exclusive cablegrams to the *News of the World*, he disclosed his plans for the future, but at the same time, left readers in no doubt as to his feelings about the British Boxing Board of Control.

The first of the three cablegrams was dated Saturday, 9 July 1938 in New York, and was published in the *News of the World* the following day. It read:

This has been a day of surprising developments in the matters of heavyweight boxing, and for me personally, a day of unexpected good fortune. Briefly, I am to have another crack at the world heavyweight title, and this time I hope there will be no mistake. Tonight Mike Jacobs gave me a definite promise that next May I shall meet Joe Louis on a day and at a place that for the moment do not matter. The all important thing is the second chance because a second chance does not come the way of every boxer.

Friends back home may be interested to know that I have signed a contract to fight either Max Baer or Tony Galento in September. My opponent depends on and if, because if Galento beats John Henry Lewis on 26th July it is long odds that he will be selected to meet me. In the meantime, there is Eddie Phillips, and the Board of Controls ultimatum that I must arrange before 5th of August, to defend my titles against him.

Let me set the minds of the Board at rest. I am more anxious to fight Eddie Phillips than any other boxer in the Empire, if only for the reason he holds against me three decisions which rattled me a little at the time. Naturally I am eager to clean up the slate, and by hook or by crook I will return to fight Phillips.

However, there must be this condition: the Board of Control is not to interfere with my end of the purse. I have been put wise to the possibility that the £750 recently awarded to Mr Syd Hulls in circumstances I need not repeat again, may be deducted. Already I have received a tentative offer to meet Eddie, and Joe Gould my manager will discuss that offer this week-end. Our immediate anxiety is connected with the match with Maurice Strickland next month. So far the promoter Mr Galbraith, has been unable to secure the Polo Ground in Toronto, and it is difficult to say at the moment whether the arrangements will go forward according to plan.

When he prepared that cablegram, Tommy clearly did not know that his appeal against the board's decision to order him to pay Sydney Hulls £750, had been dismissed. In the meantime, however, he found out, and although he was not unduly surprised, he was very angry. In a further exclusive cablegram to the *News of the World* which was published on Sunday, 17 July 1938, his tone was far more aggressive, and he made his feelings very clear:

A cable from home today brings the sad tidings that the Stewards of Appeal of the BBB of C have dismissed my appeal against the award of £750 to Mr Sydney Hulls for alleged breach of contract. They say I must pay up within six weeks, and add to the cheque ten guineas towards the costs of Mr Hulls appeal.

News of the World readers must be so well acquainted with the history of the dispute, that there is no necessity to travel the old ground all over again. Let me add however, that for the BBB of C to order Tommy Farr to pay £750 is easy, but to make Tommy Farr part up, is not quite so simple.

For the last time, let me tell this precious Board that I have never had the slightest intention of paying a penny, and I am not likely to change my mind now. Who and what are the BBB of C to dictate the business affairs of the individual. Let the Board attend to its own job with the efficiency that boxers and boxing managers attend to theirs.

Before me are two balance sheets of the BBBC, one dated December 1935 contains the item: bank overdraft – £2,011·4 shillings. The other for December 1936 discloses expenditures over income of £1,018-5 shillings-1 penny, and the overdraft has jumped to £2,305-5-5. I wonder what they would say if they had a peep at my own private account.

The BBBC is a self-appointed, self-constituted body. They make the rules and regulations for the control of the sport, but there is one thing they cannot do. They cannot stop Tommy Farr or any other British boxer from getting a living in the ring. If they think they can, well I'll give them the opportunity. Whatever happens here in America, I am coming home as soon as circumstances permit, to defend my titles, but to defend them as a free-lance fighting man. Any match or matches, will be sponsored I hope by the National Boxing Association which organised and run by unpaid officials, has made remarkable progress in the last year or two. It is an open secret that a wealthy sportsman is ready to promote the fights for me, not with the object of getting anything out of it, but to expose the impotence of the Boxing Board. No challengers are to be barred. Eddie Phillips is welcome to a fight, or anyone else who wants a go at the titles.

In the meantime, I have to fight in America. It may be Tony Galento, it may be Max Baer. Somehow I don't think it will be Maxie. And if I win, it's a certainty that I will get another crack at Joe Louis early next summer.

Tommy appeared to recognise that Phillips was the leading contender for his titles, which by this stage he was, having knocked out Ben Foord in nine rounds at Harringay on 21 June. Their fight had been recognised by the Board of Control as a final eliminator for Farr's titles.

Suddenly, and very unexpectedly, Tommy Farr solved the board's problem. In a third exclusive cablegram to the *News of the World*, he dramatically announced that he was relinquishing the British title. The story was published by the newspaper on 24 July 1938 under the headline; DAY I SURRENDER MY BRITISH HEAVYWEIGHT TITLE. In it, Tommy vented all of his anger against the Board of Control, but in doing so abused them just once too often:

My cable today was intended to take the form of an open letter to my rivals, my friend and former rival Eddie Phillips. In the light of the last minute developments however, that intention has to be revised. The British Boxing Board of Control, that precious authority which can control nobody or nothing, not even its own flagrant prejudice, and it has given me until 5th August to defend my titles. I knew, everybody knew, it would vent a bit of its own back on the rebellious upstart Tommy Farr, and now it has shown its hand.

Gentlemen of the British Boxing Board of Control, sleep easily in your beds, the rebel surrenders. Today, the News of the World gives me the opportunity publically [sic] to say that I relinquish my title as heavyweight champion of Great Britain. One day, Board or no Board, I'll come back and fight for it, but gentlemen I'll warn you. Hands off the Empire title. You're not going to mess about with that. You may have eyes to read and minds to understand, (I hope), so surely you know that Maurice Strickland has challenged me for the title of the heavyweight champion of the British Empire. We fight in Toronto on 1st September.

I have been accused, openly accused, of side stepping Eddie Phillips, and reminded that he holds three decisions against me. Very well, let us put the clock back four years and see. At Holborn Stadium in 1934, I put Phillips on the floor twice and lost on points. At Wandsworth the same year, I knocked Eddie out in the third round, but was disqualified for an alleged low blow. In February 1935, I went into the ring at Mountain Ash with the mono carpel bone in my right hand broken, but was outpointed. It was a case then of fight or forfeit, and I preferred to fight.

All this happened nearly four years ago. In the meantime, I have fought twenty-four times in Great Britain and survived the lot. Eddie naturally stakes his claim to a cut at my title on his knock out victory over Ben Foord. Who can blame him for that? I certainly do not, but however great one's patriotism in sense of loyalty, it has to be conceded that a world championship takes precedence over a British title, and in as much as I'm now in line for another go at Joe Louis, it would be madness to surrender the chance.

Now let us return for the moment to my decision to relinquish the British title, and see whether I am getting a square deal or not.

The Board of Control has already explained that I am to fix up to meet Eddie Phillips by 5th August. But why Eddie Phillips? Has the Board forgotten that last year Jock McAvoy well and truly knocked Eddie out. Does it not realise that Ben Foord, beaten by Phillips, has never recovered, and maybe never will recover from the terrible hiding Max Baer gave him at Harringay.

Before I got my own chance against Foord and the Empire championship, I had travelled a pretty rough road in boxing. Along that road I encountered every heavyweight in England, and some of them, believe me, were pretty tough. Oh, in case I forget, between the time that he knocked out Archie Sexton in October 1933, and beat Al Burke in 1935, Jock McAvoy was allowed to go twenty months without a challenge for his middleweight title. Yet I am given precisely three weeks to make up my mind about Phillips.

In April of last year, Eddie was cruiserweight champion of Great Britain, and Jock McAvoy stepping up from the middles, took the title away from him, and made no bones about it. But the Board of Control says in effect, 'Phillips is your man Farr, fight him, or throw in what you hold.' Well I'm throwing in, but I'll get it back, oh yes, I'll get it back.

In the meantime, let us hope that there'll be some kind of sorting out process among the heavies at home, and that Jack London, Len Harvey, my Welsh butty George James, and yes even Jack Doyle, will get some sort of chance at Eddie. And when they have settled anew the championship of Great Britain, I'll be ready and willing to meet the man who wears the belt.

For myself, I am lucky and unlucky. Joe Gould has mapped out a programme intended to keep me going for the next ten months at any rate. Here it is: 1st September – Maurice Strickland in Toronto. September - Galento in Philadelphia. November – Bob Pastor at Madison Square Garden. May 1939 – Louis for the world title.

Now the match with Galento has been called off, and my prospect of getting £10,000 out of that contest has vanished for the time being. The day before yesterday, 'two ton' Tony was rushed to hospital at Orange in New Jersey with a severe attack of pneumonia. This mornings reports say his temperature is up to 104 degrees, and he is battling for life in an oxygen tent. Tough luck for the man who once was ranked second to Joe Louis. I hope Tony pulls round, and that we shall have a crack at each other one day.

Tommy Farr.

The old arrogant streak in Tommy had once again come to the fore. The sad thing was that there seemed no immediate like-lihood of the fans seeing him in action. He didn't seem to appreciate that the Board of Control had a duty to order champions to defend their titles within a reasonable time. A number of good heavyweights were entitled to be considered for a title shot while Tommy earned big dollars across the Atlantic.

The board issued an official statement accepting Farr's resignation as heavyweight champion of Great Britain, and declaring the British Empire title as vacant.

The Stewards promptly nominated Len Harvey to meet Eddie Phillips for the vacant British title, and ruled that the winner of a contest between Gains and Strickland should meet the British champion for the vacant Empire title.

The board had not finished with Tommy, and in mid-October the Administrative Stewards held a meeting in London. It was decided that he had pushed his luck too far, and he would be suspended from boxing in Britain until he made full settlement of the £750 plus costs to Sydney Hulls. Not content with just banning him in Britain, they requested the controlling bodies in Europe and America to recognise the suspension as well. The board had working agreements with every controlling body in the United States except those of just three states.

As soon as he heard news of the suspension, Tommy hit back at the board. 'They are a bunch of schoolmistresses,' he retorted angrily. Referring to the money he had been ordered to pay Hulls, he said, 'I would not pay it on principle. It may be that I shall never want to go back to England, and with the board disliking me as they do, it is immaterial to me if I ever fight in England again.'

Tommy insisted that he had attempted to show the board affidavits from Mike Jacobs, Joe Gould, Max Schmeling and others, proving that it had been impossible for him to fight Schmeling in London in September 1937; he was one of the men that Schmeling had contracted not to fight before he met Joe Louis the following year.

Earlier, towards the end of August, it was reported that Tommy had failed to appear at a meeting in New York to sign contracts for the fight with Maurice Strickland.

Tommy later strenuously denied that he had ever agreed to the proposed contest with Strickland, saying that the whole business had been a publicity stunt for the New Zealander at his (Farr's) expense.

Mike Jacobs certainly didn't agree with Tommy's account, and neither did the newspapers. The fight had apparently been set for Madison Square Garden on 16 September, and according to the promoter, both boxers had agreed terms. On the day contracts were due to be signed, the promoter claimed Farr telephoned to say he had decided not to go ahead, but gave no reason.

However, a contest was being planned against Gunnar Barlund of Finland for 2 November.

Barlund was due to meet Bob Pastor at Madison Square Garden on 3 October, but when Pastor pulled out, Lou Nova substituted. The big Finn entered the ring a firm favourite, but Nova was a convincing winner, outpunching Barlund before stopping him in the seventh round. This outcome ruined plans for the proposed contest between Farr and Barlund set for November, but Mike Jacobs was unconcerned. The following day contracts were signed between Nova and Farr, and the fight set for Madison Square Garden on 16 December.

Although only a year younger than Tommy, Nova was not nearly as experienced. In three years as a professional, he had taken part in just 25 contests. The only blot on his record was a points defeat to Maxie Rosenbloom, against nineteen wins and five draws. Thirteen wins had come by knockout.

Beating Barlund put Nova into the big time, and Mike Jacobs liked what he saw. A fight with Farr would give some indication of whether he could reach the top. 'Get past Farr and you get to fight Max Baer,' the promoter told him. It was becoming obvious that Jacobs intended using Tommy as a trial horse for younger talent, knowing full well that he would always be in there trying.

Signing to meet Nova was the first piece of good news Tommy had received for some months. Not only would it provide him with another good payday, but it demonstrated that the New York State Athletic Commission had refused to recognise his suspension in Britain. However, the board later received a letter from the commission stating it was because Farr had signed the contract before the date of his suspension.

Despite his relief, there was further disturbing news for Tommy from London. Several of the Administrative Stewards of the Board of Control had decided to sue the *News of the World*, its Editor and Farr for libel over the articles which appeared under Farr's name.

The case eventually came up in the Kings Bench Division of the High Court on 30 March the following year, when the court was told that the defendants had agreed to withdraw the defamatory statements, to make a public apology, to make a substantial contribution to the boxers' pension fund, and to pay the plaintiffs' costs.

The significance of the case was that the Stewards had demonstrated very clearly that they were not prepared to tolerate libellous statements made by their licence holders in newspapers. Farr had openly challenged their authority at a time when he was a national hero, but he had gone too far.

19

MORE AMERICAN FIGHTS

As he was about to start training for his fight with Lou Nova, Tommy was feeling far from fit. His eyes were sore and watery, his chest ached and his breathing was loud and heavy. Joe Gould was extremely concerned and immediately called a doctor, who diagnosed a bout of bronchitis and ordered the Welshman to bed.

As soon as he was able to get up, Tommy went to a health farm at Garrison on the Hudson river, some miles from New York. It was owned by New York State Athletic Commissioner Bill Brown, and catered for athletes from all fields of sport. Tommy soon discovered that the programme was far harder than in a boxers' training camp.

The daily routine consisted of an early morning call at 4.30 a.m. and straight into a series of physical exercises. Then it was a cold shower followed by a good massage before breakfast. The morning was spent in the fresh air, doing several miles of hiking. After lunch there was riding, followed by an early dinner, and inmates were in bed by 8.30 p.m.

Once he was back into reasonable shape, Tommy returned to Doc Bell's training camp at Pompton Lakes intent on preparing for the fight with Nova. Doc took one look at him and told him that he was in no condition to start hard training. 'You'll never be ready in time,' said Doc. 'If you take my advice, you'll pull out of the fight now.'

Tommy thought Doc was crazy, and wouldn't hear of such a suggestion. 'I've given my word I'll fight Nova,' he replied firmly, 'so there will be no backing out now.'

Against Bell's advice, he started training, but after a couple of days was taken ill again with bronchitis and confined to bed. He was again nursed back to near fitness, but with temperatures below zero, it wasn't possible for him to do much roadwork. Doc Bell again told the stubborn Welshman to seriously consider pulling out of the fight. 'If you won't do that,' he snapped, 'at least get it put off for a couple of weeks.'

Tommy refused to listen and said he was confident he could stop Nova. Joe Gould shared his view. Nevertheless, the manager should have made a stand and postponed the fight himself, but was no doubt aware of previous rows between Farr and Ted Broadribb.

Although Nova was known to be a smart young boxer, Tommy was the betting favourite by the night of the contest. He had the respect of the fans, who, like the critics, believed his experience would win the day.

The weather was similar to when Tommy fought Jim Braddock. Freezing blizzards were blowing down the concrete canyons of New York, and promoter Mike Jacobs was not a happy man. He liked to see long queues at the box office, but on this bitterly cold night, he was sorely disappointed. By the time Farr and Nova climbed into the ring, the vast Madison Square Garden arena was only half full.

Referee Eddie Josephs quickly got the contest under way. It soon became obvious that the Welshman was not in the best of condition, and although Nova began cautiously, he settled down and looked faster than Farr. He was soon scoring well with his left jab, and Tommy's sluggish start worried Joe Gould. 'Make him mix it, Tommy,' he yelled, but Nova wouldn't have any of it. He dictated most of the early rounds, and hurt Tommy on a couple of occasions with short rights to the body. Whenever Farr did get inside trying to belt away to the body, the referee broke them up.

Farr kept plugging away in his familiar style, but needed all his experience to get inside and score with any telling blows. He did appear to have a brief success in the fifth round when Nova went to the floor, but the referee ruled that it was a slip.

Despite his efforts, Tommy wasn't scoring enough, and by the eighth, Nova was a long way ahead. 'You've got to knock this baby out,' shouted the anxious Joe Gould as Tommy returned to his corner. 'Keep fighting the way you are now, and you'll break him into little pieces.' They were desperate words, but Joe had to motivate Tommy somehow, because he wasn't the fighter who had waged war against Louis, Braddock and Baer. The speed wasn't there, the left hand wasn't working as it should be, and he just wasn't throwing enough punches. Gould must have wished that the fight had been postponed, because his man's lack of preparation was very apparent.

His words seemed to have some effect on Tommy because during the next few rounds he put more effort into his work and succeeded in pulling back some of the American's early lead. During rounds 11 and 12, he attacked with both hands, but it was again obvious that he lacked a knockout punch. His other problem was that he hadn't got the strength to hold Nova off when he hit back.

During the thirteenth, Nova looked very tired as Farr kept storming forward, pumping in good body shots which were slowing the American. Most ringside critics believed that Tommy's big effort had levelled the fight by this stage, and his experience would see him through. It had been a good round for the Welshman, and at the bell, Nova was bleeding from the nose and mouth and could hardly lift his arms. His handlers worked desperately to freshen him up, but as the fourteenth round began, Lou was still feeling the effect of the solid body shots from the previous session. 'Get stuck in and knock Farr out,' yelled manager Ray Carlin frantically, believing that his man was about to blow his big chance.

Tommy immediately carried the fight to Nova, but the American somehow found hidden reserves of strength. He changed the course of the fight with a tremendous right to the jaw which made Farr's knees buckle and his mouth drop open. The round had only just begun, but Lou forgot his own pain and tiredness and for almost the entire session bombarded the Welshman with everything he had left. Farr reeled about the ring, a helpless target, and it seemed that he would have to go down under the sheer volume of punches. At one stage, he held onto the ropes to avoid dropping to the canvas. Many ringside critics believed that had he gone down, he wouldn't have had the strength to get up.

Tommy was in desperate trouble, and as Nova moved in to try and finish it, the referee jumped in and pulled him away. Many spectators leapt to their feet thinking the fight had been stopped, but it hadn't. Instead Mr Josephs started to count over Farr, but had only reached two when the Welshman pushed him aside and stormed back at Nova. His success was brief, and he was soon under heavy fire again. Fortunately the bell was not far away, and when it sounded to end the one-sided round, Tommy was still standing, albeit on very rubbery legs. Recognising his courage, the crowd cheered him loudly as he tottered back to his corner.

The referee's action in pulling Nova away brought a storm of criticism from the fighter, his handlers and supporters because they all believed it had saved Farr from being knocked out. Although Tommy had been in terrible trouble, Mr Josephs' intervention was quite in order because a situation where a fighter was defenceless but still standing was covered in the rules of the New York Commission.

The excitement was tremendous as the final round began, with fans believing that Nova could stop Farr. Both men were weary from the gruelling pace, but as they came together in the centre of the ring, Tommy looked the fresher. He was renowned for his tremendous powers of recovery between rounds, and again staged a magnificent final rally. Yet as the round wore on it became clear that he hadn't the strength or the punches to match Nova, who lasted it better. By the close, both men were bleeding from cuts about the face, and looked relieved to end hostilities.

As they waited for the verdict, Farr and Gould were confident of victory, but then to Tommy's disgust it went to Nova on a spilt decision. Had the fight been over ten rounds, he would have won more decisively, but in the later rounds his inexperience had shown as he failed to finish Farr when he was there for the taking.

Tommy couldn't believe the decision, and turning to Joe Gould, asked, 'Joe, perhaps you'll tell me how the scoring is done here. I'm not saying I beat Louis or Baer, but I did beat Braddock, and I've just beaten Nova, and nothing will convince me I didn't.'

Gould just shook his head and replied, 'Don't ask me, Tommy. It's just too bad.'

As Tommy left the ring, he received a wonderful ovation from the crowd, who recognised him as the best import they had seen for years.

A couple of days after the fight, Tommy made special mention of the ovation. 'Nothing has ever sounded more pleasant to my ears,' he remarked. 'American fight fans are the fairest in the world. On the other side, they have no use for a loser. I'm almost as glad over the fact that I gave them a fight they liked, as I would have been had I won the decision.'

Tommy's fights with Braddock and Nova had been close affairs, and he was convinced that he was the victim of home-town decisions. The fact of the matter was, Tommy was no longer a title contender, but just a good opponent for any up-and-coming young heavyweight. Although neither he nor Mike Jacobs would openly admit it, his chances of fighting for the world title again were long gone.

Despite his anger at losing to Nova, within a few days, Tommy had talks with Mike Jacobs about having another fight. The promoter had Madison Square Garden booked for 13 January, and was considering matching Farr with either Maurice Strickland, Red Burman, Gus Dorazio or Roscoe Toles.

Before such a fight could take place, however, it would have to be sanctioned by the New York State Athletic Commission, because the British Boxing Board of Control were still seeking to have Tommy banned in the States.

When the news came that the commission was taking no action against Farr, and he was free to box in New York, Jacobs immediately matched him with Clarence 'Red' Burman. Farr had a great incentive to beat Burman because not only did he badly need a win, but he also wanted to earn some money. The Nova fight had been a disaster; he finished up with just 16 dollars from his purse after he had paid his taxes and an indebtedness to Mike Jacobs.

Once again Jacobs was talking about the possibility of the winner meeting Louis for the title. This came about because of a breakdown in talks the promoter had been having with Ancil Hoffman, the manager of Max Baer.

Back in Britain, Len Harvey had won the British title by beating Eddie Phillips. This prompted speculation that Tommy would return home to challenge Len, and it was known that various syndicates were trying to tempt him.

Tommy started training for his fight with Burman, working out at Stillman's, the most famous gymnasium in the world. Situated on New York's Eighth Avenue, it was an old-fashioned sweatshop with two rings, and large crowds gathered daily to watch him.

As he reached his peak, Tommy's schedule consisted of a six-mile run in Central Park, vigorous floor exercises in the gym, sparring and work on the heavy bag. He gave his sparring partners Abe Feldman and Francis Jacques a rough time, and they were constantly on the defensive against his heavy attacks.

During the later stages of his training, Tommy was somewhat irritable. This was thought to be due to the rigorous nature of his schedule, and the fact that he was suffering from a slight cold.

Farr weighed in at 14 stone 5½ to Burman's 13 stone 1½, giving him a weight advantage of 18 pounds. The odds, which had been 13–8 on, the day before the fight, shortened to 2–1 on by the time they climbed into the ring. It was even rumoured that a number of Burman's supporters had backed Tommy heavily.

From the opening bell, Burman attacked furiously to the body as though believing that Tommy might be fragile in that area. He did most of the forcing in the early rounds, and a right to the heart in the third clearly hurt Tommy. The American, however, became erratic, and several blows, including a heavy left hook, went low. That shot was ruled a foul by the referee, and it cost Burman the round, which he would otherwise have won.

Farr rallied strongly in the fourth, but it was noticeable that there was no power in his punches. By the fifth, he looked a spent fighter, and as the American swarmed all over him, pounding steadily with punches to the head and body, it looked as though Tommy was about to be knocked out.

As so often in the past when the going got tough, Tommy's tremendous courage shone through. Once again he fought back magnificently, and occasional good rights reddened Burman's skin. Unfortunately, most of the time Tommy was going through the motions and his punches were having little effect. By the end of the eighth, however, Burman had punched himself out trying to get rid of Farr, and he was looking extremely weary.

In the last two rounds, Tommy called on all his reserves of energy, and opened up to have the crowd of 9,756 on their feet as he went all out for a dramatic victory. Although Burman didn't have the strength to keep Farr out, there was no power in the Welshman's punches, and he was fighting on sheer heart alone. His big final effort swayed the sentiments of most people in the crowd, but not the judges. Although referee Pete Harley scored it a draw, Judge Eddie Forbes made it six rounds to three, with one even in favour of Burman, and Judge Patsy Haley scored five rounds to four with one even in favour of the American.

The decision was greeted with loud jeering, and there followed one of the worst outbursts of booing ever heard at Madison Square Garden. The din was so bad and went on for so long that it was impossible for the ring announcer to introduce the contestants for the next fight, and it was well into the second round before order was restored.

Although the fight had been close, the crowd's reaction was perhaps an indication as to the fairness of the decision. Farr and Joe Gould both thought they had been robbed again, and Gould was so angry that he said he was going to ask the New York State Athletic Commission to reverse the decision.

Gould's view was not shared by the New York Times boxing critic, who in his report of the contest the following day, remarked: 'The outburst was without justification. The decision was fair, and as a world heavyweight title contender, Tonypandy Tommy is through.'

The majority of fans, however, thought Farr was robbed, and so did the reporter from Associated Press, who gave Farr five rounds, Burman four and one even. The British press, too, were convinced that Tommy had been robbed yet again.

Although Tommy was staggered when he heard the result, he smiled and took defeat in a sporting manner. It was as though he now automatically expected to be returned a loser.

Back in his dressing room, Tommy was the perfect gentleman. He made no real complaint about the decision, although he did tell reporters that he didn't think Burman won a round. He said that the low blows in the third round for which the American was penalised had hurt him quite badly, although they hadn't slowed him down. He added that his cold, which he had tried to play down in training, had been far worse than outsiders knew.

Despite the latest upset, the energetic Mike Jacobs still had ideas for Tommy, and recognised that they still had at least one good payday ahead of them. He promptly offered him a fight with Tony Galento, and there was more talk of the winner going forward to meet Louis for the title.

Once he had come to terms with his latest defeat, Farr wasn't so keen to accept the promoter's offer. He recognised that he was at the crossroads of his career, and couldn't afford another defeat in the States. He knew that the time had come when he would soon have to make a firm decision one way or the other.

In the meantime there was still some socialising to do. There were places to go and people to see, and Tommy wanted to make the most of it while he could. His old friend Nat Gonella, the British bandleader, had arrived in the States just after Christmas while Tommy was preparing to meet Burman. The week after the fight, he took up the bandleader's invitation, and accompanied him to the Cotton Club.

That night, Harlem's famous nightspot was packed with celebrities, including Joe Louis and Max Baer. Everyone was there to say farewell to Abe Lyman, who was taking his band off to Miami for the season. At one point, Tommy was called up onto the stage and introduced, but he politely refused to sing.

Although he was still living it up in the States, meeting folk from back home didn't help Tommy's predicament. With things not going well in the ring, he had become homesick and desperately wanted to see his brothers and sisters. Things had not improved when he was joined by Billy Churchill, because stories of the folk back home made Tommy realise just how much he missed them.

Meeting up with Nat Gonella had a similar effect on his

emotions, yet helped him reach a decision. He had been away for eight months, and the defeat by Burman was the last straw. In the days that followed he became a very disillusioned young man, so somewhat reluctantly, he called Mike Jacobs and turned down the offer to meet Galento. He had decided to pack his bags and head for home.

* * *

Tommy had thought long and hard about what to do, and came to the conclusion that he had nothing more to gain by staying in America. He knew Mike Jacobs would still arrange fights for him, but they would be meaningless because he had become just an opponent for any young up-and-coming American heavyweight. Tommy Farr was too proud to become just a trial horse, so he packed his bags and announced that he would sail home on 10 February.

'I shall positively be aboard the *Queen Mary* on Friday,' he told an Associated Press reporter. 'I've got to go home. I've business to do. I've been here for nearly nine months, and I want to see my brothers and sisters.' Tommy said that he was still willing to meet Galento, and would return to America in four or five weeks. 'But I'm not postponing this trip for anything,' he added.

Apart from the money he had earned, all Tommy could really claim from his experiences in America was that he had displayed a greater degree of courage than any British heavyweight before him. Furthermore, he had finished on his feet at the end of each contest.

Tommy didn't rule out the possibility of further fights in America because there were difficulties to be overcome before he could fight in Britain again. Many of his loyal fans, however, were convinced they had seen him fight there for the very last time.

The American people had taken the Welshman into their hearts, and were with him until the end. He received hundreds of letters and messages of good luck, many of which begged him to return. Thousands lined the quay of New York harbour to bid him farewell, and as he boarded the liner he was given a magnificent send-off.

Despite everything he had said during interviews, there was scepticism in the press over the real reason why Tommy was returning to Britain. There was a strong feeling that he had been offered fights which would earn him far more money than he could now hope for in America. The speculation wasn't far wrong, because as soon as he decided to return home, Farr had cabled Sydney Hulls in London, asking him to meet him aboard the *Queen Mary* when it docked at Cherbourg. Hulls cabled back agreeing to the proposal, but their plans were kept a closely guarded secret.

Hulls managed to slip aboard completely unnoticed. He and Tommy had an amicable meeting lasting half an hour, after which they agreed to continue discussions in London. Hulls then stepped ashore and made his own way back to England.

When Tommy arrived at Southampton later that evening, he was met by a group of Fleet Street boys anxious to know about his plans. He said that the main reason for his return was so that he could attend the wedding of his younger brother Doug. He added that he intended having discussions about the possibility of future fights in London, but made no reference to his meeting with Hulls.

'I'm staying in Britain indefinitely,' said Farr, 'maybe a month or two. It depends on how quickly Mike Jacobs succeeds in signing Tony Galento for me.' Although he said that beating Galento was the best way to get another shot at Louis, Tommy was stalling to avoid revealing his discussions with Sydney Hulls. Asked who he would like to fight in Britain, Tommy said, 'I don't mind. The winner of the Gains–Harvey fight, or even Jack Doyle. He's the fellow I'd like to meet because he would draw a big crowd.'

Tommy went on to explain that his disappointments against Nova and Burman were largely due to loss of weight. 'I lost twenty-five pounds before meeting Nova,' he remarked. 'This worried me, so after fighting him, I consulted a doctor, who diagnosed lung trouble and advised treatment at Hot Springs in Arkansas. This had an excellent effect and now I feel my old self again.'

That evening, Tommy travelled to London in the company of John McAdam of the *Daily Express*, a journalist for whom he had the greatest respect. As he had no idea what the future held for him, Tommy sought McAdam's guidance and reassurance.

They eventually agreed that there appeared to be just two real options. Either Tommy returned to the United States to meet Tony Galento in Atlantic City; or – the more sensible course – he stayed at home and challenged the winner of the Harvey–Gains fight for the vacant British Empire title, scheduled for 16 March, which would give Tommy the opportunity to aim at one of the titles he never lost in the ring.

In London, it was noticed that Tommy was wearing a big diamond ring on the little finger of his left hand. At first he refused to say anything about it. Eventually, contradicting what he had told a reporter in Cherbourg, Tommy admitted he was engaged to an American girl who had given it to him as an engagement present.

'I would not tell you her name even if you offered me a thousand pounds,' said Tommy. 'All I can say is, she is an American girl of English extraction. She is still at college, and she is a brunette.'

The first indication that Farr and Hulls had put their differences behind them came one day when a reporter happened to be in Hulls' office. The telephone rang, and from Hulls' reaction, it was obvious that Farr was the caller. Although lengthy, the conversation was good-natured, and after it was over, Hulls insisted that the situation was not to become public knowledge.

Meanwhile, Job Churchill's son Billy, who had travelled home from the States with Farr, returned to Penygraig full of news of his trip. 'I have had a millionaire's holiday,' he said. 'It was a wonderful time, and I will never forget it.' He insisted that Tommy was engaged. 'I have met Tommy's fiancée. She's a marvellous girl, but I'm not going to tell you her name.'

Proudly relating some of his experiences, Billy said, 'If Farr was world champion, he could not be more popular. It is amazing the number of letters he received in America from Welsh admirers begging him to come home. When I walked down the street with him, it was like walking with royalty. Everyone wanted to shake his hand and pat him on the back. In Miami when he had a cold, practically every doctor there wrote or rang him offering to cure him. Wealthy people offered him the loan of yachts. In hotels and restaurants, waiters dropped their trays to ask him for autographs.'

Within a couple of days of Billy Churchill's return to the Rhondda, Tommy followed suit. He was particularly keen to see Job, who had been very ill.

Tommy stayed in the Rhondda for about a week before returning to London for the Eric Boon–Arthur Danahar fight being staged at Harringay by Sydney Hulls. Farr was introduced from the ring, and received a wonderful reception when he announced that he hoped to be fighting in London the following month. A few days later, Hulls accompanied Tommy to the National Sporting Club, where he was given another rousing reception.

Behind the scenes, the talks with Hulls went well, and within a few days the promoter announced that they had settled their differences, and that Farr would meet 'Red' Burman at Harringay in April.

Many critics doubted the fight would interest the fans, because Burman was the least attractive of Tommy's American opponents. A delighted Farr saw it differently, and at a press conference said, 'There is nobody I would like to meet more than Burman. I would almost be prepared to fight him for nothing so as to get even with him.'

Hulls was prepared to gamble on the fight because he believed it was important to get Tommy back into a British ring for the first time in almost two years. The fans were longing to see him again and they still talked about his epic encounters with Baer and Neusel at Harringay. Despite this, as he set off for America to get Burman to sign contracts, Hulls knew he could lose a great deal of money on the fight.

Suddenly, however, the fight took on a new meaning when the National Boxing Association world rankings for March were published. Burman had moved up to number five, whilst Farr had dropped out of the top ten. Now it looked a good fight for Tommy to take, because if he won it would push him back into the rankings.

Burman's adviser was Jack Dempsey, and knowing his popularity, Hulls persuaded him to travel to London to be at ringside for the fight. It was a good move by the promoter because once the news got around that Jack would be accompanying Burman, tickets began to sell rapidly. Hulls had, however, overlooked the fact that Farr had still not paid his debts to the Board of Control. Within hours of signing up Burman, he received a cablegram in New York from the board advising him that the Welshman was still suspended.

Tommy had always insisted that he had no intention of paying the £750 fine imposed by the board. Hulls knew he was a man of principle and unlikely to change his mind. So he cabled his secretary in London with instructions to pay the money owed to the board into Farr's bank account. Even then, Tommy would not release his cheque until he received confirmation of the deposit from his bank.

The following day, the Board of Control issued a statement confirming that Tommy had been given clearance to box in Britain again.

Burman arrived in Britain on 24 March, and Jack Dempsey was to follow a week later. Red told reporters that Farr was nothing more than a rough, tough guy with no punch. He said he had no time for a fighter who made excuses in defeat as Farr had done after their contest in New York.

Following his short break in the Rhondda, Tommy moved to Brighton and set up his training camp at the Black Lion at Patcham. His headquarters were at the Ocean Hotel at Saltdean. He said that provided he beat Burman, he would challenge Len Harvey, who had just beaten Larry Gains to take the British Empire title. 'An open-air venue during August Bank Holiday would be an ideal time for such an attractive contest,' said Tommy, 'because everyone would be free to see it.'

In the absence of Joe Gould, who was in America, Tommy started training under the supervision of Eddie Whiting and Harry Goodman, and did his roadwork on the Sussex Downs. 'The air on the Downs is wonderful,' he remarked. 'Just what a boxer wants in his lungs.'

Although he said he was determined to get himself into peak condition, the Welshman appeared to lack his usual confidence to begin with. The arrival of Job Churchill in Brighton, however, was just the tonic he needed, and the old enthusiasm was soon back. This was particularly noticeable one day in late March as he worked rigorously in front of a big crowd at the Sussex Boxing and Athletic Club in North Street in the centre of Brighton. Harry Burns, an undefeated 20-year-old Brighton amateur, and promising heavyweight George Markwick, were shown no mercy as Tommy worked to get into shape.

Whether he was boxing or not, Tommy still had a big following. This was confirmed just a week after he returned from the States, when he was presented on the BBC programme *In Town Tonight*, and also on the stage of the London Hippodrome where he appeared as a guest at an all-star concert in aid of the Lyon Hospital Aid Society.

Many spectators who visited the Black Lion were surprised to see that since going to the States, not only had Tommy's style of boxing changed, but so had his personality. A number of reporters found that his temperament and general attitude were different. Gone was the rather trying attitude that had made him difficult to deal with a couple of years earlier. Instead, he was quieter, and there was nothing arrogant or bombastic about him.

Prior to the Louis fight, Farr had been a fast and elusive boxer. His main weapon had been the famed left hand, but this seemed to have almost disappeared. Instead, he had adopted a two-fisted American style of fighting and was trying to use the heavy right

Farr, Dennis Powell and their handlers, pose with referee Ike Powell after their fight at Shrewsbury on 7 July 1951

Farr (right) mixes it at close quarters against Georges Rogiers at Brighton on 3 December 1951

South Africa's Jake Tuli (left), Farr, France's Robert Meunier, and Don Cockell at the weigh-in for their fights at Nottingham on 9 March 1953

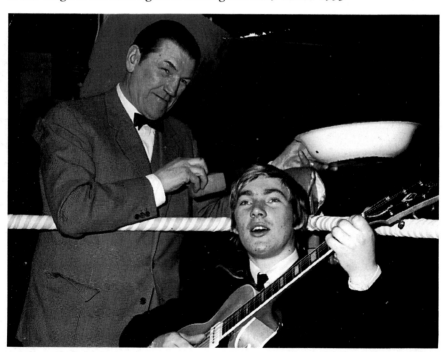

Tommy proudly observes son Gary playing his guitar at the Cambridge Gym, Earlham Street, London on 25 February 1965. Gary Farr and the T-Bones were a successful pop group in the 60s

Farr meets Muhammed Ali at his Shepherds Bush training quarters on 13 March 1966 where he prepared to meet Henry Cooper

Peter West (left), Ike Powell, Farr and Harry Carpenter, at rehearsal for the BBC Wales programme *Game and Match – Boxing* on 5 August 1967

Farr and Joe Louis square up at their reunion at the Hilton Hotel, London on 13 January 1973

Tommy meets former world heavyweight champion Joe Frazier at the Anglo American Sporting Club dinner at the Hilton Hotel in London on 14 June 1971

Tom Gummer (left), Farr, John L. Gardner, and Joe Erskine at the British Boxing Board of Control 50th Anniversary dinner at the Cafe Royal on 7 November 1979

With Mickey Barnett, mine host of the Albion Tavern, Fleet Street at the Boxing Writers dinner at the Savoy Hotel in 1979

Elder statesman pose at the age of 68 years

At Croydon Ex-Boxers Association meeting with (left – right) Johnny White, Farr, Jim Toohig and Tom Powell (President)

One of the last photos taken of Tommy. Sussex Ex-Boxers Association gathering at Hove in 1984 with Albert Starr (right), Jack 'Kid' Berg, Ernie Woodman and Glen Moody

Tommy and Monty shortly before Tommy's death in March 1986

Tommy's ashes were placed inside the grave he erected for his parents at Trealaw Cemetery more than 50 years earlier

hand more often. This was slowing him down, and some critics believed he was now easier to hit.

Joe Gould arrived in Britain at the beginning of April and immediately went to Brighton. He admitted that he had been extremely worried during Tommy's fights with Nova and Burman because the Welshman had clearly not recovered from illness. Even so, he was convinced that Tommy beat Burman in New York but was robbed of the decision. 'There will be no doubt about the outcome this time,' said Joe. 'Tommy is in such grand shape already, that I am certain he will lick Burman easily.'

In the pre-fight interviews, Joe did not deny a change in the Welshman's style during training. 'Tommy might not box prettily in the gym,' he remarked. 'That's because he does not want to outclass his sparring partners. But tonight you will see the Farr of old shooting out his left as he did before.'

Farr himself told newsmen that he was confident of reversing the decision over Burman. 'Having settled my dues with Sydney Hulls,' he added, 'I hope the Board of Control will soon give me my titles back.' Although he was extremely serious in making the remark, Tommy must have realised it would never happen. The only way he would get them back would be by winning them in the ring.

Although there had been doubts about the fight's drawing power, there was a huge demand for tickets, and receipts had exceeded £10,000. The Great Western Railway was running special trains from South Wales to Paddington, and a sell-out looked a certainty.

Two years had passed since he beat Baer and Neusel, but Farr was still a tremendous attraction. On the night of the fight, all roads leading to Harringay were heavy with slow-moving traffic as some 11,600 fans converged on the stadium. If anything, the five defeats in America had increased Tommy's popularity because, like their American counterparts, the British fans knew he had endless courage.

Job Churchill was convinced that some of Tommy's defeats in America were due to his change in style, so shortly before Farr was due in the ring, he went to the dressing room. Ignoring Joe Gould, he pleaded with Tommy to outbox Burman rather than trying to mix it with him. Farr listened intently as his philosopher told him to revert to the tactics that brought him victories over Foord, Baer and Neusel. To Job's delight, just before climbing into the ring, Tommy patted him on the shoulder saying, 'All right, Dad, I will concentrate on my left for your sake.'

As the lights dimmed and fanfares heralded his return, the crowd rose and gave the Welshman a wonderful welcome. The hero was back, and to make him feel at home, the sound of *Land of My Fathers* echoed once more around the nostalgic arena. Standing rigidly to attention, with a red dragon emblazoned on his dressing gown, Tommy seemed overawed by the occasion.

The referee for the fight was Eugene Henderson of Scotland, who was officiating in London for the first time. Although an experienced and capable official, he couldn't have had a tougher baptism in the capital, because before the fight had even started he was confronted with a somewhat difficult problem. Standing beneath the ring arc lights, sporting at least three days' growth on his face, Burman appeared to be heavily coated in grease. Mr Henderson told the American's chief second, Maxie Waxman, to remove his fighter's dressing gown. As he did so, it confirmed the official's suspicions because Burman was covered from head to waist by a thick coating of vaseline.

'Clean it off,' ordered Henderson.

Waxman made a few gentle pats with a towel, but the referee was far from satisfied. Seizing the towel, he told the American corner that the fight was under British rules, which would be strictly complied with, and he personally wiped off the grease.

At the opening bell, both fighters went to work at close quarters as though releasing tensions caused by the delay. Farr soon gave his big contingent of fans their first excitement as he rammed five straight lefts into Burman's face in quick succession. Although he was caught by a heavy right hook before the bell, Tommy's first round back in a British ring had been a winning one.

As they came out for round two, Henderson took Burman back to his corner and wiped another heavy application of grease from his face. Farr continued making good use of his left jab, and varied his work with some good shots to the body from both hands. There was one rally where both men joined in a toe-to-toe slam, throwing heavy punches, and the crowd were cheering loudly by the end of the round.

As the fight progressed, so Tommy continued to score well with his left, and his work rate was much greater than Burman's. The American was intent on landing heavy single shots, and had some success in the fourth when he bloodied Farr's nose. It had an immediate effect on the Welshman, who snarled and stormed after his opponent, and one terrific right staggered him. Sensing that Burman was in trouble, the crowd yelled for Tommy to finish it, but the American covered up and survived the round.

The fifth was a great round for Tommy as he jabbed Burman silly, and then in a two-fisted attack had him in serious trouble. There was so much excitement that Farr's corner were cautioned by the referee for continuously yelling for their man to end it. Burman was in trouble again in the sixth, but although Tommy was 19 pounds heavier, he didn't have the punch to end it.

The Welshman won the seventh and eighth rounds by wide margins as he dominated with his left. Midway through the eighth, Burman emerged from a fierce exchange with blood streaming from a nasty cut above his right eye. Sensing the danger, he launched a big attack and brought blood dripping from Farr's damaged nose.

Although Burman's injury was patched up, Tommy continued to control the fight, and by the eleventh Burman needed a knockout to win. Launching a big attack, he rocked the Welshman with several heavy shots, and for once the left hand failed to dominate. Tommy knew his chin was sound, so he stood and traded punches in a good old-fashioned slog. The crowd were on their feet, screaming with excitement as both men threw everything they had. It was Burman's best round, but Farr gave as good as he got in the heavy exchanges.

As soon as the bell sounded for the final session, both men threw everything into the attack. Burman showed that he was still strong and caught Farr flush on the nose, bringing another stream of blood dripping onto his chest. Tommy was so far ahead that he could have jabbed and run, but that was not the way he fought. Instead, he chased the American, shooting out a stream of jabs. Then as Burman countered, they indulged in another hectic exchange right up to the final bell.

The crowd were screaming, and as referee Henderson walked over and raised Tommy's arm in victory, the noise became deafening. Burman knew he had lost, and before Henderson raised his arm, threw his arm around Tommy's neck and said 'Good Luck, Tommy.' Within seconds, *Land of My Fathers* echoed loudly around Harringay once again. The referee was still holding Tommy's arm aloft when the menacing figure of Maxie Waxman strode purposefully across the ring towards him. Surprisingly it was not to rebuke, but congratulate him on his handling of the contest. Although Maxie had a reputation of being an outspoken individual, he told Henderson that he had been the first official ever to put him in his place, and there were no hard feelings.

Back in his dressing room, Farr was besieged by pressmen and photographers. In answer to questions, he said, 'I know I cannot claim to have accomplished anything by beating Burman tonight, but this victory has restored all my old confidence. It has given me new fighting heart. People didn't know it, but I was becoming very down-hearted.' Tommy admitted that the welcome from the crowd, and the singing of the Welsh National Anthem, meant more to him than beating Burman. 'It was just like old times to me,' he remarked. 'Now I'm ready to take on anyone. I shall not be going back to America for a long time. I want to do more fighting here.'

Job Churchill's advice had been sound, because although Tommy was not as fast as before going to the States, he had kept pace with his lighter opponent by sticking to orthodox boxing and accurate punching. The Welshman had shown that his left jab was as good as ever, and beat a merciless tattoo on Burman's face and body. For good measure, he had thrown plenty of solid rights to the body. They were sound tactics because the American had a good chin, and the body shots slowed him down.

Joe Gould returned to America the morning after the fight in the company of Burman and Maxie Waxman. Before leaving, he told Tommy that if he ever changed his mind and decided to have another try in the States, he would happily look after him.

After a short break in Tonypandy, Tommy returned to London for a meeting at Sydney Hulls' office. The promoter fancied the idea of trying to bring the Welshman's American conquerors to London one by one. Hulls cabled Joe Louis with an offer of £30,000 free of tax to defend his title against Farr in London during July or early August. Joe Gould, Hulls' representative in the States, discussed the proposal with Mike Jacobs. 'I do not, however, expect a final answer until after Louis has defended his title against Tony Galento on 28 June,' he said.

'Nothing would suit me finer,' said a delighted Farr when he heard the news. 'I would welcome the chance of reversing that verdict against me, and I would be prepared to fight him for nothing if they could bring him here.'

Knowing that it would be the biggest fight in the history of British boxing, Hulls looked no further than Wembley Stadium or the Arsenal Football Ground at Highbury with a view to staging the contest in the open air.

20

LARRY GAINS, WAR AND PROBLEMS

Despite his efforts, Sydney Hulls was having difficulty finding another leading American who was willing to meet Farr in Britain. Larry Gains was an extremely popular figure in the British rings, so Hulls offered him a fight with Tommy and he readily agreed.

Gains had been boxing as a professional since 1923, and had taken part in over 130 contests. He won the British Empire heavyweight title in 1931 by beating Phil Scott, and held it until 1934, when he was beaten by Jack Petersen. He still continued to fight top-class opposition, and was a household name. In the earlier years of his career, he had boxed all over the world, and one of his most notable scalps was that of Max Schmeling, whom he knocked out in two rounds in Cologne in 1925.

During 1938, the British Boxing Board of Control recognised that he was still a quality fighter, and nominated him to meet Maurice Strickland of New Zealand in a final eliminator for the vacant British Empire title (the title the board had taken from Tommy Farr). When that contest failed to materialise, they matched him with the newly crowned British heavyweight champion, Len Harvey, for the vacant title.

Larry had remained unbeaten in his last 22 contests, but sadly old age caught up with him at Harringay on 16 March 1939. When the referee examined a cut above his right eye at the end of the thirteenth round, the 38-year-old ex-champion agreed it was time to retire, not only from the fight, but from boxing. Sydney Hulls, however, persuaded him to have just one more fight.

The fight between Farr and Gains was set for Cardiff's Ninian Park on 17 May, and it would be the first time that Farr had boxed in front of his own countrymen since he beat Jim Wilde

277

for the Welsh heavyweight title in September 1936. Interest was so great that it was expected to attract crowds of international football proportions.

Although Farr and Gains agreed to the fight, the signing of contracts was delayed for several days due to a disagreement between them over its duration. Being the younger man, Farr wanted it to be over 15 rounds, but Larry on the other hand was insistent that it be over 10 rounds. Eventually, both boxers agreed to a compromise of 12 rounds.

Farr said that he had wanted to meet Gains for some time. 'A few years ago, I fought George Brennan at Leicester, and Gains was his second that night,' he recalled. 'In the fight, Gains said a few things about me which I disliked immensely.' Tommy claimed that following an exchange of words, he became so incensed that he offered to fight the Canadian there and then. Gains allegedly replied, 'Go away little boy', and Tommy told reporters that he still remembered the jibe, and badly wanted revenge.

Some years later when Larry wrote his autobiography, he recalled the same incident, but with some slight differences. He recalled how Brennan was floored in the second round and in all sorts of trouble. Gains climbed onto the ring apron and shouted, 'Stay down, Bill,' When the count reached nine, he shouted, 'Get up and claim him.' Brennan got up, hung on for dear life, and survived the round. This went on through several rounds, and each time Brennan went down or was in trouble, Larry yelled advice. Gains claimed that Farr became so angry that he leaned over the ropes and shouted, 'I can lick you.' Larry shouted back, 'You couldn't lick me if I was a lollipop.'

In his book Larry claimed that the remarks which flew back and forth between him and Tommy that night became a great joke between them in later years. Away from the ring, Farr and Gains had become firm friends, and would remain so for many years after their ring careers were over. In the weeks leading up to their fight in Cardiff, however, Tommy was telling a different story, undoubtedly doing all he could to promote maximum interest in the contest. Both men got down to serious training as soon as the fight was announced. Larry set up camp at Shoeburyness on the Essex coast, whilst Tommy returned to Patcham, where he trained to meet Burman.

Demand for tickets was tremendous, and increased a few days before the fight when Sydney Hulls decided to reduce prices of seats in the cheaper part of the arena from three shillings to two. It was a goodwill gesture to Tommy's many working-class and unemployed supporters. The Great Western Railway announced that cheap trains would run to and from all parts of South Wales, with a number of special late services being added to assist everyone to get home.

After completing his training, Tommy flew from Brighton to Cardiff Airport on 15 May aboard a Western Airways aircraft, despite Hulls' objections because of the risk involved. Tommy had become very air-minded in the United States, and regarded the trip from the south coast to Wales as 'just a small hop', despite the fact that on the day of the flight there was a terrible gale blowing.

The weigh-in took place at Tommy's hotel, and he caused some amusement by appearing in a pair of red pyjamas with a yellow stripe for a bet. Both men weighed-in at 14 stone 8½, but Farr was the younger man by 13 years.

Tommy did have one concern because he had left his lucky water bottle on the aeroplane when he arrived at Cardiff. After a few quick phone calls, the bottle was flown back from Liverpool so that he could have it in his corner.

Ninian Park was packed with almost 40,000 excited fans welcoming Tommy back into a ring in his native South Wales for the first time since 1936. With Larry Gains in the opposite corner, they were entitled to expect a classic contest, and no doubt Farr's threat of revenge had added fuel to the attraction.

Before the show began, there was community singing led by Mr Ratcliffe, who led similar entertainment before the FA Cup Finals at Wembley Stadium, and the Cardiff Transport Band played at intervals over a period of two hours before the boxing programme began. People needed to be entertained because it was a bitterly cold night and the fingers of many fans were numbed by the biting wind that blew up from the River Taff.

Eventually the long wait for the main event was over, and four trumpeters heralded the entrance to the ring, first of Larry Gains, and then Farr. Both looked in splendid condition, and they were received with deafening cheers.

As the bell sounded for the opening round, Farr sprang from his corner, showing he was intent on an early finish. He was fast and aggressive, and the experience he had gained in the States soon became obvious as he bobbed and weaved inside to bang away at the stomach of his older opponent with both hands. These were good tactics, deliberately aimed at trying to slow down Gains before he got going.

Although he was under heavy fire, Larry remained calm, and

used his left jab to try and hold off his younger opponent. Farr, though, would have none of it, and kept up a relentless attack, storming forward throughout the opening round to win it by a wide margin.

He came out for round two still clearly intent on destroying his opponent, and landed two terrific left hooks which caused Larry to give ground. At this point, the Canadian showed his immense skill and experience as he replied with a good right to the body followed by a jabbing left into Farr's face as he pressed forward.

Although the Welshman was still going for the body, intent on wearing his opponent down, he was not getting things all his own way, because at close quarters the vastly experienced Gains tied him up. At one stage in this round, he shook Tommy with a series of solid right hooks to the head, and things were beginning to look very interesting.

The third round opened with another terrific attack from the Welshman as he fired in beautiful lefts to the face, followed by more driving rights to the body. He drove Gains all over the ring, and the pace was so furious that many ringsiders were wondering just how long they could keep it up.

To the Canadian's credit, he was taking Farr's punches well, and then towards the end of the round, he started scoring with his own left to the face as Tommy stormed after him. Nevertheless, it was Farr who was setting the pace, and his tactics were winning the fight.

The Welshman began round four by again tearing straight into the attack, hooking to the body, to have Gains backing away and defending with all his might. Farr's attacks were relentless as he switched from head to body and back to the head again. There was no respite for the Canadian in this round, and he took a terrific right hook to the jaw which would have floored many lesser men. He took the punch well, and saw out the round.

Shortly after the fifth round had begun, it was clear that Larry was having trouble with his right hand. He continued to box cleverly, jabbing Farr with the left, but he was very much a one-handed fighter. Sensing that his opponent had problems, the ruthless Farr tore into him, hooking to the body with both hands. Towards the end of the round, Larry had no defence to another tremendous right to the jaw, and he was in serious trouble. He needed all his experience and courage, to survive the round without taking a count.

As the bell sounded to end the round, it was a dejected-looking Larry Gains who returned to his corner holding up his right glove.

There was a lot of talking in his corner, and towards the end of the interval, referee Moss Deyong was called over. Then Deyong strode straight across to Farr, and an almighty cheer went up as he raised his arm in victory.

'Farr is the winner,' announced MC Patsy Regan, who had been brought down from London specially for the occasion. 'Larry Gains has retired with a damaged hand.'

Tommy gave a whoop of delight and leapt into the air. Then he turned and waved to the crowd before running across to Gains to pat him sympathetically on the shoulder.

The ending was a great disappointment to the huge crowd. It gave Tommy no satisfaction either. 'Larry,' he said to Gains before leaving the ring, 'I wish there was a better way for you to go.'

The Canadian smiled and shrugged his shoulders. 'Tommy, there's never a good way to go.'

There was tremendous excitement among Tommy's supporters, and as he made his way back to his dressing room, police had to force back the huge crowds as they tried to hoist their hero shoulder high.

Farr was highly elated with his second success since returning to Britain, but he was none the less very anxious to know what the crowd thought of his performance.

'Did the crowd like my fighting?' he asked *South Wales Argus* correspondent 'Marlovian'. 'How did I fight?'

When the reporter told him that he believed he fought better than he did against Burman, Tommy replied modestly, 'I want to keep on improving, and I believe I shall. I feel much fitter since I returned from America. My confidence is returning. I feel I can still climb back to the top. I was still warming up when Gains retired.'

In Larry Gains' dressing room, it was seen that the knuckles of his right thumb and forefinger, had been badly displaced; an old injury had been damaged when he threw a heavy uppercut which caught Farr on the left elbow. It was the last time that Larry Gains fought, but despite the pre-fight stories that Tommy told, the two of them remained firm friends and frequently met at ex-boxers' conventions and association dinners. When Larry eventually died, Tommy was particularly upset.

As soon as news reached the United States that he had beaten Gains, Tommy received telephone calls from both Joe Gould and Mike Jacobs urging him to return. The Welshman's priority, however, was to prove beyond doubt that he was still the number one heavyweight in Britain. America was in the past, and now all he wanted to do was win back his old titles.

Although there was a lot of talk about an inevitable showdown between Farr and Len Harvey, most of it was without any real foundation. About a week later, Sydney Hulls announced an ambitious programme for the Welshman. He said that Tommy would meet Walter Neusel over 12 rounds at Cardiff by the end of June, and then planned to match him with Jack Doyle in London during mid-July. Should he win those fights, he would meet either Eddie Phillips or Jack London in Cardiff over the August Bank Holiday. If all went according to plan, he hoped Farr would fight Harvey in London at the end of August.

Suddenly, to the disappointment of everyone, the Board of Control threw a spanner in the works by refusing to allow Tommy to meet either Neusel or Doyle. No explanation was given for the rejection of the German, but as Doyle's only fight in the last two years had been when he was knocked out in two rounds by Eddie Phillips the previous September, the board considered him unsuitable.

Not to be outdone, Hulls reverted to his original idea, and announced that he intended bringing Lou Nova, Max Baer and James J. Braddock to London to meet Farr. In early June, Braddock accepted Hulls' offer to meet Tommy at Earls Court on 5 July, but this was later postponed. One by one Hulls' plans for Tommy fell apart.

When war loomed up, like many other leading boxers, Tommy offered himself for active service and joined the Royal Air Force. So too did Len Harvey, who jokingly remarked, 'It would be rather funny if Tommy and I were to clash in an inter-squadron battle. It could not be for the British and Empire titles, nor for the purse monies we would get in the ordinary way, but...'

In October, Tommy signed with Dublin promoter Gerald Egan to fight Manuael Abrew, which brought criticism from the press. The promoter reminded the critics that Abrew had knocked out George James, and given Len Harvey a terrific battle.

Farr took no chances as he prepared for the fight because he knew that plans were still being made for him to meet both Harvey and Joe Louis. He did not treat Abrew lightly, and engaged three sparring partners, Billy Ross and Canadian brothers Paul and Bernard Cook, to assist him. The intensive training paid off because Tommy knocked out Abrew with comparative ease after just 1 minute 18 seconds of the third round.

The crowd of 4,000 at Dublin's Theatre Royal were thoroughly disappointed, but recognised it had been a fine performance by the Welshman. He demonstrated his power as early as the first round, when punches from both hands had Abrew looking distinctly uncomfortable. It was the same in round two, and Abrew hadn't the strength to hold Tommy off as he stormed forward throwing big shots to the body. In the third he stepped up a gear and showed he was a class above the Scotsman, who was floored twice for counts of nine and eight. He rose gamely each time, but went crashing to the canvas again from a tremendous right under the heart. Although he crawled to the ropes and tried to haul himself up, Abrew was counted out, and looked in trouble for some ten minutes as his seconds worked on him.

* * *

Although Tommy volunteered for military service just three days after the declaration of war, he was also very involved in affairs of a more personal nature. Journalists who closely followed proposals for him to meet Harvey and Louis were completely unaware that the Welshman had a special lady in his life.

The affair was conducted with such secrecy that when Tommy was married on 1 November 1939, not one newspaper reported it. His marriage remained such a well-kept secret that it would not become public knowledge until three years later. By that time Tommy was the proud father of Rosalind Ann, aged two, and newly born Thomas Richard. When the story finally hit the newspapers in December 1942, neighbours couldn't understand what all the fuss was about. Tommy and his wife were just like any other married couple.

Tommy had been terrified that a blaze of publicity might cause him to lose the lady he loved. His fear stemmed from his relationship with Eileen Wenzell in America a couple of years earlier. Between fights, he and Eileen had mixed with many famous people and gone to exotic places including Hollywood. As a society figure, she made the perfect companion for Tommy at prestigious gatherings, but wherever they went, they were harassed by reporters wanting to know if their plans included marriage. Photographers were continually taking pictures because the beauty and the prize fighter made big headlines. At the time, Eileen was the only girl in the world for Tommy, but it was extremely difficult for them to find privacy. Eventually in desperation, he suggested they secretly ran away to escape the constant attention of the media. When Tommy asked Eileen to marry him, to his horror, she refused. He was convinced it was because she couldn't stand the pressure they were under. Shortly afterwards, he returned to Britain a very bitter and disappointed man. Tommy blamed the press for the break-up of his first real love affair, and was determined the same thing would never happen again.

Fortunately for Tommy, he had plenty of good friends in Britain, and shortly after returning to London he was invited to go to Olympia to watch showjumping. Among the contestants was Carol Montgomery, an attractive auburn-haired young woman from Wanton in Devon who was one of the best horsewomen in the country. After the show they were introduced on the basis that both were at the top of their fields of sport.

Tommy was stunned by Carol's charm, and invited her out to dinner at the fashionable Coq d'Or in Mayfair. The next day he sent her a love poem which he had specially written for her. He loved poetry, and being a Welshman, it was very romantic. Their friendship quickly developed into a firm love affair, and Tommy later admitted it was the poem that won him the lady.

Carol Montgomery was her stage name having been a model for fashion and advertising. She was born Muriel Montgomery Germon in British Columbia, but Tommy called her 'Monty'. She was an expert pilot, so they flew together and generally built a wonderful relationship. When they decided to get married Tommy was so excited that he wanted to telephone everyone he knew and break the news, until he remembered what had happened with Eileen Wenzell.

Tommy and Monty, as he now called her, set up home at Brighton, but had no time for a honeymoon. Not only had he enlisted with the Royal Air Force, but he was also due to fight Manuel Abrew in Dublin nine days later.

The Welshman's period with the RAF was very short-lived because within a few weeks he suffered from a series of illnesses. After examination he was declared unfit for military service and discharged on medical grounds. There were suggestions that Tommy had pulled a stroke in order to continue boxing, and the matter became of such public concern that on 21 February 1940, it was raised in the House of Commons.

Despite the doubts, Tommy suffered from extremely poor health during the next two years or so. One of the main complaints was catarrhal trouble, and in April 1940 he was admitted to Wembley hospital. There he underwent operations on his nose, right eye and ear, which were regarded as a complete success.

Whilst in hospital, Tommy received an unexpected visit from a police officer. Some weeks earlier he had been fined over a motoring offence at Gloucester, and somehow the princely sum of ninepence had been omitted and remained unpaid. The court issued a warrant for his arrest, and attempted to execute it at the hospital. With the country in the middle of war, the Welshman was full of indignation and made his feelings known.

Tommy was released from hospital after two weeks and went to Patcham in Sussex to convalesce. The air from the Downs and the sea were the perfect tonic, and he was soon well on the mend. On 6 May, he made his first public appearance since the operations, when together with Sydney Hulls, he attended a boxing show at Watford Town Hall. There he was presented with a gold watch as a token of esteem from local sportsmen for his services to British boxing.

In mid-July, the Welshman was given a great reception when he attended a boxing show at Barnstaple promoted by Dai Morgan in aid of the Mayor's Fund for the fighting forces. Mayor Charles Dart explained that Tommy had travelled at his own expense to support the show and had intimated that as soon as he was fit enough he would box on a show in aid of the fund.

True to his word, in early August Tommy met Zachy Nicholas from Cornwall, who was billed as the heavyweight champion of the West of England. Although he put up a plucky show, Nicholas was no match for the Welshman. He was floored for a count of six, and punished heavily with body punches before retiring at the end of the third round, although Tommy was nowhere near full fitness.

As his health improved, Tommy made four attempts to get back into the RAF but was always rejected on medical grounds. He was turned down by the navy when he tried to join a mine-sweeping crew, and also by the army. His continued rejection by the armed services caused such a stir that it became the subject of another, very different, debate in the House of Commons on 25 March 1942.

Tommy was still determined to do something for his country, so he built a gymnasium at the end of his garden, and started training. When he considered he was fit enough, he volunteered to travel around the countryside and entertain the troops by giving exhibitions and lectures on boxing.

Tommy proudly described his work in July 1942:

I have as many as four or five shows a week. They range from places as far apart as Hamble and Tonbridge. My visits are under the organisation of MESA, which is short for Military Entertainments for the Sussex Area. I go out to lonely gun sites where there are perhaps 80 to 100 soldiers, and I find the work extremely interesting. Some of these fellows surprise me with the knowledge they have of my career. They remember little things which have been written, and often question me about them.

Although he was unable to fight alongside the troops as he wished, Tommy at least had the satisfaction of entertaining them. They loved him for it and he received warm receptions wherever he went.

As war continued, Tommy desperately wanted to do something for the War Charity, but was still suffering from the stomach problems which had been partly responsible for his medical discharge. He was required to go on a scientific diet allowing him just one substantial meal a day. Compressed foods for breakfast and supper made him practically a vegetarian and caused him to lose weight. Tommy insisted that he felt well, but added, 'If I go on losing weight as I am, I shall soon be down to middleweight.'

Although he was nearly a stone lighter than when he fought Joe Louis, Tommy took part in bouts to aid the War Charity. But after watching him in an exhibition with George Markwick, Job Churchill was so concerned that he told Tommy to stay permanently retired.

Against Markwick, Tommy had looked very drawn, and although he showed flashes of skill, general opinion was that he should forget about boxing until he had abandoned his diet and gained at least a stone. Despite the warnings, the Welshman remained determined to help the War Charity, and at the back of his mind was still the possibility of a fight with Len Harvey.

In view of Tommy's stubbornness, it was as well that Harvey unwittingly solved the problem by meeting Freddie Mills in London in July 1942. Len had also gone backwards, and was knocked out in the second round by the young, fresh challenger from Bournemouth, who took his British and Empire light heavyweight titles. Len never fought again, ending once and for all any hopes Farr had of meeting him.

Throughout this time, Tommy continued to live at Brighton with Monty and their daughter. Then in December 1942, their second child, Thomas Richard, was born.

When he retired from the ring, Tommy was a rich man as fighters went, and was fortunate to have a good business brain. He bought a large old house in Upper Drive, Hove, which he named Glovers, and this became the family home. After his discharge from the RAF, he invested some of his hard-earned capital by speculating in a number of valuable properties, particularly along the seafront at Hove. He took over the Royal Standard public house in Queens Road close to Brighton railway station, decked the walls with boxing photographs, and it became known as Tommy Farr's Bar.

Next door he opened a restaurant and called it Tommy Farr's Pantry. Along with the pub, it was run by his brothers Doug and John. Tommy also operated a successful bookmaker's business, South Coast Commissions Limited, also situated in Queens Road. The three ventures operated successfully for several years, but in 1945, Tommy lost his publican's licence after being convicted of assault at the Royal Standard.

Situated on the main road between the station and seafront, the pub was very popular, and frequented by a number of individuals who liked to boast that they drank in Tommy Farr's pub. As is often the case, a well-known figure can sometimes attract trouble, which is exactly what happened to Tommy on the night of 17 January 1945.

A group of young sailors drinking in the bar were reluctant to leave at closing time. As Tommy tried to get them out, a scuffle developed and one lad allegedly sustained a fractured nose. The incident was reported to the police, and Tommy duly received a summons alleging assault occasioning actual bodily harm. He appeared at Brighton Magistrates' Court on 6 February, and pleaded Not Guilty to the charge.

In evidence, Tommy stated that the sailors were behaving in a boisterous manner in the bar and he had occasion to speak to them about bad language. When he called 'last orders' one of them shouted, 'We don't take orders from third-rate fighting punks.' There was also a remark made about broken glasses.

Tommy said that eventually the sailors were the only three people left in the bar so he told them that if they didn't leave he would throw them out. At that point all three surrounded him and became threatening. In view of the threat of broken glasses, Tommy struck out at one of the men catching him a blow on the shoulder. He fell to the floor but got up and all three left the bar.

In cross examination, Tommy strongly denied using the full force of his fists. When asked about how the victim sustained a broken nose, Farr said he believed he already had the injury when he arrived at the Royal Standard.

Farr's solicitor submitted that if any assault had occurred it had

287

been in self-defence. Despite his denial, Tommy was found guilty and was fined £5 and ordered to pay 5 guineas costs and £1 witness expenses. He was very angry at being convicted, especially when the brewery decided to take away his licence as a result of it.

This was the second time that Tommy's name had appeared in the lists at Brighton Magistrates' Court in recent years for minor breaches of the law. On 29 January 1941, he had been fined £1 for breach of curfew regulations, having been stopped by a constable in the street at 3.45 a.m. two weeks earlier. He pleaded guilty by letter.

* * *

After his discharge from the RAF, Tommy began to take a genuine interest in local life. In 1942, his popularity led to him being nominated as a candidate for the Hanover Ward of the Brighton Town Council. His nomination caused a great deal of interest, and when asked about it, he said, 'I was asked by several councillors if I would stand, and replied that I would be only too glad to do what I could to help the working classes.' He said there was a great deal of poverty in Brighton, especially in Kemp Town. 'I think if I got on the council, I might help alleviate it,' he continued. 'Welshmen take to politics like ducks to water.'

Having spent his younger days in the coalfields of South Wales, Tommy was well aware of what it was like to be poor, and felt it was now time for him to try to help others. He took his nomination very seriously, and invited all serving councillors to a meeting at the Royal Pavilion so that he could put his views to them.

Most councillors attended the meeting, during which Tommy explained that he would be nominated as an Independent, and would give his vote to whatever he considered was righteous and just. He emphasised that he would fully represent the cause of working-class people. As a matter of courtesy, he had sent canvassers around the ward. 'As a result, I have received many letters expressing the hope that the council will co-opt me,' he remarked.

By the time of the meeting, signatures collected on his behalf exceeded 1,600. Tommy said that according to the last register, a total of 3,984 people were entitled to vote, and the number of signatures exceeded the total number of votes ever recorded in previous elections within the ward.

When answering questions put to him, Tommy refused to duck issues of a contentious nature, and most councillors were impressed by his sincerity and the eloquence of his replies. However, in a three-cornered election he managed to poll only four votes.

Tommy's efforts were not in vain because he was soon appointed to the Social Committee of the newly formed Brighton National Welfare Association, and worked alongside a Church of England minister and a Nonconformist pastor. Their object was to deal with complaints of old-aged pensioners, and to press for an allowance of £2 per week, plus £1 for married people.

When war ended in 1945 and life got back to normal, Tommy became very sought after. He was still a hero because people remembered his stand against Louis almost a decade earlier. He opened shops and fêtes, and one evening played the opening frame of snooker on a new table installed at a working men's club at Burgess Hill. He became a regular member of the *Sussex Daily News* sports team, which travelled all over the county, and was frequently called upon to talk about his fight with Louis. By this time, he had a second son, Gary, who had been born in December 1944.

In January 1949, he took part in a BBC programme called *Can Britain Win at Sport.* Discussing the fight game, he said he believed British boxers would do much better if they were properly supervised during the early stages of their careers, and if more gymnasiums were available.

Tommy was extremely popular with local reporters, and was frequently interviewed about boxing and its personalities. He was convinced that the sport would only improve when promoters put the interests of boxers first.

As his businesses built up, Tommy became more involved in local life, and everything pointed to him enjoying a successful retirement from the ring. By the autumn of 1949, however, there were signs that his funds had diminished considerably. The first indications came when he sold the lavish Glovers and moved to a smaller property at Wilbury Road in Hove. Glovers had once been described as one of the finest properties in Brighton, with three servants and a gardener.

Then in January 1950, Tommy appeared in the Chancery Division of the High Court in London on a motion for the appointment of a receiver of assets in respect of Tommy Farr's Pantry, and on 3 March, a receiving order was made against him. Three days later details were published in the *London Gazette,* where he was described as a restaurant proprietor and commissions agent. The story hit most national newspapers under headlines such as TOMMY FARR IS BROKE, but the Welshman insisted he would prove his solvency within a few days.

On 5 May, a public examination hearing at Brighton Bankruptcy Court was adjourned, and later that month the receiving order was rescinded, 'it appearing to the Court that his affairs are just and equitable'.

Shortly after the bankruptcy hearing, Tommy received an offer to tour Australia and South Africa and take part in exhibitions with veteran American heavyweight Jersey Joe Walcott. Despite having been out of the ring for more than ten years, he was only six pounds above his best fighting weight. But he eventually declined the tour due to financial problems.

Although he had the consolation of not being declared bankrupt, the profits had been eaten away and debts were steadily mounting. He had once dreamed of becoming a millionaire before he was 40, and had invested huge sums of money in converting property into flats. The dream, however, became a nightmare with the introduction of the Land Development Act and the Town and Country Planning Act in 1947. Tommy admitted, 'The interest rates were strangling me, and I had to get out and leave my share behind.'

Amongst properties Tommy bought was a huge building on the seafront at Hove. He put a great deal of money into it with the idea of developing it into the 'Jockey Club of Brighton'. When the law changed, the end was in sight. He had also lost a great deal of money on the Derby the year it was won by Dante.

To try and ease the situation, Tommy gave up the restaurant business at the beginning of 1950, but his other ventures were not bringing in the money of previous years. Tommy was well aware of the seriousness of the situation and desperately needed to get money from somewhere. He could think of only one way by which to survive, and that was by making a comeback to the ring.

At first he kept the idea to himself, but trained secretly, doing roadwork, skipping, and shadow boxing. Most of the running was done early in the morning around the inside of the county cricket ground at Hove, and people who did see him were not unduly surprised. Tommy was a well-known fitness fanatic, and it was something he had done regularly since moving to Sussex.

21

COMEBACK

Tommy Farr had a comfortable home, but was desperate for cash. He was determined that his wife and three children would never have to endure hardship he knew as a youngster. He had followed the fight game closely and was convinced that he could beat the current crop of British heavyweights, and plenty from abroad as well. The more he thought about returning to the ring, the more convinced he became that he should do it.

The tough Welshman desperately wanted to share his secret with somebody, and could think of nobody better than his old pal Frank Butler. At the time he was writing a boxing column in the *News of the World*, but he and Tommy went back a long way. So one Sunday morning in April 1950, the Welshman telephoned Frank and invited him to his Brighton home for lunch.

'I'm making a comeback, Frank,' he said. 'I know I can beat the present bunch of heavyweights.'

'If you have to fight, I suppose you must,' replied Butler, 'but you know, Tommy, they just never come back.'

This was the oldest and truest saying in the fight game, but Tommy would have none of it.

'Listen, Frank Butler,' he retorted, 'Do you mean to tell me you don't think I can beat the likes of Gardner, Williams, and the rest? As for Savold and Baski, they're just made for me.'

'They wouldn't have placed a glove on the old Tommy Farr,' admitted Butler, 'but you can collect plenty of ring rust in ten years.'

Butler was well aware of Tommy's financial problems but was genuinely concerned for him and his family. 'Think it over again Tommy,' he pleaded. 'You know your own business, but I hope you find another way of solving your problems.'

* * *

It was during the early summer of 1950, that rumours started to circulate. Tommy was known to be putting in some intensive training at Brighton, and it was therefore believed that he was contemplating a comeback. Then in July, Tonypandy promoter Albert Davies announced that Farr would fight in South Wales within a month or so. Tommy angrily denounced the suggestion. 'I have no arrangement with Davies,' he said, 'and nothing has been settled about a contest for me.'

He did, however, indicate that there was some substance in the rumours. 'I want first of all to satisfy myself completely that I am fit enough to make a comeback, for my comeback fight will not be against somebody who does not really matter. I don't propose to go into the ring with a loser, but with a fighter of reputation.'

A couple of days later, it was revealed that Tommy had secretly taken part in a two-round gymnasium contest with ex-guardsman Jack Gardner at the Crown and Anchor pub in Brighton. Jack was due to meet Johnny Williams of Rugby in a final eliminator for the British and Empire heavyweight titles about ten days later. The bout had in fact been a two-fold exercise. Gardner wanted a good workout prior to meeting Williams, and it gave Tommy the chance to test himself against one of the country's leading heavyweights.

Weighing 14 stone 6½, which he considered to be his best fighting weight, Tommy looked extremely fit. Although his timing was out, he moved well and many of his old moves were still there.

Tommy continued to train at the Crown and Anchor, which was situated on the north side of Brighton at Preston Park. During mid-July, scores of holidaymakers intrigued by the comeback rumours packed in each afternoon to watch him. Starting at 2.30 p.m. he did the equivalent of ten rounds, and as the days passed, so the training intensified. Tommy pushed himself to the limit doing floor exercises, bag work and sparring in his efforts to build up his strength and stamina.

Tommy Farr was still a household name, and the man who almost beat Joe Louis more than a decade earlier was suddenly big news again. Reporters travelled to Brighton in numbers trying to get an exclusive interview. 'I'm feeling fine,' Tommy told a group of them one hot afternoon, 'but I cannot definitely say that I will be coming back into boxing.' He said he had medical certificates to prove his fitness, but added, 'I would not come back if I didn't think I could do it. The British boxing public have been long-suffering enough, and I would not think of imposing myself on them if I were not confident.'

Tommy explained that his old nose and stomach problems had cleared up, and revealed that he had been on a course designed by the Swiss physical culture expert Arthur Abplanalp. Four months earlier he had bought a book written by Mr Abplanalp entitled *In Perfect Shape All Your Life*, and practised the instructions at home. He was so pleased with the results – his weight had been reduced and his stamina remarkably improved – that he had written to thank the author.

Farr was finally convinced that he could make a successful comeback. The training had gone well, he was down to his best fighting weight, and was satisfied that his strength, stamina and old fighting skills had returned. So he applied to the Board of Control for the renewal of his licence.

Shortly after his licence was granted, it was announced that Tommy would box an exhibition at Porthcawl on 23 August. Within hours, the Colney Beach ticket office was invaded by fans wanting tickets, and on the night 10,000 packed in. They cheered wildly as Tommy climbed into the ring clad in a brilliant white dressing gown. Weighing 14 stone, he showed that he had lost little of his old skill as he boxed three fast rounds with Bill Brennan of Manchester. With Bill being rather cumbersome, Farr was able to demonstrate speed of punching combined with good footwork. His long left leads continually found Brennan's face, and he followed up with plenty of right crosses as well.

The fans loved it, and at the end Tommy took the microphone and thanked them for the tremendous welcome they had given him. He invited them to go along to Pontypridd and see his real comeback fight in September.

Determined that the comeback would be a success, Tommy was soon looking beyond his first fight. Amongst people he contacted was Jack Solomons, the country's leading promoter. Tommy met Jack in London because he knew that was where the big money was to be had. Intending to be his own manager, the Welshman wanted to know if Solomons was interested in using him on his big shows. Jack told him that if he won a couple of fights in the provinces, the crowds would queue overnight for tickets for a fight between him and Bruce Woodcock for the heavyweight title.

'I'm still not interested in your Woodcocks,' he snapped. 'I want the men who have beaten him. Mauriello, Baski and Savold. And if my old pal Joe Louis is really coming back, nothing would give me greater pleasure than a repeat of our 1937 rendezvous.'

Louis had announced that he was also to embark on a comeback. Like Tommy, he had serious money problems, owing the taxman alone $41,000. The two old warriors will long be remembered for their epic battle of 1937, so it was quite incredible that debts would force both to announce comebacks during the same month. Even more incredibly, their comeback fights would both take place on the same night.

Farr's comeback created considerable interest, particularly because of the length of time he had been away. For him to make a return after ten years was thought to be a record, surpassing that of Jim Jeffries, who had returned in 1910 after a six-year absence to fight Jack Johnson. Even then the trade saying that 'they never come back' had stood firm, because Jeffries was badly beaten.

American Pat Comisky was tipped as the man most likely to oppose Tommy. He was an ambitious young heavyweight from New Jersey who had made a successful British debut by stopping Johnny Williams at the White City in June.

Despite Farr's denial that he had any agreement with Albert Davies, the Welsh promoter announced that Tommy would meet Comisky at Pontypridd on 6 September. This brought about a strong protest from Jack Solomons. The London promoter was staging a fight between Eddie Thomas and Cliff Curvis at Swansea for the British welterweight title a week later. He argued that the gate for the championship contest would be seriously affected.

As soon as he became aware of the problem, Albert Davies offered to postpone his show. In any case, Pat Comisky had suddenly pulled out of the fight with Farr. One source claimed that he had returned to America for family reasons, whilst others said that Pat had received a better offer to fight back home.

Davies secured the services of Dutch heavyweight champion Jan Klein as the new opponent for Farr. Although he had been beaten by moderate continentals such as Piet Wilde, Robert Eugene and Kurt Scheigel, he was a solid performer. It was thought that he would give the Welshman a good test at this stage. Many people considered him a more suitable choice than Comisky.

Farr himself raised no objection to the new choice of opponent, and in fact conceded that it was sensible to see how things went before getting carried away by taking on the big names.

With his comeback date now set at 27 September, Farr trained intensely every day. He did miles of running and many rounds of sparring. In the early stages he concentrated on speed with Brighton light heavyweight Brian Anders. Then with three weeks to go, he enlisted the help of heavyweights Don Mogard – the first man to take Rocky Marciano to a points decision – and Bill Brennan, and light heavyweight Mark Hart. By the time his training came to an end, Tommy claimed to have sparred more than 250 rounds.

Whilst Tommy's comeback was catching the imagination of the public in Britain, so too was that of Joe Louis some 3,000 miles away. The Brown Bomber had last fought in June 1948 when he successfully defended his title against Jersey Joe Walcott. It was not until March the following year that he announced his retirement, although he continued to take part in dozens of exhibition bouts. In announcing his comeback, Joe said he wanted to become the first retired heavyweight champion of the world to regain his title – and it was necessary to clear his tax arrears to the United States Government.

The enforced comebacks of Louis and Farr were viewed with a tinge of sadness by the followers of boxing. The Brown Bomber was regarded as having been the greatest heavyweight champion of all time, whilst the Welshman was without doubt the best British heavyweight since the days of Bob Fitzsimmons. Both had earned well from their ring careers, but now they were broke.

Louis had been out of the ring for a mere two years, and was to carry on where he had left off. For his return contest, he was matched with Ezzard Charles, the man who had succeeded him as champion. Joe was reported to be fit and punching well in training. In fact, there was a general feeling in the States that he was the one man who just might come back. The bookies shared that confidence and installed him as the 11–5 on betting favourite.

For Tommy Farr, it was like turning the clock back to 1926 when he was a 13-year-old fighting for a square meal. Now at the age of 37, he was prepared to spill more blood and endure pain and suffering for the sake of his wife and children.

The history of boxing is spattered with stories of fighters great and not so great who have been forced back into the ring because they were broke. That is one of the sadder sides of the game.

* * *

Farr travelled by train to Wales the day before his fight with Jan Klein. Crowds were waiting as he arrived at Brighton Station and they cheered loudly as his train pulled away. En route to Wales he received hundreds of goodwill messages. People recognised him at Victoria and Paddington stations, and as he waited for the Cardiff train, dozens queued for autographs and the chance to shake his hand. A large crowd greeted him as he arrived at Cardiff, and at least a dozen car owners offered to drive him to his hotel. Tommy was in such demand that before he went to bed, he signed autographs for every guest at the hotel.

The weigh-in for the fight was at 1 p.m. the following day. Klein, who had trained at Newport, made onlookers gasp as his weight was called at 15 stone 8¼. Farr was a mere 14 stone, and the Dutchman was also much taller at 6 foot 4.

At about 6 p.m. that evening, a huge crowd gathered outside Tommy's hotel to see him leave to make the short journey up the valley to Pontypridd. Men, women and children cheered and wished him luck as he set off.

Despite the fact that rain had poured down almost continuously for over 12 hours, more than 20,000 fans packed into Ystradgyn-lan Park, the home of Pontypridd Rugby Club. It had rained every day for almost a week, and the River Taff, which spectators had to cross to get into the park, was swollen and over its banks. The ground was a beauty spot situated between mountains and two coal tips. Yet it was a thoroughly depressing setting as the driving rain failed to let up.

The scene was only brightened by the unquenchable enthusiasm of Tommy's ardent supporters. Many stood ankle-deep in mud, whilst others sat on soaking-wet seats as they waited to see their hero make his historic return to the ring. The event should have been called off, but that would have caused an uproar. The venue was only a few miles from Tommy's old home town of Tonypandy, and his fans didn't care about the conditions.

Suddenly the moment everyone had been waiting for arrived. A fanfare of trumpets heralded one of the most famous returns ever to a British ring. Jan Klein led the way, followed by Farr, who was tightly wrapped in a spotless white dressing gown. It was a long walk from the dressing rooms to the ring, and the route was treacherous. Farr wore a pair of thick-soled bedroom slippers over his boxing boots to keep them free from mud, whilst Klein wore ordinary shoes and carried his ring boots.

Tommy was cheered ecstatically all the way to the ring, and he responded by smiling and waving confidently. As he climbed the steps of the ring, one of the last people to wish him luck was Jack Petersen, who was seated near to Tommy's corner.

The boxers took some time to change their footwear, and even then it looked as though their efforts would be in vain. The canvas was not only soaked from the rain that had lashed down, but was also covered in rosin, sawdust and mud from officials' boots. The place looked more like a ploughed field than a boxing ring, and it was obvious that the fighters would have difficulty in maintaining a foothold.

As they were called to the centre of the ring for the referee's final instructions, the Dutchman's physical advantages were clear for all to see. Farr, however, was unconcerned, and had no intention of letting down those thousands of wet fans.

From the opening bell, Tommy set a fast pace, and got his left jab working. A good left hook to the body in the first seconds showed that he had a real appetite for the job ahead. It had the big Dutchman hanging on desperately, for which he drew a caution from the referee.

During the first session, Klein lashed out with his own punches, but the Welshman was able to avoid them with ease. By the end of the round the Dutchman's nose was bloodied from the accuracy of Farr's left jab.

Tommy had easily won the first round, and he took the next two as well. By repeatedly moving inside his taller opponent, he dictated the contest with his left. Klein's face was covered in blood, and just before the end of round two, he was badly shaken by two vicious right hooks from Farr.

During the third, the Welshman sensibly took a breather, but stepped up the pace again in the fourth. He was growing in confidence, and in this round defended brilliantly. He avoided almost every punch that Klein threw, and took others on his arms and shoulders. The Dutchman was never allowed to use his greater reach, and was completely outmanouvred.

Ringsiders could sense that the skilful Farr was trying to set Klein up for a big right hand. In the fifth, the Dutchman went down for a count of two from such a punch, but did not seem unduly hurt. Before the end of the session, he came back with good shots of his own, and raised a large bruise on Farr's left cheekbone.

Tommy stormed out for the sixth, determined to finish matters. He caught the Dutchman flush on the chin with a peach of a right hand, and then set him up for the kill. A vicious two-fisted attack followed, and then he neatly stepped back and fired a solid left hook to the liver. Klein was badly hurt, his face twisted in agony.

Farr stepped back again, and this time threw a perfect right hook to the jaw. The big Dutchman fell in a heap in his own corner, and the count was a formality. The end came after 72 seconds of round six.

It had been a creditable win, albeit against a somewhat limited opponent. Farr's intensive training had paid off because he was superbly fit and strong. To return to the professional ring after so long was no mean feat, and he had done it in style.

The crowd cheered wildly because Tommy had shown glimpses of his former self. There was a feeling amongst many that with proper handling, he could become a threat to the current crop of British heavyweights.

As Tommy tried to leave the ring and head back to the dressing room hundreds of excited fans surged forward. The scenes were incredible, and he had to battle all the way amid hugs and back-slapping.

As soon as he reached his dressing room, Tommy telephoned Monty, who was sitting at home anxiously waiting for news of the fight. He also arranged for a telegram to be sent to Joe Louis. *I have just won my comeback fight*, it read. *I hope you win yours. Your old opponent, Tommy Farr.*

Unbeknown to Tommy, shortly after he had finished talking to her on the phone, Monty made an unexpected dash from their Brighton home to join him at a celebration party at his Cardiff hotel. It was a total surprise when she arrived because Tommy had no idea of her intentions. He was overwhelmed when he saw her, and remarked, 'This makes everything perfect.'

*   *   *

Across the Atlantic, Joe Louis did not have the same good fortune as Farr, and was beaten on points over 15 rounds by Ezzard Charles. Instead of sensibly taking a series of warm-up fights, Joe had been persuaded to go straight into a fight for his old title. It must have been a decision he deeply regretted.

Charles had won the vacant title in June 1949 by outpointing Jersey Joe Walcott following Louis's retirement. He had success-fully defended it three times before agreeing to put it up against the old champion. Joe had been out of the ring for a little over two years, a relatively short time compared to Farr, but still long enough for the ring rust to set in.

When Farr heard the result, he admitted being sad because he clearly held great affection for the old champion. He was also somewhat critical. 'It took me ten months to get ready and to satisfy myself that I was completely fit for my first comeback fight. Yet Louis, out of the game for two years, took on Charles, seven years his junior and a clever boxer, after a ballyhoo training period that lasted only six weeks.'

Tommy was absolutely right in what he said, but nobody could ever make Tommy Farr do something he didn't want to do. He alone made all the decisions regarding his comeback, and always maintained that he would never have got back into the ring again unless he was convinced that he could make a go of it. Louis, on the other hand, was a soft, placid man who could be manipulated into a situation.

The comeback fates of Farr and Louis differed tremendously. Whilst over 20,000 people sat in the pouring rain at a muddy park in a small Welsh town to see Tommy box a relatively unknown Dutchman, a similar crowd sat amid fine weather in New York to watch Joe attempt to win back the heavyweight championship of the world. After ten years out of the ring, Farr returned like a man possessed with a new will and ambition, and showed that he had lost little of his natural ability, whereas Louis fought like a tired old man. Whilst it appeared to be the end of the road for Louis, plans were already being made for Tommy Farr's next fight.

* * *

Tommy admitted that he needed a couple more fights before taking on stiffer opposition, and eventually signed to meet Piet Wilde of Belgium at the Granby Halls, Leicester. Wilde had boxed in Britain on a number of occasions, but rarely emerged victorious. Nevertheless, all 4,500 seats were sold within a few days of the fight being announced, leaving standing room only for a further 4,000 on the night.

Meanwhile, Tommy offered to box in Glasgow to raise money for the dependents of a mining tragedy. During early October, a terrible disaster occurred at the Knockshinnock Castle Colliery in Ayrshire, when 128 men were trapped underground as a result of a landslide. Thirteen lost their lives, and as soon as Tommy heard about it, he was anxious to help.

As he set off from his Brighton home the day before the fight with Wilde, Tommy was given all the incentive he needed for victory. As he said goodbye, his four-year-old son Gary told him, 'I will love you just the same if you lose, Daddy, but it won't be the same.'

The fight with Wilde quickly settled into a pattern as the

299

Belgian, a 6 foot 3 giant with dark curly hair, poked a long left hand into Tommy's face with ease. He followed up with an occasional right swing, and during the first session opened a slight cut over the Welshman's left eye. Later a swelling appeared below it. With an advantage of nine and a half pounds, Wilde outpaced and outsmarted Tommy, making him look slow and unimpressive.

The Belgian clearly won the first two rounds, but then in the third he went down heavily when Farr caught him with a short right uppercut to the jaw. The crowd roared with excitement as he hit the canvas, but when it appeared that he was not badly hurt yet making no effort to rise, that excitement turned to anger.

For the first couple of seconds he was on the floor, Wilde blinked and looked towards his cornermen, who were anxiously gesturing for him to get to his knees. He sat in the centre of the ring, and only when the count reached eight did he slowly begin to pick himself up. There was so much noise that the count was inaudible.

People were amazed when referee Moss Deyong signalled 'out' with a sweep of his hands whilst the Belgian was still in the act of rising. He appeared in no distress, and later claimed he had not heard the count after it reached six.

The crowd were not happy at the way the ending came, and jeered long and hard, with most of their venom being directed at Wilde. There was a feeling among a number of pressmen that Wilde was automatically obeying a Continental ruling that a fighter who is knocked down shall not rise before the count of eight.

The whole affair was a great disappointment, especially to Farr, who had looked less impressive than he had against Jan Klein. Having received a magnificent reception after that fight, the contrast on this occasion couldn't have been greater. He was treated as though the outcome was his fault.

The controversy continued when it was later learned that the timekeeper, Charlie Freer, and the referee had apparently been at a variance over the count. Freer remarked that he was one beat (one second) behind the referee. If this was so, then with Wilde rising at the signal of 'out', he had in fact beaten the count by rising at nine.

The British Boxing Board of Control were sufficiently concerned over the outcome of the contest to hold an enquiry a few days later. Farr was amongst those invited to attend. There was no official statement. However, a motion tabled for the agenda of the next general meeting attempted to enforce the retirement age of

65 upon referees and timekeepers. Moss Deyong, the Farr–Wilde referee, was 73 and timekeeper Charlie Freer allegedly older.

* * *

As Tommy's comeback continued on its winning way, the British and Empire heavyweight titles changed hands. The holder, Bruce Woodcock, was decisively beaten in 11 rounds by Jack Gardner, and afterwards announced his retirement from the ring.

Across the Atlantic, Joe Louis, having decided to continue with his comeback, won a ten-rounds points decision over the 23-year-old Argentinian Caesar Brion in Chicago. It was described as a dull fight, but got Joe back on the winning trail.

* * *

Welsh promoter Albert Davies matched Farr with American veteran Lloyd Marshall at the Market Hall, Carmarthen, on 4 December. Although the British Boxing Board of Control approved the contest, they told Tommy that they would have preferred him to meet a British boxer.

Marshall, a Californian, had the unique claim of having beaten five world champions past and present at every weight from welter to heavyweight. The fight therefore looked a good one for Farr to take. Lloyd was no stranger to Britain, usually boxing at light heavyweight. He had recently put up a credible performance against British champion Don Cockell before being disqualified in the seventh round.

Tommy travelled to Wales by rail the day before the fight. Even though his train arrived at Cardiff nearly two hours late, huge crowds waited at the station and outside his hotel to greet him. People were singing and waving, slapping him on the back and shaking his hand to wish him good luck. The scenes were incredible considering he was taking part in a non-title fight amidst a comeback campaign. Tommy was treated like a national hero; the Piet Wilde affair was clearly history.

Lloyd Marshall had travelled from London on the same train as Tommy, but the Welshman was not aware of it until he reached his hotel. Farr was staying at the 400-year-old Boar's Head in Carmarthen, and was told that the room he would be sleeping in had frequently been used by Lord Nelson. When he sat down for breakfast on the morning of the fight, Tommy told a group of well-wishers, 'Wales expects every man this night to do his duty, and I will try to do mine.'

Shortly after the Welshman left his hotel early in the evening, things started to go wrong. As he approached Market Hall, he found it impossible to get his car through the dense crowds outside the building. The gates had been shut, but once he was recognised, hundreds of fans waving tickets, surrounded his car screaming for him to help get them in. Tommy promised to do what he could, but first of all he had to get inside himself.

Tommy was accompanied by his trainer Snowy Buckingham and a reporter from the Brighton *Argus*, but the crowd was so dense that they couldn't move. Almost an hour passed before police officers arrived and ushered them into the building.

Marshall experienced similar problems, and the situation was so bad that his manager took him back to their hotel. They only reached Market Hall when escorted through the crowds by a large posse of policemen.

Inside the hall, there were some ugly crowd scenes as many fans became restless while several supporting bouts were put on and everyone waited impatiently for the main event. At one stage an empty whisky bottle was thrown into the ring, and several angry spectators tried to climb in.

Then finally came the moment everyone had been waiting for, the appearance of Farr and Marshall. As soon as they were in the ring, the scenes became very emotional with the crowd rising as one to spontaneously sing *The Star-Spangled Banner* followed by *Land of My Fathers*, throughout which Tommy stood rigidly in his corner.

For the first time in his comeback, Farr would start a contest with a weight advantage, being 14 stone 0¾ to Marshall's 12 stone 10½. Although the Welshman weaved, feinted, blocked punches and smothered with some success in the early rounds, it became clear that the years out of the ring had caught up with him. During the course of the fight, he suffered extremely rough treatment at the hands of the experienced American journeyman, and he did well to survive the full ten rounds to lose on points by a wide margin.

Marshall was too fast, too strong and too rough for the ageing Welshman, and only Tommy's superb defence and ringcraft saved him from being stopped. His normally effective left jab had little effect as the American repeatedly scored with crude swings from both hands.

Tommy produced his best boxing during the first three rounds, but in the fourth Marshall started to liven things up. His heavier punches brought blood from the Welshman's nose. By the halfway stage, his right eye was closed, there was blood smeared all over his face, and his cheeks were red from the effect of the American's constant left jab.

When Tommy attacked, he had little effect on his lighter opponent, and at the same time was getting caught by heavy punches. During the seventh he was blowing hard, whilst Marshall was composed and strong.

Big punches brought blood streaming from the Welshman's nose in the ninth, and throughout the last round, he boxed on the retreat as Marshall attacked with flurries of vicious punches. Farr's only consolation was that he went down fighting.

Back in his dressing room, Tommy refused to admit he was finished. 'Of course I'm going on,' he said. 'That was just the sort of work I needed. Marshall is a strong and clever fellow, and he has licked me into better shape.' He said that the American was too small and quick to suit his style, and in future he would take on bigger men.

Tommy's wife was shocked when she heard the result of the fight. 'That's awful,' she gasped. 'I will do all I can to persuade him to give up boxing now. I was very much against him taking it up again in the first place, but you can't discourage a Welshman.'

The next morning, Tommy found his Welsh fans were still very supportive. His send-off was as warm and sincere as his welcome. He made no secret of the fact that the defeat by Marshall was a setback, but said he had got a verbal agreement from the American for a return. A couple of weeks later, however, Tommy learned that efforts to stage the return with Marshall had failed.

The critics were unanimous in their opinions that Farr should now retire, but he stubbornly refused to listen and continued to train daily over the Christmas period because he expected to box at Porth on 22 January. The show was eventually cancelled because a suitable opponent for Farr couldn't be found.

The Welsh Area Council nominated Tommy as the official challenger for the Welsh heavyweight title held by Dennis Powell. Farr reacted by saying that he had everything to lose and nothing to gain by fighting Powell, and the fight failed to attract any outstanding bids from promoters. Tommy was out of action for three months before Albert Davies matched him with Frank Bell of Barnoldswick over ten rounds at Porth on 21 March 1951. The venue was a large converted garage owned by the promoter.

The contest meant a great deal to both men, in particular Farr, who had received attractive offers from places as far afield as the

United States and Malta.

Although he was 24 years of age, Bell had taken part in only 13 contests since turning professional in August 1949. Of his ten wins, seven had come inside the distance, so there was no doubting his punching power. Although the promoter applied to the Board of Control for the contest to be recognised as an eliminator for the British title, this was rejected by the Stewards.

Only 5,000 fans turned up on the night of the fight, which was surprising considering that the venue was almost within walking distance of Tonypandy. It was surely an indication that many considered Tommy was pursuing a lost cause.

Farr weighed 14 stone 4 – his heaviest since returning to the ring – which gave him a three-pound advantage over his younger opponent. He began the fight as though he was going to completely outbox Bell, and within the first minute caught him with a right hook which almost had the Yorkshireman on the floor.

The Welshman's stiff jabs were repeatedly pumping into his opponent's face, and Bell's nose was bleeding quite heavily before the fight was two minutes old. Although Frank tried his right hand on a number of occasions, Farr was able to avoid it with ease, apart from one which caught him under the heart just before the end of the round.

Tommy began the second round by again pushing his left jab into Bell's face, and then landed a hard right which buckled the Yorkshireman's knees. A fierce exchange followed, and as Tommy moved away so Bell let go a tremendous right, catching him on the side of the jaw. He went down, but to everyone's amazement, got up at the count of two. He gave himself no time to gather his senses, and was clearly very dazed.

Sensing a dramatic victory, Bell charged straight at Farr, throwing heavy punches to head and body with both hands. The body punches made Tommy sag forward, and then another big right hook to the head knocked him flat on his face. He remained there until the count reached six, when he rolled over panting loudly. He tried to rise but hadn't the strength, and by nine was only in a sitting position. He was counted out after 55 seconds of the round. Tommy was badly hurt, and it was some time before he was fit to leave the ring.

The outcome couldn't have been more disastrous for the Welshman. Not only was it the first time he had been knocked out since he was a mere novice, but it was also his second successive defeat. The punch which brought the fight to a close was completely against the run of things, and the old Tommy Farr would never have been caught by it. It was sad he should suffer such embarrassment at the hands of a comparative novice.

Tommy was very dejected by the defeat. 'I do not know whether to go on or not,' he said. 'I shall sleep on it.'

A couple of days passed before the stubborn Welshman announced that he had decided to carry on. He contacted London promoter Jack Solomons, asking that an opponent be found for him on the show at Harringay on 24 April. Solomons agreed, on condition that Tommy retired for good if he was beaten again. Reluctantly he agreed, so the promoter matched him with Irish heavyweight champion Gerry McDermott.

22

ALMOST THE END

If Tommy Farr was to have just one more fight, there could be no more fitting venue than Harringay. If this was to be the end for the man who brought respectability back to heavyweight boxing in Britain, then at least he could go out in dignity. It was perhaps with some compassion that Jack Solomons therefore agreed to get him just one more fight. Harringay was the finest arena in the country, and the scene of Tommy's greatest victories. It would be better to bow out here than at some obscure town hall venue in the provinces.

Top of the bill that night was a contest between British and European light heavyweight champion Don Cockell and the American Freddie Beshore. Cockell was being groomed for a world title fight and had a big following in London, so a large crowd was in attendance.

Tommy was given a wonderful reception as he strode down the famous aisle to the ring. As he climbed into the ring, there was a mixture of nostalgia and sadness because here was the man who back in 1937 had warmed the hearts of British boxing fans after the disappointments of so many heavyweights before him. Many people present were convinced this was the night when the old warrior would finally say farewell to boxing.

Tommy had trained hard to get into condition for this fight, and looked extremely fit. As the opening bell sounded, it was clear that he intended putting the defeats by Marshall and Bell behind him. He took command of the fight from the start, setting a fast pace, which was exactly the right tactics because McDermott had been inactive for some months. Weighing just 13 stone, the Irishman appeared somewhat apprehensive of Farr, instead of forcing the fight and attempting to tire him out.

McDermott occasionally landed stiff punches, but failed to follow up any advantage, and Farr's speed took him away from danger. Whenever big punches landed from either boxer, it was the Irishman who looked in trouble. A cut opened under his left eye in the second round and bled throughout the fight. In the fifth, Farr landed big punches which had his opponent in all sorts of trouble, and he was only saved by the bell. Farr was putting on a winning performance, and McDermott's only success was a big right in the fourth which shook the Welshman, but it wasn't followed up.

At the end of the ten rounds, Tommy was a clear points winner. Those who saw his performance must have asked what he would have done to the present group of heavyweights had he been 15 years younger. He gave McDermott a complete boxing lesson, and even in the final round when he was extremely tired, he still demonstrated many of his old skills. He feinted, jabbed, bobbed and weaved, avoiding many wild swings as the Irishman desperately tried to pull out a dramatic victory. At the end, McDermott was much the worse for wear. He had cuts over both eyes and a big lump under the left one. Farr did have a cut over his left eye, but apart from that, tiredness was his only problem at the end.

The crowd gave him a tremendous ovation when his arm was raised. They had witnessed a first-class exhibition of boxing, demonstrating how the standards of British heavyweights had declined since the war years. Despite this, the sentimentalists still wanted Tommy to call it a day, but the jubilant Welshman announced soon afterwards that he would continue.

In June Tommy agreed to meet Dennis Powell of Four Crosses at the West Midlands Show Ground, Shrewsbury, on a show staged by DRG Promotions. The Welsh Area Council announced that the contest would be over 12 rounds and that Powell's Welsh heavyweight title would be at stake.

Tommy took the fight to show just how determined he was about his comeback. If he beat Powell, he had been promised a fight with Johnny Williams of Rugby in a final eliminator for the British and Empire titles held by Jack Gardner.

Powell also held the Welsh light heavyweight title, but had not defended his heavyweight crown since winning it in August 1949. The contest with Farr was of particular importance because if he won, he would be able to concentrate on whichever division he chose.

Farr trained for the fight at the Crown and Anchor, and sparred with Brian Anders and Sammy Wilde, a welterweight from Nigeria, boxing three rounds with each man daily.

The day before the fight, as Farr was buying his ticket at Paddington Station, a Welsh voice suddenly called out from behind him, 'Good luck, Tommy bach.' Turning round, he saw the smiling face of labour MP Nye Bevan. After passing the time of day and thanking him for his good wishes, Tommy smiled to himself and thought, 'If you hadn't made properties a liability with that Land Development Act of yours, I wouldn't be making this trip'.

Dennis Powell was clearly only a light heavyweight, scaling just 12 stone 12 to Farr's 14 stone 4. Yet contrary to expectations, he dictated matters early on. In the opening round Powell scored with crisp lefts to the body and being 11 years younger, was able to move around the ring quickly thereby avoiding the heavier punches of the bigger man. These were good tactics because Farr would be expected to tire the quicker.

Powell was also more aggressive, and landed several good left hooks to the jaw, which shook Tommy in the second and third rounds. In the fourth, Farr went to the floor following a body punch, but the referee ruled that it was low and warned Dennis to keep his punches up.

Farr showed more initiative in this round, and began to move around well. He showed much of his old defensive skill and ringcraft, especially in the fifth, when he stood up to two of Powell's best punches without flinching. Tommy's face, however, was beginning to show signs of damage from the attention of Powell's left hand, which was repeatedly finding its target. Sheer courage kept Tommy going when it appeared that youth was going to have the final say.

In the sixth round, Powell landed a right that shook Tommy badly. He seemed to suddenly realise the fight was going against him, and cut loose, hitting out with both hands. There was a hectic exchange of good punches, many of which caught Powell about the head, and he emerged with blood streaming from a cut over his left eye. By the end of the round, he was covered in blood, and referee Mr I.K. Powell of Bargoed took one look at the damage and decided that it was too bad for Dennis to continue.

The crowd were ecstatic because Tommy had regained the title that he first won 15 years earlier and never lost in the ring. Many tried to climb into the ring to embrace him, and the scene was one of genuine emotion and excitement. As he tried to leave the ring, Tommy was mobbed. It was impossible for him to climb through the ropes until an appeal was made.

Tommy was jubilant. He said retirement was the furthest thing from his mind, and if anything, he was now on course for a fight for the British heavyweight title.

'I felt better than at any time since I came back, and now I'm looking for more fights,' he added. 'I'm Welsh champion again after fifteen years, and I don't intend to be an idle one.'

* * *

Outside the ring, Tommy had again become involved in legal proceedings stemming from his financial problems. On 16 July 1951, he appeared at Sussex Assizes at Lewes, having been sued by a Brighton widow, Mrs Emma Elizabeth May Corby, of Wakefield Road, for the repayment of £200. Mrs Corby alleged that the money had been the subject of a loan to Farr by her husband. South Coast Commissions Limited, a bookmaking company, of Queens Road, Brighton, of which Tommy was said to be the Director, were also sued by Mrs Corby in respect of a cheque alleged to have been dishonoured.

The court was told that Mr Corby had given a cheque to Farr who, at the time, was in considerable financial difficulty. Corby had since committed suicide but in his will had referred to the money owed to him by Farr.

In evidence, Tommy denied that the money was owing. He claimed that in January 1950, South Coast Commissions owed Corby amounts of £94 and £100 which represented winning bets on horses. The company was in difficulty, so Corby expressed an interest in becoming involved and gave Tommy cash against a postdated cheque for £200. Tommy stated that Corby agreed it could be paid back when the company finances improved.

Mr Justice Parker said he was satisfied that £106 represented a loan by Corby to the company and therefore gave judgement against Farr in that amount plus costs. The sum of £94, however, was a gaming debt and therefore irrecoverable. The claim against South Coast Commissions was dismissed.

Three months later, South Coast Commissions Limited was summoned by the Board of Trade for failing to submit annual returns to the Registrar of Companies. Tommy's brother Doug, a director of the company, appeared at Bow Street Magistrates' Court on 24 October and pleaded guilty to the allegation. Tommy Farr did not attend the hearing but was represented by Counsel. The court was told that he took full responsibility for what had occurred, and the company had since been wound up. He asked that his brother should not suffer for what had been his fault. Doug Farr was fined £1 and ordered to pay one guinea costs.

* * *

Back on the boxing scene, Farr kept himself in strict training, and promoter Albert Davies, who was keen to keep his comeback going, was planning to use Farr on a show at Bangor City Football ground on 30 August, which was to be the first big open-air boxing show to be staged in North Wales. Farr was matched with the American Steve McCall, who was based on the Continent. He had a reputation of being an extremely rough fighter, and although he had been beaten in London on two occasions, had defeated such men as Jan Klein, Robert Eugene and Carl Nielsen, and was considered a dangerous opponent for Farr.

At 14 stone 8¼, Farr had an advantage of 5¾ pounds over the American. After spending the first round sizing up his opponent, Tommy proceeded to put on his finest display since returning to the ring. He delighted the 18,000 crowd with a masterful display of boxing, and showed that he was still an accomplished boxer, despite being 14 years younger than McCall. He jabbed beautifully with his left and frequently threw good left hooks which shook the American. Whilst adopting his familiar crouching stance, he made McCall miss badly and look a very ordinary fighter.

Although the American attacked throughout, he had little success with his big rights apart from briefly in round six. This was due to the skilful display by Farr, who surprisingly landed the best punch of the fight in round eight when he caught McCall with a tremendous right to the jaw. The American was in serious trouble and did well to hang on and survive the round.

At the end Farr was a clear winner, having won virtually every round. McCall finished with a badly swollen left eye, and his face was raw red from the constant attention of the Welshman's brilliant left hand. The crowd, who had been thoroughly absorbed with the fight, gave Tommy a tremendous ovation. At the end they broke into the familiar singing of the Welsh National Anthem, and mobbed their hero as he left the ring.

The crowd reaction to Tommy Farr was still quite incredible considering his fights were of little significance except to himself. He was loudly cheered into and out of the ring, and invariably there was spontaneous singing from most of the fans. The attendances to see him box mediocre opposition surpassed those of most modern-day title fights in Britain.

Tommy was delighted with his latest performance, and said afterwards that he wanted another fight as soon as possible. He had recovered well from the Marshall and Bell setbacks, and was now rated sixth in the *Boxing News* heavyweight rankings in Britain.

Within a day or so, it was just like old times for Tommy, as offers flooded in for him to fight in Ireland, Canada, South Africa and of course Wales. He was suddenly a very sought-after commodity again. He decided, however, that things had to be put into perspective, and set off for Torquay for a holiday with his family.

Albert Davies then reached agreement with the Belgian Robert Eugene and he met Farr at the New Sophia Gardens Pavilion, Cardiff, on 4 October.

Eugene was a solid performer who had beaten Frank Bell but been outpointed by Jack Gardner in 1949 and 1950. He had been around the Continental rings for some time, and had the advantage of being 12 years younger than Farr. He was also taller, with a much longer reach, and on the night of the fight climbed into the ring weighing a massive 16 stone 4, against the Welshman's 14 stone 7¾ .

Despite all his advantages, the Belgian was never allowed to make them count, and Farr once again ran out a very clear points winner. His superb ringcraft and defensive skills were the deciding factors, and he delighted the 3,000-strong crowd. At times Tommy had Eugene so completely baffled that he must have thought he was chasing shadows.

Farr sustained cuts above and below his left eye early in the fight, and despite the apparent ease of his victory, described the fight as one of the most difficult of his comeback campaign, while Eugene considered Farr the best British heavyweight he had ever met.

Tommy's comeback was being watched by promoters up and down the country, and no sooner had he beaten Eugene, than Albert Davies booked him for a fight at Abergavenny on 5 November. When the show fell through, he agreed to meet the American Al Hoosman at Belle View, Manchester, on 16 November. Before the fight even took place, Tommy agreed to box Georges Rogiers of Belgium at Brighton for local promoter Ralph Barber on 3 December.

At 6 foot 4, and with a weight advantage of 5¾ pounds, Hoosman was a difficult character. He was well-known on the Continent, having boxed out of Germany for about a year. The

311

American started the fight as though he fancied an early night, chasing Tommy and flooring him with a big right. He had an unusual style, similar to that of many modern-day American heavyweights. He looked lazy, boxed for only part of each round, and spent a lot of time holding and spoiling. At one stage the referee asked him for more action.

Realising that the American did not punch his weight, Farr attacked more as the fight wore on, but every so often Hoosman would counterpunch and slow Tommy down. He looked particularly uncomfortable against some solid punching to the ribs. Tommy made a big effort in the latter stages of the fight, but had no visible effect on the American. In a desperate last round rally, an old injury over his left eye opened, and by the end, it was bleeding badly.

Hooseman got the decision, much to the annoyance of the crowd, who booed loudly, but it was a correct one. Although Tommy had done all he could, he made no impression on the big, strong and unorthodox American.

Despite his cut left eye, Tommy was fit enough to go through with the fight against Georges Rogiers at the Brighton Sports Stadium two weeks later. More than 5,000 fans gave him a royal reception as he stepped into the ring in his adopted home town for the first time. He didn't disappoint them, punching out a decisive points win which some critics thought was the best of his comeback.

The Belgian had possessed a good left hand, which he used well during the first six rounds, cutting Farr under his left eye in the fourth and over it later in the fight. The Welshman came more into it during the middle stages as Rogiers tired, and in rounds eight and nine his two-fisted attacks had Rogiers reeling.

As soon as the decision was announced, there was a great deal of booing, perhaps from the betting boys who had descended on the stadium in numbers. They had been very active both before and during the fight, and many had backed the Belgian to win.

Shortly after Farr left the ring, the master of ceremonies appealed for local chiropractor Mr Parnell Bradbury to go to the Welshman's dressing room. Tommy was one of his patients, and early in the fight he had strained an arm. Mr Bradbury later confirmed that Tommy suffered from a crick in the neck which often caused him to fight with his head on one side, and that was very possibly what caused the strain.

One of the first people to congratulate Tommy on his victory was his old friend the comedian Max Miller, who was a keen fight fan. 'In my opinion, Tommy won comfortably.' said Max, 'and I was amazed that some people should have taken the decision so badly. Tommy has done a lot for boxing, and one thing to remember is that he has got himself into superb condition, and always gives the spectators value for money. I was in my three guinea seat and certainly had my money's worth.'

After the fight, there was a celebration party in Tommy's honour at the Royal Albion Hotel. In the days of Edward VII, the hotel, situated opposite the Palace Pier, was the scene of many big boxing gatherings. Many of the greatest boxers of all time attended as guests of honour.

On 14 December, Tommy Farr was the main attraction at the Regent Theatre in Brighton when he presented a cheque for £30 to Mr E. Infield-Willis, Chairman and Managing Director of the publishers of the *Sussex Daily News*. Tommy was generously doing his part for the newspaper's Christmas appeal for children in need. Tommy had wanted to make a donation from his purse from the Rogiers fight without publicity, but was convinced by the organisers that his lead was one which other sporting figures would probably wish to follow.

* * *

As Tommy Farr continued along the comeback road, so the career of Joe Louis came to a dramatic end. On 26 October 1951 in New York, the Brown Bomber was stopped by the up-and-coming Rocky Marciano. Both he and the Welshman had been superb boxers, and it is extremely unlikely that the likes of Marciano and Frank Bell would have laid a glove on them at their peaks.

* * *

At the beginning of 1952, Tommy was confident that by the end of the year, he would either have won the British heavyweight title, or at the very least be only one fight away from it. He was so confident that he said he wanted to eliminate all other contenders one by one, starting with Frank Bell.

Bell was the natural opponent for Tommy if he was to progress towards the title, because he had to avenge that stunning knock-out defeat. Frank himself was more than willing to meet Farr again, but he was contracted to meet American Steve McCall. Bell beat McCall at Leeds, and was given a return fight with Robert Eugene at Manchester two weeks later, earning a draw, but none of this was helping Farr's cause.

In March, Tommy's fortune changed. Not only did he sign to meet the Italian Giorgio Milan at Cardiff, but he was also nominated by the Welsh Area Council as a contender for the British title. During the same month, it was announced that Sydney Hulls had died in Nice. Although there had been differences between them, Tommy admitted being saddened at the loss of the man who put on his big fights in London back in 1937.

Meanwhile, the British and Empire heavyweight titles changed hands when Johnny Williams beat Jack Gardner after a rough fight. The outcome was of great interest to Farr, because having been nominated as a contender for the British title, he knew that a contest with Williams in the open air in Wales during the summer would be a real moneyspinner.

Against Giorgio Milan, Tommy ran out a clear points winner, but only after a dull fight. The Italian was strong and rugged, and Farr needed all of his skills to keep out of trouble, especially in the eighth round when he sustained a badly cut left eye. The crowd of 4,500 appreciated Tommy's fine ringcraft, and to many younger fans his skill was a revelation. Although Milan was 11 pounds lighter, he was not as fast as Farr, and after the fight was full of praise for his conqueror.

Albert Davies next matched Tommy with another Italian, Alfredo Oldonini, said to be the official challenger for the Italian title. The fight was set for the Market Hall, Abergavenny, on 19 May, but a few days later the bout was cancelled. The venue was certainly proving a bogey for Tommy. This was the third time a proposed fight for him there had to be called off. Mr Davies did, however, save the show on this occasion, by putting it back a week and matching Farr with Georges Rogiers. The Belgian had been seeking a rematch ever since Tommy beat him at Brighton the previous December.

The Welsh fans knew it had been a good fight, and a crowd of more than 3,000 turned up for the return. They were not disappointed because Farr boxed brilliantly, and ran out a clear points winner. He won the first eight rounds, showing just what a skilful and scientific boxer he was, and demonstrated plenty of his earlier greatness.

Tommy boxed as well as in any of his comeback fights, against a very awkward opponent who did his best to tire out the veteran by repeatedly laying on. Eleven years younger than the Welshman, Rogiers looked much the worse for wear at the end when both carried swollen left eyes.

If Tommy needed any convincing that 39 years of age was no

314

barrier to being a top-class fighter, he had to look no further than the new world heavyweight champion, Jersey Joe Walcott. He was 37 when he won the title in July the previous year, knocking out Ezzard Charles in the seventh round.

Albert Davies realised that if Tommy was to secure a title shot, he must beat opponents of some standing. He therefore matched him with former European heavyweight champion Jo Weidin of Austria. The significance of this fight was that Johnny Williams had beaten the Austrian in six rounds the previous year. If Tommy could beat him more impressively, then Williams would be forced to give him a shot at the title.

Farr's fight with Weidin took place in the open air at the Worcester City football ground before a large Saturday night crowd on 26 July. As in most of his comeback fights, Tommy's skill and cagey tactics were decisive, and they took him to an easy points victory. His left hand was once again the fight winner, although his most dangerous punch was a right swing which split the Austrian's left eyebrow in the fourth round. Tommy boxed brilliantly and at times his opponent was completely bewildered, and the Welshman won nearly every round.

Tommy did have one anxious moment in round seven, when good punches from Weidin put him on the floor, but he was up without a count. He did not escape unscathed either, because in the fifth a chopping right hand discoloured his left cheekbone.

It was a fine performance, and some observers remarked that Tommy had boxed in the style reminiscent of 1937 when he won the British title. Officials of the Welsh Area Council were also extremely impressed, and announced they would back Tommy's claim for a British title fight against Johnny Williams.

Farr had now won four fights in succession, all in good style, and wanted nothing more than a fight with Williams. At the age of 39 he was rapidly becoming the only logical contender for the title.

Tommy was anxious to keep active, and he was persuaded to try and reverse the decision he had lost to American Al Hoosman. He was convinced he could do it, and promoter Alex Griffiths put the fight on at the Maindy Stadium, Cardiff, on 10 September.

A capacity crowd of 8,000 turned out to see the Welshman take a clear points decision over ten rounds. He was the master throughout, and ended the fight unmarked, whilst the American was bleeding profusely from a cut left eyelid sustained in the fifth round. As usual, Tommy dictated the fight with his left hand, and the American had no answer to it, unlike in their first fight.

Hoosman was clearly not the same fighter, and received a number of warnings from the referee for not punching correctly. The reason for this, however, would not become clear until after the fight.

There was an amusing situation at the end of the seventh round when the American's trunks split at the front. The damage was so bad that a replacement pair were urgently needed, but Hoosman's spares were in a locked dressing room. The regulation one-minute interval had to be extended to five and a half minutes, while the American tried on three pairs of trunks before finding a pair to fit. In the end, he wore swimming trunks over the damaged garment, and a third pair over those.

Whilst all this was going on, Farr sat in his corner huddled under a blanket lent to him by someone in the audience, to keep out the biting wind. The prolonged stoppage did not help the American's cause and Farr continued to dictate the terms. He finished the fight completely unmarked, a tribute to his remarkable skill against a rugged opponent.

Hoosman had, however, been badly hampered from the third round by a broken finger in his right hand. During the fight this was disguised to such an extent that only his manager and second knew about it.

Farr had now won nine of his last ten contests, and was generally considered to be the number one contender for the British and Empire titles. Despite this, he was still being overlooked. At last, on 21 October 1952, the British Boxing Board of Control officially nominated Farr, Don Cockell and Frank Bell as contenders for the British title. Cockell was the surprise nomination because he had only boxed once as a heavyweight.

On 2 November, Farr was matched with Werner Wiegand of Luxembourg at Dortmund in a non-title fight. It was Tommy's first contest abroad since 1939, but he wasn't at all concerned. Although the referee had him in front at the end, both judges scored in favour of Wiegand. Tommy was disgusted when the decision was announced, and paced angrily around the ring. He was not alone in believing he had been robbed, and there was an outburst of booing from the 10,000 crowd when the verdict was announced. Many people, including several hundred British soldiers, thought he had won clearly. British reporters at the ringside shared the view.

Farr had gone into the fight at 15 stone 3¾, the heaviest of his comeback, and during the first three rounds it appeared as though the extra weight had slowed him down as Wiegand got on top.

Tommy came back well, however, to take the next three when Wiegand, a massive man of 16 stone 11¾, slowed considerably. He sustained a bad cut over his left eye towards the end of the third, and his corner were unable to stem the bleeding, making him much more cautious.

Although the Luxembourger attacked more from the sixth round onwards, Tommy took many of the blows on his arms and gloves, while picking up points himself with his left jab. Wiegand then rallied well in the final two rounds, which apparently influenced the two judges.

The cut over Wiegand's eye bled profusely from the third round onwards, and immediately after the fight he went to hospital to have it treated. It was generally agreed that had the fight been in England, it would have been stopped in Farr's favour.

* * *

Towards the end of November 1952 came the news Tommy had been waiting for. The British Boxing Board of Control announced that he would meet Don Cockell in an eliminator for the British and Empire heavyweight titles. Williams had won the titles in March of that year, but had not defended the British title. His only defence of the Empire title was when he beat Johnny Arthur in October.

Cockell, a former blacksmith from Battersea, had held the British, European and Empire light heavyweight titles, and had been a highly rated fighter at that weight. Yet his nomination to box the eliminator came as a surprise to many critics as he had moved up to heavyweight just two months earlier.

In October, returning to the ring as a full-blown heavyweight, Don beat Irishman Paddy Slavin in two rounds at Streatham Ice Rink. Boxing followers were shocked when it was discovered that he was carrying two stone more than when he had fought Randolph Turpin just four months earlier. Three weeks later, Cockell was in action against Farr's old conqueror Frank Bell. It was a real brawl in which Bell was on the floor several times before the referee stopped the fight in Cockell's favour in the eighth round. The two wins hardly qualified Cockell for a title eliminator, but with Farr on a fairly successful comeback, the contest between them was an intriguing one. Tommy was still a fast and skilful boxer, whereas Cockell was carrying too much weight for his height, and was considered to be only a blown-up heavyweight, but was younger and heavier punching.

317

There was expected to be a battle between promoters to stage the contest, but nobody seemed particularly interested. The Board of Control may have been to blame because, when announcing the fight, they introduced a ridiculous proviso. Having said it would be a title eliminator, they added that they would only decide after the fight if the winner was a worthy challenger to Johnny Williams.

Both Farr and John Simpson, the manager of Cockell, were angry with the board over a number of aspects. They were convinced that the proviso made it sound less attractive thereby scaring off some of the top promoters from the start. 'Naturally I'm delighted at having the opportunity of fighting again for the title I never lost,' said Tommy. 'However, I don't like the board's stipulation that the stewards will decide after seeing the contest whether Johnny Williams shall be called upon to meet the winner.'

Farr and Simpson were convinced that promoters thought they would be signing up a fight which had little or no bearing on the domestic heavyweight scene. They were also annoyed that the board wanted the fight to be staged at a time when most of the big arenas in London had been booked for circuses or panto-mimes. It ruled out the possibility of bids from Jack Solomons to stage the fight at either Harringay or Earls Court, or from Freddie Mills who was promoting at the Empress Hall.

Tommy believed that the fight should be held over until the warmer weather, and staged at an open-air venue in Wales, where it would draw a crowd of at least 30,000 which would mean more money for him and his opponent. Having returned to the ring because of his financial problems, he wanted to secure the best possible pay-day for himself. Now that he was being given the chance to fight in a title eliminator, it should provide him with the biggest purse of his comeback. Farr was realistic enough to know he could lose the fight, and thereby reach the end of his career. He had every reason to be angry with the board because he believed that with proper organisation and publicity, he could come out of the situation very well financially. Jack Simpson was equally anxious to get the best possible deal from his man, and openly shared Farr's thoughts on the whole business.

Despite arguments put forward by both camps, the fight went to purse offers. Only promoters with access to large venues outside London showed any interest, the main ones being Joe Jacobs at Leicester, and Reg King in Nottingham. The board eventually announced that King's bid of £2,050 was the largest received, so the fight would take place at Nottingham Ice Rink on 9 March 1953.

Both boxers trained at the Crown and Anchor in Brighton. It was an unusual situation, but by mutual consent they staggered their training times to avoid meeting each other.

Tommy started training shortly after Christmas. In the weeks leading up to the fight he was running five miles daily, and was in tremendous shape. He packed the same suitcase that he took to America for the Louis fight, and included the trunks and boxing boots that he wore during that memorable contest.

A crowd of 6,000 turned up at the Nottingham Ice Rink with mixed feelings and emotions, the sentimentalists hoping Tommy would win because he was looked upon as a legend. He was still extremely popular and Reg King had to return money sent in by thousands of applicants for tickets.

Farr looked extremely fit, whilst Cockell at less than a pound lighter appeared strong but rather fleshy. The fight began at a rapid pace, which was to be expected from Tommy. He moved around the ring flicking left jabs into Cockell's face as the Battersea man moved forward trying to make openings for his own stiff punches. The Welshman ducked and weaved in his old familiar style, but it soon became apparent that it was not the Tommy Farr of old. His rhythm was not there, and he was continually caught with hard punches which in previous contests he would have avoided.

The fight settled into a pattern, particularly at close quarters. Cockell opened up, throwing big punches from both hands at Farr's midriff, whilst the Welshman punched away at Don's bulging waistline. Although there was little power in Tommy's punches, Cockell did at times look apprehensive, and moved away just as he appeared to be getting on top.

As the fight progressed, it was Cockell who was boxing more consistently, and his left jabs were tiring Tommy, and when he unleashed his heavy left hooks, he had the veteran reeling away. Don was so in command that there were occasions in each round when he had Farr cornered and under heavy fire and it was only the Welshman's superb skill that enabled him to escape.

By the fifth round, Tommy was slowing badly and looked extremely tired, and the crowd sensed it was only a matter of time before Cockell stopped him. His badly cut face was evidence of the power Don was putting into his punches. Yet it was during this round that Farr landed his best punch of the fight, when he let go a thumping right to the chin. His supporters were reminded briefly of the night he brought Walter Neusel down with a similar punch some 16 years earlier, but their hopes were short lived. Not only did Cockell take it well, but he stormed back almost immediately and floored Farr. There was a count of two but the referee ruled it was not a knock down.

In the sixth, Tommy was cornered for long periods and punished almost at will. The Battersea man was showing no sign of tiring, and despite his appearance had obviously trained extremely hard. He was boxing sensibly and carefully, and this was particularly noticeable when he had Farr in trouble. Instead of going all out to finish it, he stood off and picked his punches, making every one count. At the same time he made sure he did not tire himself out because he knew Farr was brave and durable, and wouldn't drop easily.

By round seven, Tommy's resistance had almost gone, and when he was cornered again, he didn't have the strength to box his way free. His arms and legs were heavy as Cockell punched him solidly to the head with both hands, taking nothing in return. Only the Welshman's amazing courage kept him on his feet, and the referee would have been justified in stepping in at this point.

When the bell came to his rescue, Tommy was still standing, but his face was a mask of blood. Even his most ardent supporters knew there was no point in him continuing. Referee Eugene Henderson followed Farr to his corner and examined his injuries, and it came as no surprise when he signalled that the fight was over.

Tommy protested bitterly at the stoppage, which was officially announced as being due to a bad cut over his left eye. Afterwards he said he was in no danger of being knocked out, which was probably true because his durability had never been in question. The action of the referee, however, was absolutely correct because Tommy was taking a tremendous amount of punishment in a fight he had no chance of winning. He was just a shell of a once great fighter, and nobody wanted to see him absorb punishment which could have left its mark for the rest of his life.

It was the most important fight of his comeback, but he was always fighting an uphill battle. He moved like a tired old man, retaining only his courage and toughness, combined with a little skill. Fans who knew Tommy from his glory days were saddened at his final attempt to get back into the big time.

So the dream of Tommy Farr had not come true. He would never again fight for the British title.

Cockell duly met Johnny Williams for the British and Empire

titles, and in that fight again surprised the critics by out-speeding the champion to win a points decision after 15 rounds. Don continued to progress as a heavyweight, beating good Americans Harry Matthews (three times) and Roland La Starza. These victories steered him to a shot at the world title held by Rocky Marciano, making him the first Briton to challenge for the crown since Farr met Louis. Cockell showed that, like Tommy, he possessed tremendous courage as he stood up to a fearful battering from the champion before being stopped in the ninth round.

To his credit, Tommy took defeat like the truly sporting man he was. Before leaving the ring, he took the microphone and sang *Land of My Fathers* as though he was leading a massive Welsh choir in victory. The atmosphere was very emotional, and there were many in the crowd with lumps in their throats. But it was a sad occasion, and obviously the end of the career of a wonderful fighting man, the likes of whom may never be seen again.

Three days later, it was Tommy's fortieth birthday, and at 7 a.m. that morning he was awoken by his three children anxious to give him their presents. He was a very loving father, and was moved by the experience.

A couple of months passed, and still there was no indication of what Farr's plans were. Behind the scenes however, he was carefully and quietly planning his future. Then, without warning, he announced his retirement from the ring in an exclusive story published in the *Sunday Pictorial* on 17 May 1953. It would soon become clear just why he had chosen that particular newspaper in which to make the announcement.

He gave a moving account of his career, and revealed that, having watched the films of his fights with Louis and then Cockell, he was convinced he had nothing left.

'I have quit boxing,' he said, 'for I realise that nobody can lick Father Time. Whatever I have, I owe to boxing. This great sport doesn't owe me one single little thing, and as I quit, I'd like you to know that if I could turn that clock back, I'd be inside the ring again,' he added. 'As long as I can remember, I've had three dreams. The first was to be a great fighter, and I came near to greatness against Baer. The second was to be a singer; at least I make a pleasant noise. And third, was to do some writing. That chance is coming now. You may like to read more about it on page 18.'

It was a quiet retirement, and without the emotion that goes with a public announcement from the ring.

During his comeback, Tommy showed the moves of a real

master, and made many of his opponents look silly. But sadly, as Tommy put it, nobody can beat Father Time.

* * *

Tommy's comeback was the result of the money problems which arose a few years earlier, and although he claimed it had enabled him to pay off many of his debts, there were still outstanding matters to be resolved.

On 24 February 1954, the Welshman appeared at the High Court in London to defend an action brought against him by solicitor Jack George Woodman. It was alleged that Mr Woodman had given Farr £1,325 to place as bets on a racehorse named Trapini. It was claimed that the bets were never laid, and the money should therefore be returned.

This was not the first dispute involving the horse because on 26 October 1951, Tommy's wife Monty was the defendant when Woodman applied for an injunction to restrain her from running Trapini in races. The solicitor claimed that he owned Trapini in partnership with Mrs Farr, having paid £700 for a half share. The partnership had since been dissolved and Mrs Farr was training the horse against his wishes. He further alleged that she intended to run it in a steeplechase the following week.

Dismissing the ex-parte application, Mr Justice Roxburgh said there was no evidence that the partnership had been dissolved.

The action in 1954 was heard in the Queens Bench Division of the High Court and lasted for three days. Counsel for Mr Woodman told the court that in 1950, Farr's wife, as his nominee, held a share in the horse, the other half having been sold to Woodman during August the same year. Agreement had been reached between Woodman and Tommy Farr that the horse would be trained at their joint expense, and when they were confident it had a good chance of winning, they would lay considerable bets on it.

The horse was trained at Lewes and ran in one or two races. It looked very promising for a betting coup early in 1951, and the date eventually agreed upon was 13 January 1951 at Lingfield. Woodman claimed that on 11 January he sent a bankers draft for £975 payable to Farr, who received it the next day. The draft was not paid into his account but into that of his wife. On the morning of the race there was a telephone conversation between them during which Farr said that he had placed Woodman's money (£500 each way) with bookmakers in Glasgow and

Liverpool. He claimed to have put up £25 of his own money to make up total bets of £1,000.

Trapini ran at Lingfield but fell at the second fence, and consequently there were no winnings to collect. It was Woodman's contention, however, that Farr had converted the bankers draft to his own use, as he had further amounts of £250 and £100 entrusted to him for other bets.

Farr told the court that Trapini was bought in France in 1947 for his wife for £2,160. Between 1947 and 1949 it won only one race in England. Tommy said that all cheques received in connection with racing were paid into his wife's account because, for income tax purposes, he did not want payments from his fights to get mixed up.

Tommy said a jockey had introduced him to Woodman, and they first discussed betting on Trapini in November and December 1950. It was agreed that the placing of all bets would be left to his discretion. He dealt mainly with Jack Powell of Bridgend, and when he visited Brighton on 18 or 19 January 1951, Mr Powell was paid £1,290 which included the bet by Woodman – £600 was laid to win and £300 for a place; the outstanding £75 was laid with A. Risden Limited.

Tommy said that £250 was placed with Mr Powell backing Trapini to win at Windsor on 28 February, and £100 was placed on the horse to win on 12 May as part of a larger bet. All the money was lost. The evidence given by Farr was corroborated by Jack Powell and Albert Risden who were called as witnesses on his behalf.

Mr Justice Hilbery said that he had to determine whether the monies entrusted to Farr by Woodman to place as bets on Trapini, were placed in accordance with instructions. In considering the financial transactions between the parties, the judge said he had no hesitation in accepting Woodman's evidence and preferring it to that of Farr. The sum of £900 had been duly placed, £600 to win and £300 for a place. The judge said that Farr did not deny receiving the equivalent of £1,000 to put on Trapini at Lingfield on Mr Woodman's instructions.

'I think it is established that on 13 January 1951, Mr Farr did make a bet of £600 to win and £300 for a place on Trapini with Mr Powell,' the judge found.

The judge also found that Tommy had been given discretion as to how the bets should be laid, and Woodman could therefore not complain because the money was not placed each way. Regarding the balance of £100 the judge was not satisfied that it was laid in bets as Farr had asserted, and Woodman was therefore entitled to recover that amount.

Mr Justice Hilbery said that Woodman had his fingers burned to the tune of £1,000, yet he was still prepared to risk another £200 (£100 each way), which he later gave instructions to raise to £125 each way. 'That race was on 1 March, and Mr Farr said that he finally put the whole £250 on to win,' said the judge. 'This he was not entitled to do. The horse ran second, so on his claim Mr Woodman is entitled to recover £125.'

On the third claim for £100, the judge said there had never been any defence, and Woodman was therefore entitled to recover the full sum. There would be an overall judgement for Mr Woodman in the sum of £325.

The case turned out to be just the start of a series of civil actions brought against Tommy in respect of alleged debts and in February 1955 he was sued by Horace Aldrich, a former mayor of Brighton. At a preliminary hearing it was alleged that Farr owed Mr Aldrich £1,700. The court was told that the case would be strenuously defended, but due to the ill health of the complainant the case did not proceed.

In November the same year, Tommy again appeared in the Chancery Division of the High Court in London, this time to answer a judgement summons in the sum of £600 allegedly owed to William Little of the Albany Club, Savile Row, London. Counsel appearing on behalf of Mr Little, told the court that the summons was for the balance of a judgement obtained in August 1950 for £1,054, monies which had been lent to Farr. Counsel said that Farr had on two occasions unsuccessfully attempted to set aside the judgement which had been entered in default of appearance. It appeared that Farr had no goods on which a writ could be levied, and the summons was the only means by which to obtain payment.

Tommy told the court he was unable to make an offer of repayment. 'I really did think all of this money had been paid off,' he said, 'because five garnishee orders were put on my last five comeback fights.'

He said his house in Wilbury Road, Hove, was bought on a mortgage in October 1949 and cost £7,750. The monthly instalments to the building society were £38, and all the furniture in the house belonged to his wife. He said he had a regular engagement to write for a Sunday newspaper, and agreed that he had received a substantial sum of money from his comeback fights but added that he did have large expenses.

He also admitted having received between £5 and £10 a time for appearances on radio programmes. He had appeared on a television programme called *Face the Music* for which he was paid £10 or £12, and received about £20 for *Desert Island Discs*.

'What is that?' enquired Mr Justice Harman.

'It is a programme of records that people would like to take with them on a desert island,' said counsel.

'Who on earth wants to take records to a desert island,' remarked the judge, to the amusement of everyone in the court.

Tommy said he took five of his comeback fights to clear a particular debt. He admitted that his outgoings at home were in excess of his earnings. He had tried desperately to pay off his debts, and this had gone on since 1947. He said his house had been up for sale for a couple of years, but nobody was interested.

The case was adjourned for two weeks and when it resumed on 21 November, the court was told that Farr had agreed on a weekly sum by instalments.

In February 1957, Tommy was summoned to appear at Brighton County Court concerning an alleged debt of £100 to Mr Edwin Williams, who owned a butcher's shop in Hove. Mr Williams said that by 1952 he had known Farr for two years and they often had dinner together at Tommy's house. In April that year Tommy told him he was having trouble trying to pay his children's school fees. Mr Williams agreed to lend him £100, but no money was ever returned. Tommy, however, denied borrowing any money.

The judge said that Farr and Williams, who were once good friends, were now 'at daggers drawn'. The recollection of them both was distorted, but he found against Farr, ordering him to pay Mr Williams the £100 claimed, together with costs.

Although the majority of Tommy's court appearances were between 1954 and 1957, the debts had been incurred some years earlier. He had been forced to fight again, and by doing so had cleared most of them. Those which were outstanding, or disputed, were heard in the courts, and attracted publicity of a disturbing nature.

23

MAN OF WORDS

When he retired from the ring, Tommy knew there were plenty of ways to occupy his time. Most importantly, he intended spending more time with his children, who, by this time were growing up fast. Without the pressures of a strenuous training routine, and worries about mounting debts, he was less moody.

Shortly after his defeat by Cockell, Tommy was invited to become a regular contributor to the *Sunday Pictorial*, commenting on boxing and boxers of the day. His column 'Tommy Farr's Corner' gave readers his forthright opinions for several years. He was no slouch with the pen, and wrote with passion about men such as Cockell, Turpin, Gardner and Williams. He paid tribute to Harry Levene, and his old pal and foe, Larry Gains.

Tommy's first trip as a *Sunday Pictorial* correspondent was to Gwrych Castle in North Wales, where Randolph Turpin was training to meet Charles Humez in a world middleweight title eliminator, and he was very critical of Turpin's preparation.

One of Tommy's most entertaining trips for the *Pictorial* was in 1959 when he travelled to Indianapolis to cover the world heavyweight title fight between Brian London and Floyd Patterson. It was his first trip to the States since his fight with Red Burman 20 years earlier. Brian gave him an exclusive interview, and a few minutes before the fight, Tommy went to London's dressing room for a five-minute chat. Unfortunately, London's performance was well below his best, and he was knocked out in the eleventh round.

After the fight, Tommy persuaded Frank Butler to accompany him to New York for a couple of nights on the town. Farr loved reliving old memories in New York. They went to the fashionable Latin Quarter, where he had entertained Eileen Wenzell on a number of occasions some 20 years earlier. During the evening one particular waiter made a great fuss of Tommy, and eventually plucking up courage, remarked, 'That was a very brave display you put up against Patterson. I am honoured to meet you.' He had genuinely mistaken Farr for Brian London, and the Welshman was furious. Frank Butler, however, saw the funny side of the incident, and quickly calmed Tommy down.

Whilst in New York, Tommy appeared on the Ed Sullivan Show, co-starring with Maurice Chevalier.

As a writer of boxing, Tommy was always straight and factual, but never short of witty or controversial comment. His column in the *Pictorial* was popular and kept him in touch with the fight game until his contract ended in 1961. He had a natural, dry sense of humour, but his style of writing stemmed from the education given to him by Job Churchill when he was a youngster. He once explained, 'In between fights, Job fed me with books. I saw in him Don Quixote come to life, with myself as Sancho Panza.'

Farr was also a wonderful conversationalist, and created a great impression with the American writer A.J. Liebling when they met in May 1955 aboard an Aer Lingus flight between Heathrow and Dublin. They were on the way to cover the European feather-weight title fight between Ray Famechon of France, and British champion, Billy 'Spider' Kelly. After boarding the plane, Tommy discovered there was only one spare seat and it happened to be next to Liebling. Although the writer had seen Farr fight in America, they had never met. Nevertheless, he was so fascinated by the conversation he had with the Welshman during their flight to Dublin, that he paid tribute to him in his book *The Sweet Science* published the following year. In a chapter entitled 'Donnybrook Farr', Liebling recalled the memorable flight and the evening that followed.

Tommy was never afraid to speak his mind, and after leaving the *Pictorial* he was often asked to comment on controversies in the fight game.

There was a typical instance after he had been invited to act as Master of Ceremonies at an amateur boxing show at the Brighton Dome on 29 October 1953. The event was being staged to raise funds for the General Orde Wingate Children's and Youth Aliyah which cared for disabled youngsters. Tommy was delighted to be invited, but a few days later, he discovered that the Sussex Amateur Boxing Association had refused to allow him to act as MC. They regarded him as a professional, and their rules did not allow professionals into the ring at any of their shows. Farr was furious, and said he was being prevented from helping a good cause by 'the antiquated rules of the Sussex ABA'.

'I don't know what the British Boxing Board of Control would think if they heard me referred to as a professional,' he remarked angrily. 'The Sussex ABA might have remembered that I have retired. Surely for such a wonderful cause as this, they could relax their antiquated ruling.'

However, despite the attitude of the Sussex ABA, Tommy still attended the event and gave it his support.

Farr was not short of words after Floyd Patterson lost his world heavyweight title to Sonny Liston in 1962. 'I don't want to be cheeky, but if I were in my prime, Liston would hold no fears for me. Tickle him like a trout, that's the answer.'

When Liston defended his title against the loud-mouthed young Cassius Clay in February 1964, and retired at the end of the sixth round, Farr observed: 'Clay fought a perfect fight...the boy is loaded with natural talent, and made a laughing stock of the so-called boxing experts. He made Liston look like a cart horse, and from the first second to the last, Liston showed me nothing. He is greatly overrated.'

In the years that followed, Tommy took a dislike to Clay, who had changed his name to Muhammad Ali. 'I just hope someone takes him to one side. His lip is getting a bit too much for boxing,' he remarked. 'As far as Clay is concerned as a fighter, I would say it is a case of slow horses seen to run past fast trees. Clay, in my humble opinion, is a great detriment to boxing. He has brought politics and religion into it, and that is unforgivable.'

In August 1983, when there was great concern about the former world champion's health, Tommy was asked if he thought Ali had taken one punch too many. 'You've got to be joking,' he snapped. 'He's not had enough bloody fights. In my day, I was fighting for one shilling and sixpence for six rounds, and sometimes took on three men in a night and still had to struggle to make a living.'

In May 1963, Tommy spoke out publicly against Baroness Edith Summerskill, at the time one of boxing's most committed opponents. 'I had 295 fights, and boxed from every weight from paper to heavy. If she or her doctors can find anything wrong with my faculties, I shall be surprised. I think the honourable lady likes publicity. I know with some people it can grow like cancer. The noble lady would do well to turn her attentions to something else. Boxing has been a whip donkey for too long. Why not try motor racing?'

Although he had left the *Pictorial*, Tommy still had bills to pay, and in 1964 became a sales representative for the United Paint Company. He worked extremely long hours, and learned fast. He travelled all over the country, sometimes doing as many as 2,000 miles in a week with only Sundays off. Most of the time, Monty accompanied him. 'She does most of the driving,' he explained. 'When we get home, we are up to our ears in contracts and letters. Then I do the dictating, and she does the typing.' After about seven years, Tommy's hard work was rewarded, and he was appointed an executive director of the company. He remained with United Paint for 16 years, and once remarked, 'If boxing was as competitive as selling paint, it would be bang on.'

After he finished with boxing, Tommy was careful not to allow good living to take over. He kept himself fit by running and swimming, and even when he was 65, got up at 5.45 a.m. each morning and went for a swim in the sea.

He still constantly received invitations to attend boxing events. One was to the last night at Harringay Arena on 28 October 1958, when the nostalgic arena in North London closed its doors to boxing to be converted into a warehouse. Jack Solomons decided that the occasion of his last promotion there warranted something special, and therefore arranged a parade of champions. Before the main event of the evening, a fanfare of trumpets blazed away and many of the greats who had graced the ring since Harringay opened to boxing more than 20 years earlier climbed through the ropes just one more time.

The popularity of Tommy Farr never diminished, and he was frequently asked to attend charity functions, especially those with a boxing connection. He always made every effort to support fund-raising events in aid of children because he never forgot the hardships he endured as a child.

Tommy loved attending Ex-Boxers Association meetings and conventions where he could meet up with old opponents and friends, and talk of days gone by. He was a regular at events organised by Sussex Ex-Boxers Association which for several years were held at the County Cricket Ground Suite at Hove. He was also a guest at similar meetings of London and Croydon Associations, and was invariably accompanied by his wife Monty. Tommy and Monty shared a very happy marriage, and he constantly talked about her in romantic terms. They had survived hard times together, including worries of the collapsed businesses and the enforced comeback. Once everything was behind them, they began to enjoy life to the full, and in 1979 celebrated their ruby wedding anniversary. 'I adore Montgomery my wife,' Tommy once remarked. 'I always say I knew Monty before the General was heard of. She is my pal, my lover, and my secretary.'

They lived in and around Brighton and Hove for over 40 years, firstly at the stylish Glovers on Upper Drive, then in Wilbury Road. They later moved to a smaller property in Goldstone Crescent, before finally settling at Shoreham in 1971. There they bought a smart white bungalow in Old Fort Road, where they lived happily until Tommy died in 1986. The bungalow was beautifully furnished, and Tommy was always the perfect host. Visitors were treated to a variety of home-made sherries and wines which had been brewed by Monty.

As he entered old age, Tommy was very contented. He was extremely domesticated, and enjoyed most of the household chores. He did lots of cooking, and often said that had he not been a fighter, he would loved to have been a chef. He was as much at home in the kitchen as he had been in the boxing ring, and the big moment of the week in later life was cooking the Sunday dinner. Tommy also loved music and spent many hours at home relaxing at his ivory grand piano.

In the years that followed his retirement from the ring, Farr was frequently asked about the fight with Joe Louis. It was clear that he not only had great respect for Louis, but was also extremely fond of him as a person. He always rated Louis as the greatest heavyweight champion of all time. 'He was a methodically perfect fighter who could flatten you with both hands,' he remarked. 'But he was such a gentleman.'

In February 1948 when Louis visited London to box exhibition bouts at the Health and Holiday Exhibition at Earls Court, he specifically asked to meet Tommy socially. The Welshman was delighted to oblige.

When Louis travelled to London again in January 1973, the Anglo American Sporting Club arranged a reunion at the Hilton Hotel, where Joe was staying with his wife Martha. Joe and Tommy were genuinely pleased to meet again. It was a nostalgic occasion, and although both looked fit and well, Joe, at 18 stone, out-weighed Tommy by nearly four stones. Accompanied by their wives, they posed for photographs and answered questions from invited journalists.

Although Tommy had mellowed with age, he was still not a man to cross, and if he believed somebody had taken a liberty, he would soon make his feelings known. A classic example was in November 1979, when the old warrior was 66 and became extremely angry about Radio Brighton's plans to broadcast a commentary of a computer fight between himself and Henry Cooper. The programme was the idea of Derek Leney, the station's boxing correspondent.

Leney, intrigued by a computer fight staged between Muhammad Ali and Rocky Marciano in 1969, was convinced that Farr against Cooper was the ideal choice because Tommy was unquestionably one of the hardest and most courageous British heavyweights of all time and Cooper was a modern-day favourite, having turned professional in 1954, more than a year after Tommy finally retired. By the time he retired in 1971, he had won three Lonsdale Belts outright, won the European title twice, and fought Ali for the world heavyweight title.

When the idea was quite new in Derek Leney's mind, he happened to bump into Farr one Sunday morning at a Sussex Ex-Boxers Convention, and according to Leney, Tommy agreed with it in principle.

The Radio Brighton team studied old films of fights involving Farr and Cooper, got details of their weight, height, types of punch, contrasting styles, records – every conceivable piece of information about them. It was all fed into a computer at Sussex University. The project stretched over four years, and was carried out in total secrecy.

The commentary of 'the fight' was due to be broadcast on 22 November 1979, and would sound like a live contest. A few days before the broadcast was due, however, Farr claimed he knew nothing about it, and angrily hit out at the idea, saying it was absolutely farcical. He insisted he had not given his consent either verbally or in writing, and in his anger threatened to sue Radio Brighton.

Although Tommy continued to maintain that he didn't want to know anything about the fight, and insisted he would not listen to the commentary, Derek Leney found it hard to believe that curiosity would not get the better of him. So, on the evening of the broadcast, an interviewer from Radio Brighton parked his car outside Tommy's house at Shoreham. He sat in the car listening to the commentary, but as the sixth round began, he went and knocked on Tommy's front door. Monty answered and said Tommy wasn't available, but the man heard what he had come for. The commentary of the fight was coming over loud and clear from a radio in the living room, and the interviewer was convinced Tommy was in there listening to it.

The result was in fact a seventh-round knockout victory for Farr. Afterwards, Leney stressed that the programme was only an experiment. 'It was what could have happened, not what would have happened,' he explained. 'We don't want to put anyone's reputation on the line. It was an interesting experiment, and one which I think paid off.'

In the years that followed, Farr and Leney met on many occasions and discussed boxing. They got on well, but never once did Tommy mention the radio broadcast. He showed no animosity, and didn't sue Radio Brighton as he had threatened. Perhaps it was an indication that he actually agreed with the result.

Tommy Farr's life had been full of ups and downs, and his career as a boxer had been spectacular. It was therefore not surprising that he was constantly approached by writers anxious to write his story. He always refused, but in 1979 announced that he had written his autobiography. 'It's called *Thus Farr*,' he told a journalist from a Sussex paper. 'Publishers beg me to publish it, but it is locked in the vaults. It will not be published until after my death. Blind men sing for money, but there is a limit to what I regard as decent earnings. If you are going to publish the truth, there are a lot of people who are going to be hurt. My book tells the truth. I'm not a goody-goody, and I have my principles.'

True to Tommy's word, *Thus Farr* was published after his death, and released on general sale in the United Kingdom in April 1990. Although it had apparently been edited by Tommy's youngest son, Gary, it was clear that the script had been written by Tommy long before he made his comeback in 1950. The basics of the story had already been published in a series of articles in the *News of the World* under the title 'Philosophy of a Pugilist'. Tommy had signed a contract with the newspaper for his story to be published, and the articles appeared weekly between 13 December 1942 and 7 March 1943. At the end of that final article, there was a footnote: 'To meet the wishes of the countless correspondents who have written to him during publication of the series of articles in the *News of the World*, Tommy Farr has arranged for his reminiscences, greatly extended of course, to be published in book form shortly.'

When the promised book eventually materialised, there was a great deal missing. Perhaps Tommy was just too modest.

* * *

Tommy died at his Sussex home on St David's Day 1986, just 11 days short of his seventy-third birthday. He had cancer, but mercifully his illness had been a short one. When his death was announced there was a feeling of real sadness, especially in the towns and villages of the Rhondda Valley. In Tonypandy, the name of Tommy Farr still had a magical air about it because many people remembered the pride he brought to Wales the night he fought Joe Louis. Although he had left more than 50 years earlier, Tommy had kept in touch with many of his old mates.

The following week, more than 150 mourners gathered in the little chapel of Worthing Crematorium to pay their final respects. Many were people from Shoreham and Brighton, mourning the loss of a dear friend. Others came from the world of boxing to pay respect to a truly great fighter who had brought honour and dignity to a sport which is so often criticised. Many were members of Ex-Boxers Associations throughout the country, particularly those in Wales, London and Sussex. Tommy had regularly attended meetings of the Sussex EBA until two months before his death.

Inside the chapel, Tommy's coffin stood in a corner above a deep blue pile carpet. The service was conducted by the 83-year-old Reverend Sydney Dyer, who lived only a few doors away from the Farrs in Shoreham. Describing Tommy as a titanic character, Mr Dyer said:

'He was a very special human being with charisma. One of Nature's gentlemen, and the epitome of personal honour. With the same hands that he wrote beautiful poetry to Monty and played the piano, he floored giants in the ring. The ring was his throne. In the ring he was king, not only because he was such a star himself, but because he made others see stars in conflict. To see this artist in action was sheer poetry, sheer magic.'

It was always Tommy's wish to be buried beside his mother and father. Therefore almost 60 years after he set out to pursue a career which would turn him into a household name, his ashes were taken to the Rhondda. More than 200 people gathered at St Andrews Church in Tonypandy to say goodbye to the man who once said that in his heart of hearts he had never been away from the valley. Members of his family were joined by friends, civic dignitaries and former boxers, including Jack Petersen, Glen Moody, Eddie Thomas and Howard Winstone. They sat in silence as the Rev. Leuan James Owen recalled the days when he and Tommy were boys growing up together:

'I remember he used to be a tough little guy. He used to sell vinegar from a grocery trailer, and used to compel us to push it around for him. He was a tough little guy but he grew up into a graceful giant. He became a great and graceful gentleman.'

The final farewell to the great Welsh warrior of the prize ring was so emotional that many people fought back the tears. Hymns were sung in Welsh by the Cambrian Male Voice Choir to make the occasion a traditional Welsh valley funeral. After the service a casket containing Tommy's ashes was taken to Trealaw Cemetery, situated on a gentle hillside just a mile from his birthplace. There it was gently lowered into his parents' grave beneath a marble monument inscribed *In Death United* which Tommy had erected many years earlier. Alongside it were placed a number of wreaths, including two in the shape of boxing rings. It was fitting that Tommy should finally come to rest in the valley where he had once struggled to survive.

Quite rightly, Tommy was recognised in many areas for who he was and what he had achieved. An indication of his immense popularity was demonstrated back in 1937 when he was approached with a view to a wax model of him being exhibited at Madam Tussauds in London. As with all models displayed in this world famous tourist attraction, the personality must be very much in the public eye. Tussauds clearly recognised his achievements and tremendous popularity. His courageous battle against Joe Louis which followed his spectacular wins over Baer and Neusel, had confirmed that he was by no means a 'one hit wonder'.

Tommy readily agreed to the proposal, and gave a lengthy sitting to one of the sculptors in order that measurements and photographs could be taken to enable an accurate likeness to be achieved. The wax portrait of Tommy Farr went on display in the Madam Tussauds exhibition in 1938 and remained there until it was removed in 1952.

In 1981, the BBC paid tribute to Tommy in a half-hour programme in the series *Maestro – Reminiscences of a Sports Star*. Narrated by Tim Gudgin, it showed clips of his fights with Foord, Baer, Neusel, Louis and Gains.

During interviews with Frank Keating, the old Welsh warrior came over well. He frequently dropped into his old poses, and demonstrated the once famous left jab as he recalled particular big fights. Tommy was alert and articulate, displayed a warm, dry sense of humour, and showed no signs of punchiness that the opponents of the noble art would no doubt love to have seen.

The programme was a moving insight into the life and career of the best British heavyweight of all time, and Tommy's true character came shining through. Most of the filming and interviews had been done in Tommy's home at Shoreham. Apart from the boxing side, it also featured his musical talents and a bronze statuette of him which had at one time been displayed in the Royal Academy.

It is fitting that one of the finest tributes ever paid to Tommy Farr came from none other than Joe Louis. In his book entitled *My Life*, published in 1978, the old champion said:

> Farr stayed 15 rounds with me when everyone thought he couldn't do it. He was probably the best conditioned heavyweight to come out of England. He was tough and had a lot of heart. He took a punch as well as anyone I ever hit.

Even today, Tommy is still a legend in Wales and is remembered as one of the country's finest ever sporting heroes. In appreciation of his achievements, an invited audience of 600 assembled at the Rhondda Sports Centre at Ystrad on 24 November 1994 to celebrate his inauguration into the Rhondda Hall of Fame. There were many sporting giants present, and among the boxers were Eddie Thomas, Cliff Curvis, Colin Jones, Pat Thomas, Robbie Regan and WBO featherweight champion Steve Robinson, who accepted a posthumous award on Tommy's behalf. Old opponent Charlie Bundy was also a guest. World Boxing Council President Jose Sulaiman, donated a belt in memory of Tommy 'for an outstanding boxing career and his contest with Joe Louis'. In making the award, TV commentator Harry Carpenter gave a moving speech in which he described Farr as 'a gentleman and a wonderful boxer'.

Tommy Farr was without doubt a man of courage, and it is worth recalling his own words: 'I fought from almost the time I was born. I was so young, in fact, that I don't remember my first fight. It had to be that way, for I was born in a tiny mining village between the mountains where the standard of living was so low that it was worse than poverty. Life was a constant battle for survival and when I gave all I had in the ring, I wanted to come out of boxing with my share.'

He was a credit to the hard world of professional boxing and will be remembered for as long as the sport survives.

Rest in peace, old champ.

BIBLIOGRAPHY

Books

Astor, Gerald, *And a Credit to His Race*, Dutton, New York, 1974.

Broadribb, Ted, *Fighting is My Life*, Frederick Muller, 1951.

Butler, Frank, *A History of Boxing in Britain*, Arthur Barker, 1972.

Butler, Frank, and Butler, James, *The Fight Game*, Worlds Works, 1954.

Carpenter, Harry, *Masters of Boxing*, Heinemann, 1964.

Carpentier, Georges, *My Fighting Life*, Cassell, 1920.

Cooper, Henry, *The Great Fights*, Hamlyn, 1978.

Diamond, Wilfred, *How Great was Joe Louis*, Worlds Works, 1955.

Fleischer, Nat, *50 Years at the Ringside*, Fleet, New York, 1958.

Fleischer, Nat, *Ring Record Book & Encyclopedia*, Ring Bookshop, New York, 1969.

Gains, Larry, *The Impossible Dream*, Leisure, 1976.

Gutteridge, Reg, *Boxing, the Great Ones*, Pelham, 1975.

Hails, Jack, *Classic Moments in Boxing*, Moorland, 1983.

Helliwell, Arthur, *Private Lives of Famous Fighters*, Day & Mason, 1949.

Louis, Joe, *My Fighting Life*, Eldon Press, 1947.

Louis, Joe, with Rust, Edna, and Rust, Art, *Joe Louis – My Life*, Angus & Robertson, 1978.

Miller, Margery, *Joe Louis – American*, Current Books, New York, 1945.

Mills, Freddie, *Forward the Light Heavies*, Stanley Paul, 1956.

Odd, Gilbert, *Boxing – the Great Champions*, Hamlyn, 1974.

Odd, Gilbert, *Great Moments in Sport – Heavyweight Boxing*, Pelham, 1975.

Odd, Gilbert, *Ring Battles of the Century*, Nicholson & Watson, 1948.

Wood, Don, *Great Moments in Boxing*, Queen Anne Press, 1973.

BIBLIOGRAPHY

Newspapers

Boxing News

Brighton and Hove Leader

Daily Express

Daily Mirror

Daily Telegraph

Eastbourne Chronicle

Liberty Magazine

Montreal Gazette

Newcastle Evening Chronicle

New York Herald Tribune

New York Times

The People

Slough Observer

South Wales Argus

South Wales Echo

Sunday Chronicle

Sunday Graphic

Sunday Pictorial

The Times

Toronto Star

APPENDIX

Tommy Farr's Fighting Record 1926–1953

Date		Opponent	Result		Venue
1926					
Dec	18	Jack Jones	W Pts	6	Tonypandy
Dec	26	Young Snowball	W Pts	6	Tonypandy
1927					
Jan	15	Kid Denham	Drew	6	Tonypandy
Feb	18	Cliff Smith	Drew	6	Tonypandy
Mar	12	Dai Davies	ND	4	Cwmparc
Apr	2	Albert Davies	L Pts	6	Gilfach Goch
Apr	15	Kid Summers	ND	6	Dinas
July	16	Cliff Smith	W Pts	6	Trealaw
July	23	Cliff Smith	W Pts	6	Trealaw
Aug	26	Young Wilkins	W Pts	6	Bridgend
Aug	27	Cliff Smith	Drew	6	Trealaw
Aug	30	Evan Lane	L Pts	8	Treorchy
Sept	3	Dai James	Exh	3	Trealaw
Sept	9	Evan Lane	Drew	6	Penygraig
Sept	10	Jackie Moody	L Pts	6	Pontypridd
Oct	14	Young Battling Smith	ND	6	Trealaw
Nov	4	Cliff Smith	L Ret	4	Tonyrefrail
Nov	7	Kid Evans	ND	4	Tonypandy
Nov	19	Cliff Smith	Drew	6	Tonyrefrail
Nov	26	Dave Flowers	Drew	6	Pontypridd
Dec	2	Sam Rees	ND	4	Treharris
Dec	12	Cliff Smith	W Pts	6	Cardiff
Dec	23	Albert Davies	L Pts	6	Gilfach Goch
1928					
Jan	6	Ted Evans	ND	6	Tonypandy
Jan	16	Ted Evans	ND	6	Tonypandy
Jan	20	Evan Lane	L Pts	6	Trealaw
Jan	28	Young Hazell	W Pts	6	Pontypridd
Jan	30	Young Howe	ND	6	Pontypridd
Feb	25	Young Billy Grocutt	Drew	6	Bridgend
Apr	9	Young Billy Grocutt	L Pts	6	Porthcawl

338

May	3	Evan Lane	L Pts	8	Treorchy
May	18	Young Hazell	Drew	8	Treorchy
June	1	Hector Parry	ND	6	Trealaw
June	2	Dixie Kid	W Pts	6	Ogmore Vale
June	22	Dixie Kid	W Pts	6	Ogmore Vale
June	30	Young Baldock	Drew	6	Ogmore Vale
July	2	Young Parry	W Pts	10	Clydach Vale
July	4	Evan Lane	L Ret	5	Blaengwynfi
Sept	29	Albert Davies	L Ret	4	Gilfach Goch
Dec	1	Danny Andrews	L KO	6	Llanelli

1929

Feb	8	Idris Pugh	L Pts	6	Treherbert
Feb	23	Eddie Thomas	W Pts	6	Ystrad
Mar	23	Len Jones	Drew	6	Porth
Apr	27	George Kid Spurdle	L Pts	6	Porth
May	4	Idris Pugh	Drew	10	Mardy
May	8	Herbie Hill	W Pts	6	Blaengwynfi
May	18	Trevor Herbert	W Pts	8	Ferndale
June	1	Trevor Herbert	Drew	8	Ferndale
June	12	Johnny 'Dooner' Davies	W Pts	10	Nant-y-moel
June	15	Idris Pugh	L Pts	10	Ferndale
Aug	9	Idris Pugh	L Pts	10	Llanelli
Sept	14	Kid Evans	W Pts	10	Tonypandy
Sept	28	Eddie Norton	W RSF	5	Porth
Sept	30	Billy Hazell	W Pts	10	Pontypridd
Oct	4	Rees Owen	ND	6	Treherbert
Oct	5	Trevor Herbert	Drew	6	Porth
Oct	12	George Williams	ND	6	Treherbert
Oct	26	Young Jim Driscoll	L Pts	10	Ynyshir
Nov	16	Billy Howley	W Pts	10	Tonypandy
Dec	7	Young Baldock	W Pts	10	Nanthr
Dec	14	Phil Gardner	W Pts	10	Pontycymer
Dec	21	Billy Jones	W Pts	110	Tonypandy
Dec	26	Cliff Llewellyn	W Pts	10	Newport

1930

Jan	18	Billy Pritchard	Drew	10	Blaengarw
Jan	24	Rees Owen	W RSF	6	Blaengarw
Jan	25	Llew Haydn	L Pts	15	Clydach Vale
Feb	28	Billy Pritchard	L Pts	10	Penygraig
Apr	5	Billy Thomas	W Ret	4	Penygraig
Apr	12	Emlyn Jones	W Pts	10	Tonypandy
Apr	19	Billy Saunders	L Pts	10	Tonypandy
Apr	21	Emlyn Jones	L KO	4	Tonypandy
June	14	Josh Sullivan	L Ret	7	Llanelli

Nov	20	Windsor Williams	ND	6	Penygraig
Dec	26	Herbie Nurse	W Pts	10	Penygraig

1931

Feb	2	Jack Powell	W Disq	3	Ebbw Vale
Feb	7	Bryn Powell	Drew	10	Blackwood
Mar	14	Chris Shea	Drew	10	Bargoed
Mar	28	Jack Powell	W Pts	12	Bargoed
May	23	Steve Donoghue	W Pts	10	Tonypandy

1932

Aug	2	Ashton Jones	Drew	10	Tredegar
Aug	8	Bunny Eddington	Drew	10	Pontycymer
Aug	20	Albert Donovan	L Pts	12	Tredegar
Aug	27	Bob Jarrett	W Pts	10	Aberavon
Sept	15	Hopkin Harry	L RSF	5	Clydach Vale
Sept	19	Tiger Ellis	L RSF	5	Ystrad
Nov	25	Bert Mallin	W Pts	10	Pontardulais
Dec	10	Jim Wilde	W Pts	12	Pontardulais
Dec	30	Jerry Daley	Drew	15	Trealaw
Dec	31	Charlie Bundy	W Pts	15	Treherbert

1933

Feb	18	Billy Thomas	L Pts	15	Bargoed
Mar	3	Glen Moody	ND	3	Pontypridd
Mar	25	Bunny Eddington	W Pts	15	Trealaw
Apr	8	Dai Benyon	W KO	2	Gorseinon
Apr	21	Jerry Daley	W Pts	15	Trealaw
May	2	Jim Wilde	ND	4	Tonypandy
May	2	Charlie Bundy	ND	4	Tonypandy
May	2	Ashton Jones	ND	4	Tonypandy
May	2	Guardsman Francis	ND	4	Tonypandy
May	6	Randy Jones	W RET	6	Merthyr
May	13	Charlie Bundy	W Pts	15	Bargoed
May	15	Eddie Steele	L RET	7	Crystal Palace
May	20	Billy Thomas	W Pts	15	Trealaw
May	22	Tony Arpino	W Pts	15	Pontypridd
June	3	George Smith	W Pts	15	Merthyr
June	26	Gunner Mick Bennett	W RET	8	Cardiff
July	1	Tiger Ellis	W Pts	15	Tredegar
July	8	Ernie Simmons	W Pts	15	Merthyr
July	15	Bunny Eddington	W Pts	15	Ebbw Vale
July	22	Randy Jones	W Pts	15	Tonypandy
		(Welsh Light Heavyweight title)			
July	29	Jack O'Brien	W RET	5	Belfast
Sept	23	Tom Benjamin	W Pts	15	Trealaw

Sept	30	Charlie Chetwynd	W RET 9	Swansea
Oct	7	Jack Marshall	W RSF 7	Merthyr
Oct	28	Seaman Albert Harvey	W Pts 15	Trealaw
Nov	4	Steve McCall	W RET 12	Merthyr
Nov	6	Ernie Simmons	L Pts 10	Blackpool
Dec	2	Leo Evans	W Pts 15	Merthyr

1934

Jan	14	Walter 'Kid' Scott	W KO 1	Belfast
Feb	1	Eddie Phillips	L Pts 15	Holborn
Mar	6	Johnny Farr	ND 4	Penygraig
Mar	26	Jim Winters	W Pts 15	Cardiff

(British Light Heavyweight title elim.)

Apr	23	Jack Casey	L Pts 12	Newcastle
May	7	Charlie Belanger	L Pts 12	Newcastle
June	13	Eddie Phillips	L DISQ 3	Wandsworth

(British Light Heavyweight title, final eliminator)

July	6	Selwyn Ford	EXH 4	Pontypridd
July	27	Johnny Farr	EXH 4	Ystrad
Aug	9	Ernie Simmons	Drew 10	Wimbledon
Aug	22	Charlie Belanger	W Pts 10	Wandsworth
Sept	3	Del Fontaine	W Pts 12	Swansea
Sept	14	Charlie Bundy	W Pts 15	Trealaw

(Welsh Light Heavyweight title)

Sept	19	Dave Carstens	L Pts 10	Wandsworth
Oct	20	Seaman Albert Harvey	W RET 9	Llanelli
Oct	22	Eddie Pierce	W Pts 12	Bradford
Dec	21	Pat McAuliffe	W KO 2	Trealaw

1935

Jan	11	Arthur Novell	W KO 1	Trealaw
Feb	4	Eddie Phillips	L Pts 15	Mountain Ash

(Vacant British Light Heavyweight title)

Mar	8	Johnny Farr	ND 4	Maesteg
May	8	Manuel Abrew	W RET 6	White City
May	13	Eddie Wenstob	W Pts 6	Holborn
June	28	Presidio Pavesi	W Pts 10	Paris
July	20	George Brennan	W Pts 8	Leicester
Aug	14	Frank Moody	Drew 15	Cardiff
Oct	25	George Brennan	W Pts 10	Leicester
Nov	15	Presidio Pavesi	W KO 4	Paris
Dec	2	Eddie Wenstob	W Pts 10	Blackfriars
Dec	16	Rhenus de Boer	W Pts 12	Bristol
Dec	21	Frank Moody	W KO 4	Cardiff

1936

Jan	15	Tommy Loughran	W Pts 10	Albert Hall

Mar	5	Peter Van Goole	W Pts	12	Swansea
April	2	Bob Olin	W Pts	10	Albert Hall
May	18	Jim Wilde	Drew	12	Swansea
Sept	14	Jim Wilde	W KO	7	Swansea
		(Welsh Heavyweight title and final eliminator for British title)			
Dec	21	Charles Rutz	W Pts	12	Earls Court

1937
Feb	8	Joe Zeeman	W KO	8	Bristol
Mar	15	Ben Foord	W Pts	15	Harringay
		(British & Empire Heavyweight titles)			
Apr	15	Max Baer	W Pts	12	Harringay
June	15	Walter Neusel	W KO	3	Harringay
June	28	Bob Rowlands	Exh	2	Earls Court
June	28	Bob Scally	Exh	2	Earls Court
Aug	30	Joe Louis	L Pts	15	New York
		(World Heavyweight title)			
Nov	1	Gunner Mick Bennett	Exh	3	Birmingham
Dec	6	George Markwick	Exh	2	Mountain Ash
Dec	6	Gunner Mick Bennett	Exh	2	Mountain Ash
Dec	6	Ex- PC Dick Power	Exh	2	Mountain Ash
Dec	6	Johnny Carr	Exh	2	Mountain Ash

1938
Jan	21	James J Braddock	L Pts	10	New York
Mar	11	Max Baer	L Pts	15	New York
June	10	Abe Feldman	Exh	4	Gloucester
Dec	16	Lou Nova	L Pts	15	New York

1939
Jan	13	Clarence 'Red' Burman	L Pts	10	New York
Apr	13	Clarence 'Red' Burman	W Pts	12	Harringay
May	17	Larry Gains	W RET	5	Cardiff
Nov	10	Manuel Abrew	W KO	3	Dublin

1940
Feb	26	Danny Paul	Exh	3	Nottingham
Feb	26	Packey Paul	Exh	3	Nottingham
Aug	7	Zachy Nicholas	W RET	3	Barnstable

1941   INACTIVE

1942
April	19	George Markwick	Exh	3	Liverpool
April	20	George Markwick	Exh	3	Liverpool
April	21	Jack Fox	Exh	3	Liverpool

APPENDIX

1950

Aug	23	Bill Brennan	Exh	3	Porthcawl
Sept	27	Jan Klein	W KO	6	Pontypridd
Nov	6	Piet Wilde	W KO	4	Leicester
Dec	4	Lloyd Marshall	L Pts	10	Carmarthen

1951

Jan	29	Don Mogard	Exh	3	Watford
Mar	21	Frank Bell	L KO	2	Porth
April	24	Gerry McDermott	W Pts	10	Harringay
July	7	Dennis Powell	W RSF	6	Shewsbury
		(Welsh Heavyweight title)			
Aug	30	Steve McCall	W Pts	10	Bangor
Oct	4	Robert Eugene	W Pts	10	Cardiff
Nov	16	Al Hoosman	L Pts	10	Manchester
Dec	3	Georges Rogiers	W Pts	10	Brighton

1952

Mar	17	Georgio Milan	W Pts	10	Cardiff
May	26	Georges Rogiers	W Pts	10	Abergavenny
July	26	Jo Weidin	W Pts	10	Worcester
Sept	10	Al Hoosman	W Pts	10	Cardiff
Nov	2	Werner Wiegand	L Pts	10	Dortmund

1953

Mar	9	Don Cockell	L RSF	7	Nottingham
		(Final eliminator for British Heavyweight title)			

Career Summary

Bouts Taken	197
Won	95
Lost	43
Drawn	22
No Decision	19
Exhibition	18
Wins inside the distance	27

After losing to Eddie Phillips for the British Cruiserweight title, Farr issued a
challenge to allcomers in February 1935 (*Boxing,* 27 February 1935)

Poster advertising Farr's fight with Charles Rutz (France)

344

ROYAL ALBERT HALL

Manager ... ... C. B. COCHRAN

THURSDAY, APRIL 2nd at 8

JEFF DICKSON SPORTS PROMOTIONS, Ltd.

Important Anglo-American 10 (3-min.) Rounds Contest

BOB OLIN

(America). Ex-Lt.-Heavy-weight Champion of the World

vs.

TOMMY FARR

(Wales). One of the most promising of the younger British Heavy-weights

Referee ... ... C. B. THOMAS, Esq.

Great International 10 (3-min.) Rounds Contest

ERICH SEELIG

(Germany). The exiled Middle-wt. and Cruiser-wt. Champion of Germany.

vs.

EDDIE PEIRCE

South African Cruiser-weight Champion

Referee ... ... WILFRED SMITH, Esq.

Watch out for the usual Strong Supporting Bouts between Picked Men

POPULAR PUBLIC PRICES (including Tax)

Gallery	B'cony	Boxes	Orch.	Loggias	Stalls	Ringside
3/6	5/- & 7/6	12/-	15/-	18/-	24/-	30/-

Seats can be booked at Jeff Dickson's Offices, 8 and 10, Cecil Court, Charing Cross Road, W.C.2 (Temple Bar 5523 & 8922), and at Royal Albert Hall; Messrs. Keith Prowse; Alfred Hays; District Messengers; Webster & Waddington; Webster & Girling; and all agencies: BIRMINGHAM: J. Murphy, Farcroft Hotel, Handsworth. CARDIFF: Messrs. Pickfords, 122, Queen Street.

Poster advertising Farr's fight against ex-world champion, Bob Olin

Posters hung inside and outside The Green Man public house at Blackheath where Farr trained in April 1937

BOXING EVERY WEDNESDAY

BRITISH CHAMPION CAN BEAT MAX BAER

In the build-up to the Louis fight, Tommy was frequently the subject of cartoons. This was one of the more complimentary ones

A copy of the poster advertising Farr's contest with Joe Louis for the World Heavyweight Championship

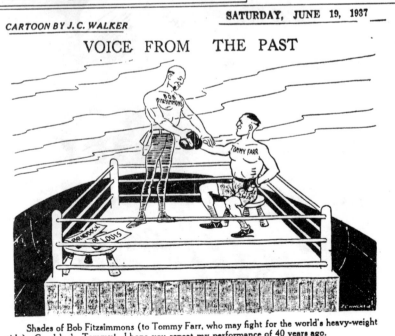

Shades of Bob Fitzsimmons (to Tommy Farr, who may fight for the world's heavy-weight title): Good luck, Tommy! I hope you repeat my performance of 40 years ago.

Tommy became involved in product advertising

348

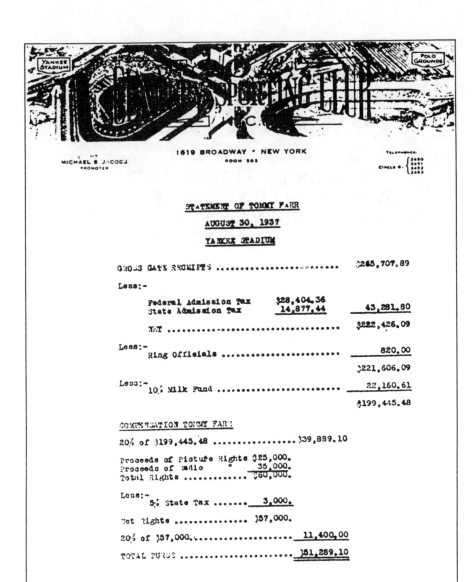

THE 'PAY-OFF' FOR THE JOE LOUIS-TOMMY FARR FIGHT.

A copy of Mike Jacobs' statement of finances and details of Farr's purse for the Louis fight

After his fight with Louis, Tommy was challenged by Larry Gains (*Boxing,* 27 October 1937)

Although they were locked in dispute, Broadribb made it clear that Farr was still under contract to him (*Boxing,* 25 October 1937)

A Reg King Presentation

MONDAY, 9th MARCH, 1953

=ICE STADIUM=

FIGHTS

12 (3-min.) ROUNDS HEAVYWEIGHT CONTEST
HEAVYWEIGHT CHAMPIONSHIP OF GREAT BRITAIN ELIMINATOR

TOMMY FARR v. DON COCKELL
(Wales) (Battersea)

---

8 (3-min.) ROUNDS LIGHTWEIGHT CONTEST at 8st. 4lb.
JAKE TULI v. ROBERT MEUNIER
(Zulu) (France)

8 (3-min.) ROUNDS FLYWEIGHT CONTEST
TERRY McDONALD v. GEORGE NUTHALL
(Doncaster) (Stockport)

8 (3-min.) ROUNDS MIDDLEWEIGHT CONTEST at 11st. 9lb.
WALLY BECKETT v. ROCCO KING
(London) (Doncaster

6 (2-min.) ROUNDS LIGHT HEAVYWEIGHT CONTEST
BONNY FOORD v. BRIAN ANDERS
(South Africa) (Brighton)

6 (2-min.) ROUNDS HEAVYWEIGHT CONTEST
RON HARMAN v. MARIE BUSH
(Brighton) (London)

4 (2-min) ROUNDS LIGHTWEIGHT CONTEST
BILLY COBB v. JACK CRAWLEY
(Chesterfield) (Portsmouth)

OFFICIALS

REFEREES: Farr v. Cockell, Mr. **EUGENE HENDERSON**; for other contests appointed by B.B.B. of C.

M.C.: Mr. FRANK YEXLEY

TIMEKEEPER: Mr. CHARLES TOWN

INSPECTORS: Mr. G. A. MUSSON and Mr. A. CUNNINGHAM

MEDICAL OFFICER: Dr. W. D. CLARKE

All Officials appointed by the B.B.B. of C.

Programme advertising Farr's contest with Don Cockell

351

BOXING!

GESS PAVILION, FAIRGROUND, Pontardulais!

FRIDAY, NOV. 25th

TEN ROUND CONTEST

KID PARR, Tonypandy, who put up such a splendid fight against Hopkin Harry a few weeks ago, and has a win over Bunny Eddington, Pentyrymmer.

v.

DICK SMITH, Neath, the Glamorgan Middleweight Champion and runner-up in the Territorial Championship 1932, since turning professional he has won all his contests with a knock-out, including Bob Jarrott, Abrahams Ben Mellin, Neath; Jim Henderson, London, and several others.

SIX ROUNDS CONTEST

JEM SMITH v. KID MORRIS
GLYNNEATH   BRITON FERRY

ALSO FOUR ROUNDS CONTEST

Doors open 7.00 p.m., first bout 8 p.m. prompt

ADMISSION (TAX INCLUDED) — SIXPENCE

SATURDAY, NOVEMBER 26th.

TEN ROUNDS CONTEST,

BRYN EDWARDS, Garnant,
Without doubt one of the best lads in West Wales at his weight, who has defeated some of the best feather-weights in England and Wales

v.

BILLY EVANS, Ystrad,
Ex-Featherweight Champion of Wales, who last Wednesday defeated Dan Carey, Featherweight Champion of Scotland at Manchester. This will prove a big contest, as he is known as a fighting man.

SIX ROUNDS CONTEST

Young Brace, Treorchy v. Ed. Evans, Pontypridd

SIX ROUNDS

Bertie Davies, Garnant, v. Kid Jones, Ammanford.

Referee - Mr. PARRY, Porth.

Admission 1/- (including Tax).   Doors open 7.30, first contest 8 prompt

Read the "Western Mail" for all Boxing Results

"South Wales Voice," Ystalyfera

Fight bill advertising the Joe Gess Booth

352